by Lynn Beighley

Wiley Publishing, Inc.

Drupal For Dummies®

Published by
Wiley Publishing, Inc.
111 River Street
Hoboken, NJ 07030-5774

www.wiley.com

Published by Wiley Publishing, Inc., Indianapolis, Indiana

Published simultaneously in Canada

For general information on our other products and services, please contact our Customer Care Department within the U.S. at 877-762-2974, outside the U.S. at 317-572-3993, or fax 317-572-4002.

For technical support, please visit www.wiley.com/techsupport.

Wiley also publishes its books in a variety of electronic formats. Some content that appears in print may not be available in electronic books.

Library of Congress Control Number: 2009941353

ISBN: 978-0-470-55611-5

Manufactured in the United States of America

10 9 8 7 6 5 4 3 2 1

About the Author

Lynn Beighley has been a computer book author for a very long time, and this is her tenth book. She's written about SQL, PHP, Flash, Photoshop, and Dreamweaver, and finds that they all have connections to Drupal. In fact, like Kevin Bacon, she thinks maybe everything is connected to Drupal. Or perhaps Drupal is connected to everything. Either way, she loves it.

Lynn lives in a sleepy New Jersey town, and doesn't know anyone named Tony. She shares her slightly off-kilter 1920's home with her husband, Drew, and an 80-pound lap dog named Wroxton.

Dedication

To Drew.

Author's Acknowledgments

I'd like to thank Kyle Looper for giving me the opportunity to write a Dummies book on such a great topic, and Pat O'Brien for shepherding me through the process. Thanks also to Debbye Butler for her superb copy editing. I also thank the whole crew at Wiley who helped with this edition.

Publisher's Acknowledgments

We're proud of this book; please send us your comments at `http://dummies.custhelp.com`. For other comments, please contact our Customer Care Department within the U.S. at 877-762-2974, outside the U.S. at 317-572-3993, or fax 317-572-4002.

Some of the people who helped bring this book to market include the following:

Acquisitions, Editorial, and Media Development

Project Editor: Pat O'Brien

Acquisitions Editor: Kyle Looper

Copy Editor: Debbye Butler

Technical Editor: Todd Kelsey

Editorial Manager: Kevin Kirschner

Media Development Project Manager: Laura Moss-Hollister

Media Development Assistant Project Manager: Jenny Swisher

Media Development Associate Producers: Josh Frank, Marilyn Hummel, Douglas Kuhn, and Shawn Patrick

Editorial Assistant: Amanda Graham

Sr. Editorial Assistant: Cherie Case

Cartoons: Rich Tennant (`www.the5thwave.com`)

Composition Services

Project Coordinator: Patrick Redmond

Layout and Graphics: Ashley Chamberlain, Joyce Haughey, Melissa K.Jester

Proofreaders: Christopher M. Jones, Jessica Kramer

Indexer: Potomac Indexing, LLC

Publishing and Editorial for Technology Dummies

Richard Swadley, Vice President and Executive Group Publisher

Andy Cummings, Vice President and Publisher

Mary Bednarek, Executive Acquisitions Director

Mary C. Corder, Editorial Director

Publishing for Consumer Dummies

Diane Graves Steele, Vice President and Publisher

Composition Services

Debbie Stailey, Director of Composition Services

Contents at a Glance

Table of Contents

Introduction

Welcome to the first edition of *Drupal For Dummies,* the book written especially for people who want to have their own Web sites but haven't a clue about how to start or where to begin.

Are you frustrated because the kid next door has five Web sites to your none? Are you tired of trying to find someone to build your site for you for free? Do you hear stories about how much a Web site has picked up your dentist's business? You need Drupal!

Or maybe you already have a Web site, but you have one problem: The guy who built it isn't around to help when things break. And he built it in Javanese HRH or some other gibberish you can't even remember the name of, much less decipher. Makes you want to scream.

Either way, you've found the right book. Help is here, within these humble pages.

This book talks about building a Web site from scratch using Drupal in everyday language. It doesn't assume you know how to create Web pages. You don't need to know code, either; in fact, you can create your site without a single line of computer code. The language is friendly; you don't need a graduate education to get through it. The goal is to show you how to build your own site with the features you want, without coding, without deciphering technical jargon, and without pulling a single hair from your head in frustration.

About This Book

There are a couple of ways to use this book, depending on your preferences and experience.

If you're a content management, Web site, or Drupal newbie, you can start reading and working with Chapter 1 and keep going until you reach the Index at the end. Everything falls in sequence as you build experience and knowledge. I explain the concepts and give you practical instructions. It has

17 chapters, each one covering a specific aspect of building a Web site with Drupal — such as installing Drupal, building a basic site with a blog and forum, using images and video on your site, or building an online store.

But you don't have to memorize anything in this book. It's a need-to-know book: You can pick it up when you need to know something. Need to know how to put a YouTube video on your Drupal site? Pick up the book. Need to know how to create a contact form for your customers? Pick up the book.

How to Use This Book

This book works like a reference. Start with the topic you want to find out about. Look for it in the table of contents or in the index to get going. The table of contents is detailed enough that you should be able to find most of the topics you're looking for. If not, turn to the index, where you can find even more detail.

After you find your topic in the table of contents or the index, turn to the area of interest and read as much as you need or want. Then close the book and get on with it.

Of course, this book is loaded with information, so if you want to take a brief excursion into your topic, you're more than welcome. If you want to know the ins and outs of building an online store, read the whole chapter on storefronts. If you just want to know how to post a product on your site, read just the section on adding products. You get the idea.

This book rarely directs you elsewhere for information — just about everything that you need to know about Drupal is right here. If you find the need for additional information on related topics, plenty of other *For Dummies* books can help.

What You Don't Need to Read

Aside from the topics you can use right away, some of this book is skippable. I carefully placed extra-technical information in self-contained sidebars and clearly marked them so that you can steer clear of them. Don't read this stuff unless you're really into technical explanations and want to know a little of what's going on behind the scenes. Don't worry; my feelings won't be hurt if you don't read every word.

Foolish Assumptions

I'm making only one assumption about who you are: You're someone who wants to build a Web site and has heard that Drupal is a good choice.

Macintosh and Windows users can all use this book.

How This Book Is Organized

Inside this book, you find chapters arranged in five parts. Each chapter breaks down into sections that cover various aspects of the chapter's main subject. The chapters are in a logical sequence, so reading them in order (if you want to read the whole thing) makes sense. But the book is modular enough that you can pick it up and start reading at any point.

Here's the lowdown on what's in each of the five parts.

Part I: Getting Started with Drupal

The chapters in this part present a layperson's introduction to what Drupal is all about, where to get it, and how to install it. This part is a good place to start if you don't have the Drupal software already installed for you. It's also a great place to start if you've looked at Drupal but have no idea what all those infernal links do.

The best thing about this part is that it starts at the very beginning and doesn't assume you know how to download and upload and extract and install software. It also suggests simple solutions on how to get started. In other words, this part is aimed at ordinary people who know almost nothing about how Web sites come to exist.

Part II: Your First Drupal Site

The goal of the chapters in this section is to show you how to build your first Web site quickly and easily. And it takes you beyond simply building a site, into fun stuff such as changing the appearance and building a site with a blog, forum, and user comments.

Part III: Bending Drupal to Your Will

After you get a basic Web site up and running, the chapters in this part show you how to add on to it and really control it. You find out all about safely allowing others to use your site and controlling what they can and can't do. You also spend time making your site even more your own by customizing colors, logos, and artwork.

Part IV: Taking Drupal to the Next Level

This part really takes your site to a whole new level. You discover how to pull content and data from other Web sites, how to build a storefront, and how to create an image gallery. And those are just a few of the many new features you can add to your site using Drupal's modular design.

Part V: The Part of Tens

This wouldn't be a *For Dummies* book without a collection of lists of interesting snippets: Ten modules (or add-ons) for your Drupal site and ten sites you can visit to learn even more about Drupal.

Icons Used in This Book

Those nifty little pictures in the margin aren't there just to pretty up the place. They have practical functions:

Hold it — technical details lurk just around the corner. Read on only if you have a pocket protector.

Pay special attention to this icon; it lets you know that some particularly useful tidbit is at hand — perhaps a shortcut or a little-used command that pays off big.

Did I tell you about the memory course I took?

Danger, Will Robinson! This icon highlights information that may help you avert disaster.

Where to Go from Here

Yes, you can get there from here. With this book in hand, you're ready to build your own robust and useful Web site with Drupal. Browse through the table of contents and decide where you want to start. Be bold! Be courageous! Be adventurous! Above all, have fun!

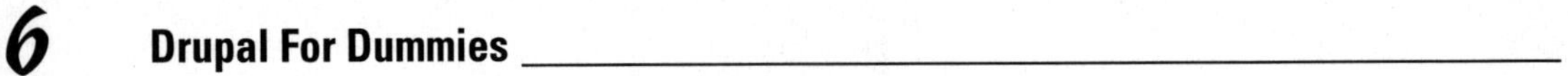

Part I
Getting Started with Drupal

"Run Nigel! It's the mummy's cursor!"

In this part . . .

You want a Web site. But the kid next door doesn't know enough to build what you need and the Web design company wants to charge you an arm and a leg. Just when you are about to give in and pay too much, you overhear a conversation about Drupal, and how you can build a Web site with it.

But when you try it, you don't find it easy. The documentation is hard to follow, and you can't find anything in the Drupal interface.

If this has happened to you, you'll appreciate the chapters in this part. They provide a gentle introduction to building your first Web site with Drupal.

What if you don't even have Drupal and need to install it? Then the chapters in this part take you to the very beginning. That way, your site will be up and ready to be enhanced by the great stuff in the chapters in Parts II and beyond.

Chapter 1

The Big Picture

In This Chapter

- Understanding open source software
- Comparing Content Management Systems
- Developing a Web site with Drupal
- Knowing Drupal's potential

In the past, if you wanted to create a fully featured Web site with forms, a blog, and a message board, you practically had to be a computer programmer. You needed to know how to write HTML and possibly JavaScript and CSS, and to accomplish anything dynamic, yet another language such as PHP or ASP. You probably would have needed to know SQL, the language that allows Web sites to store and retrieve information.

Over the years, Web developers began freely sharing code. If you knew some HTML and a few other things, you could use the work of other people to knit your site together. No longer did you need to write code every time you wanted a contact form or poll or image library on your Web site.

Today, we have entire robust and powerful Web applications, supported by communities of Web developers. Enter Drupal. Drupal is one of a class of applications that do nearly all the work for you. You can build a site with Drupal without ever writing a line of code. Indeed, that is the ultimate goal of Drupal: to free you from the inner workings of the code and instead let you focus on the layout and content of your site. There are other, similar applications you can use that also accomplish this, but Drupal is one of the best open source applications for quick, code-free Web site creation.

Before I get into the installation and use of Drupal, I think it's helpful to start by introducing the features of Drupal. The more you understand about what Drupal is, the better you can plan and use it to your advantage.

What Drupal Is

The official Drupal Web site, http://drupal.org, describes Drupal as "a free software package that allows an individual or a community of users to easily publish, manage and organize a wide variety of content on a website." This is a great description of this application. It's free, as long as you follow certain rules that I mention later in this chapter. Drupal allows for a wide variety of content, making it extremely flexible and customizable. The fact that more than one individual can publish and manage content makes it a Content Management System, or CMS. I explain each of these important characteristics of Drupal in more detail.

Free

Drupal is distributed as *open source* software. This means that you can get a copy of the program and install it on your Web server, modify the appearance of the pages and layout to suit your needs, and add your content to it without paying for the program. It seems too good to be true!

Software designated as open source essentially means it's "free," but it does have certain legal obligations associated with it. If you were a programmer and made changes to the code itself and then provided the new code to other people, there would be certain rules you would have to follow under Drupal's license. You can learn more about it here: http://www.gnu.org/copyleft/gpl.html.

If you really like Drupal or the great Drupal site you build helps your company make lots of money, you can contribute to the efforts of the many great programmers who have created this software by visiting http://drupal.org/contribute.

Flexible

Drupal sites are completely flexible. This means you can do things like:

- **Modify the layout of your pages:** With the use of blocks, you can move your navigation links to the side, top, or anywhere else on your pages you wish. You can put all your content in one column or choose multiple-column layouts.
- **Remove or replace the default Drupal logo:** By default, your Drupal site will have the official Drupal logo. You can easily remove it or replace it with your own logo.

- **Add and remove pages:** Drupal wouldn't be of much use to you if you were stuck with a specific set of pages. Drupal gives you complete flexibility to create as many pages as your site will need, as well as freedom to choose where page links will appear.
- **Hide content and pages from certain users:** You can, if you choose, allow only logged-in users or even a subset of users to see certain pages on your site. You can even hide content *within* a page from certain users.
- **Allow users to choose their own layout:** You can let individual users choose their own layouts. When they log in, they will see the layout they chose.

Customizable

One of the best things about Drupal is the ease with which you can customize your site features. Drupal comes with lots of great features you can turn on with the click of a button. If you want a forum or a poll or a blog, for example, it comes with the Drupal application and you can easily include or exclude it in your site. Your site can contain precisely what you want it to, and you can turn off features you don't want.

Beyond the features, or modules, included with the program, many Web developers have created and made freely available to you *thousands* more modules you can download and install! I recommend you take a minute to check out the third-party modules here: `http://drupal.org/project/modules`. Some great add-ons are in there. If you aren't already excited about the potential Drupal offers, you will be. For example, free modules allow you to integrate Facebook and Twitter information into your site, turn your site into an online store, or create photo galleries. I tell you about some especially useful and interesting third-party modules later in this book.

Content Management System

At its heart, Drupal is all about *managing content.* Drupal belongs to a class of applications known as Web *Content Management Systems* (CMS). These applications are designed to separate the content on a Web site from the presentation of that content. In other words, you can manage the text and graphics on your site through the Drupal interface as easily as you can create a Microsoft Word document.

After you set your site up, you don't have to worry about looking at HTML code and putting your desired text into some sort of Web format. You can simply type in a text box on a form and press a button. Your new content will show up on your site. Behind the scenes, Drupal handles the conversion of your text into a format viewable on the Web. Drupal will also, in the case of a blog style page, save any old content previously published and provide a link to it for your users.

But the real power of CMS applications is that you can give specific users the permission to easily post, edit, and/or delete content on your site, without having permission to change the layout or features of your site. You can even allow certain users to create content, but not allow it to be published on the site until you've had a chance to approve it. All of this control allows your site content to be maintained, while your site structure remains safe from possible harm.

What Drupal Isn't

Drupal is a great application for creating a robust CMS Web site. But it's not perfect. You may encounter a few difficulties as you work with it:

- **Drupal isn't so easy to install:** Probably the most difficult part of building a Drupal Web site is installing Drupal in the first place. You have to understand its requirements, make a few decisions, and gather required information to get it installed correctly.

  Chapter 2 covers the ins and outs of installation.

- **Your site isn't automatically ready to go after you finish installing Drupal:** You will be modifying the configuration of the site, changing the layout, and adding your own content. You will also need to spend time deciding on the best site structure for your Web site.

  I show you how to customize your site in great detail in Part II.

- **You have limited ability to change the appearance or function of modules:** Any modules you use will have some configurable options, but there may be things you want to change that aren't configurable. This is the case with any of the open source CMS applications you will encounter and isn't simply a limitation of Drupal. The developers of modules generally do their best to anticipate what you might want to configure, but they can't read your mind. Fortunately, because of the beauty of open source, you have the code and your specific needs can be addressed.

  I don't discuss programming in this book, but after you get your site running, you may want to learn more about the code side of Drupal. In Chapter 17, I recommend some sites where you can get programming help as you delve into the messy business of modifying the code.

- **Drupal's interface can be a bit confusing:** Drupal administration menus are not intuitive — which is why you bought this book, right? I show you where everything is and explain Drupal's language for things throughout this book.

What Drupal Can Do for Your Site

From Web polls to blogs and shopping carts, your site can be full of great features without any need for you to get into the actual Web programming side of things. As you look through the features, think about creative ways you can use them for the sites you are building.

You won't have to build all of these at once; you can always add new features to and remove features from your site any time.

Polls

A poll is a question posed to visitors on your site that users can answer. Polls are great for getting your community of users involved in discussions. Drupal has a simple interface that allows you to create custom polls, such as the one shown in Figure 1-1.

Should dogs be allowed around the pool?
Submitted by Lynn Beighley on Thu, 05/28/2009 - 15:01
Definitely not!
Sure, why not?
I don't care.
Vote
» Add new comment

Figure 1-1: A poll.

After a registered user has voted, he will see a tally of the current voting results (see Figure 1-2) and have the option of cancelling his vote. He can then vote again if he wishes. His vote counts only once.

Should dogs be allowed around the pool?
Submitted by Lynn Beighley on Thu, 05/28/2009 - 15:01
Definitely not!
0% (0 votes)
Sure, why not?
100% (1 vote)
I don't care.
0% (0 votes)
Total votes: 1
Cancel your vote
» Add new comment

Figure 1-2: Poll results with Cancel your vote button.

Blogs

One of the primary reasons Web Content Management Systems are extremely popular is the ease with which you can create blogs. Drupal provides full-featured blogging, complete with

- Automatically archived past entries
- A simple-to-use interface for creating new blog entries
- An optional comment system for site visitors to contribute their thoughts (see Figure 1-3)

Blogs aren't used just to document someone's daily activities. Companies leverage blogs to keep the content on their sites fresh. Instead of having to create new HTML Web pages every time they publish a press release, for example, they can blog the information.

Not only is it incredibly easy to create blog entries, but you also develop a history of all your blog postings over time. And all this information, and any other content posted on your site in any other location, including forums, static pages, and comments, can be made searchable — an incredibly useful feature! (Notice the search box in the upper-right-hand corner of Figure 1-3.) It's also a built-in module you activate.

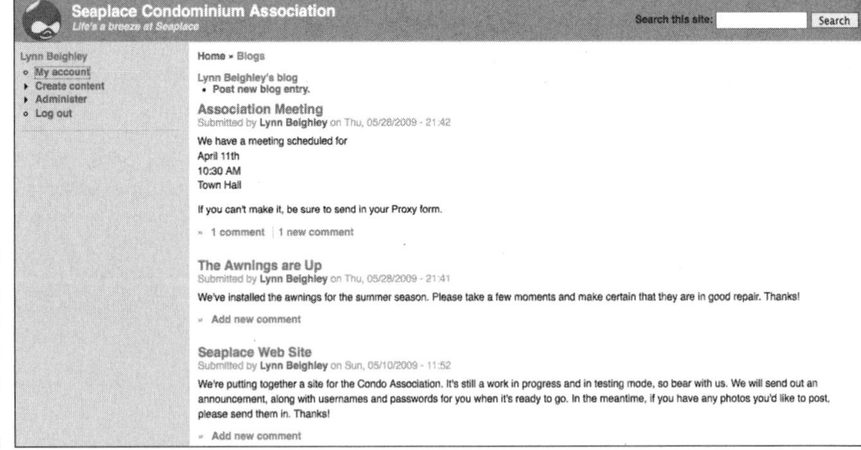

Figure 1-3: Blog entries with comments enabled.

Contact forms

It isn't the most exciting feature of a Web site, but it is an important one: Your site visitors need a way to get in touch with you. In the past, if you didn't have programming skill, you might have used an HTML *mailto* link on a Web page that never reliably worked. Drupal takes care of the contact form for you and creates a Web form:

- The form sends the content to your e-mail address, or wherever else you tell Drupal to send it, when the form is submitted (see Figure 1-4).
- You can configure the form to automatically send a custom confirmation message to the e-mail address of the person who submits the form.

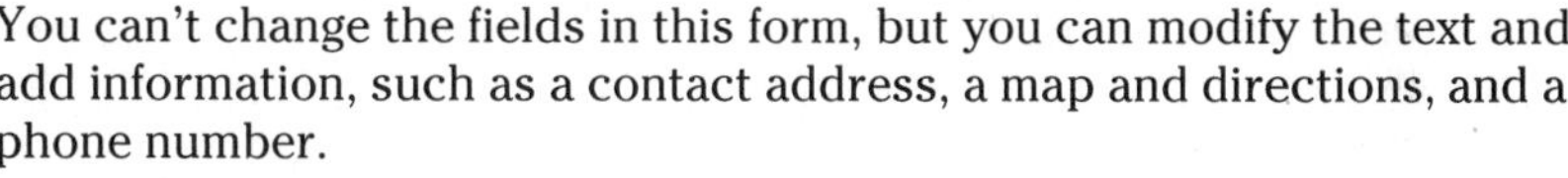

You can't change the fields in this form, but you can modify the text and add information, such as a contact address, a map and directions, and a phone number.

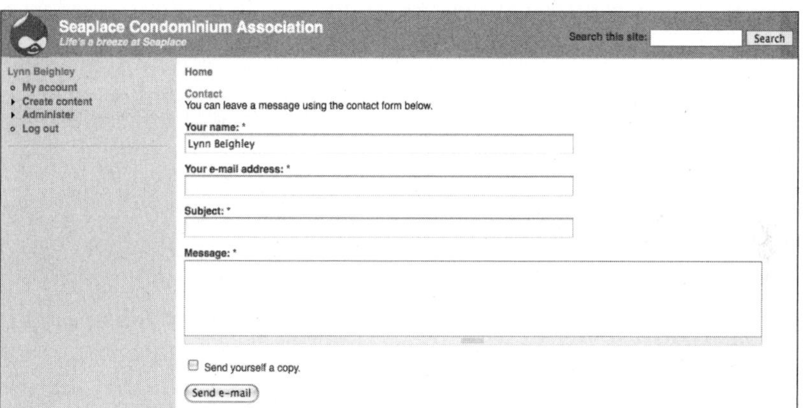

Figure 1-4: A contact form.

Forums

A blog is generally used to share large amounts of information with your users, with the information flowing one way, from you to your site visitors. A forum is most often used to allow your site visitors to chat amongst themselves. If it's important to you to build community interaction and encourage communication among the users of your site, you should consider adding a forum.

A forum consists of a set of *discussions,* as shown in Figure 1-5:

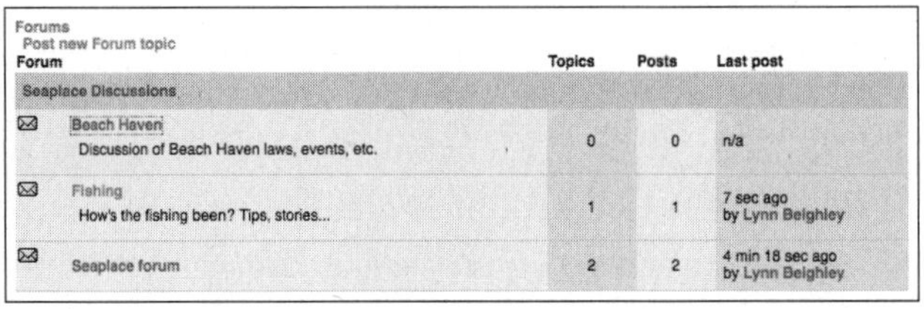

Forums
Post new Forum topic

Forum	Topics	Posts	Last post
Seaplace Discussions			
Beach Haven Discussion of Beach Haven laws, events, etc.	0	0	n/a
Fishing How's the fishing been? Tips, stories...	1	1	7 sec ago by Lynn Beighley
Seaplace forum	2	2	4 min 18 sec ago by Lynn Beighley

Figure 1-5: A forum containing a set of discussions.

- Inside each discussion is a set of topics (see Figure 1-6).
- Inside each topic, your users post their comments and replies to each other's comments.

  After you drill down into a discussion, you see all posts for that discussion. You also see a small icon indicating postings you have not read since you last visited the forum.

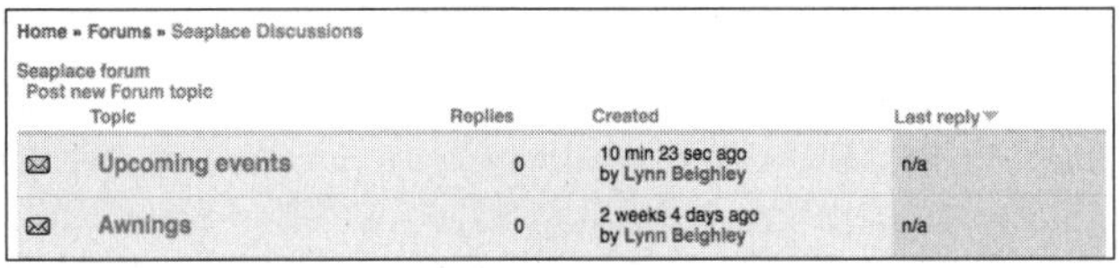

Home » Forums » Seaplace Discussions

Seaplace forum
Post new Forum topic

Topic	Replies	Created	Last reply
Upcoming events	0	10 min 23 sec ago by Lynn Beighley	n/a
Awnings	0	2 weeks 4 days ago by Lynn Beighley	n/a

Figure 1-6: Topics within a discussion.

Like many of Drupal's features, the forum configuration settings give you a great deal of control over the permissions you give your users. You can either

- Maintain complete control over discussion topics.
- Allow your users to create topics.

You can even delegate specific people to be forum moderators and help you share the workload.

Image galleries

While sites like Flickr allow you to share your photographs or video, there are reasons why you may not want to upload them there:

- There's always the possibility that you don't want your work publicly viewable.
- After your media is on a Web site not your own, the site might keep a copy of it, even if you try to delete it.

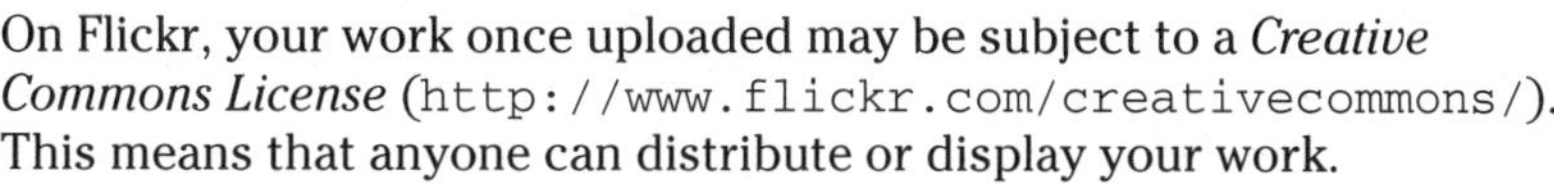

On Flickr, your work once uploaded may be subject to a *Creative Commons License* (`http://www.flickr.com/creativecommons/`). This means that anyone can distribute or display your work.

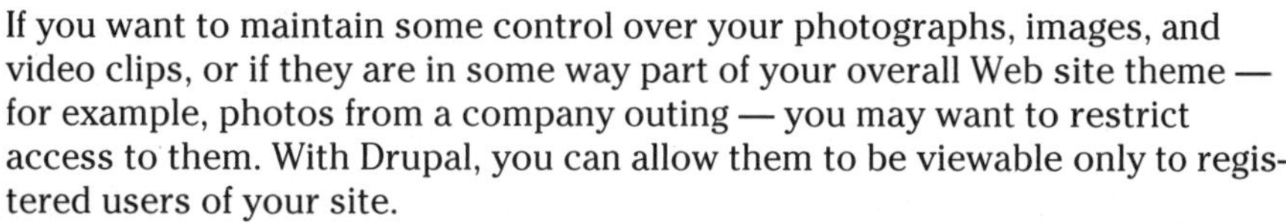

If you want to maintain some control over your photographs, images, and video clips, or if they are in some way part of your overall Web site theme — for example, photos from a company outing — you may want to restrict access to them. With Drupal, you can allow them to be viewable only to registered users of your site.

Although Drupal doesn't come with an image gallery module, there are several great third-party free modules available. I like one named, appropriately enough, Gallery2 (see Figure 1-7).

The gallery integrates with your Web site, allowing you to control whether site visitors have to be logged in to view images. It also allows your users to upload their own images if you choose to allow that.

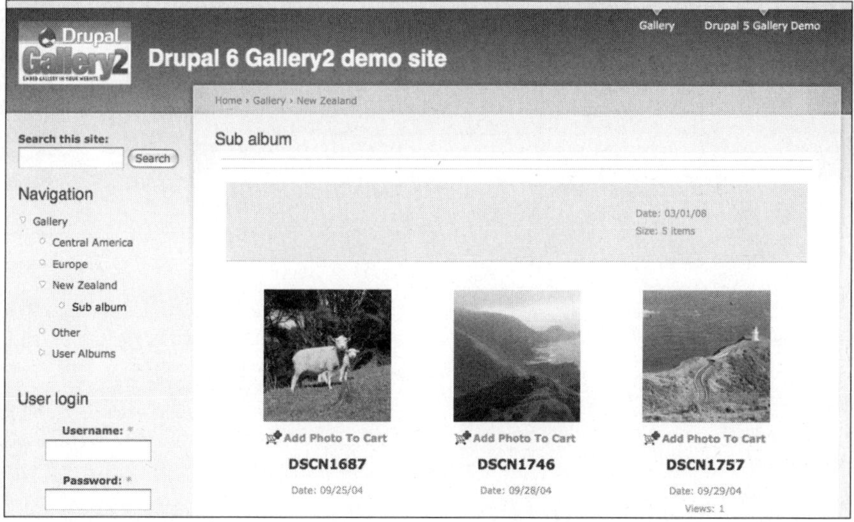

Figure 1-7: Gallery2 module for Drupal.

Examples of Drupal sites

Are you excited about your Web site? You should be. Following are a few really nice sites built using Drupal. Take a look and you'll see why I recommend them.

Drupal.org

It would very odd if Drupal's own site wasn't built with Drupal. Drupal.org (see Figure 1-8) is, and you can see many of the features I mention in use there, from blogs to forums and a search box, along with quite a few more.

Zappos.com

Zappos is a major online retailer that has leveraged Drupal to create a robust online store. Although it customizes the Drupal code base, much of the core Drupal code is used.

Figure 1-8: The home of Drupal.

Drupalmuseum.com and Drupalsites.net

These two Drupal sites exist to showcase other Drupal sites:

- Drupalmuseum.com (see Figure 1-9)
- Drupalsites.net

Figure 1-9: Drupalmuseum.com features attractive Drupal sites.

Most of the featured sites have substantially customized their appearance, but the code behind them is all Drupal.

Chapter 2

Getting and Installing Drupal

In This Chapter

- Downloading Drupal
- Putting Drupal on a Web server
- Gathering database information
- Configuring Drupal

Before you can use Drupal, you have to install it. Manual installation can be the trickiest part of the Drupal experience. Once you've got it up and running, getting your site going will seem rather easy. Just push on through this part, keeping in mind that it does get simpler.

You have several options. If you want to go the easy route, you can sign up for an account with an Internet service provider (ISP) that will do the dirty work of installing it for you. I highly recommend this, and in this chapter, I offer you the names of a few ISPs I've had accounts with. However, in case you are more ambitious and want to install it yourself, I cover that here as well.

To begin the installation, you need to decide where you want your Drupal site to be installed and understand why you might not necessarily install it on that computer sitting in front of you. This chapter shows you the ins and outs.

Deciding Where Your Site Will Live

The purpose of a Web site is to share information with the people who browse to that site. The first decision you need to make is *where* (on what Web server) your Drupal installation will run because that governs if and how people can view it.

The term *Web server* can mean either

- Web server software, like Apache or Internet Information Server (IIS). These programs send Web pages over the Internet to Web browsers when users request them.
- The computer where the Web server software runs.

In this book, Web server refers to the computer, not the software.

Getting on the Web

As you may guess, a useful Drupal installation requires a computer with an Internet connection, unless you want to build a tiny network of your own. But it also requires other resources.

Internet connection

Drupal needs to be installed on a Web server for the rest of the world to see it. Usually, this means that you have an account with an ISP such as GreenGeeks (`www.greengeeks.com`) or GoDaddy (`www.godaddy.com`).

If you download the Drupal software and install it on the computer sitting on your desk, you would probably be the only person who could browse to the site. Unless your computer has been specifically configured for the Internet as a Web server, it can't send your Drupal pages out to the Web.

Other software

Drupal requires other programs on the Web Server before you install it:

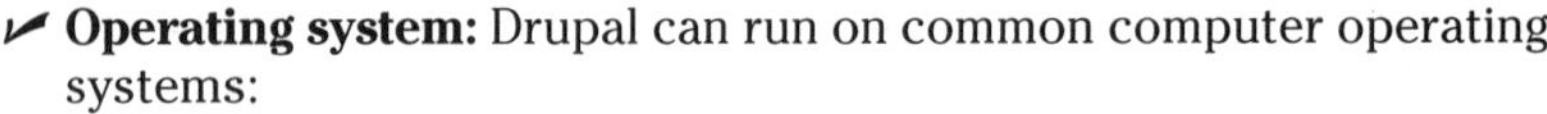

- **Operating system:** Drupal can run on common computer operating systems:

  - UNIX/Linux

    Older UNIX/Linux releases may not be able to run Drupal
  - Mac OS X
  - Windows versions with IIS 5 (or newer)
- **Web server software:** Drupal runs on either of these packages:
  - **Apache Web server `(www.apache.org)`**

    With Drupal 6, I recommend using Apache 2.0 (or newer). Drupal 6 can run on versions as old as Apache 1.3.

Apache is the only Web server software option for UNIX, Linux, or Mac.

- **Internet Information Services** (`www.microsoft.com/iis`)

  With Drupal 6, I recommend using IIS 7 (or newer). Drupal 6 can run on versions as old as IIS 5.

  IIS only runs on Windows.

- **MySQL database** (`www.mysql.com`)

  With Drupal 6, I recommend using MySQL 5.0 (or newer). Drupal 6 can run on versions as old as MySQL 4.1.

- **PHP scripting language** (`www.php.net`)

  With Drupal 6, I recommend using PHP 5.2 (or newer). Drupal 6 can run on versions as old as PHP 4.35.

ISPs that make Drupal easy to install

Here are a few ISPs I use and recommend. Most allow you to install Drupal with just a few clicks using Fantastico:

- GreenGeeks (`www.greengeeks.com`): Offers great customer support and is committed to offering quality service with an eye toward environmental friendliness.

  GreenGeeks hosts my own site, `drupalfordummies.com`.

- Site5 (`www.site5.com`): Focus is on guaranteed performance and talented tech support. Winner of dozens of industry awards, including Best Shared Webhost.

- Cirtex (`www.cirtexhosting.com`): If you plan on uploading videos on your site and allowing users to stream videos online, then CirtexHosting is a good choice.

  CirtexHosting specializes in ffmpeg video hosting, which allows Drupal to convert videos into flash videos online for your visitors to stream. Learn more about ffmpeg at `www.drupal.org/project/ffmpeg`.

- GoDaddy (`www.godaddy.com`): This is a very popular hosting service.

  GoDaddy doesn't use Fantastico, but its own installation script is very similar and very easy to use to get Drupal running.

- Nexcess (`www.nexcess.net`): You'll have to install Drupal manually if you use this ISP. They pride themselves on being simple, affordable, and reliable.

You don't have to worry about these requirements if you put your Drupal site on an ISP that offers easy Drupal installation. I mention some great choices of Drupal-friendly ISPs in the next section. Ask your ISP which versions it runs.

Internet service providers

Internet service providers offer you access to a Web server where you can install Drupal and make your site visible on the Web. Some companies install Drupal for you or provide you with one-click install, saving you a bit of effort.

If you decide to skip installing Drupal yourself, consider getting an account with one of these.

The following sidebar recommends a few ISPs I have worked with. Most of these use a program called Fantastico, which I walk through in this section.

Installing on an ISP with Fantastico

Many ISPs offer a super easy install for Drupal using a program called Fantastico. If your ISP uses Fantastico, this section shows you how it works.

The Drupal community doesn't recommend installing Drupal with Fantastico. It can make upgrading difficult and can potentially cause problems with your databases that store all your site data. I suggest you use Fantastico to create your first site quickly to help you learn how to use Drupal. Then I strongly recommend you follow the instructions later in this chapter to manually install Drupal on your ISP account when you are ready to build the site you want to present to your customers or site visitors.

Any of the ISPs that use Fantastico will have the correct versions of PHP, MySQL, and Apache installed. This means that you can do a manual install of Drupal and not use Fantastico.

To install Drupal with Fantastico, if your ISP supports it, follow these steps:

1. **Locate the e-mail from your ISP that has your username, password, and login information. Browse to the site and log in.**

   You will see a page of options for your new site (see Figure 2-1).

2. **Locate the Fantastico or Fantastico De Luxe icon and click on it.**

   You will probably have to scroll down the page to find it. (In Figure 2-1, it's the blue smiley face on the right of the page.) The Fantastico program now opens, as shown in Figure 2-2.

3. **Click on the Drupal link on the left side of the screen, located under the "Content Management" section.**

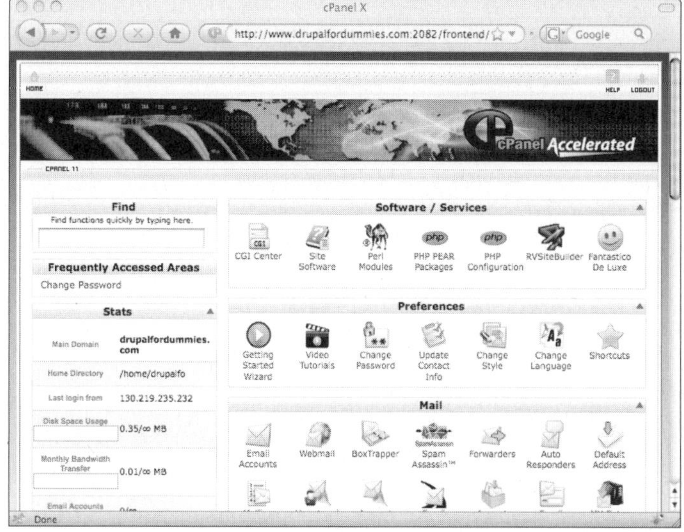

Figure 2-1: Web site control panel with Fantastico icon.

4. **Click on the New Installation link in the center of the page.**

   Your screen now displays a form (see Figure 2-3). This is where you enter a username and password for your new Drupal site and where you decide where on your site Drupal will run.

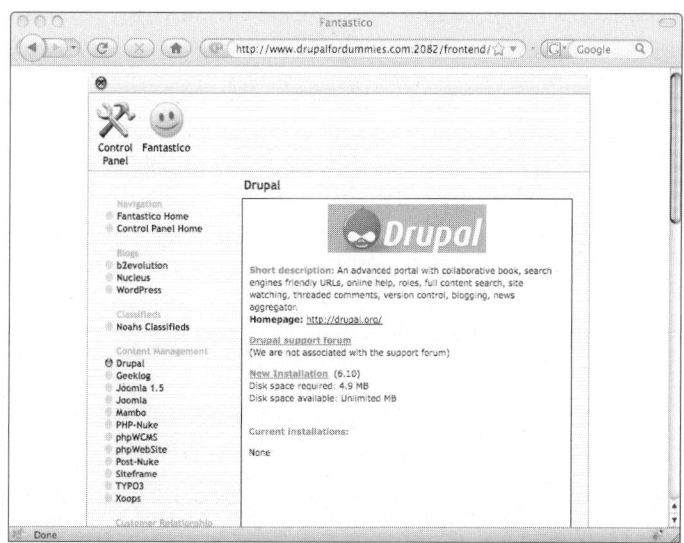

Figure 2-2: Fantastico application with Drupal link on left selected.

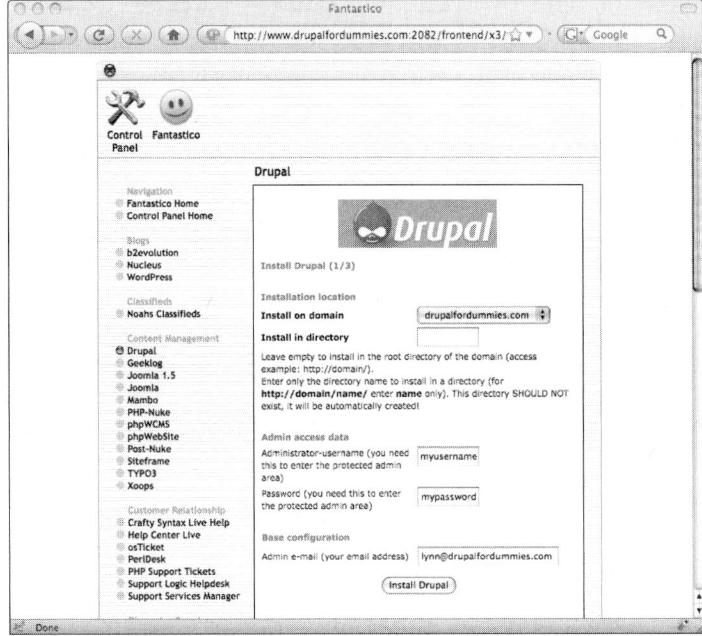

Figure 2-3: The first of three Fantastico screens for installing Drupal.

5. **Enter a directory where you want Drupal to appear on your Web site in the top blank.**

   This appears a bit confusing, but don't let it throw you. Suppose you have requested the domain `myshinynewdrupalsite.com` from your ISP. If you want your Drupal site to be the first thing people see when they browse to `www.myshinynewdrupalsite.com`, leave the blank empty. If, however, you plan on having multiple sites, or just want to play with this first Drupal site, you can put it in a directory on your site, such as **test**. Then when people go to `www.myshinynewdrupalsite.com/test`, they see your site.

6. **Enter a username and password of your choice in the Admin Access section.**

   These will be a username and password, chosen by you, that allow you to administer and customize your site.

   Choose a good password; otherwise, you risk someone hacking your site.

7. **Enter your e-mail address and click the Install Drupal button.**

   Figure 2-4 shows you the next screen. This gives you a bit more information about the databases Drupal will create. This is just for your information. (I talk more about databases and Drupal a bit later.)

Testing on your local machine

You can install Drupal on a computer in your office or in your home. You can't share your site with anyone on the Web, but you can build a site and gain experience. This also allows you to experiment without worrying about

- Your site being hacked
- Embarrassing mistakes

You can't use Fantastico to install on your local machine. You have to do a manual install. Follow the instructions in this chapter, beginning with the section "Installing Drupal on a local machine."

8. **Click the Finish Installation button.**

   Your site is installing. It may take a moment, so don't bother reloading. You will see a confirmation screen when it finishes, and you will be e-mailed a confirmation that your site has been installed.

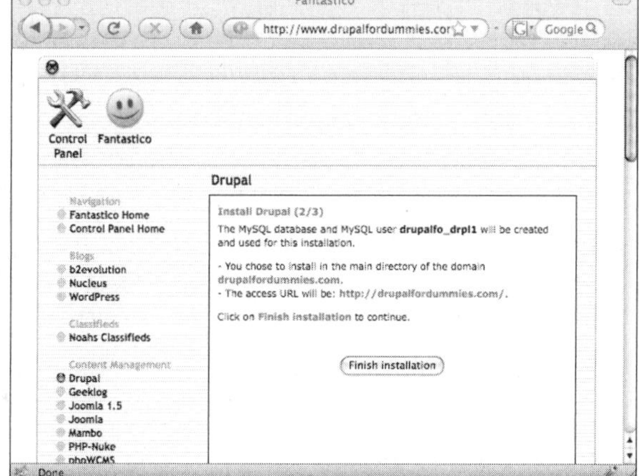

Figure 2-4: The second of three Fantastico screens for installing Drupal.

9. **In a browser, click the link shown on the screen to your site.**

   The link reads something like, "The full URL to the admin area (Bookmark this!): `http://drupalfordummies.com/`." Of course, the link will be to whichever domain you set up (for example, `http://myshinynewdrupalsite.com/test`).

You're finished. When you click the link, you will see the main page of your new Drupal site (see Figure 2-5). If you want to log in, use the username and password you specified on the first of the Fantastico screens.

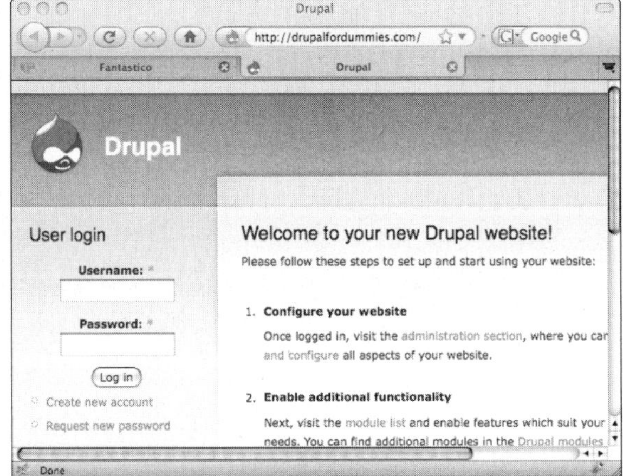

Figure 2-5: Your new Drupal Web site after installation.

Obtaining Drupal

If you aren't using an ISP with Fantastico, you have to get a copy of the latest version of Drupal, copy it to your ISP, and extract it yourself:

Downloading the package

Getting a copy of the Drupal software is free and easy. Follow these steps:

1. **Browse to `www.drupal.org`.**

   A link to download the most current stable release is on the right side of the page just under the Search box.

   As I write this, the most current version of Drupal, and the version this text is based on, is 6.12. In general, this book applies to the 6.12 version or later.

2. **Click the link Download the latest version.**

   You will be taken to a News and Announcements page with a link to actually begin the download.

   The file will be named something like `drupal-6.12.tar.gz`.

3. **Save this file to a directory you will remember.**

Uploading the package

When you download Drupal, it comes as a single, compressed `tar.gz` file, but it actually consists of many files and folders. All these files need to be located in a Web directory on your ISP. Here's how you can upload the single `tar.gz` file to your Web directory on most ISPs. (In the next section, I show you how to uncompress it.)

Don't extract the `tar.gz` until you upload it. I recommend that you extract the files in the final Web directory where you want them. Otherwise, you may find it difficult to upload all the files and keep them in their appropriate locations in the Drupal directory.

The screen shots I show use a program called Fileman, but your ISP may have a different program that handles file management. In general, these file manager programs do similar things. If you are familiar using an FTP program, feel free to use that instead.

To upload the `tar.gz` file from your computer, follow these steps:

1. **Locate the e-mail from your ISP that has your username, password, and login information. Browse to the ISP's site and log in.**

   You will see some sort of control panel with options for your new Web site. It may look like Figure 2-1, or it may look more like Figure 2-6.

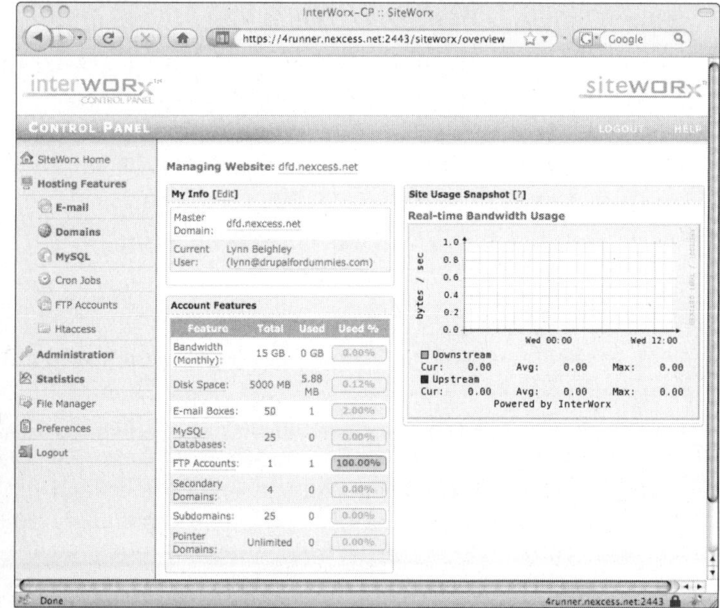

Figure 2-6: An ISP control panel for your site.

2. **Find and click the link to a file manager.**

   You need a file manager so that you can select the Drupal `tar.gz` file and put it in the correct directory on your ISP's site. After you click the file manager, you will see a screen similar to Figure 2-7. This shows your files on your ISP's Web server.

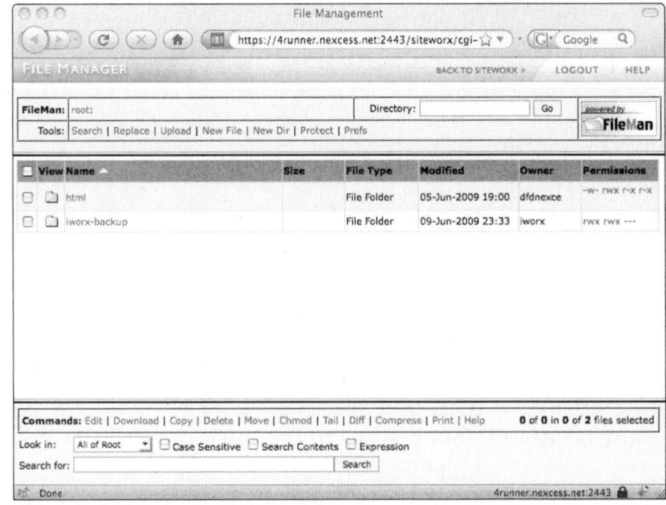

Figure 2-7: An example of a file manager application on an ISP.

3. **You should see a single folder or directory named "html," "www," or "htdocs." Click on its name to open it.**

   There may be several directories, but the one for your Web site should be easy to spot. This is where all your Web pages belong and where you need to install Drupal.

   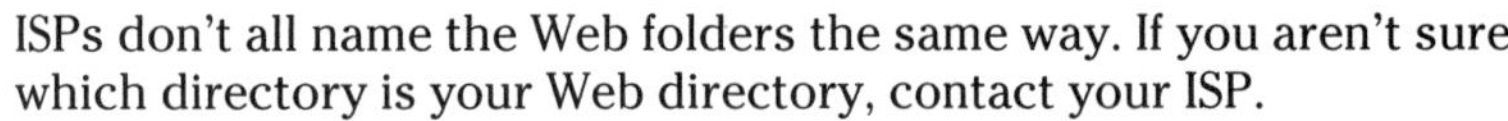

   ISPs don't all name the Web folders the same way. If you aren't sure which directory is your Web directory, contact your ISP.

4. **Locate and click the upload link on your file manager.**

   You should see an upload form with a Browse button, as shown at the bottom of Figure 2-8.

5. **Click Browse and find the Drupal `tar.gz` file you downloaded from drupal.org. Click Upload.**

   Your file is now on your site. The following section shows to extract it.

If you accidentally click on one of the directories or folders and end up inside that folder in your file manager, look for the Parent Directory link near the top of the file listing and click on it to navigate out of the folder you are in to the parent folder one level above.

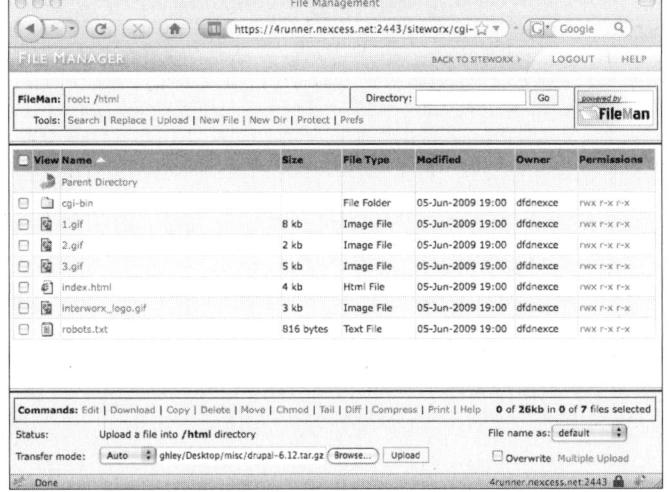

Figure 2-8: An upload form on a file manager.

Extracting Drupal

The file extension `tar.gz` indicates that the files are compressed into a single file. You may be familiar with `.zip` files on Windows. `Tar.gz` is similar to `.zip`. It's also a file compression type often used on Linux and other UNIX systems. Fortunately, most file managers can extract your Drupal file for you. Here's an example of how it works. Your version may differ, so contact your ISP for help if you can't find the same functions on your file manager.

1. **Find the Drupal `tar.gz` file you just uploaded to your Web directory and select it, as shown in Figure 2-9. Select the file name to open the file.**

   You will see a list of files stored inside your `tar.gz` file (see Figure 2-10). They will all be selected.

2. **You should see an option to uncompress your files, as shown at the bottom of Figure 2-10. Leave the selection box set to uncompress All and click the Go button.**

   This will uncompress your single `tar.gz` file into a folder with the same name (for example, `drupal-6.12`). This will take you back to the main directory. You will see both the compressed file (for example, `drupal-6.12.tar.gz`) and the uncompressed files in a new directory (for example, a folder named `drupal-6.12`).

   As things stand now, visitors coming to your Web site (for example, if your site is `www.myshinynewwebsite.com`) will only get to the Drupal site if they type something like **myshinynewwebsite.com/drupal-6.12**. This is not a great URL. You should move your Drupal files to your main site or a different folder.

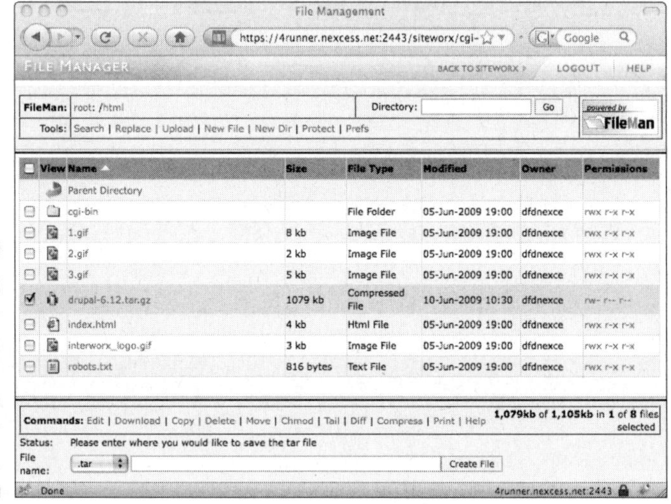

Figure 2-9: Select the Drupal `tar.gz` file in the file manager program.

3. **Select the new folder (for example `drupal-6.12`), and click on the Move command in your file manager.**

   You should see a form (refer to the bottom of Figure 2-10) that asks you to type in a directory name. This will become the new name of the folder in which your Drupal files are stored. For example, if you type in **test**, and choose Move, the contents of your `drupal-6.12` directory will be moved to a directory named `test`. Visitors to your site will need type your domain name and this directory to get to the Drupal site (say `myshinynewdrupalsite.com/test`).

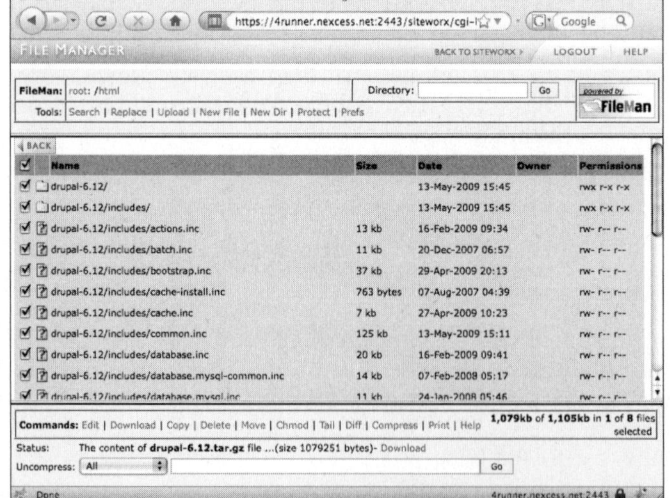

Figure 2-10: File manager showing the selected contents of the Drupal `tar.gz` file.

If you want your Drupal site to be visible when people browse to your main site (for example, `www.myshinynewdrupalsite.com`), the process can be a little trickier. You first need to select the Drupal directory to see all the files and folders in it (see Figure 2-11). Everything in the folder needs to be selected, which you can tell by looking at the check boxes on the left. If it isn't, you need to select all the files. There's usually a Select all option somewhere in the file manager. Click the very top check box on the left, which will select all the files. With everything selected, type **/html** in the Move box, where "html" is the name of your Web directory. (Remember, yours may be named www or htdocs or something else.) This will move all the files in the Drupal directory immediately under your main Web directory.

Use this option with caution; it's painful to delete all those files if you change your mind later.

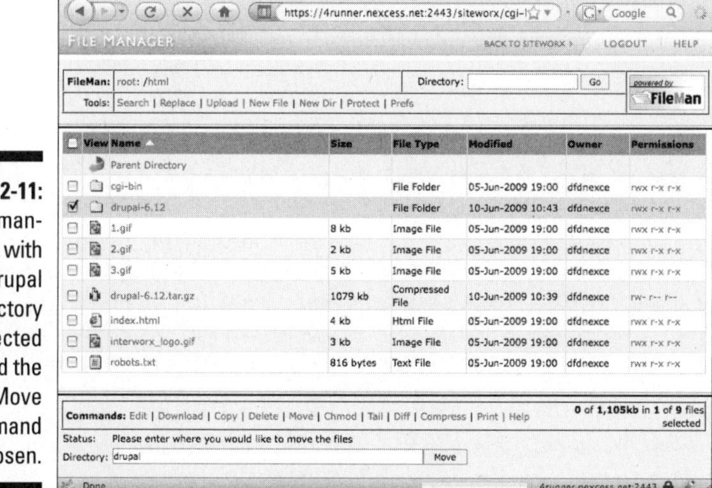

Figure 2-11: File manager with the Drupal directory selected and the Move command chosen.

Setting Up a Database

Before I walk you through the Drupal setup script, there's one more major bit of work that needs to be done. You need to set up a database. It's not difficult, but like the last few steps, your own ISP may have different software showing than what I demonstrate below, making things very confusing.

You should be able to find the same commands somewhere in your particular interface, even if your setup doesn't match the screen shots in this chapter.

What a database is and why you need one

A *database* is a set of files stored in a special format that contain data. You come in contact with databases all the time. For example, every time you look up something on Google, a computer program compares what you typed in the Search box to information stored in a database. The program that communicates with a database is called a *database server.*

Drupal uses a database to keep track of all kinds of data. Chapter 1 explains that Drupal can create a forum for your users, for example. All the messages your users type are stored in the Drupal database. And the people you allow to log in to your site have their usernames and passwords stored in your Drupal database.

To allow Drupal to save all this information, Drupal needs its own database that it can write information into and read information from. Fortunately, most ISPs provide an application that lets you talk to the database your Drupal program needs. I show you how to create a database that Drupal can use for its data below.

Creating a database for Drupal

Although databases are sometimes located on the same computer as your Web site, sometimes they aren't. Your ISP may need to tell you where and how to create a database and what username and password you need to use to connect to it. The steps below assume that your MySQL program is located on the same machine as your Drupal files. This is the most common setup and is the case with all the ISPs I have mentioned.

Drupal needs its own database, and you have to create one if you aren't using Fantastico. You may also have to create a database username and password. This varies tremendously from one ISP to another, but here are the general steps to follow:

1. **Locate the e-mail from your ISP that has your username, password, and login information. Browse to the ISP's site and log in.**

   You will see some sort of control panel with options for your new Web site. It may look like Figure 2-1, or it may look more like Figure 2-6.

2. **This step is a little vague. Find and click on a link that refers to MySQL as part of the name.**

You're looking for a way to create a database. ISPs vary in how they allow you to do this. For example, look at Figure 2-6 and notice the *MySQL* link on the left. Clicking on that causes a link to Databases to appear. And then clicking on the Databases link gives you a form on the right where you type in the name of a new database.

3. **Type in the name of your new database. Call it *drupal* and click the Add button.**

Applications that allow you to create databases are fairly common, but if you don't find one, you may have to contact the technical support department of your ISP. Other programs that allow you to create databases may be called things like *MySQL Databases* or *MySQL Database Wizard.* The whole point is to find an application that lets you create a database.

4. **Also, you may have to add a database username and password if your ISP didn't send any. Locate an application in your control panel that lets you add users to MySQL.**

I wish this step was easier to explain, but every ISP is different. Some may have a simple link called *Users* that opens a form where you enter a username and password. Some ISPs send you a username and password just for MySQL. And some use the same username and password you were assigned to access your site's control panel. If you can't find them, consult your ISP's help documentation and technical support.

Installing Drupal on a Web Host

Now that you've uploaded and extracted Drupal, and created a database named *drupal* for it to use to store its data, you are ready to begin the setup.

Browsing to your Drupal site

By now, you are probably eager to see your Drupal site. It's out there on the Web, waiting for you to go through the installation. To reach it, browse to your domain and the directory where you installed it. For example, if your Web site is `www.myshinynewdrupalsite.com`, and you installed it in a directory called `test`, browse to `myshinynewdrupalsite.com/test`. You should see the Welcome screen, as shown in Figure 2-12.

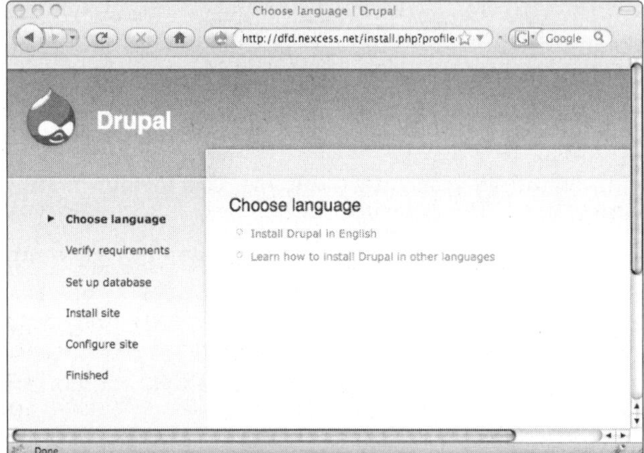

Figure 2-12: The first Drupal setup screen.

Running the installation

Drupal will now take you through a series of forms. Click on the Install Drupal in English link. You will see the message shown in Figure 2-13, indicating that there is a Requirements problem. You can't proceed without creating a configuration file.

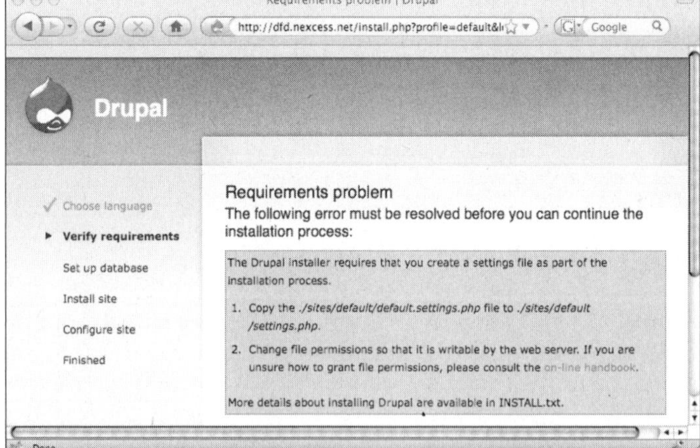

Figure 2-13: Message indicating that you need to create a configuration file.

Creating the configuration file

To create the configuration file, open the file manager on your ISP's site, and copy and rename a file in the Drupal directory in the directory `sites/default/`. Follow these steps:

1. **Locate the e-mail from your ISP that has your username, password, and login information. Browse to the ISP's site and log in.**
2. **Find and click the link to a file manager.**
3. **Select the Web directory and then the directory containing all the Drupal files.**
4. **Locate the `sites` directory and select it. Choose the `default` directory.**
5. **Select the only file in this directory, named `default.settings.php`. Locate and select the Copy function in your file manager.**
6. **If your file manager asks you to enter a directory for the new file, type in *./settings.php* and click Copy.**

   Your file manager may simply make a copy of the file, and you may have a function that allows you to rename the file to `settings.php`.

Verify requirements

Browse back to your Drupal site and reload the page. The error message should be gone, and you should see the form shown in Figure 2-14.

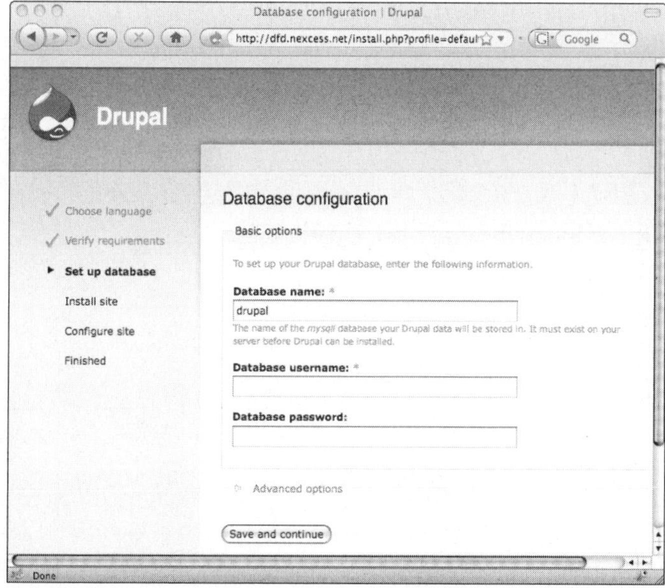

Figure 2-14: The Setup database screen of the Drupal configuration.

Setup database

Enter the name of the database you created earlier, ***drupal***, in the Database name field. For the database username and password, enter the username and password I discuss in Step 4 in the section "Creating a database for Drupal." Click the *Save and continue* button and cross your fingers. If everything goes well, your Drupal site is installed and you move on to configuring it (see Figure 2-15).

There's a very good chance you will have a problem creating a database, adding a database username and password, or giving that username permission to communicate with the database you created. These are not trivial tasks and are probably the hardest part of the Drupal experience. It would take much of this book to explain the way databases, users, and database permissions work and to describe the most common setups for MySQL on popular ISPs. I *strongly* encourage you to read through the process as I describe and contact your ISP for help with these steps if you encounter any problems. You can also visit `www.drupalfordummies.com` and post questions on the forum, where other readers of this book can help you figure out how to solve your database problems.

Configure site

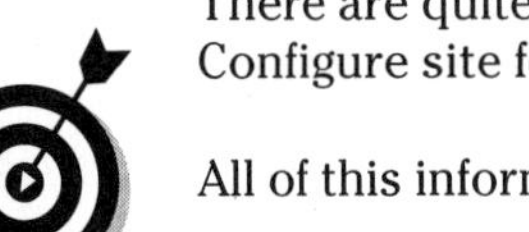

There are quite a few bits of information you need to provide on the Configure site form shown in Figure 2-15.

All of this information can be modified later.

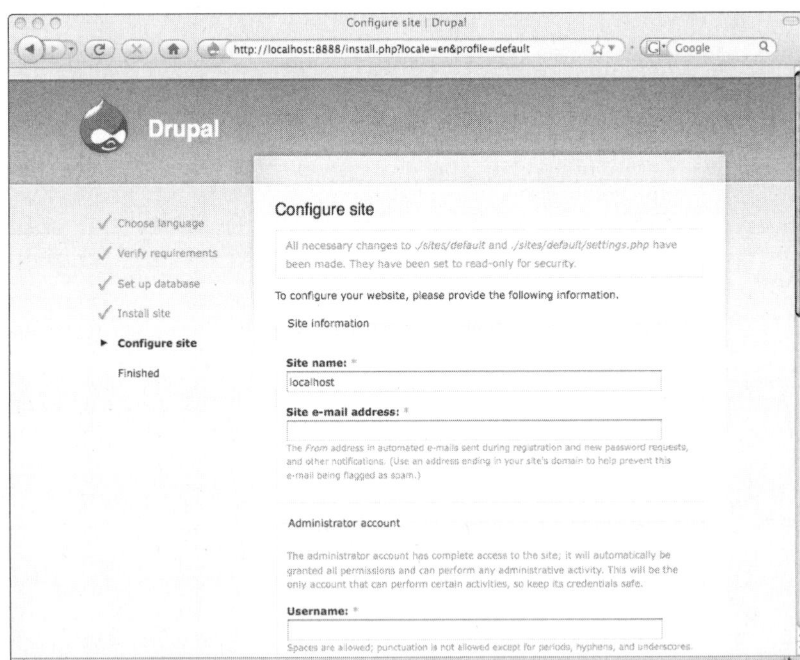

Figure 2-15: Configure site setup screen.

Here's the list of text boxes and options you fill out:

- **Site name:** This field is pre-filled with the domain name of your Drupal site. It's actually going to show up at the top of all the pages on your site instead of the current large white heading, "Drupal."

  Change this to a title that makes sense for your current site. If you don't know what you want to call your site, you can set this later.

- **Site e-mail address:** Drupal can automatically send e-mails when certain things happen, such as a new user signing up. This e-mail address appears as the sender (the From address) on these e-mails.
- **Administrator username:** This is the username (yes, yet another username) that you use to connect to your Drupal administrative functions. You need this username to do anything to your site, from changing the appearance to adding new pages. Enter a username of your choice. Make this a name you will remember.
- **Administrator e-mail address:** Enter an e-mail address where you want to receive e-mails from the Drupal system.
- **Administrator password:** Enter a password to be used with your Administrative login.

  Make it a difficult-to-guess password, but one that you will remember.

- **Administrator confirm password:** Type the password again to confirm.
- **Default time zone:** Anything you do with Drupal that has a time associated with it will use this time zone. For example, if you post to a blog on the site, the time posted will use this time zone.
- **Clean URLs:** Without this enabled, the URLs to the pages on your site will look similar to this: `http://www.drupalfordummies.com/?q=node/55`. If you are can use Clean URLs, your URLs will be a little shorter and leave out the `?q=` (for example, `http://www.drupalfordummies.com/node/55`.

  Use the Clean URLs option if you can, but it really doesn't make much difference.

  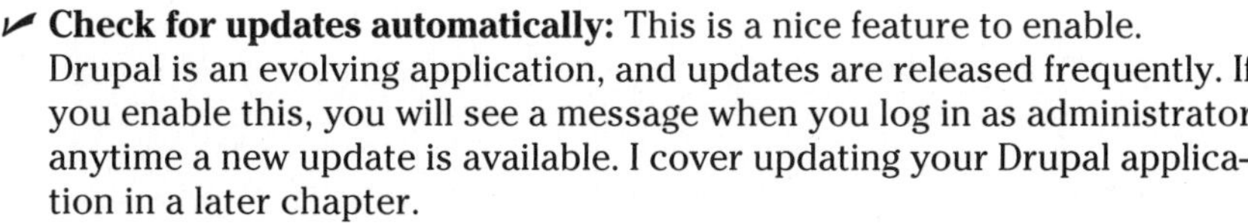

- **Check for updates automatically:** This is a nice feature to enable. Drupal is an evolving application, and updates are released frequently. If you enable this, you will see a message when you log in as administrator anytime a new update is available. I cover updating your Drupal application in a later chapter.

After you fill out and submit the configuration form, you see a final screen letting you know configuration is complete (see Figure 2-16).

Congratulations!

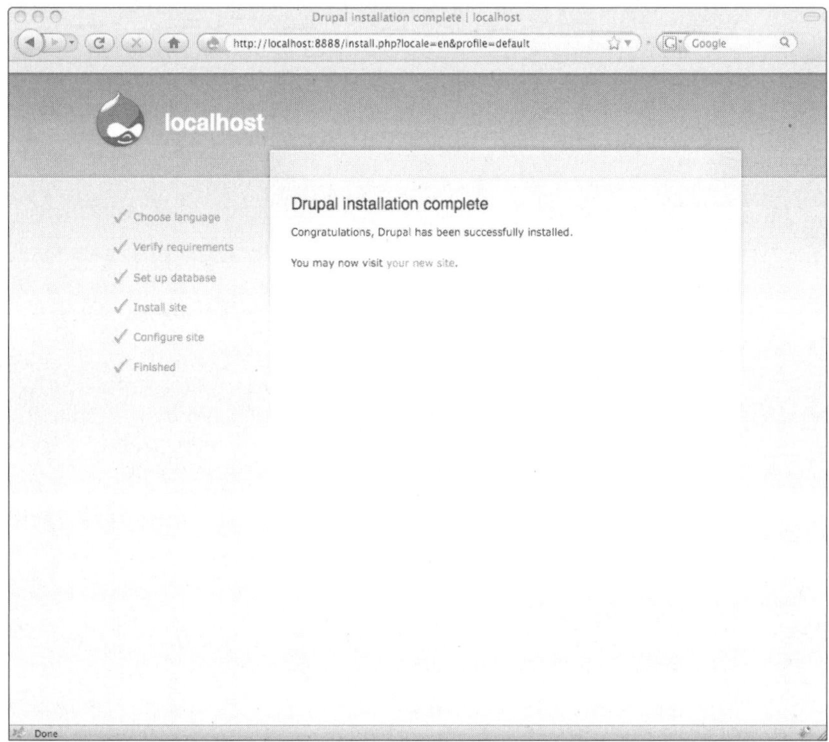

Figure 2-16: The final screen of the Drupal setup.

If you don't want to run Drupal on your own computer, you can skip from here to Chapter 3.

Installing Drupal on a Local Machine

Running Drupal on your personal computer can be helpful if you want to learn how to use Drupal without the expense of signing up with an ISP.

While installing Drupal on your local machine is similar to the manual installation I describe, you have the added steps of installing the correct Apache, MySQL, and PHP versions. If you are using IIS on a Windows machine, consult your documentation for information on using PHP applications, such as Drupal.

What you need

Drupal needs Apache, MySQL, and PHP. You have to install these first, and installing each one involves downloading the software, extracting it in the correct location, making any file configuration changes, and testing it. You should install MySQL (`mysql.com`) first, then Apache (`apache.org`), then PHP (`php.net`).

Walking through the installation of these three products is outside the scope of this book and rather involved. Fortunately, some developers have put together applications that install all three of these packages at the same time for you.

Getting Apache, MySQL, and PHP

Several companies have taken the hard work out of installing these individual packages. These companies provide a single program that installs all three applications for you. I recommend either of these:

- XAMPP (see Figure 2-17) describes itself as "an easy to install Apache distribution containing MySQL, PHP and Perl. XAMPP is really very easy to install and to use — just download, extract and start." It can be installed on Linux, Windows, and Mac OS X. The home page for XAMPP is located here:

  ```
  www.apachefriends.org/en/xampp.html
  ```

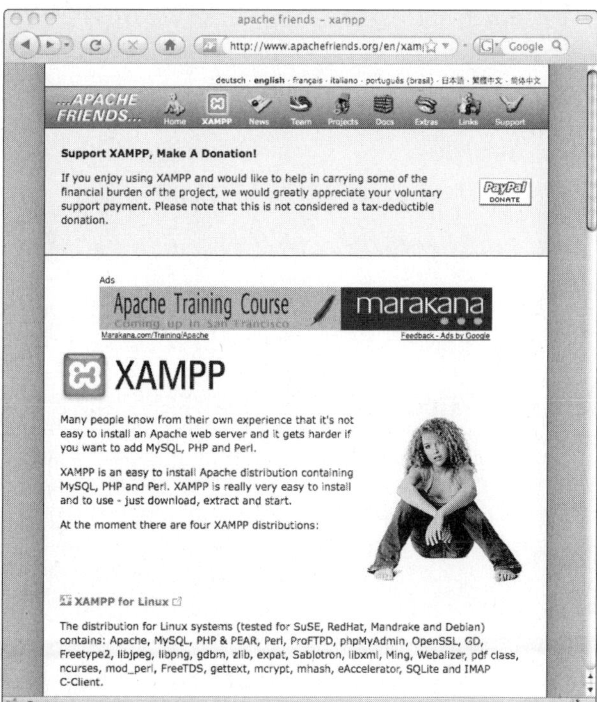

Figure 2-17: The home page of XAMPP.

- WAMP is a Windows option. The home page is

```
http://www.wampserver.com
```

- MAMP (see Figure 2-18) is a great option created just for Mac OS X. The home page is

```
http://www.mamp.info.
```

- They have commercial and free versions of the software.

Figure 2-18: The home page of MAMP.

Finishing a local machine install

After you've got MySQL, PHP, and Apache running, whether individually or through XAMPP or MAMP, you are ready to set up a database and install Drupal.

To set up a database and install Drupal on a local machine, follow these steps:

1. **Locate and open the phpMyAdmin program installed by XAMPP or MAMP.**

2. **Locate the Create a new database field on the right side of the phpMyAdmin screen.**
3. **Type in the name of your new database. Call it *drupal* and click the Add button.**

Now you need to download the Drupal software and install it on your local machine under the Web directory. Follow these steps:

1. **Browse to `www.drupal.org`.**

   A link to download the most current stable release is on the right side of the page just under the Search box.

2. **Click the Download the latest version link.**

   You will be taken to a News and Announcements page with a link to actually begin the download.

   The file will be named something like `drupal-6.12.tar.gz`.

3. **Save this file to a directory you will remember.**
4. **Double-click the Drupal `.tar.gz` file to extract it.**

   It will be extracted as a single folder.

5. **If necessary, rename the extracted folder `drupal`.**
6. **Copy the `drupal` folder to your local Web server directory.**

   Move this new folder to your local Web server directory. This location depends on which package you used to install Apache. Consult the documentation for your particular package to find the Web directory on your machine.

Now you are ready to run the installation. To reach it, browse to `http://localhost/drupal`.

Running the installation

Drupal will take you through a series of forms. Click on the Install Drupal in English link. Your first step is to create a configuration file.

Creating the configuration file

To create the configuration file, open the `drupal` directory on your local Web server directory, and copy and rename a file in the directory `sites/default/`. To do so, follow these steps:

1. **Using Explorer on Windows or Finder on the Mac, open your Web server directory, and then the `drupal` directory.**

2. **Locate and open the `sites` directory. Open the `default` directory.**
3. **Select the only file in this directory, `default.settings.php`.**
4. **Rename this file `settings.php`.**

Verify requirements

Browse back to your Drupal site and reload the page.

Set up database

Enter the name of the database you created earlier, `drupal`, in the Database name field. For the database username and password, enter the username *root* and leave the password blank, as I discuss in Step 4 in the section "Creating a database for Drupal." Click the *Save and continue* button.

Your MySQL database username may not be *root.* If this doesn't work, consult the documentation for your particular installation software (XAMPP, MAMP, or WAMP).

Configure site

There are quite a few bits of information you need to provide on the Configure site form.

Here's the list of text boxes and options you fill out:

- **Site name:** This field is pre-filled with the domain name of your Drupal site. It's actually going to show up at the top of all the pages on your site instead of the current large white heading, "Drupal."

  Change this to a title that makes sense for your current site. If you don't know what you want to call your site, you can set this later.
- **Site e-mail address**
- **Administrator username:** This is the username that you use to connect to your Drupal administrative functions.
- **Administrator e-mail address:** Enter an e-mail address where you want to receive e-mails from the Drupal system.
- **Administrator password:** Enter a password to be used with your Administrative login.
- **Administrator confirm password:** Type the password again to confirm.
- **Default time zone**
- **Clean URLs**
- **Check for updates automatically**

Chapter 3

Essential Administration

In This Chapter

- Deciding where to begin
- Understanding modules
- Figuring out tasks
- Becoming comfortable with Drupal terminology
- Configuring Drupal

You just finished the hardest part of Drupal — getting the software installed correctly. It wasn't easy. You had to decide where to install it; integrate your Drupal application with an Apache Web server, PHP, and a MySQL database server; and configure various settings. This is quite a bit of work. Now I move on to more interesting Drupal administration details.

In this chapter, I show you some easier but essential tasks to get your site into shape. This chapter is fun. You get to dive in and start shaping your Web site. You make changes and immediately get to see the results of those changes.

I cover some of the nitty gritty Drupal configuration settings that you need to know. And I introduce *Drupalese* — that is, I go over some of the language that Drupal uses and explain what it means in nontechnical terms. This is especially important because these terms are used frequently in the rest of the chapters. Understand them here, and you won't be in the dark later.

Setting a Strategy for Your Drupal Site

It's never too early to think about the purpose of your site. The site I use to illustrate concepts in this chapter is `drupalfordummies.com`. In my case, this site exists to support this book and give readers a place to discuss information in the book and Drupal in general. It helps create a sense of community.

In this chapter, when you see screen shots of `drupalfordummies.com`, they are early ones, taken when the site was first being put together. I was still considering the site configuration options that Drupal offers and which choices made the most sense for this particular site. With every decision I made, I had to consider the purpose of the site and the audience of the site.

When you visit the site now, you see the finished product, complete with a blog where I share my personal Drupal experiences, and forums that allow site visitors to discuss book topics. But before I could build those into `drupalfordummies.com`, I had to become familiar with the Drupal administrative menus and take care of some initial administrative tasks. As I made my preliminary decisions, I had to keep in mind my eventual objective: a Web site to help me build a community for readers of this book. Your objective might be to raise awareness of a cause or to sell a product. These things matter as you make your decisions. Throughout this chapter, I mention how my personal site goals influenced my administrative decisions.

Using Your New Site Sections

You've installed and done some initial configuration of your site. Now it's time to get down to work and customize this site to suit your needs. But before you can, you have to become familiar with the interface. Browse to your new Drupal Web site and take a look at the current default home page (see Figure 3-1).

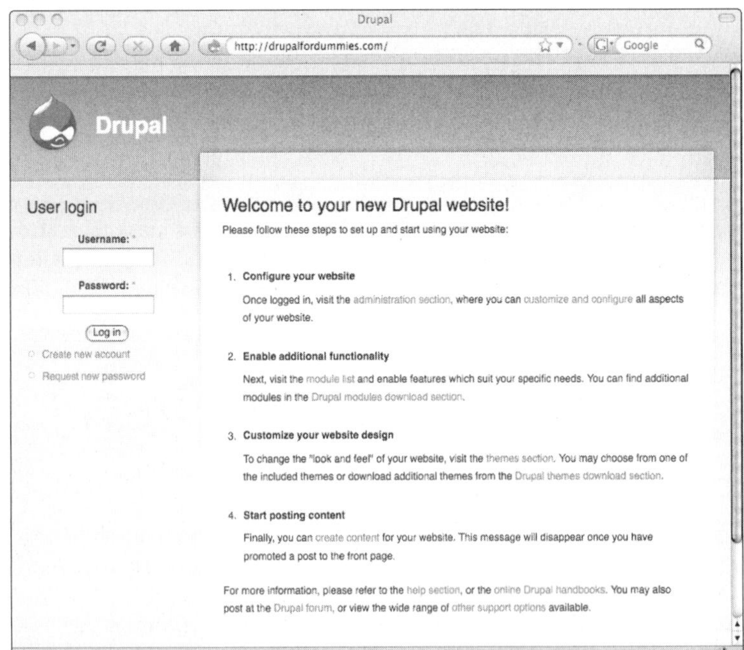

Figure 3-1: Your new Drupal site before any administrative changes.

There's not much to see yet. It's still a default Drupal installation and needs lots of work. To do everything in this chapter, begin by logging in with the administrative username and password you set up in Chapter 2.

Log out and log in

Everything begins by logging in. Type your administrative username and password that you chose when you installed Drupal and click Log in. You will now see your username above a new menu on the left where the user login form was (see Figure 3-2).

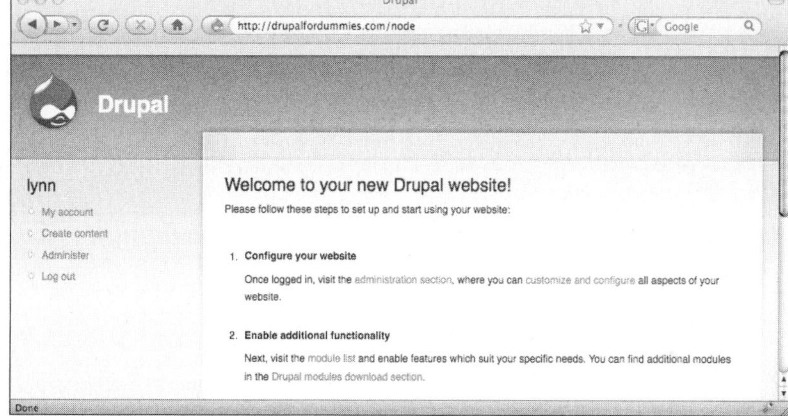

Figure 3-2: The main menu on the left appears when you log in to the site.

This menu contains four links:

- **My account:** Click on this to access your personal information. You can also edit it by clicking the Edit tab on the right side of the screen (see Figure 3-3). All users see this link.
- **Create content:** Clicking on this link opens up several links underneath it. This is where you go to add, edit, or delete any content on the site. Only when you are logged in as the administrator will you see this link.
- **Administer:** This also expands into many more links when clicked. This section is concerned with how the site behaves and looks rather than the content on it. Only when you are logged in as the administrator will you see this link.
- **Log out:** This does exactly what you think it does — logs you out. Make sure to log out if you plan on leaving your computer unattended in a public place for any length of time. All users see this link.

That's the overview of the main menu. Now you should take a closer look at each menu item.

Editing your account

This link takes you to your personal settings. When you click on it, you see your basic information. Locate the Edit link on the right and click on it to edit your personal settings, as seen in Figure 3-3.

Even though you are logged in as the administrator, the account settings shown on this page are the same ones any registered user will be able to control. When a user clicks on the My account link and then the Edit tab, he will be able to make changes to his personal account.

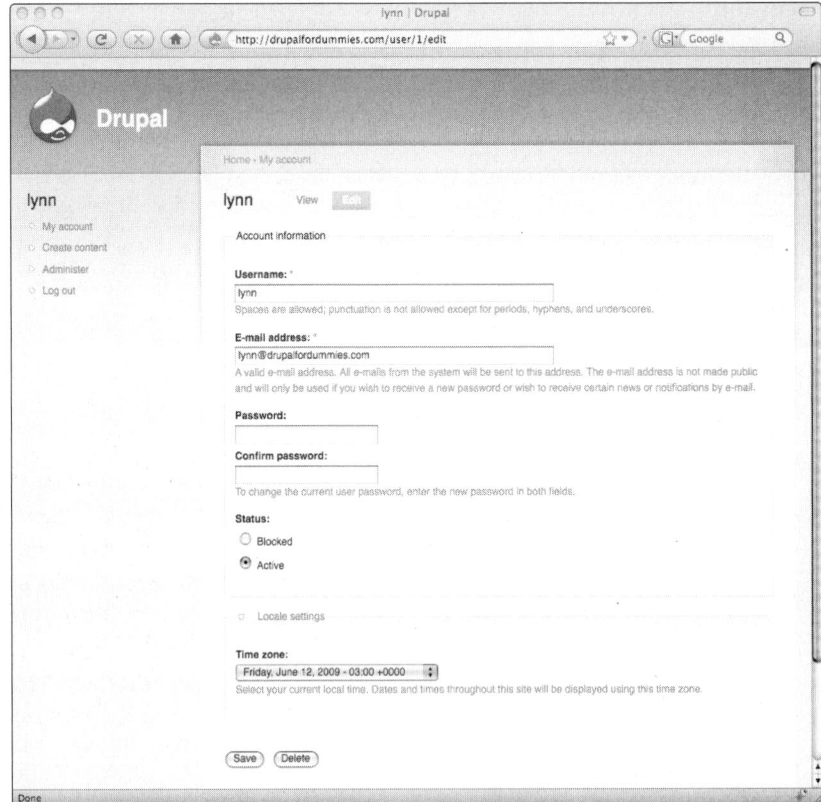

Figure 3-3: The Edit tab of the Account information page.

The settings are:

- **Username:** You can change your current username here.
- **E-mail address:** This is the e-mail address for the current user.
- **Password:** If you want to change the password for this account, enter it here.
- **Confirm password:** Type the new password again to confirm.
- **Status:** You can change the status here from Active, which allows you to post on the site, to Blocked, where you can't. There isn't any reason to change this setting in this menu. Another section of the site that I talk about later allows you, as an administrator, to manage the setting for any user on the site.
- **Time zone:** Remember the time zone you set in the last chapter during the manual install? No matter what the site time zone is set to, when you are logged in you will see the time zone selected here.

Creating your first content

Enough about the important, but not very interesting, account settings. After setting up and administering your site in the first two chapters, you're ready to make a visual change to your Drupal site. I discuss the content link in this section and show how to add some content to the site.

I cover content creation in much more detail in Chapter 5.

Understanding pages and stories

In Drupal, a *page* is generally content that seldom changes. In the case of my `drupalfordummies.com` site, I might create a page with my contact information on it.

A *story* is more like a news article or blog. You can allow users comments on an individual story, which a page, by default, doesn't allow you to do.

Creating a story

To add your first story to the home page of your Drupal site, follow these steps:

1. **If you aren't logged in to the site, log in with your administrator username and password.**

2. **Click the Create content link on the left.**

   You see two new links appear on the left, *Page* and *Story.*

3. **Click the Story link on the left.**

   You see a form that allows you to create your first story (see Figure 3-4). There are lots of other options and settings on this form, but I won't discuss those until Chapter 5.

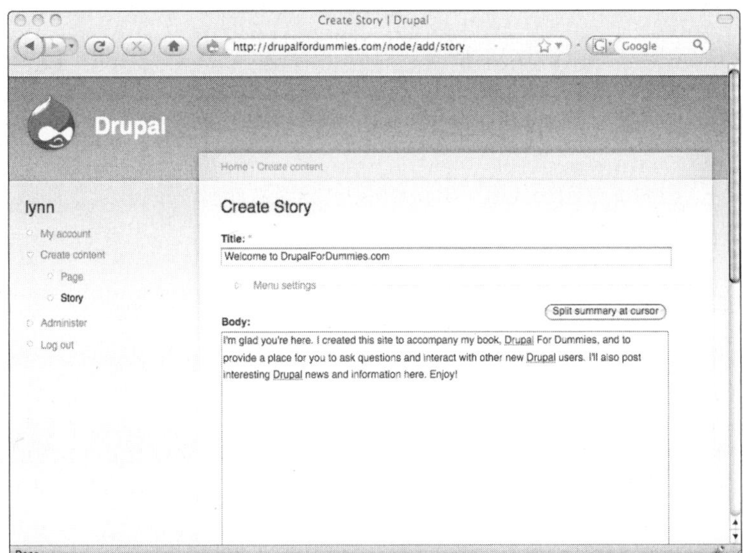

Figure 3-4: The Create Story page.

4. **Type something in the title and body text boxes. Scroll down to the very bottom of the page, and click the Preview button.**

   You will see a preview of your story (see Figure 3-5).

   Your story will not yet appear on your Web site; this just gives you an idea of what it will look like when it is published and gives you the chance to make changes before it appears on your Web site.

5. **After you've made any additions or changes to it, and when you are happy with it, click the Save button at the bottom of the page.**

You can use the Preview button again and again as you change the story. Preview your story as often as you wish without saving it. It won't appear on your Web site until you click the Save button.

That's it! You will see a confirmation message in green (see Figure 3-6) that your story has been published, but that message won't show up on the site when you reload, and anybody else visiting your site will not see the green text.

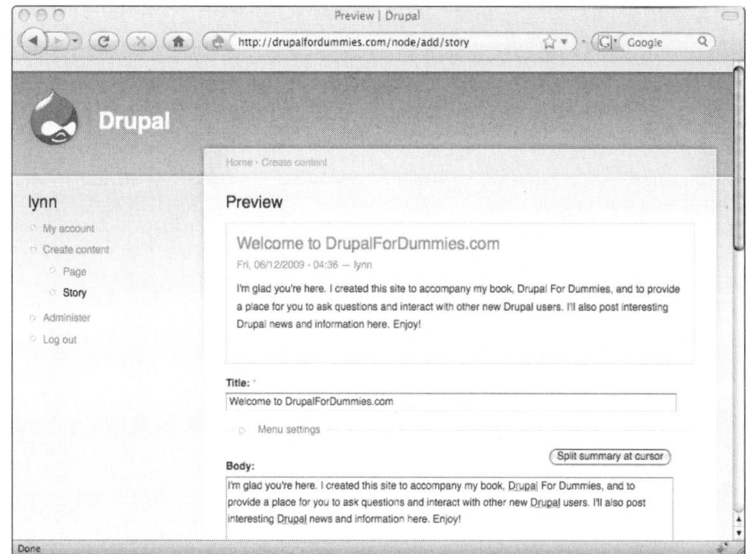

Figure 3-5: A preview of your first story.

To see your new story, reload the browser. Your story is visible to anyone who browses to your site, whether or not they are logged in.

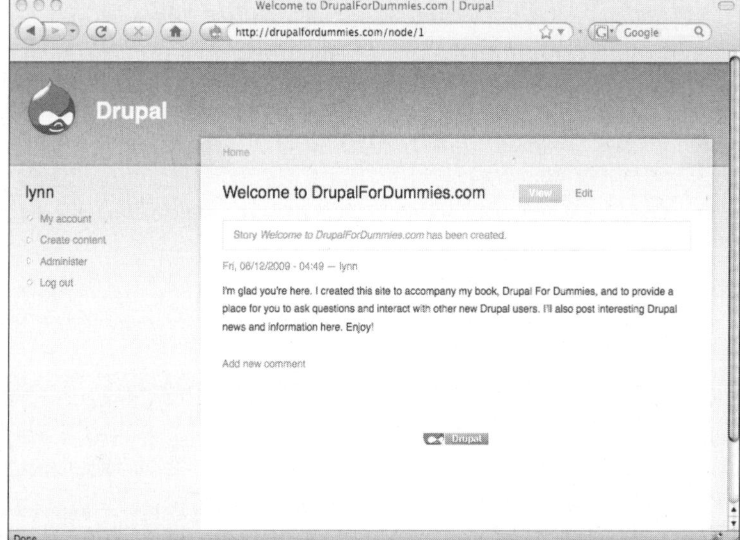

Figure 3-6: The story you created now appears on the home page of your site.

By default, your story has a comment link. Only registered users can add comments.

Administering Options

The Administer menu has a few interesting menu items you may want to play with right now.

I cover the Administer menu in detail in Chapter 4.

Log in with your administrator username and password, and click the Administer link. For now I focus on the menu on the left:

- **Content management:** The menu options available under this section control everything to do with the appearance and management of your content. While you would use the Create content link to create new content, this section allows you to edit existing content.

  This is where you change how and where your content appears.
- **Site building:** Here's where you change the appearance of your site. You can change the overall look by selecting a new theme, and you can change where on the page various content types will appear. For example, I could move the new story I created in the left-hand column and move the menu items to the right if I wished. There's no good reason to do so, but there will be changes to the interface you will wish to make. This is also the area that controls navigation links and where they appear. This is where you would create a link to a Contact Us page, for example. You would create the page itself by clicking the Create Content link.
- **Site configuration:** In the preceding chapter, you set some of the Site Configuration options when you installed Drupal manually. If you used Fantastico, you haven't made any configuration changes yet. This section controls some basic but important options that control how your site operates.

  The section "Configuring your site," below, shows a few important site configuration options you should set.

Embracing Drupal terminology

You've already encountered the words *page* and *story* to describe types of content. And you probably have an idea of what *theme* means now.

A few Drupal expressions that you should know at this point are:

- Page: A type of content primarily used for news. This type allows registered users of the site to add comments.
- Story: A type of content primarily used for information that doesn't change very often.
- Menu: A Drupal menu means a collection of links.
- Theme: This is a set of styles, graphics, and layouts.

- **User management:** If you want to add, edit, or delete users, this is the place to do it. You can also control what the user can see on the site and what he can't.
- **Reports:** The reports section helps you keep tabs on how much and what kind of activity is happening on your site.

  This becomes very important as your site gets more visitors.

- **Help:** If you get stumped as you administer your site, you may find some help in this section.

It's not much fun to read about all these menu items and not get a chance to do anything. While I go through all this in more detail later in the book, here's one fun thing you can change on your site, buried in the Administer menu section:

1. **Choose Administer⇨Site Building⇨Themes.**
2. **Scroll down and find the Chameleon theme. Select the check box and radio button to the right of Chameleon (see Figure 3-7).**
3. **Click the Save configuration button at the bottom of the page.**

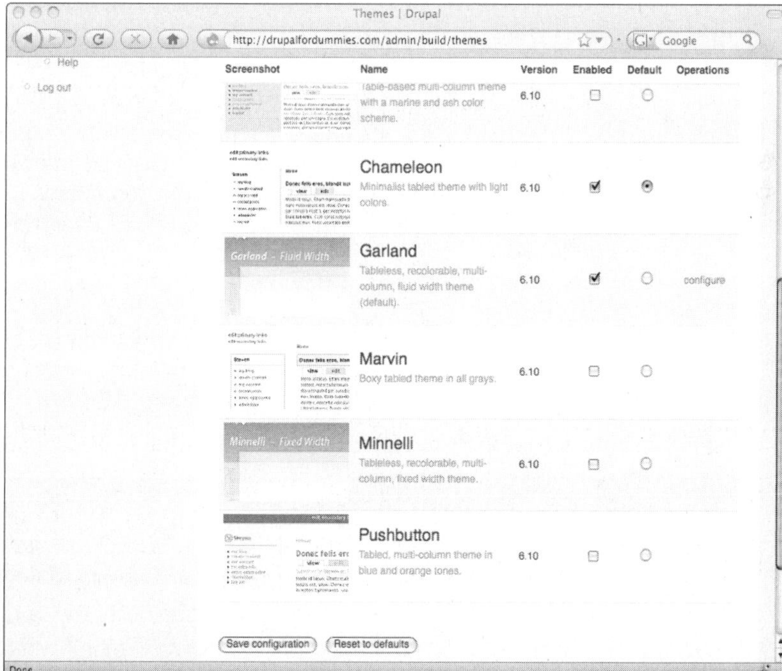

Figure 3-7: Changing the default theme to Chameleon.

Suddenly your site has changed to a new theme (see Figure 3-8). Only the appearance has changed. The content is still there, and the layout is even the same.

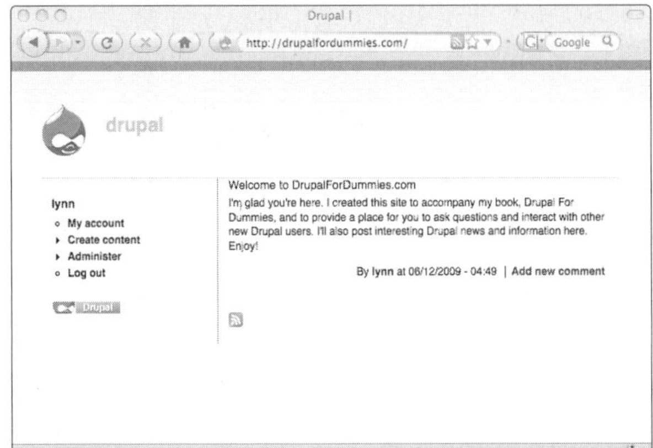

Figure 3-8: Drupal site using the Chameleon theme.

If you don't like the new theme, you can return it to the Garland theme by selecting the radio button to the right of the Garland theme on the Themes page. Or try one of the others. You can change it back if you don't like it.

Configuring Your Site

You may not have manually installed your Drupal site, choosing to go the Fantastico route instead. If so, the name of your site is still "Drupal." It's time to change that, as well as a few other important configuration options. I begin by looking at all the options under the Site configuration menu. To get there, choose Administer⇨Site configuration.

Here are the options you are most likely to use at some point:

- **Actions:** Suppose you wanted Drupal to send you an e-mail whenever someone comments on your story. Sending that e-mail to you is a type of *action*. Clicking this link allows you to create new actions.
- **Administration theme:** If you want just the administrative pages (that is, all the links under the Administer menu) to use a different theme than the rest of the site, you can set it here.
- **Clean URLs:** Many Drupal URLs look like this: `http://drupalfordummies.com/?q=node/1`. Enabling this makes them look like this: `http://drupalfordummies.com/node/1`.
- **Date and time:** Here's where you can change the default time zone for your site.

  You can also control how dates appear on the site. For example, if you look at the story you created earlier in this chapter, it has a byline with your username followed by a time and date. This form lets you change the appearance of that information.

- **Error reporting:** Settings here control what happens when a visitor tries to go to a page on your site that doesn't exist.
- **File system:** These settings control where files uploaded by users are kept and how Drupal handles those uploads.
- **Image toolkit:** You can control the quality of images and how they are handled if you add an image gallery or similar feature on your site.
- **Site information:** This contains a number of text boxes where you can enter information that will, if you wish, appear on every page of your site. I explain this in more depth later in this chapter.
- **Site maintenance:** If you want to work on your site but don't want anyone to see the changes or log in while you are making them, you can take your site offline here. This means that visitors will see a message about the site being unavailable. You will still be able to see the site when you log in with your administrator username and password.

Setting your site information

There are quite a few settings in the Site information form you should fill out. This is where you can put your own name on the site as well as additional information that appears on every page of your site.

To customize your site information, follow these steps:

1. **Logged in with your administrator username and password, choose Administer⇨Site configuration. You see the form shown in Figure 3-9.**

   I am currently using the Chameleon theme. You may be using a different theme, so your screen doesn't look like mine. Don't let that throw you; all the same form fields are on all versions.

2. **Enter your site name in the Name text box. Also, if you don't have an e-mail address in the E-mail address field, enter one now. Click Save Configuration.**

   For now, just change the site name and save it. Look at the top of your page. Instead of the word "Drupal," the name you entered is displayed. In my case, my site now has a title.

3. **Navigate back to the Site configuration page and add a Footer message. Click Save Configuration.**

Your site will now have a title and a footer (see Figure 3-10).

Later in this book, I show you how to make the slogan and mission statements appear on the site.

At this point, your site should begin to look like your site, not the default Drupal site. It only gets better from here on out!

Figure 3-9: Site configuration settings.

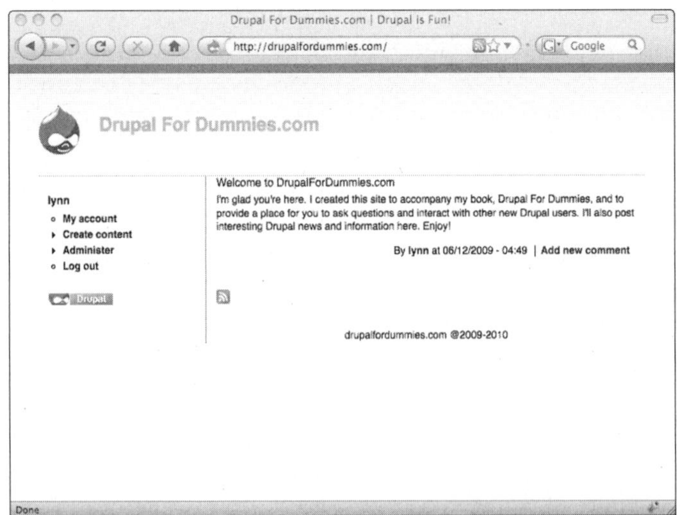

Figure 3-10: Site with a title and footer.

Chapter 4

Tackling User Management

In This Chapter

- Securing your administrator account
- Understanding roles
- Controlling site registrations
- Keeping tabs on your users

When the business of installing and configuring Drupal is complete, people can visit your site. Now it's time to consider how these visitors to your site will be treated. Part of that involves the decision whether to even allow users to register on your site and, if so, the privileges they get as registered users.

This chapter is about making your own administrator account a bit more secure, managing whether your visitors can register and log in, how that process takes place, and the privileges both unregistered and registered users get on your site.

Managing Your Administrator Account

The administrator account is the username and password you set up when you installed Drupal. This account is your key to the kingdom: The administrator account allows you complete control over everything on your site.

Editing administrator settings

To change settings for your administrator account, log in and click the My account link. You will see basic information about how long your account has existed under the View tab (See Figure 4-1).

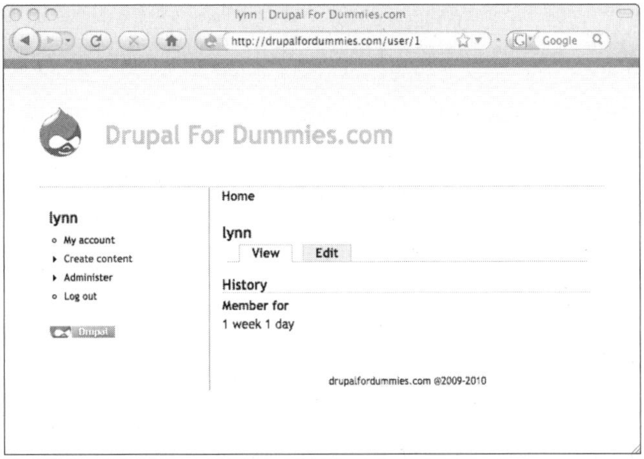

Figure 4-1: The View tab under the My account page.

You can't configure anything on this page; it states your history. Click the Edit tab (See Figure 4-2).

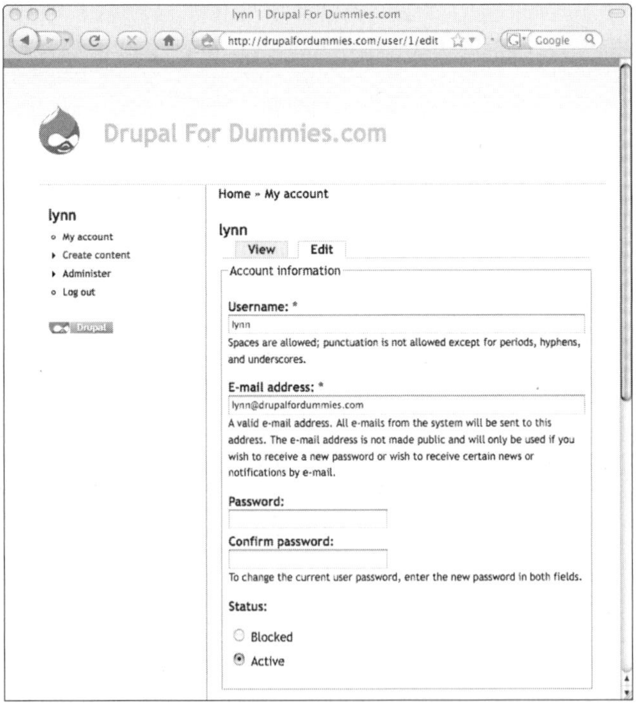

Figure 4-2: The Edit tab of the My account page.

Initial user setup

Drupal allows two types of users by default when you first install it:

- Unregistered users are visitors to your site who don't log in.

  By default, unregistered users can view the content on your site, located in pages, stories, and comments, but they can't contribute any content themselves. If they try to comment, they will be told they must log in to do so.

- Registered users have set up a username and password on the system.

  By default, registered users can view all the content and are allowed to add comments.

These are the "out of the box" settings for unregistered and registered users, but you can change these settings to your liking.

The My account page opens up a much longer page with options for you to change your *status* (which I explain in a moment), username, e-mail password, and account password. There are also sections for Theme configuration and Locale settings (See Figure 4-3).

These two tabbed pages show up for all registered users on your site. They can control their own passwords and, by default, control the same options that your administrator account can change here. You can control what your users can change on the Edit tab:

- **Username:** You can change your administrator username here.
- **E-mail address:** This is the address associated with your administrator account.

  This isn't the e-mail address you set up to be your Web site e-mail address used for automatically generated e-mails.
- **Password and Confirm Password:** If you didn't set a strong password when you set up the Drupal site, here's where you can change it.
- **Status:** This setting controls whether this user, in this case, you the administrator, can log in.

  Don't change Status to blocked! If an account is blocked, that user will not be able to log in to the site.

Don't change Status to blocked when you are looking at your own account. I can't stress this strongly enough. If you change it to blocked, you will lock yourself out of your own site! There is no easy way to recover from this. At best, you'll have to dig around and change a setting in the MySQL database behind the scenes, which is tricky.

Although the status setting appears on your own administrator setting page, it only applies if you aren't looking at that administrator setting page. Later in this chapter, I show you how to view other user accounts and reach this settings page. That's the only time you need to use this setting.

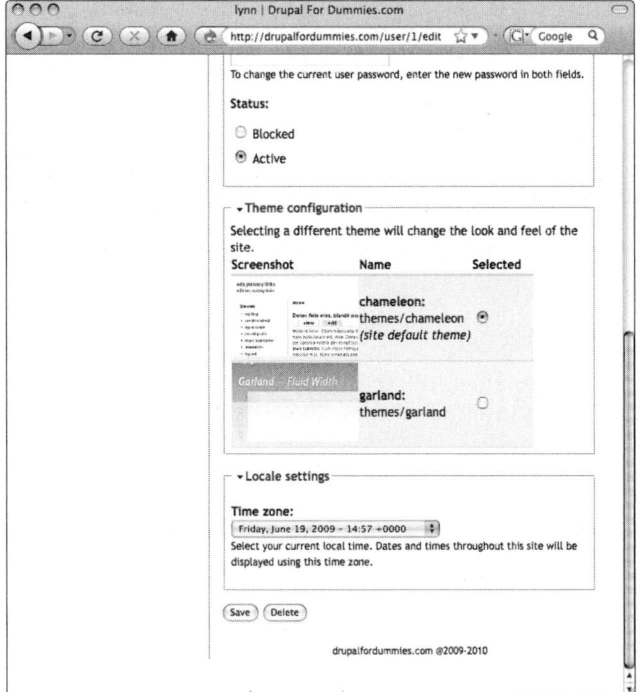

Figure 4-3: The bottom half of the Edit tab under the My account page.

The two remaining sections of the My account page are

- Theme configuration controls which theme this user (in this case, you the administrator) will see when logged in to the site. I spend lots of time talking about themes in Chapter 7.

  This is where users can change the theme that only they see. Chapter 7 explains how to turn this option off for other users if you want them to see only the theme you choose.

- Locale settings override the time zone you set when you configured the site for everything this user sees.

Drupal uses a menuing system that can hide page sections. Clicking on the title Theme configuration, for example, hides the content in the square just underneath it. You can click on the title again to display it. This behavior shows up in lots of places, so if you don't see sections of the site displayed that you think you should, make sure they aren't hidden under their titles.

Maintaining security

Your administrator account controls everything, and I mean *everything,* to do with your Drupal site. Keep your administrator account safe at all times:

- If you started with a simple password, consider changing it to something with at least 7 characters, using both numbers and letters.

  Changing your password is easy. Click the My account link, then the Edit tab on the right. Type in your new, stronger password, and type it again. Then press the Save button.
- Consider changing your username if you've used something predictable like "admin" or your first name, as I have in the examples in this chapter.

  Change your username on the Edit tab of the My account page. You can use your full name (for example, Lynn Beighley) as your username. This is a nice choice, because when you post to your site blog or write comments, your full name will appear as the author.

Allowing Public Registrations

As Drupal is set when you first install it, anyone can register for an account on the site without having to be approved by you. You can set up your own user account and see how user registration currently works:

1. **If you are currently logged in, click the log-out link at the bottom of the left menu.**

   You will see a log-in form on the left. Under that are two links: Create new account and Request new password.
2. **Click the Create new account link.**

   You will see the User account page with the Create new account form (see Figure 4-4).

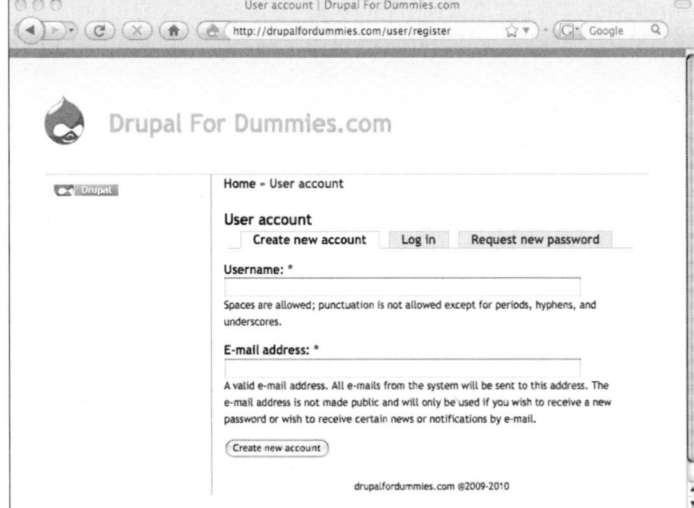

Figure 4-4: New user account request form.

3. **Enter a username and a valid e-mail address, and then click Create new account.**

   You will receive an e-mail at that address in a few minutes (see Figure 4-5).

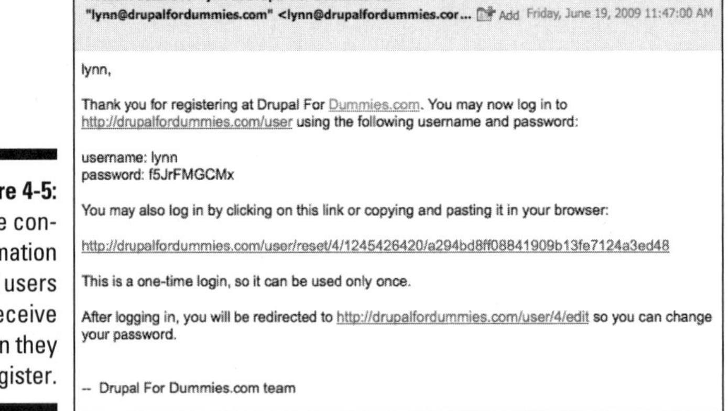

Account details for lynn at Drupal For Dummies.com Standard Header
"lynn@drupalfordummies.com" <lynn@drupalfordummies.cor... Add Friday, June 19, 2009 11:47:00 AM

lynn,

Thank you for registering at Drupal For Dummies.com. You may now log in to http://drupalfordummies.com/user using the following username and password:

username: lynn
password: f5JrFMGCMx

You may also log in by clicking on this link or copying and pasting it in your browser:

http://drupalfordummies.com/user/reset/4/1245426420/a294bd8ff08841909b13fe7124a3ed48

This is a one-time login, so it can be used only once.

After logging in, you will be redirected to http://drupalfordummies.com/user/4/edit so you can change your password.

-- Drupal For Dummies.com team

Figure 4-5: The confirmation e-mail users receive when they register.

Use a different e-mail address for your test user account than the address you used with your administrator account. Drupal identifies users on the site by e-mail address; only one user to an e-mail address is allowed.

The text of this e-mail is up to you. (I show you where you can change it in the "User e-mail settings" section, later in this chapter.)

The user account has now been set up. You can click the link in the e-mail you received and see how the rest of the registration process works.

Now you have a registered user account in addition to your administrator account. Take advantage of this new user account to see how the site looks to your registered users. You should also preview your site completely logged out as you work through the chapters of this book.

Sensible registration guidelines

Users can create their own accounts (as I explained previously in this chapter). As things stand now, the site administrator (you) won't necessarily know when a new user registers. However, there are a couple of settings that can help you control new registrations:

- You can control how you are notified when users register.
- More importantly, you can control whether new users have to be approved by you first.

To control user registrations and a few other settings involved with new user creation, you can visit the User management page (see Figure 4-6).

Figure 4-6: The User settings section of the User management page.

To get to the user settings section, log in with your administrator username and password. Click Administer⇨User management.

The Public registration set of radio buttons controls how users can register. The options are:

- **Only site administrators can create new user accounts:** If you select this option, you must create new accounts yourself. The link that invites visitors to create a new account won't show.

  To create new accounts, you will need to use the add user form that I discuss in the section "Adding, Editing, and Deleting users."

- **Visitors can create accounts and no administrator approval is required:** This is the default setting when you first install Drupal. You've already seen how this works for users:
  - Provide the system with a username and e-mail.
  - Receive an e-mail from the system with a temporary password and a link to log in.
- **Visitors can create accounts, but administrator approval is required:** If you select this, Drupal will send an e-mail to your administrator account password asking you to approve the new user registration. If you follow the link in the e-mail and approve the user, he will be able to log in. If not, then Drupal throws away his information.

  Use the administrator approval required setting, at least until you finish designing your site.

The next option on the page is a check box that asks you if you want to require e-mail verification when a visitor creates an account. It's checked by default. This option causes the new registering user to get an e-mail like the one shown in Figure 4-5.

Leave this option checked. It prevents users from registering with a fake e-mail address. They have to use the password provided in the e-mail they receive, which proves that they have access to a real e-mail account and aren't spammers who want to fill your site up with spam advertisements.

The last text box in this section gives you a place to enter your own message to users filling out the user registration form. It shows up when visitors click the Create new account link. It's a good place to let them know what to expect if they register. If you choose to approve all registrations, for example, you can use this box to tell them that it may take up to 2 days to be approved.

User e-mail settings

The User e-mail settings section on this page contains a long form on which you can customize e-mails that get sent out to users by Drupal when certain things happen. For example, here is where you can change the text sent to people who register and get e-mailed a password (refer to Figure 4-5). Figure 4-7 shows the list of e-mails. (In this figure, you're just seeing the title bars for most of the User e-mail settings.)

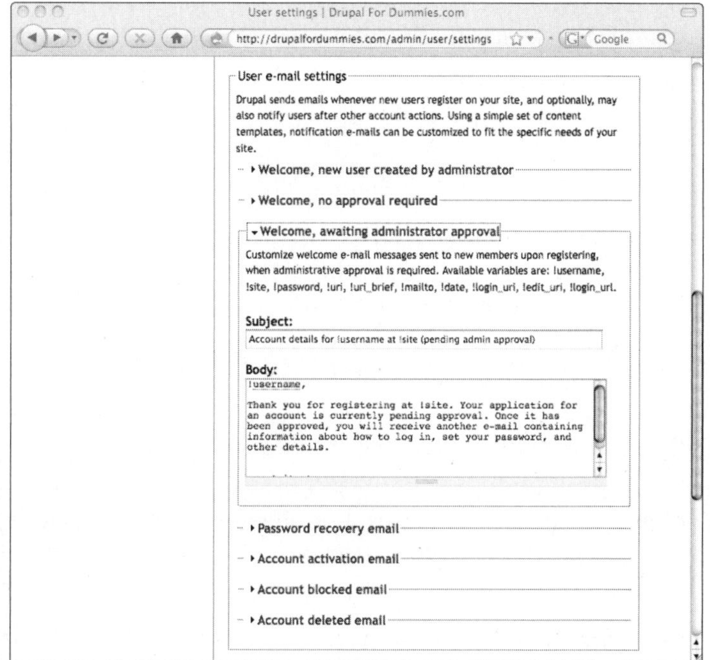

Figure 4-7: User e-mail settings portion of User management page.

To open the form for any individual e-mail form, click on its title bar.

Take a close look at the e-mail listed under Welcome, awaiting administrator approval. It starts with the word *!username*. Any time you see a word preceded by an exclamation point in these e-mails, the word is a stand-in. Since this e-mail is meant to go to any new registering user, Drupal uses !username and then replaces it with the appropriate username when it sends an e-mail to a specific user.

If you edit these e-mails, pay special attention to any words that are placeholders. The most commonly used are:

- **!username:** The username of the e-mail recipient
- **!site:** The site name that you set in the site configuration settings discussed in the preceding chapter
- **!password:** The e-mail recipient's password
- **!uri_brief:** A URL that takes the new user directly to the Edit tab of the My account page where he can change his password
- **!mailto:** The e-mail address of the e-mail recipient
- **!date:** The current date
- **!login_url:** The URL of the site

There are seven e-mails you can modify here:

- **Welcome, new user created by administrator:** If you select the first option under the user registration settings, shown in Figure 4-7, this is the e-mail that gets sent to the user.
- **Welcome, no approval required:** Sent to users if you select the second option under the user registration settings.

  This is the e-mail you received, shown in Figure 4-5, when you created the user account earlier in this chapter.

  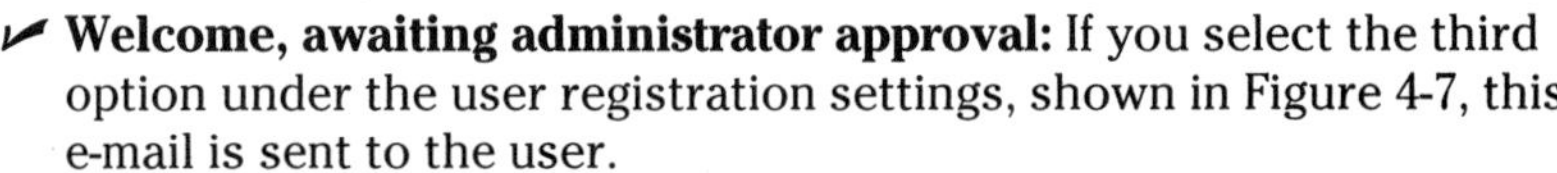
- **Welcome, awaiting administrator approval:** If you select the third option under the user registration settings, shown in Figure 4-7, this e-mail is sent to the user.

  Edit this e-mail to let the user know how long the approval will take.
- **Password recovery e-mail:** When visitors aren't logged in, they see a link to request a new password. After they enter their username or e-mail, this is the e-mail they are sent. It contains a link to a page on which they can reset the password.
- **Account activation e-mail:** If you are using the third option under user registration settings (administrator approval required), this gets sent to the user when you approve his account.
- **Account blocked e-mail:** If you block a user account, this e-mail informs him that he won't be able to log in to the site.

  I show you how to block users in the section "Adding, Editing, and Deleting users."
- **Account deleted e-mail:** If you delete a user account, that user receives this e-mail. I show you how to delete users in the section "Adding, Editing, and Deleting users."

If you accidentally change any of these e-mails, or anything else on this page, and you don't like what you've done or you've left out one of the placeholder words, you can restore everything to Drupal's default settings. Click the Reset to defaults button at the bottom of this page.

There are two more sections on this page: Signatures and Pictures. I discuss these in Chapter 9, where I show you how to add a forum to your site.

Assigning user permissions

By default, logged-in registered users can add comments to your postings, but unregistered users can't. This setting, and many other settings, is controlled by the Permissions form under User management (see Figure 4-8).

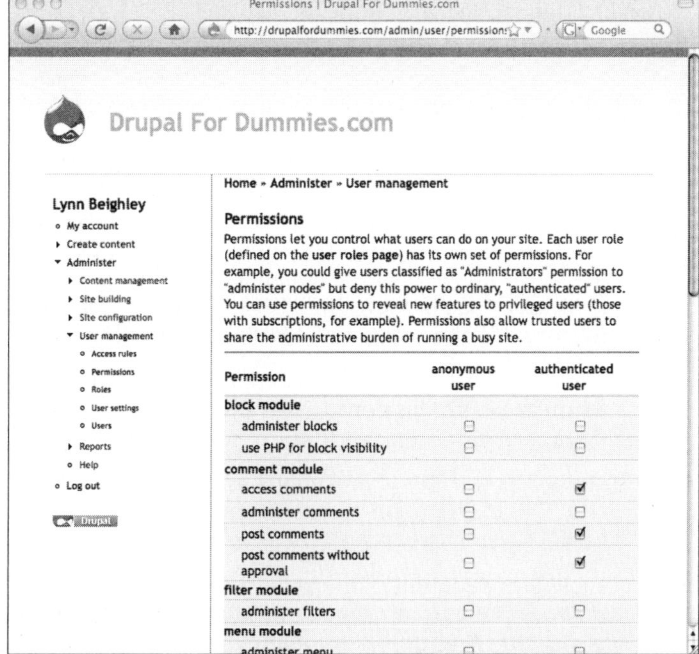

Figure 4-8: The Permissions form controls what users can do.

Drupal calls users who are logged in to the site authenticated users. From this point on, I use **authenticated users** to mean users who are logged in to the system, and **anonymous users** to refer to users who are not logged in.

To get to the Permissions page, log in with your administrator account and click Administer➪User management➪Permissions. Along the top of the table on this page, there are the table headings anonymous user and authenticated user. Anything you check under anonymous user will only apply to anyone who visits the site without signing in. Anything checked under authenticated users will only apply to users who sign in. There are lots of options here, but for now I only discuss a few of them.

It seems odd, but if you check anonymous user and not authenticated user on one of these options, only people who haven't logged in will have that privilege. Generally,, if an anonymous user can do something, an authenticated user should be able to do it as well. Make sure both check boxes are checked when the anonymous user box is checked.

Most of these permission settings are covered in detail elsewhere in the book as I show you more Drupal modules. You should know about these permission settings right now:

- **Comment Module:** This section controls whether users can view, create, or administer comments.
  - Access comments: Controls if users can see comments.
  - Administer comments: If selected, users can edit or delete comments.
  - Post comments: If this is selected, users can post comments, but they have to be approved by you first.
  - Post comments without approval: If you want users to post without prior approval, check this. In general, it's a good idea to not allow anonymous users to comment or, if so, make sure this is checked for you to view them first. Spammers frequently take advantage of comments to advertise their wares.
- **Node Module:** Nodes contain all the content on a Drupal site. I discuss only a few of these permissions that will be familiar to you at this point. Be cautious about granting permission for most of these.
  - Access content: This is probably the one permission you will always grant. This allows visitors to see content on your site. They can't do anything except view it, so it's safe to give to anonymous users as well.
  - Create story content: You may recall that the text I entered that appears on the front page of drupalfordummies.com is a *story.* This permission allows users to add their own stories to the site. You probably won't do this.
  - Edit any story content: Granting this allows users to edit stories posted to the site. For example, with this checked, a user could change the text posted to the front page of drupalfordummies.com.
  - Edit own story content: If you allow users to enter stories, you may want to enable this to allow them to edit only stories they have created.

- **User Module:** This controls the administration of users.
  - Access user profiles: Allows a user to view other users' profiles.
  - Administer permission: If selected, users can edit the page I am discussing right now. It is never a good idea to give users that much authority.
  - Administer users: You will allow your users to do all of the things I talk about in the section "Adding, Editing, and Deleting Users." This is likely not something you will want to do.
  - Change own username: If you check this, users will be able to change their usernames using the Edit tab of the My account page, as shown in Figure 4-2. It makes no sense to check this for an anonymous user, but you may wish to allow authenticated users to do so.

You can see many more permissions available here, but until you have an understanding of these modules and features (for example, blocks and filters), you shouldn't modify the permissions for them. You can always come back to this page and tweak permissions later. In general, it's best to start with as few permissions as possible and add more only when needed.

Adding, Editing, and Deleting Users

Drupal gives the administrator (you) complete control over the registered users on your site. This means you can add new users, edit all user information, and delete users.

Adding users

To add a new registered user to your site, log in as the site administrator and click on Administer⇨User management⇨Users. Then click the Add user tab on the right-hand side of the screen. You will see the Add user form (see Figure 4-9).

This is much like the Edit tab of the My account page. But rather than editing an existing user, this creates a new user. Enter a username, e-mail address, password, and status on this page. If you set the status to Active, the new user will be able to log in, and if you check the box next to Notify user of new account, an e-mail will be sent to the e-mail address you entered for this new user. The e-mail will inform him that his account has been created and explain where he can log in.

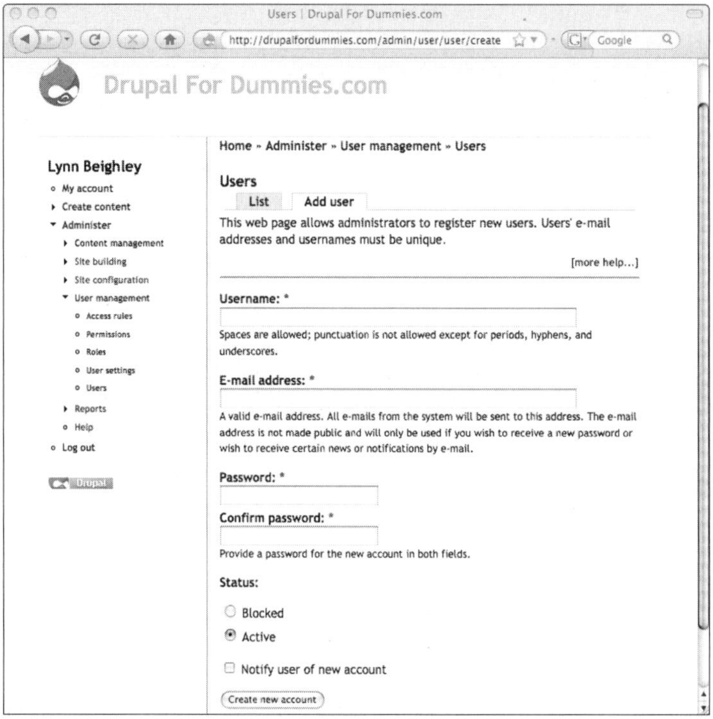

Figure 4-9: Add new user form.

Editing user information

Before you can edit user information for a particular user, you need to see a list of your users to select the correct account. To edit information for a user, log in as the site administrator and click on Administer⇨User management⇨Users. The list of users appears (see Figure 4-10).

Over time, your user list will get longer and longer. The table that lists your users can be sorted using the links at the top. For example, if you click on Username, the list will be alphabetized by username, A to Z. If you click it again, it will be ordered from Z to A. You may also find it useful to sort by the Member for heading if you are looking for a user who has just joined.

The section with the Filter button (as shown in Figure 4-10) allows you to view only users who satisfy particular criteria. You can choose to view a list of users based on the permissions you have granted them. Or if you need to see just your blocked users, use the status option.

To edit an individual user, click the edit link under the Operations heading. You will then be on the Edit tab of the My account link for that user (see Figure 4-11).

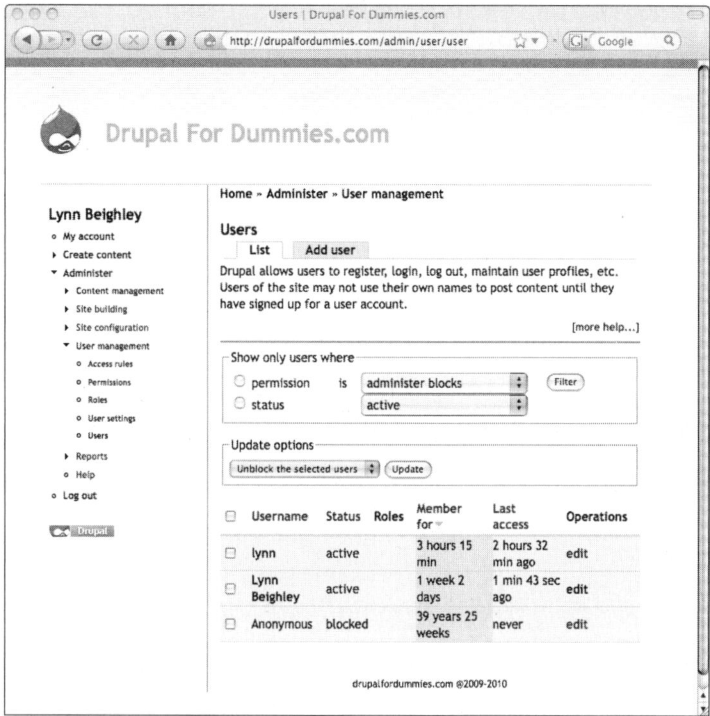

Figure 4-10: User management page with list of users.

For each registered user, Drupal keeps track of a username, password, e-mail address, a status (active or blocked), locale, and choice of theme. It also keeps track of roles, which I discuss in the next section. This is information that you, as administrator, can change. Drupal also records information such as when the last time a user logged in and comments a user has made. You can't edit this information. You can modify everything else that shows up on the Edit tab of the My accounts link.

The user edit page you as administrator see is basically the same as the edit page the user sees, with a few exceptions:

- The status section isn't available to the user. Only the administrator can control a user's status.
- The administrator can change the theme the user sees.
- The administrator can specify which *roles* (explained later in this chapter) the user has.

If you are ever asked to reset a user's password, this is the place to do it. But Drupal provides a link, Request new password, on your home page. This link sends the user an e-mail with a randomly generated password that allows him to log in and change his password himself.

Account information

Username: *

lynn

Spaces are allowed; punctuation is not allowed except for periods, hyphens, and underscores.

E-mail address: *

lynntestuser@drupalfordummies.com

A valid e-mail address. All e-mails from the system will be sent to this address. The e-mail address is not made public and will only be used if you wish to receive a new password or wish to receive certain news or notifications by e-mail.

Password:

Confirm password:

To change the current user password, enter the new password in both fields.

Status:

Blocked

Active

Roles:

authenticated user

story editors

Theme configuration

Selecting a different theme will change the look and feel of the site.

Screenshot	Name	Selected
	chameleon: themes/chameleon *(site default theme)*	(selected)
Garland – Fluid Width	**garland:** themes/garland	

Locale settings

Time zone:

Sunday, June 21, 2009 - 08:12 -0400

Select your current local time. Dates and times throughout this site will be displayed using this time zone.

Figure 4-11: The Edit user page the administrator sees.

Deleting users

To delete users, follow these steps:

1. **Log in as the site administrator and click on Administer➪User management➪Users.**

   You will see the list of users (refer to Figure 4-10).

2. **Click the box next to the user you wish to delete.**

3. **In the section Update options, click on the drop-down list box, and choose Delete the selected users.**
4. **Press the Update button to delete all the users you have selected.**

Understanding User Roles

Drupal allows you to create new user types with different permissions than anonymous or authenticated users. Drupal refers to these special groups of users as user *roles*. For example, imagine that you want to allow a group of people permission to create new stories, but you don't want your average authenticated user to have permission to do this.

Creating roles

To create a new role, log in as administrator, and then choose Administer➪User Management➪Roles (see Figure 4-12).

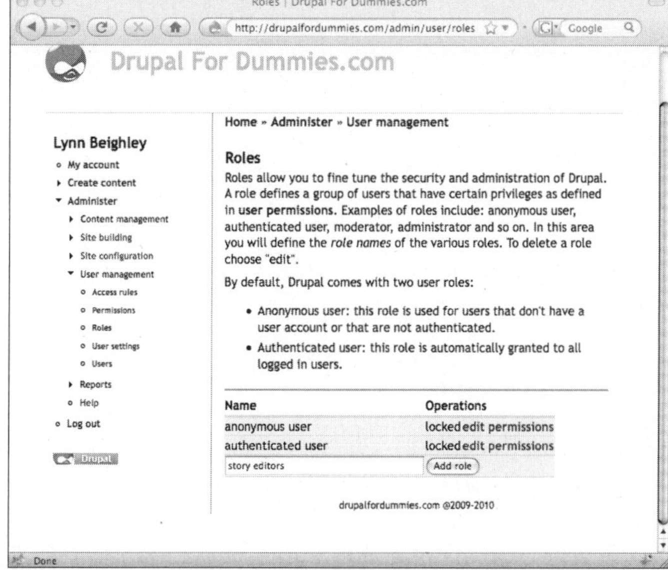

Figure 4-12: Adding a new role on the Roles page under User management.

To create a new role, type a name for your role in the text box and click the Add role button.

At this point, you have a new role, but it has exactly the same permissions the authenticated user role has. In my example, I created the story editor role to allow people with that role permission to create stories on the site. First, the new role doesn't have any permissions, and second, I haven't assigned this role to any users. To fix the first part, and modify a new role to have the right permissions, click the edit permissions link that appears to the right of the role name. You will see a page very much like the Permissions page you saw earlier (refer to Figure 4-8), only with a single column (see Figure 4-13). You can add the appropriate permissions here.

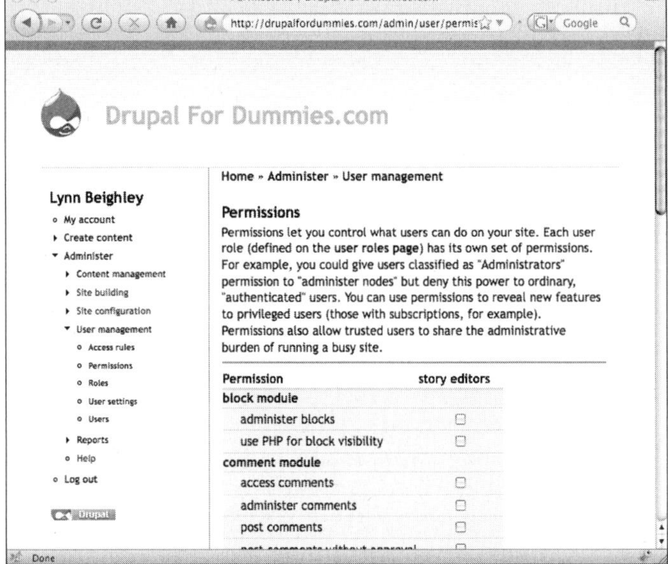

Figure 4-13: Permission editing for a new administrator-created role.

Although you can edit permissions for your new roles by clicking the edit permissions link, it's actually better to click on Administer⇨User management⇨Permissions. This page lets you see all your roles and permissions at once, making it much easier to ensure your new role has the basic permissions that an authenticated user has in addition to the new permissions (for example, *create story content,* which my story editors need).

Assigning roles to users

Users can have as many roles as you wish to give them. There are two ways to give users an additional role. To assign roles, follow these steps:

1. **Navigate to Administer⇨User Management⇨Users.**
2. **Click on the check box to the left of the user you are assigning the new role to.**
3. **Click on the drop-down box under the Update options section and select your new role from the list.**

or

1. **Navigate to Administer⇨User Management⇨Users.**
2. **Click the edit link to the right of the username in the list.**

   Since you created a new role, Drupal displays a Roles listing in the Account information section of the Edit page. Only the administrator can see this section. By default, all users are authenticated, so you can't uncheck the check box.
3. **Check the box next to the name of your new role and click the Save button at the bottom of the page.**

Part II
Your First Drupal Site

"This should unstick the keys a little."

In this part . . .

You discover how to take control of your new site, which includes creating and publishing content, changing the appearance of the site, and building menus. You learn how to post more images to your site. And to top it all off, you discover the secret to Drupal: modules.

Things are a tad more complicated here, but the rewards are great. By the end of this part, you'll have built a site with lots of fun features.

Chapter 5

Creating Content: Pages and Stories

In This Chapter

- Understanding nodes
- Beginning content creation
- Organizing your content
- Telling stories
- Creating pages

What's the point of creating a Web site without content? The primary reason to have a Web site is to communicate. You need content to get your message across, be it to sell something, to teach something, or to build a community. This chapter is all about content creation and organization.

The term *content* in this book refers to text, images, and other media intended to communicate information to site visitors. In this chapter, I focus on creating pages and adding text and image content to the pages of your site.

Understanding Drupal Nodes

Drupal has several types of content. In this chapter, I discuss two types: pages and stories. Each page or story you create for your Drupal site is stored as a structure called a *node.* Think of a node as a block of content, be it a page, story, or blog posting.

Don't confuse a Drupal page with a Web page. Drupal uses the word *page* to describe a block of content that doesn't allow comments and is largely static. And while you can view a page node as though it were a single Web page, you can do the same with a story node or any of the Drupal node types discussed in this book.

Making basic pages

At this point, your site has a home page. Chances are you need additional content on your site for things such as contact information and information about your company or group. Drupal *pages* contain information you want on your site that:

- Is necessary to have available to visitors
- Doesn't need to be on the main page of your site
- Doesn't change very often

Examples of appropriate information for Drupal pages include directions to your office; contact information; background information about your company; Frequently Asked Questions (FAQs); legal terms and policies; and biographies of your management team.

Content on a Drupal page doesn't allow visitors to add comments. If you want to allow your site users to comment, you need to create a story instead of a page. I cover stories later in this chapter.

Accessing content creation

To get to the content creation pages, you need to log in as the site administrator and click the Create content link (see Figure 5-1).

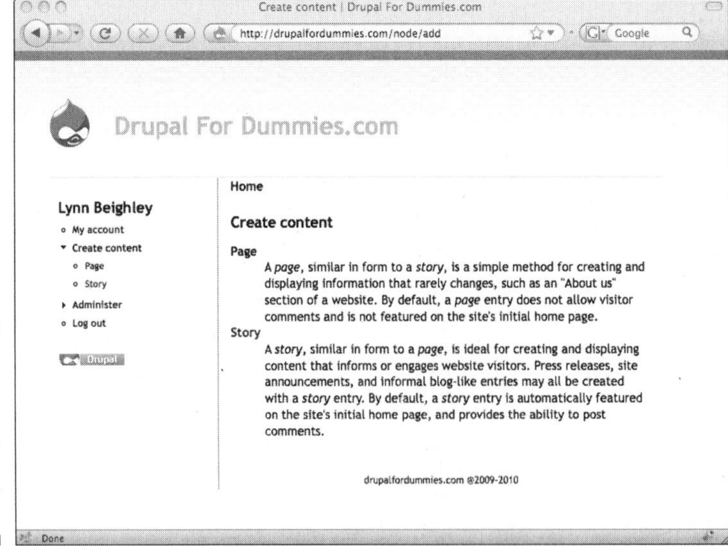

Create content | Drupal For Dummies.com
http://drupalfordummies.com/node/add
Google
Drupal For Dummies.com
Home
Lynn Beighley
My account
Create content
Page
Story
Administer
Log out
Drupal
Create content
Page
A *page*, similar in form to a *story*, is a simple method for creating and displaying information that rarely changes, such as an "About us" section of a website. By default, a *page* entry does not allow visitor comments and is not featured on the site's initial home page.
Story
A *story*, similar in form to a *page*, is ideal for creating and displaying content that informs or engages website visitors. Press releases, site announcements, and informal blog-like entries may all be created with a *story* entry. By default, a *story* entry is automatically featured on the site's initial home page, and provides the ability to post comments.
drupalfordummies.com ©2009-2010
Done

Figure 5-1: The Create content section of the administrator site.

You see a menu allowing you to create a page or a story along with some text to help you understand the difference between a story and a page. The important differences between the two are:

- Stories allow user comments; pages do not.
- Stories appear on the home page of your site. Pages are created as unique pages on your site with their own URLs.
- Stories are best for content that changes over time, such as news. Pages are best for static content.

Adding a page

You create a new page by clicking on the Page link under the Create content section. Follow these steps:

1. **Log in to your site as administrator.**
2. **Click the Create content link on the left.**
3. **Click on the Page link.**

   You see the Create Page form (see Figure 5-2).

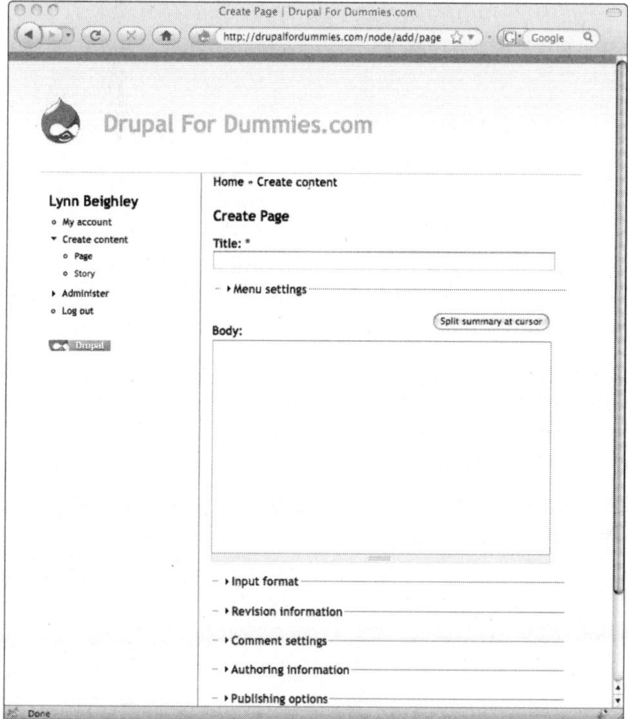

Figure 5-2: Create Page form.

4. **Enter the title of your page in the Title blank.**
5. **Enter some sample content in the Body section of the form.**

   Figure 5-3 shows sample content for a contact page.

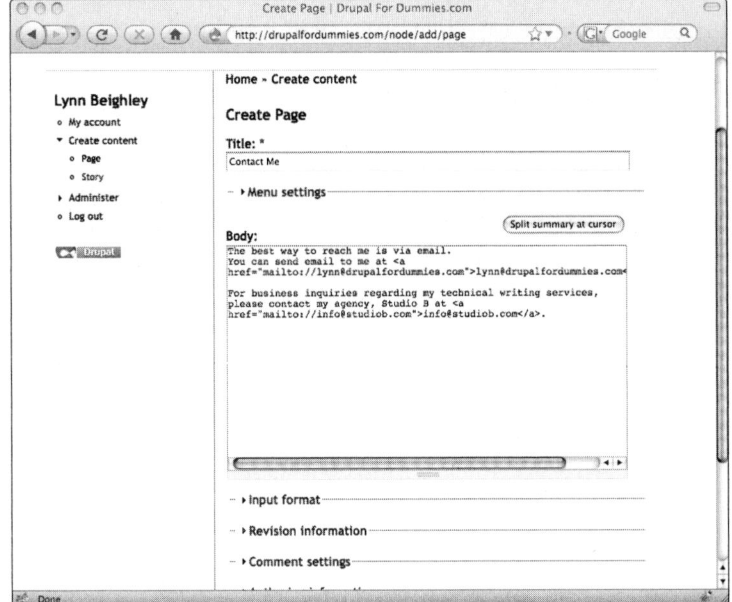

Figure 5-3: The Create Page form with the Title and Body fields filled out.

I've used some HTML code in my sample. This code turns my e-mail addresses into links on the page I'm creating. Don't let this throw you. You don't need to use HTML in your pages, but you can if you wish. I discuss this in more detail in Chapter 6.

6. **Scroll to the bottom of the form and click Preview.** If you click Save, your page will be automatically published to the Web. Preview allows you to see what your page will look like before it is published.

   Figure 5-4 shows you a preview of the new page you created. If you wish to change anything, scroll down and make your changes in the Create Page form. The same two buttons, Save and Preview, are at the bottom of the page.

7. **When you are happy with the content on your new page, click the Save button.**

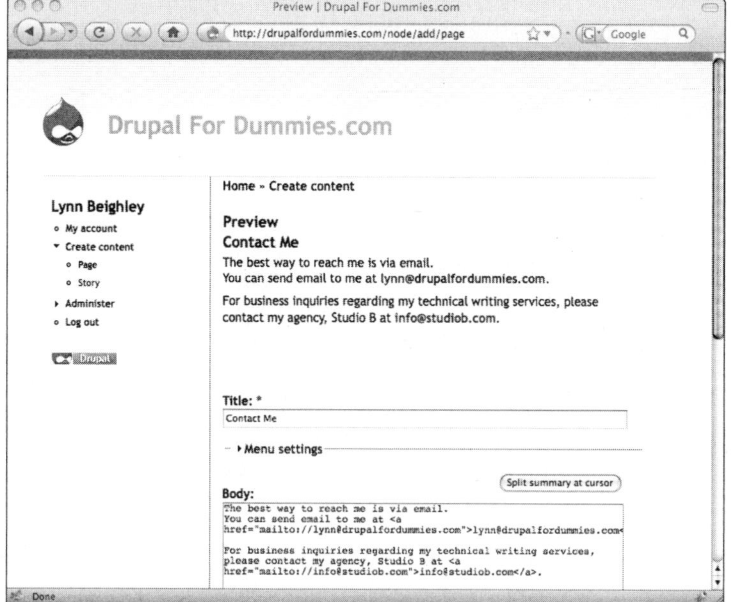

Figure 5-4: The Create Page form with a preview of the page.

When you save your new page, you see your new page with a status message, "Page *Contact Me* has been created." (See Figure 5-5.) The status message appears only once after you save your new page. You won't see it again when you later visit the page, and your site visitors will never see it.

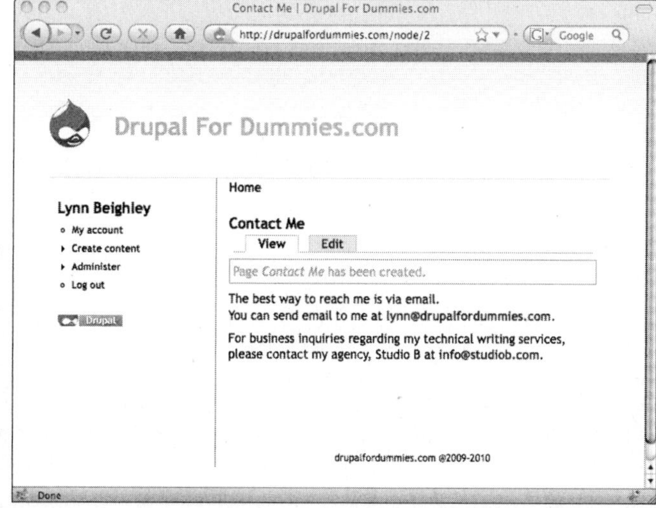

Figure 5-5: You see your new page with a status message after you save it.

The title you gave your page will appear near the top of your new page as well as part of the title bar at the top of the browser when the page is viewed.

Editing a page

When you view a page you create, your page has an Edit tab (refer to Figure 5-5). Site visitors will not see this tab. It exists to allow you, the site administrator, to make changes to the content on your page. In the example I created, I left out a comma that I now want to add. I can go back and edit the page to fix this. To edit your page, follow these steps:

1. **Log in to the site as the administrator.**
2. **Click on Administer⇨Content Manager⇨Content.** You see a list of pages, including the home page and the new one you just created (see Figure 5-6).

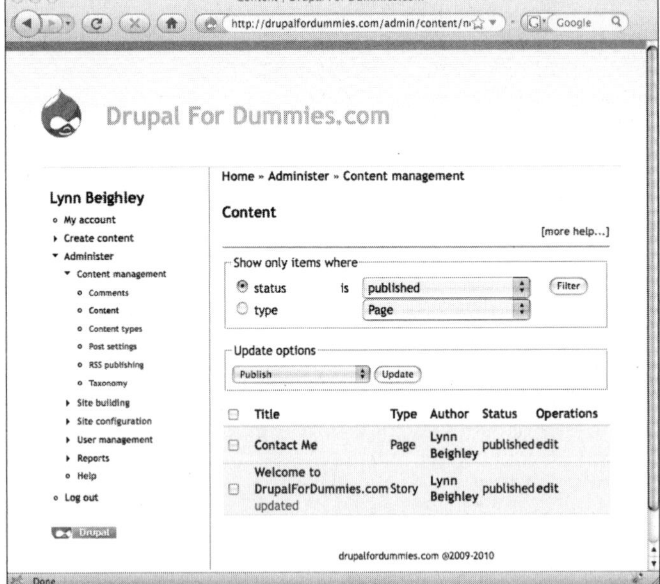

Figure 5-6: The Content management section with a listing of pages.

If you ever create a page and click the Preview button, but never click the Save button, you can get back to that page. Click on the drop-down menu next to the label *status* and choose *not published*. Then click the Filter button. You will see a list of any pages you have previewed but not saved.

3. **Click on the edit link next to the page you wish to edit.** You will see the same form you used to create the page, but this version has two tabs: a View tab and the currently selected Edit tab (see Figure 5-7).

Only you, as the administrator, will see the Edit and View tabs. Site visitors will not see them.

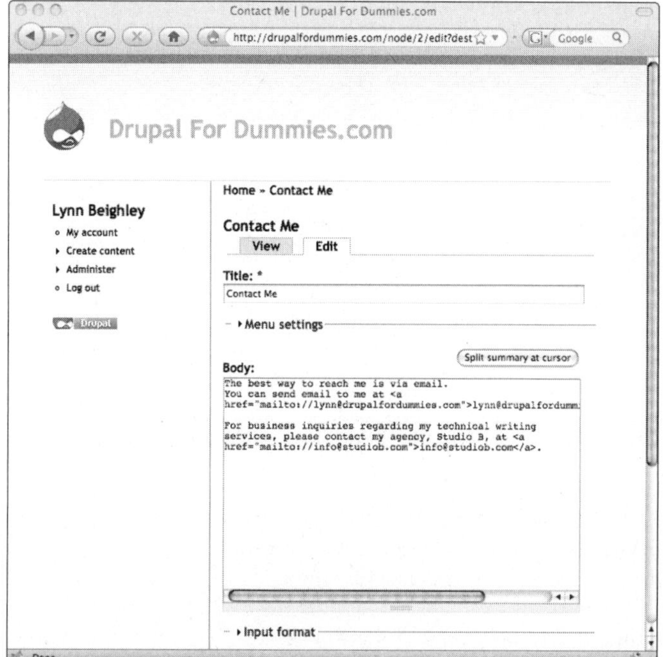

Figure 5-7: Edit tab on your page.

4. **Make your desired changes and choose Save or Preview until you are happy with your changes.**

Deleting a page

Deleting a page is done from the same content management section shown in Figure 5-6. To delete a page, follow these steps:

1. **Log in to the site as the administrator.**
2. **Click on Administer➪Content Manager➪Content.** You see a list of pages, including the home page and the new one you just created (refer to Figure 5-6).
3. **Click on the check box to the left of the title of the page you wish to delete** (see Figure 5-8).

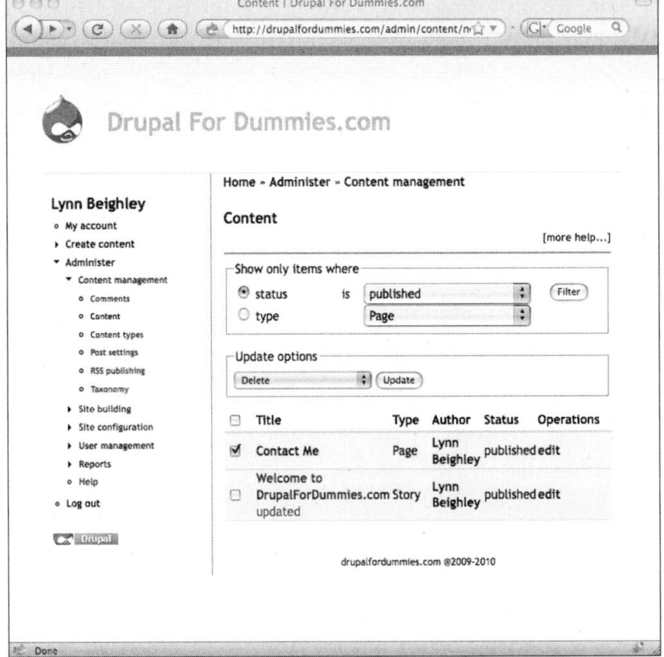

Figure 5-8: Click the check box next to the page you wish to delete.

4. **Choose Delete from the Update options drop-down box and click the Update button.** You will be asked to confirm the deletion. Click the Delete all button to delete your page.

You can delete as many pages as you wish at the same time. You can click in the check boxes next to any pages you wish to delete at the same time.

Accessing your page

If you go to the home page of your site, you won't see a link to your new page. Even though your page exists on the Web, your site doesn't give visitors a link to get to it.

Later in this chapter, you add a page to a site menu that will contain links to pages you create and will show up on every page of your site.

For now, you can get to your page by clicking on the page title on the Content page (refer to Figure 5-8).

To see how your page will look to visitors to your site, follow these steps:

1. **Click the page title on the Content page.**
2. **Copy the URL from the address bar in your browser.**

   The URL will probably be like `http://drupalfordummies.com/node/2`.
3. **Log out of the site and then browse to the URL you just copied.**

   You will see the page as site visitors will see it.

Telling a Story

I created a Drupal *story* in Chapter 3. This bit of content appears on the home page of my site by default. It also allows logged-in users to comment on it.

Even though a story can allow user comments, it doesn't necessarily have to. You may want your story to contain news from your company, but not be interested in user feedback on that news. Sometimes comments can clutter up a site and are better left for pages other than the home page.

You can have more than one story on the home page and turn off comments. Follow these steps:

1. **Log in to your site as administrator.**
2. **Click on Create Content⇨Story.**

   The Create Story form appears (see Figure 5-9).

   The Title field for a story behaves differently than the title field for a page. A page title is the actual title on a page and appears both at the top of the page and in the title bar of the viewer's browser. The title of a story appears directly above the story, but the page the story is on has its own title.
3. **Add a title and body for your new story.**
4. **Scroll down to the Comment settings link lower on this page. Click the Comment settings link to expand this section.**

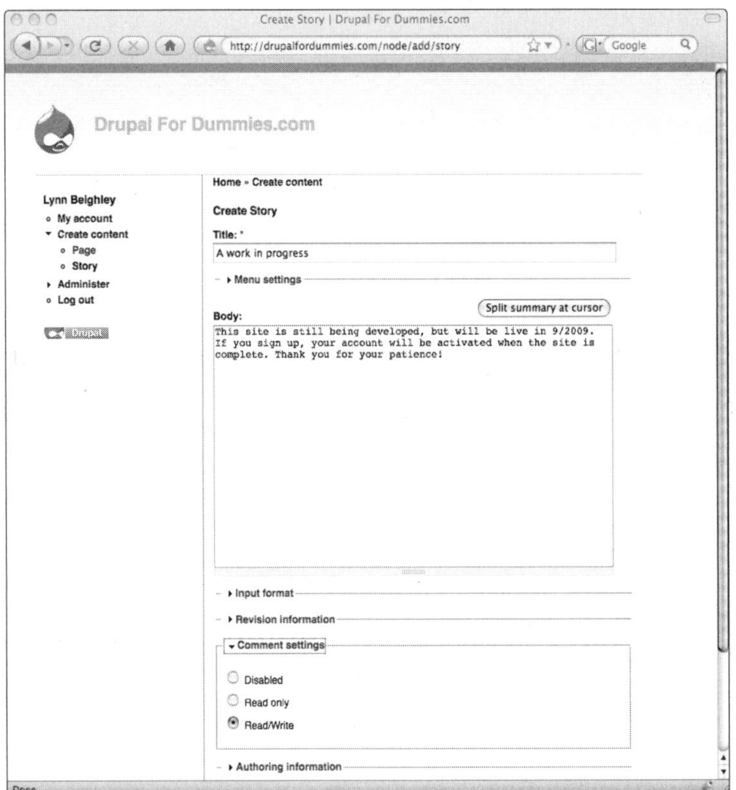

Figure 5-9: Create Story form.

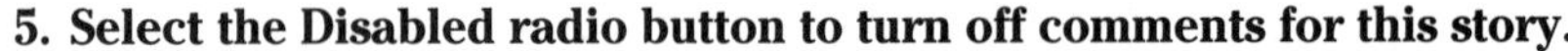

5. **Select the Disabled radio button to turn off comments for this story.**

If you select the second option, Read Only, any comments that have been made will still be visible, but new comments will not be allowed. If comments already exist and you choose Disabled, none of the comments will show.

6. **Click the Save button at the bottom of this page to publish your new story.** Your new story will appear above any you created earlier and won't have a comment link (see Figure 5-10).

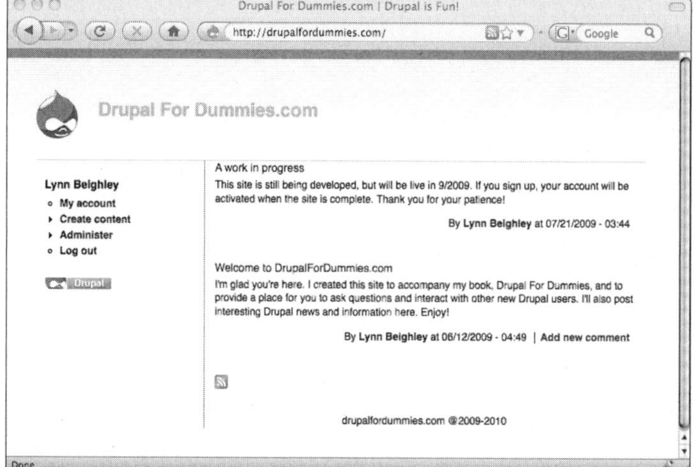

Figure 5-10: Home page with two published stories.

Editing and deleting stories

You edit and delete stories exactly the same way as you edit and delete pages. Follow these steps:

1. **Log in to the site as the administrator.**
2. **Click on Administer⇨Content Manager⇨Content.**
   - To edit, click the edit link next to the story you want to edit.
   - To delete a story, click the check box next to the story you want to delete. Choose Delete from the Update options drop-down box and click the Update button.

Ordering your content

The default behavior of a story is to show up on the home page. New stories are at the top; older ones move to the bottom of the home page. However, say you create a story that you want always to appear at the top of the home page. You can accomplish this by setting the story as *sticky.* Follow these steps:

1. **Log in to the site as the administrator.**
2. **Click on Administer⇨Content Manager⇨Content.**
3. **Click in the check box next to the story you want to always appear at the top of the page.**
4. **Choose Make sticky from the drop-down box in the Update options section (see Figure 5-11). Click Update.**

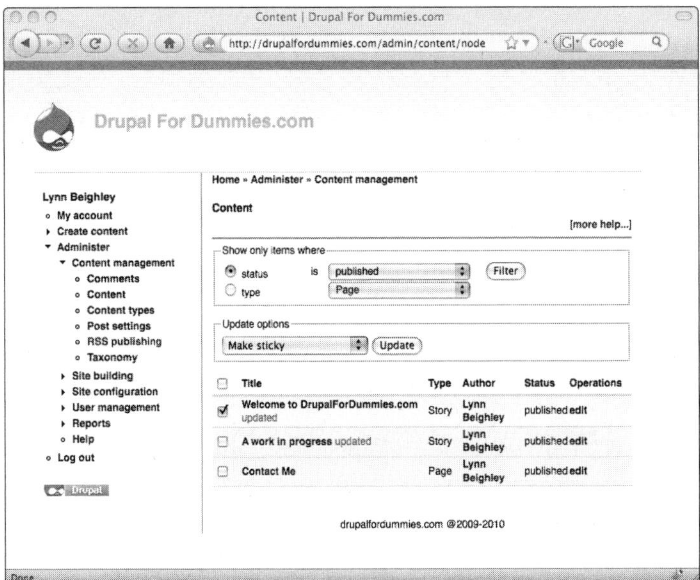

Figure 5-11: Setting a story as sticky.

If you no longer want your story to be sticky, unset this option by choosing Remove stickiness from the Update options drop-down box.

Managing story length

If you create a particularly long story, Drupal automatically shortens it for you and provides a Read more link if users want to read the entire story. Instead of a long post taking up the entire screen, and users having to scroll down to see other content on the page, the first few sentences of the post are displayed. To see a shortened story, look at Figure 5-12.

Figure 5-12: Truncated story post on the home page.

When your post is really long, it can use up all of your screen real estate. The first post on the home page is fairly long, but it doesn't bump down the other posts on the page. Figure 5-13 shows what this page would look like if the first post was not truncated.

There's nothing inherently wrong with having a long post, except that visitors to your site are forced to scroll down the page to see additional content and might not bother. Therefore, it may be better to truncate the visible part of your post by clicking after the first sentence or so and clicking the Split summary at cursor button.

You can control how many characters Drupal displays when it truncates your stories. Follow these steps:

1. **Log in to the site as the administrator.**
2. **Click on Administer⇨Content Manager⇨Post settings.** The Post settings form appears (see Figure 5-14).

Figure 5-13: Home page with long first story.

3. **To change how many characters are displayed, change the value of the Length of trimmed posts drop-down and choose Save configuration.**

Figure 5-14: Post settings form.

To force Drupal to display entire stories rather than truncate them, choose Unlimited.

When you change the Length of trimmed posts setting, it doesn't have any effect on stories that you have already published. However, anything published after you change this setting will reflect it. If you want old stories to be shortened to the new setting, you have to edit and save them in order for the new length setting to take affect.

The Post settings form also lets you control how many stories will be displayed on the main page. By default, 10 stories are displayed.

Setting Menu Options for a Page Node

If you haven't created a page, now is a good time to do so. If you have, click on Administer⇨Content Manager⇨Content and click the edit link next to your page. Look back at Figure 5-2; you see a link, Menu settings, between the title and body fields of the form. Click this link to open the Menu settings form (see Figure 5-15).

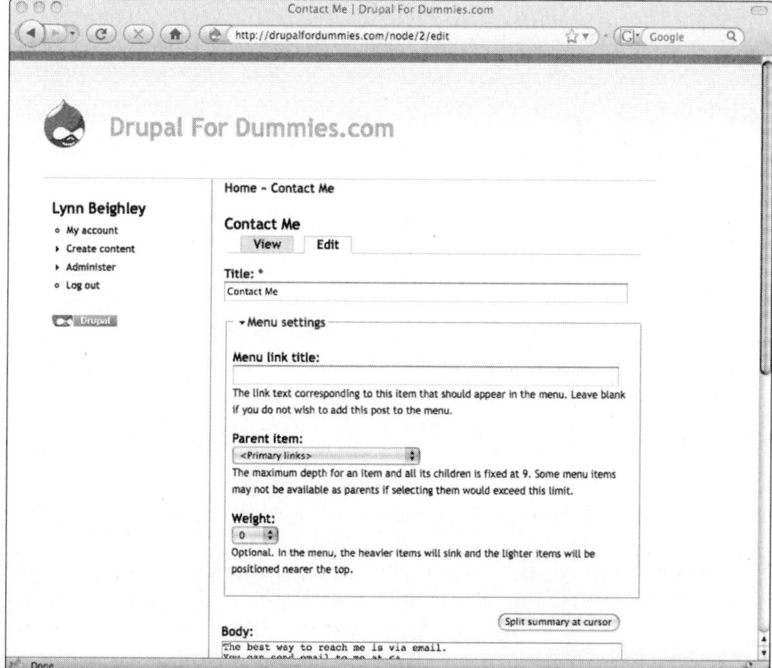

Figure 5-15: Menu settings in page editing form.

These settings allow you to put a link to your page in a menu that will appear on every page of your site.

Giving your node a menu link title

Your page already has a title. In my example, my page title is Contact Me. The Menu link title field is where you specify what text to use to link to your page. In my case, Contact Me is appropriate. Most of the time, your page title will be the perfect text to use as the link. It's possible, however, that your page title is too long to be a good link title, and this is how you can reword it to be more succinct.

Enter some sort of title in the Menu link title field. If you don't enter text here, your page will not have a link in the main site menu.

Choosing a parent item

The menu you want to put your current page link in is called the *primary menu.* The primary menu appears on every page of the site. It isn't visible right now because it contains no links. When I add this link, it will appear just under the site header (see Figure 5-16). Your new link will appear in a menu after you complete this form and save your page.

Choose the option `<Primary links>` from the Parent item drop-down menu. This puts your new link to your page in the primary menu.

Setting the link weight

The weight setting controls where in the menu your link appears. If you choose -50 from this menu, your link will be at the top of the primary menu. Choosing 50 will make your link appear on the bottom of the menu. In my case, it makes sense to choose a higher number, or heavier weight, so my link will always be the last one in my primary menu.

When choosing a weight for your menu items, consider the big picture. Will your site have several primary links? Does it make sense to put the About Us link in front of the Contact Us link? Make a list of links and assign a weight to each before you actually create them. If you know you want Contact Us to always be the rightmost link, give it a weight of 50. If you know you want your Products link to always appear on the left, because people will see it first, give it a weight of -50.

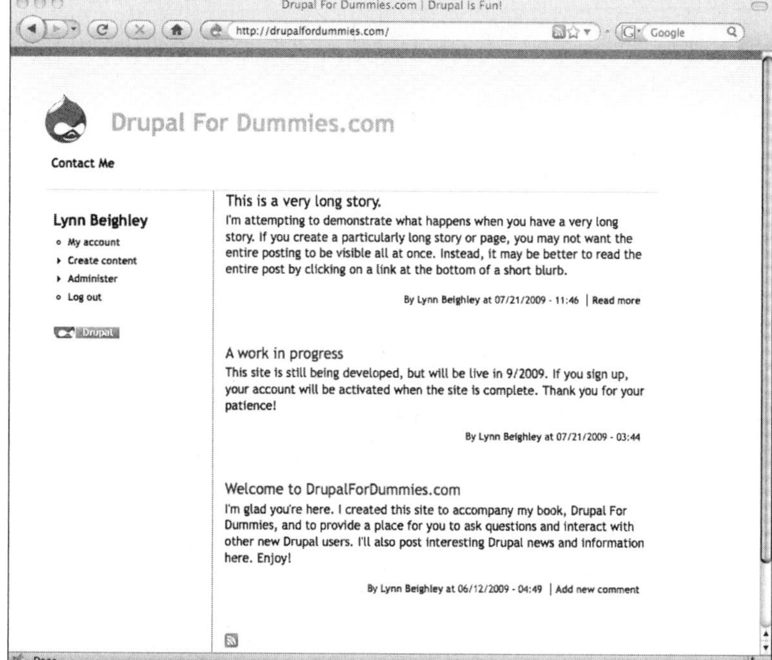

Figure 5-16: The primary menu appears under the Drupal logo with a single link to the Contact Me page.

When you create or edit a story node, you also have a Menu settings section on the form. It works exactly the same way as it does for Drupal pages.

There are lots of additional options for managing the content you create, and I discuss them in Chapter 6.

Chapter 6

Managing Your Content

In This Chapter

- Controlling HTML in your content
- Hiding content from logged-out visitors
- Managing comments
- Creating pages

Drupal offers you a number of options that allow you to customize the appearance of your content. This chapter shows you how to leverage Drupal's options to refine your content further. You see how to include HTML code, images, and even Flash movies in your posts. Also, I discuss the comment system and how to control the appearance and behavior of comments. I also show you how to temporarily hide posts while you continue to work on them and how to control who can see them when they are published. Along the way, I include information about a few other optional tweaks to the presentation of your content that Drupal gives you. There's a lot of good stuff in this chapter to help you fine-tune your nodes.

The tweaks and settings discussed in this chapter apply to both pages and stories. They also apply to other node types, including polls, blog posts, and forum posts I discuss in Chapter 9.

Most of the settings I discuss in this chapter are accessed from the form used to create or edit content. They are accessed by clicking on the links under the large Body text box (see Figure 6-1).

You get to the content editing form for any of your pages or stories by logging in as administrator and clicking on Administer⇨Content Management⇨Content. Locate the content you want to edit and click the appropriate edit link. The options I discuss in this chapter are also accessible when you first create content by selecting the Create content link and choosing Page or Story.

The links are Input format, Revision information, Comment settings, Authoring information, and Publishing options.

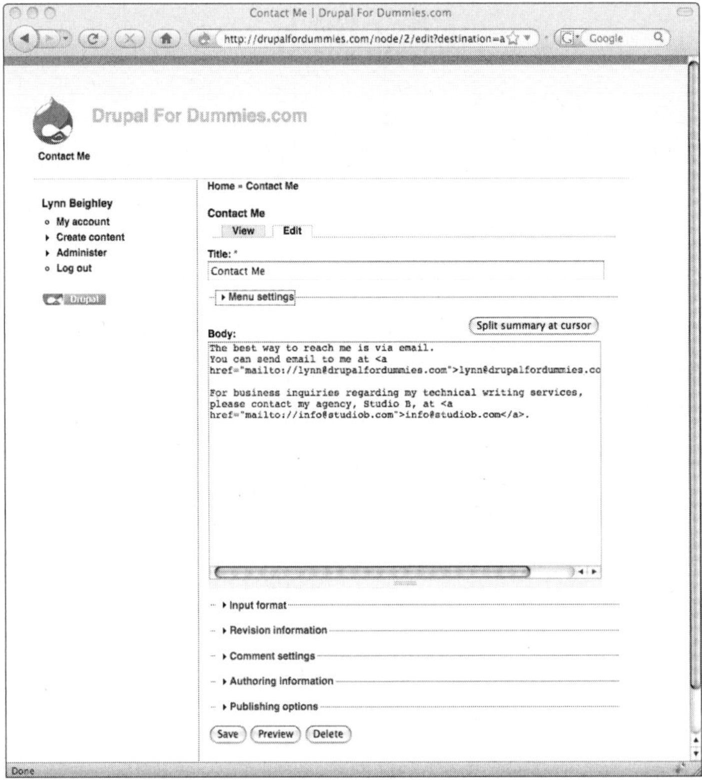

Figure 6-1: Content editing page with option links below the Body text box.

Handling HTML Content

If you aren't familiar with HTML, you're in luck. You don't need to know how to code in HTML to create links with Drupal.

To see that you don't need to know HTML, consider the text in these two versions of the Contact Me page node I created: one with HTML and one without.

- With HTML code:

  The best way to reach me is via e-mail. You can send e-mail to me at <a href="mailto://lynn@drupalfordummies.com">lynn@drupalfordummies.com</a>. For business inquiries regarding my technical writing services, please contact my agency, Studio B, at <a href="mailto://info@studiob.com">info@studiob.com</a>.

- Without HTML code:

  The best way to reach me is via e-mail. You can send e-mail to me at lynn@drupalfordummies.com. For business inquiries regarding my technical writing services, please contact my agency, Studio B, at info@studiob.com.

Both versions give you the same end result, linked e-mail addresses (see Figure 6-2). The first version, with HTML tags, is a little tricky to type and definitely not as easy to edit if, for example, my e-mail address were to change.

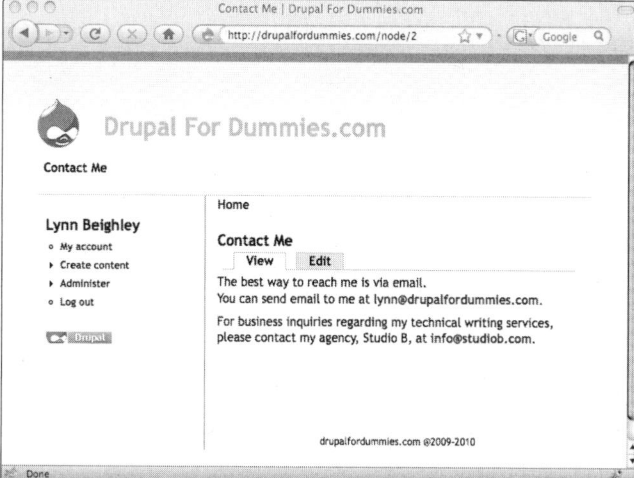

Figure 6-2: Hyperlinked e-mail address automatically created by Drupal.

Drupal does the dirty work for you. This also applies to Web addresses and URLs. To create an HTML link, you would ordinarily have to type:

```
<a href="http://drupalfordummies.com">http://drupalfor
dummies.com</a>
```

Instead, Drupal will automatically convert `http://drupalfordummies.com` into a link.

HTML requires tags to create paragraph and line breaks. Drupal handles this for you, behind the scenes, so you don't need to include `<P>` or `<BR>` tags in your content.

This automatic formatting takes some of the work out of your content creation. When you create or edit your content by typing text in the Body field of a page or story, it's very readable.

Choosing an input format

If you know HTML, you can use it in your posts. Drupal offers you two choices: Filtered HTML or Full HTML. Choose from the Input format section when you create or edit content (see Figure 6-3).

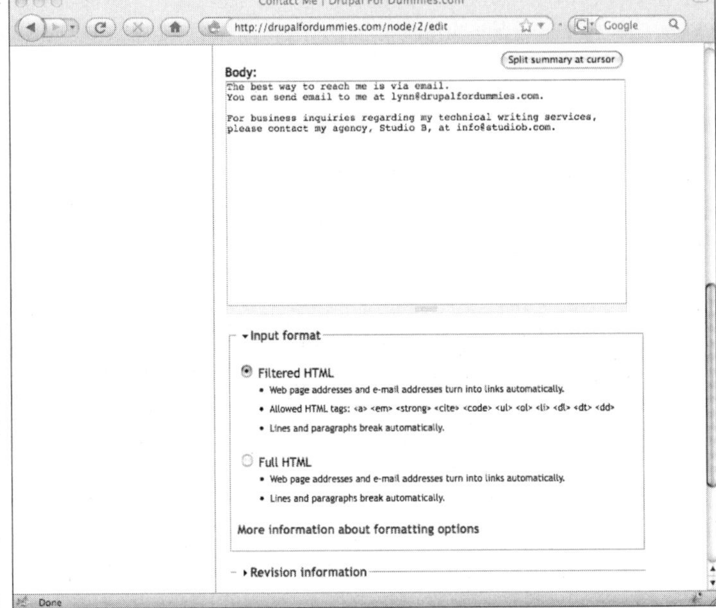

Figure 6-3: The Input format settings available when you create or edit content.

By default, Filtered HTML is selected.

Using filtered HTML

Filtered HTML allows you to use only certain tags, as listed in Table 6-1.

Table 6-1 Tags Allowed by HTML Filtering

HTML tag	*Function*
<a>	Create a link from words in your text, like <a href="http://drupalfordummies.com">Drupal for Dummies</a>.
<em>	Italicize.
<cite>	Italicize.
<strong>	Boldface.
<code>	Display as computer code.
<ol>	Start an ordered (numbered) list of items.
<ul>	Start an unordered (bulleted) list of items.
<li>	Identify an item in a numbered or bulleted list.
<dl>	Start a definition list.

HTML tag	Function
<dt>	Define a term in a definition list.
<dd>	Create a definition in a definition list.

Using full HTML

Unfiltered HTML allows you to use any HTML tag you wish. When you edit or create a page or story, you decide which to use.

Only choose the Unfiltered HTML option if you have to. If you ever give another user the ability to edit posts, as discussed later in this book, keeping your content filtered prevents inadvertent code mistakes or the inclusion of tags that give the content an appearance inconsistent with other content on your site.

Drupal ignores certain tags that are potentially dangerous, such as JavaScript PHP tags.

Controlling Revision Information

Things change. Maybe you made a mistake, leaving out some important bit of information. Maybe something new happened, making the current content inaccurate. Drupal allows you to revise your content and keep track of both

- The original version
- All revisions you make to it

To create a revision, follow these steps:

1. **Log in to your site as administrator.**
2. **Click on Administer⇨Content management ⇨Content.**
3. **Choose a page or story you created earlier and click edit.**
4. **Make a change in your content.**
5. **Scroll down to the Revision information link and click on it. (See Figure 6-4.)**
6. **Click the Create new revision check box and type something in the Log message box that explains changes you have made to the content. Click Save.**

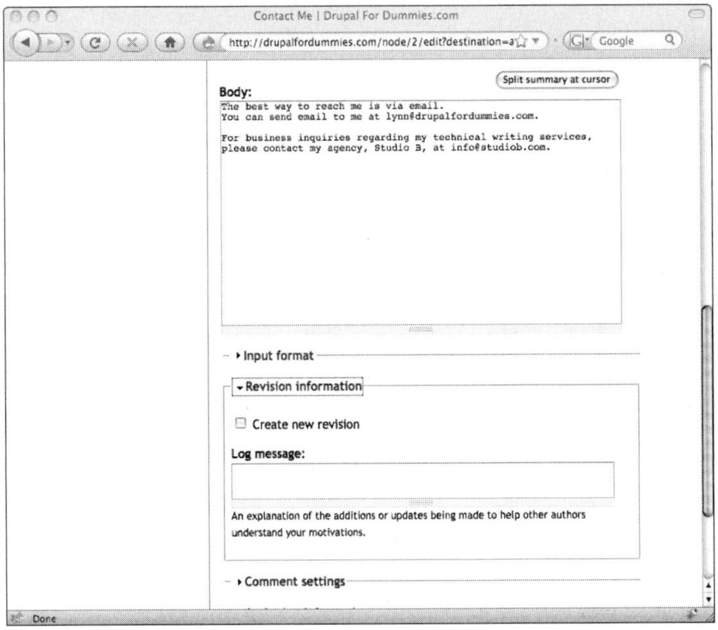

Figure 6-4: The Revision information settings available when you create or edit content.

Your revision has been saved, and you will now see a new Revisions tab that you can click to see all saved revisions (see Figure 6-5).

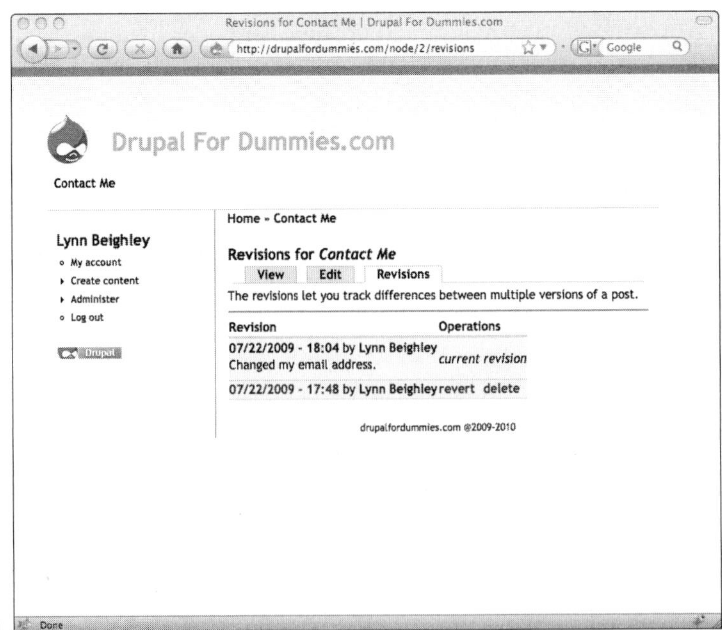

Figure 6-5: Revision history of content.

Next time you edit the content, you will see the current revision. If you wish to edit the current revision but not create a new revision, don't use the revision settings when editing. To go back to the original version, click on the revert link on the Revisions tab.

Revisions are great for keeping track of changes to the content:

- If you need to make a temporary change to content on your site but eventually want to go back to the original, you can create a revision and then click revert when you no longer need the latest change.
- When more than one person works on the same site, revisions can record when someone else changed something and why.

Managing Comment Settings

You can allow users to submit their thoughts about your content by allowing comments. When you create or edit content, you control whether registered users can add comments by using the Comment settings (see Figure 6-6).

When you allow comments, a link appears at the end of your post. When comments are posted, a link to view the comments is visible, as shown in Figure 6-7.

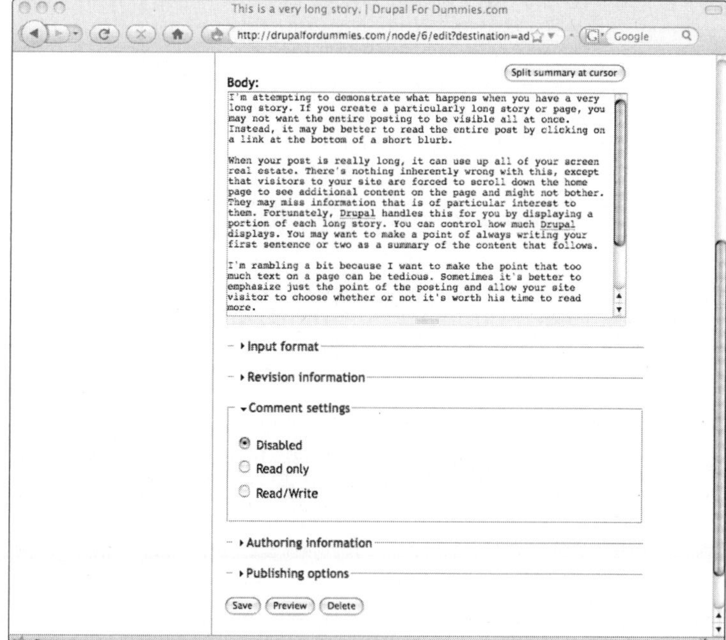

Figure 6-6: The Comment settings available when you create or edit content.

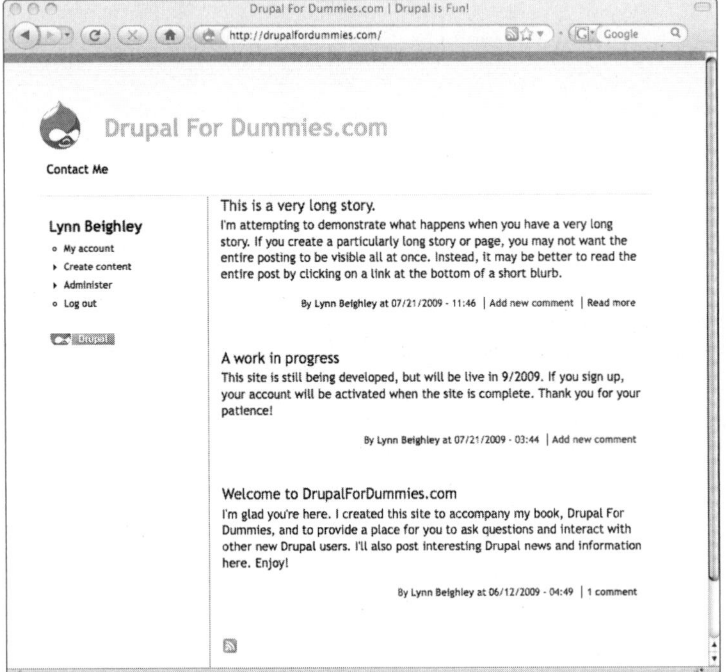

Figure 6-7: Posts with comments allowed and comment links.

To view comments on a post, click on the comment link or the title of the posting. This opens the story or page node in its own page with the comments visible and a link for users to add a new comment (see Figure 6-8).

The user who posted the comment will see links to delete or edit the comment. Users can also reply to comments.

Considerations of allowing comments

Every node you create (for example, each page and story) has the option of allowing users to comment. For some types of content, this doesn't make sense. My Contact Me page doesn't need to allow comments. But some content you create may be appropriate for allowing user comments.

A setting under User management➪Permissions allows you to permit anonymous users (site visitors who are not logged in) to post comments. Do not allow anonymous users to post comments. You leave yourself open to spammers. It's best to allow only authenticated users (people who are logged in) to post comments.

Figure 6-8: View of a single post with comment.

Disabling comments

If you disable comments for your post, no comments will be allowed. The link to Add new comment won't be present. If you edit a post and change the option from Read/Write to disabled, all the current comments will be hidden. They will not be deleted; they will show up again if you choose Read only or Read/Write.

This is the default setting for pages.

Allowing Read only comments

The Read only setting removes the Add new comments link and the reply link. Existing comments are readable, but no new ones can be added. Users can't delete comments they have posted.

The Read only setting can be useful when new comments won't add any value to the discussion.

Permitting read/write comments

This allows registered users to post comments and reply to other people's comments. Users can also delete or edit comments they have posted. This is the default setting for stories.

A primary difference between pages and stories is whether comments are permitted. Pages don't allow comments; stories do. The Comment settings are how that is controlled by default:

- When you create a page, comments are disabled.
- When you create a story, read/write comments are permitted.

Changing Authoring Information

Every time you post a story, Drupal includes information about when the content was posted and who posted it. (Refer to Figure 6-7.) The poster's username (in this case, Lynn Beighley) appears, along with the time and date the story was posted.

By default, stories include this information and pages do not.

You can fine-tune your control over this with the Authoring information section when you create or edit your story (see Figure 6-9).

Modifying Authored by information

By default, your username will appear here. You can change it or leave it blank if you don't want an author name to appear.

Modifying Authored on date

This allows you to change the date of the posting. The date is in the format year-month-day hour:minutes:seconds. When you save your post, Drupal takes that date and reformats it to a date in a format like 07/21/2009 – 11:46.

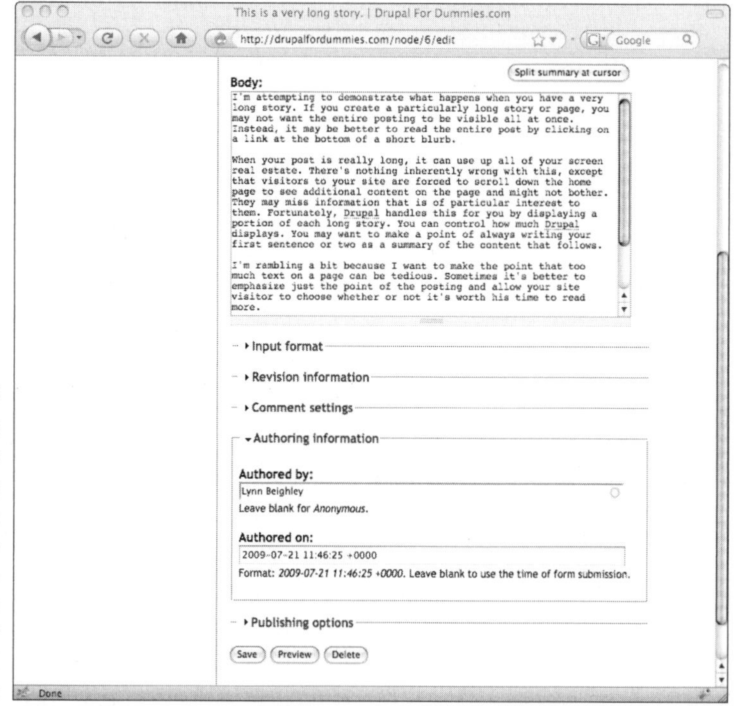

Figure 6-9: The Authoring information settings available when you create or edit content.

To change the format of this date, follow these steps:

1. **Logged in as administrator, click on Administer⇨Site configuration⇨ Date and time.** The Date and Time configuration page appears (see Figure 6-10).
2. **Locate the Short date format, in the bottom half of the page. Click on the drop-down menu and select a new format.**

   This is the format used as the Authored on date.
3. **Click Save configuration.**

You can fine-tune the appearance even further by selecting Custom format from the list. This causes a text box to appear, where you can precisely customize the date (see Figure 6-11).

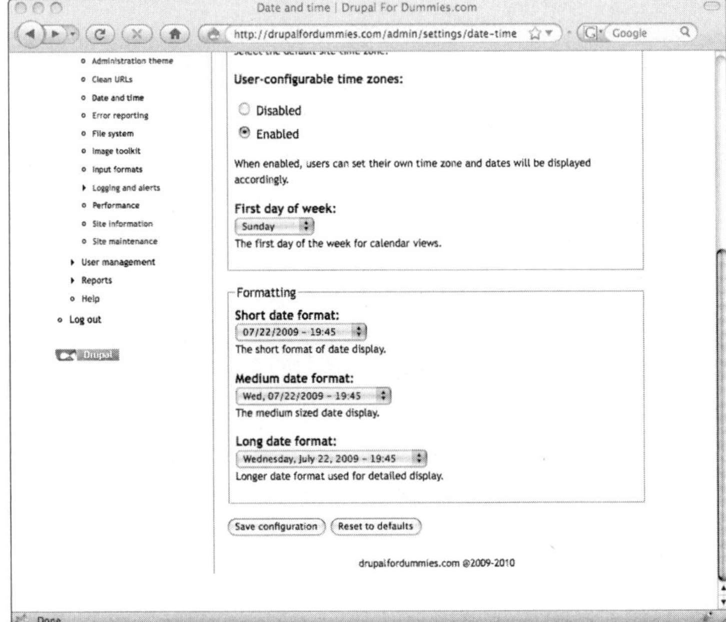

Figure 6-10: The date and time configuration formatting page.

If you are determined to create a custom date format, I recommend visiting this page: `www.tizag.com/phpT/phpdate.php`. Scroll down to the heading "Reference" and use the information there to build your date.

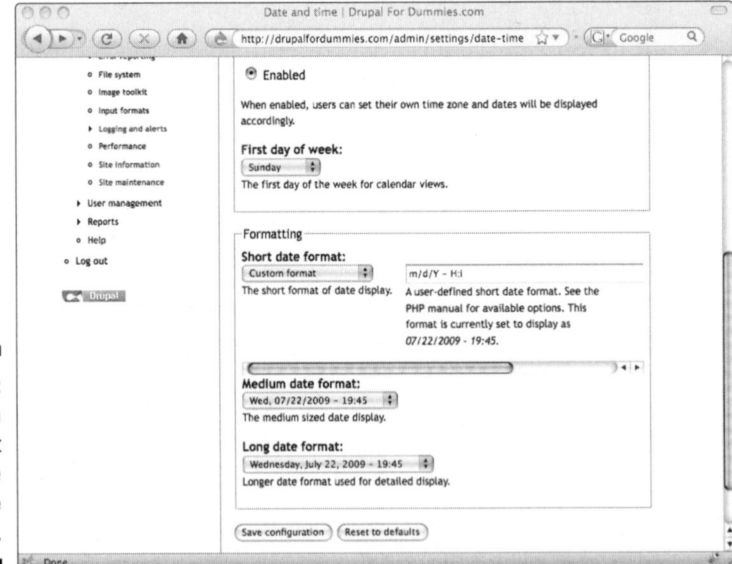

Figure 6-11: The Custom format option of the Short date format.

Publishing Options

When you write stories, they appear on the home page when you click Save (refer to Chapter 5). When they are published, pages and stories can be visited directly by anyone. But you don't have to automatically publish your content to the Web. You may want to write content but publish it at a later time. The Publishing options section lets you control what happens after you create content. This section is available when you create or edit your story (see Figure 6-12).

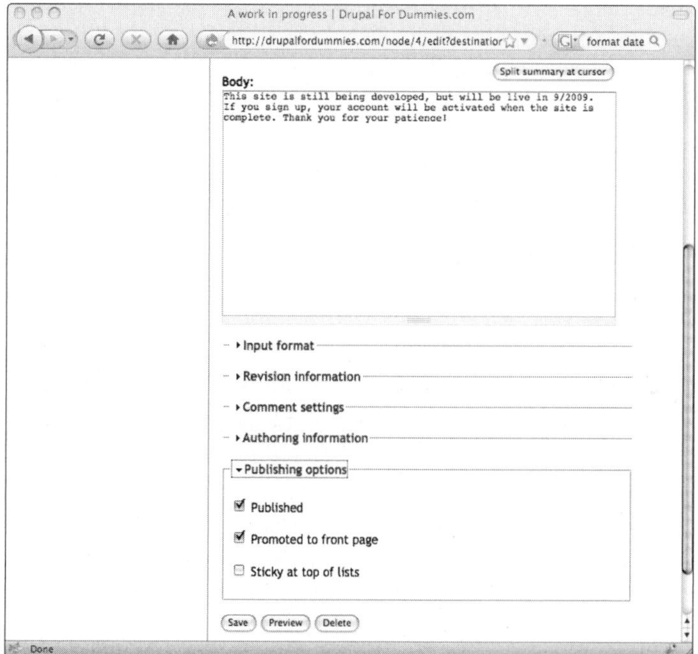

Figure 6-12: The Publishing options available when you create or edit content.

The options you select here control what happens when you click the Save button.

Publishing

By default, for both pages and stories, the Published check box is selected. This means that your content will be made live on the Web when you click Save.

If you uncheck this box and click Save, your content is saved but not actually published. No one but you, logged in as administrator, will be able to see it. To access unpublished content, log in as administrator, and click on Administer⇨Content management⇨Content. You will see all of your content with the publishing status listed next to it. If it is unpublished, it will have a Status of *not published* (see Figure 6-13).

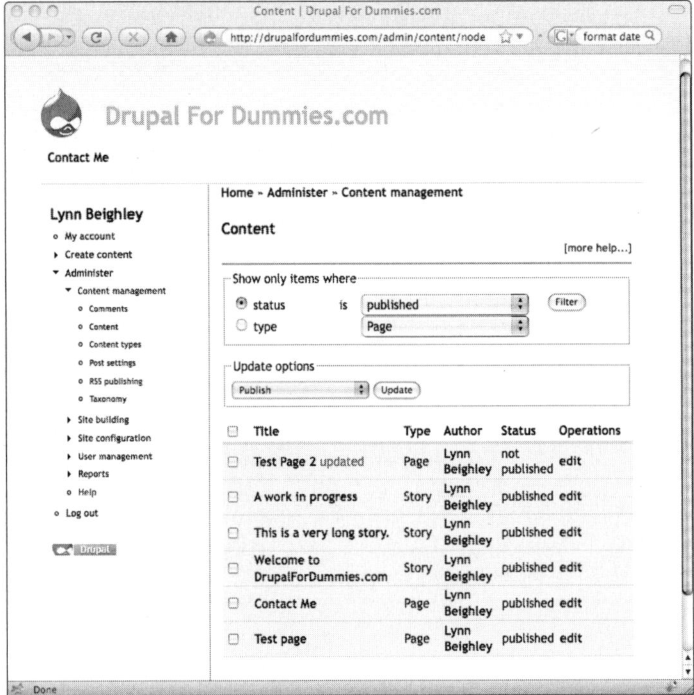

Figure 6-13: The Content page lists the publication status of all content.

To publish your content without any changes, click in the check box next to its title, choose Publish from the Update options drop-down menu, and click Update. To make changes to the content before publishing, click Edit, make your changes, under Publishing options click the Published check box, and click Save.

Promoting to front page

Stories appear on the home page by default; pages do not. But if you change the Promoted to front page check box, you can change this behavior regardless of node type.

Making content sticky in lists

When you create a new story and post it to the home page, it ends up as the one on top. Stories are ordered from newest to oldest. Chapter 5 explains how to use the Content page to set a story as sticky, so that it always appears at the top of the home page even when newer stories are published. This check box accomplishes the same thing as modifying the stickiness in the Content page.

Splitting your content

The Split summary at cursor button lets you specify precisely where to break your post to create a blurb. It's located just above the Body text box (see Figure 6-14).

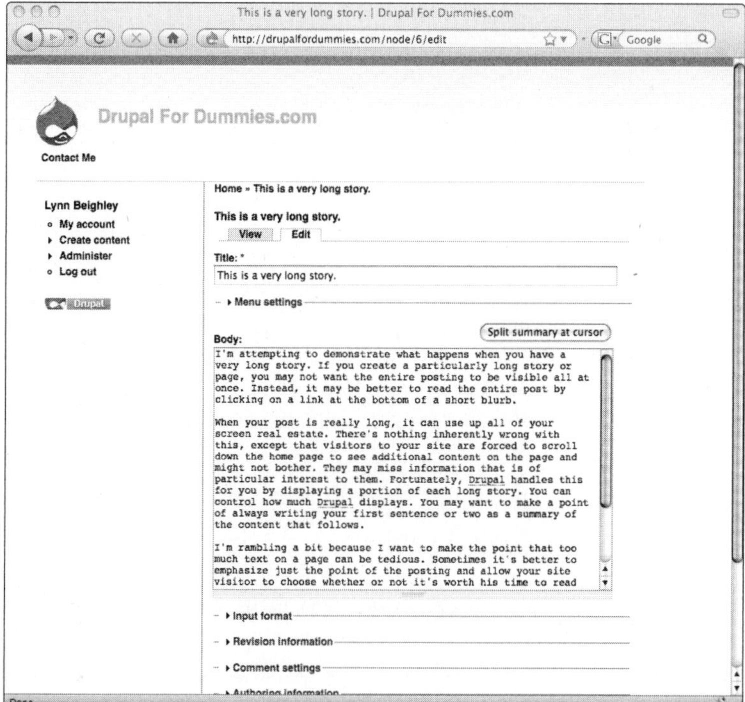

Figure 6-14: The Split summary at cursor button.

This button overrides the Length of trimmed post setting that's covered in Chapter 5.

To use the Split summary at cursor button, follow these steps:

1. **As administrator, open a story you have posted to the home page in edit mode.**
2. **Inside the Body text block, locate a good spot to trim your content.** Generally, this will be after the first or second sentence.
3. **Move your cursor to this spot and click.**
4. **Without clicking anywhere else on the page, move your mouse to the Split summary at cursor button and click it.** Your page changes to show your Body text now split into two fields (see Figure 6-15).

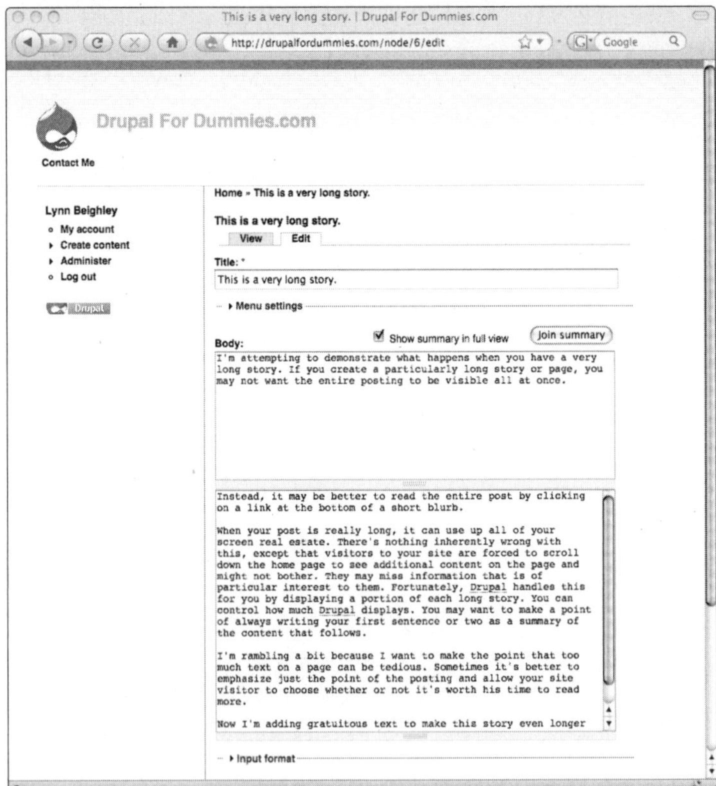

Figure 6-15: The body content is split in two after you click Split summary at cursor.

5. **Save your content.** Your home page now reflects the new blurb length.

If you edit an existing posting and use the Split summary at cursor option, make sure you click Save to republish your content. You may have to reload the home page to see the changes.

Depending on your content, you may want to write a specific blurb to show up on the home page. You can create a summary of your content in the top box and keep all your content together in the bottom box. If you uncheck the Show summary in full view check box, the summary blurb will only show up in the shortened home page version, and only the larger content will appear when someone chooses to view the entire content.

If you decide later that you don't want to split your content, you can rejoin it by clicking the Join summary button.

When you rejoin your content, you may end up with an extra line feed or carriage return at the spot where you originally split your content. Just remove the space and click Save.

Adding Images

You may be eager to include images in your pages. This section involves a bit of HTML coding, but the code is fairly easy to follow and generally is only a line or so. The rest of this chapter shows you how to add images to your pages with HTML code.

If you don't want to use HTML code, you can add images and other media with Drupal *modules.* Modules are extensions to Drupal that make it easy to do various things. Chapter 13 shows you how.

If you are going to use HTML code, make sure you select the Full HTML option under the Input format section of your content option (discussed in the "Handling HTML Content" section, earlier in this chapter). Otherwise, your content will ignore some of the code you place in your content.

Image hosting

Before you can add an image to your content, it needs to be on your Web server. Your Web hosting company should have a simple way for you to upload images to your Web server.

Chapter 2 discusses how to get files on your Web server using a file manager application on your hosting company's Web site.

I will use an image from my site for this example. If you want to test with my image, feel free, but please delete the story or page with the image when you are finished testing!

You should only use images that you have put on your own Web server. When you use an image that is on someone else's Web server, it's like watering your lawn with your neighbor's hose connected to his faucet. He has to pay for what you are using for your own purposes.

To add an image to your content using HTML, follow these steps:

1. **As administrator, create a new story by selecting Create content⇨Story.**
2. **Enter a title such as *Posting an Image*.**
3. **In the Body section, enter the following code** (see Figure 6-16):

```
<img src="http://lynnbeighley.com/lynn.jpg">
```

4. **Click on Input format and select the Full HTML option.**

   Without Full HTML selected, Drupal will ignore the HTML code.

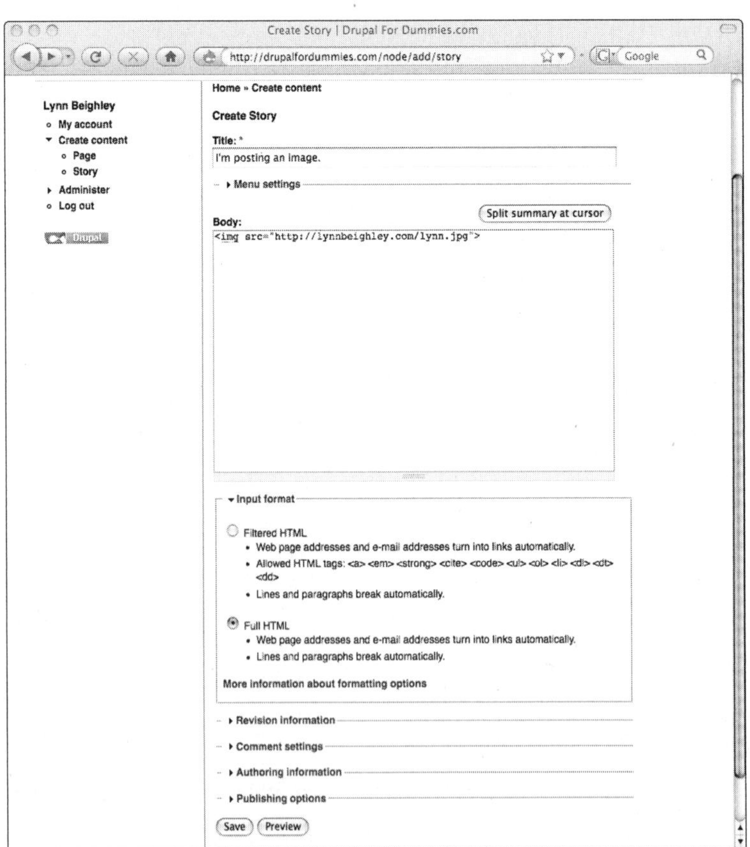

Figure 6-16: Adding an image to a story with HTML.

5. **Click Preview to see the image in your content, then click Save to view it on your home page.** Figure 6-17 shows the image on the home page.

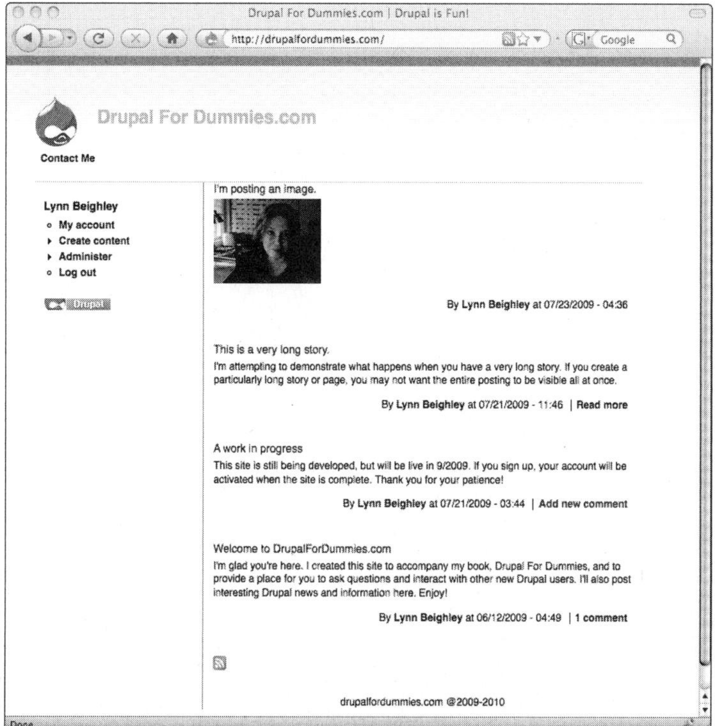

Figure 6-17: Homepage with a story containing an HTML coded image.

The HTML code you used is known as an image tag. Here's the syntax again:

```
<img src="http://lynnbeighley.com/lynn.jpg">
```

This code consists of an open and close angle bracket containing:

- The code word *img*, which stands for image and tells the Web browser to display an image.
- The code word *src*, which stands for the word source and tells the Web browser that the image location or URL follows the equal sign.
- The Web address or URL of an image in quotes.

You aren't confined to posting a single image in a story with no text. You can add text above or below the image tag, but make sure to place a carriage return or two between your text and the image. Otherwise, the text runs into the edge of the image and can be difficult to read.

Chapter 7

Changing Themes

In This Chapter

- Getting new themes
- Changing themes
- Configuring themes

In Drupal, the look and layout of the site is dependent on a set of files collectively called a *theme.* A Drupal theme is a bit like a skin or a Windows desktop theme. In Drupal, a theme controls the appearance of the fonts, how many columns are displayed, background colors, and the appearance of logos, buttons, and menu items.

When you first install Drupal, it is using a theme named Garland. While it's a perfectly nice theme, you aren't obligated to continue using it. Not only is it good to know how to change themes, but it's also fun to see your site change appearance with just the click of a button. In this chapter, you see how to change from the default theme to others of the preinstalled themes. I show you where you can preview and download even more themes. You find out how to quickly swap between themes while you are developing your site. Finally, you discover how to configure your theme.

Changing Themes

Getting and changing your Drupal theme is one of the simplest administration tasks in Drupal. Preinstalled themes can be enabled to change the look of your site by changing a simple administrative setting.

The default theme

By default, Drupal uses the Garland theme. Take a moment to look at it. Every page on your site uses it.

The Garland theme has two columns:

- The left column contains a form for logging in and user specific site navigation.

  When you aren't logged in to the site, the login form appears in the left column.

  When you are logged in as the administrator, you see the administration links.

- The larger right column contains all the site content.

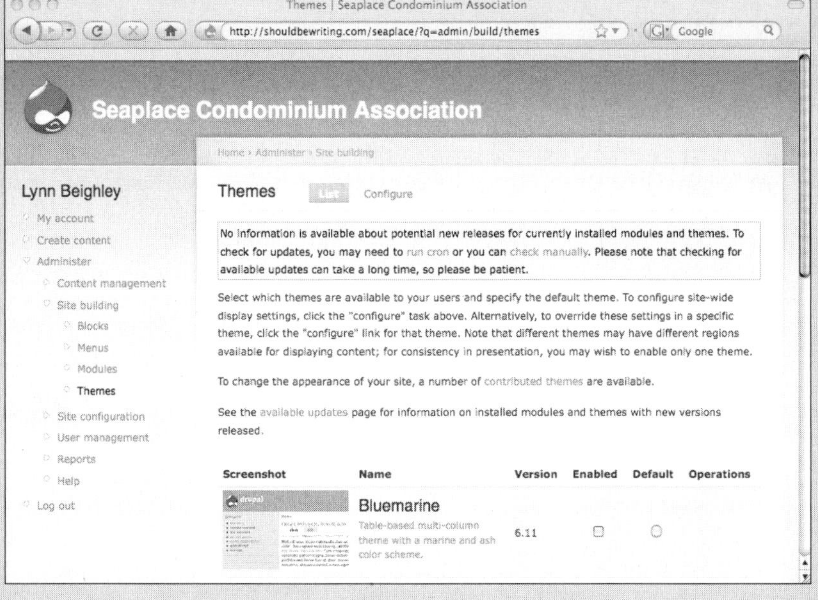

Enabling a theme

Before you can use a theme, you must enable it. Enabling it means that you can easily turn it on whenever you want to use it.

In addition to the default theme, Garland, Drupal provides you with a number of preinstalled themes. They are installed but not enabled.

To enable and view the other preinstalled themes, follow these steps:

1. **If you aren't logged in, log in to your site with your administrator username and password.**
2. **In the left column, click on Administer➪Site Building➪Themes.**

   You see a list of themes with thumbnail views.
3. **Select the Enabled check box next to each theme in the list.**

   Garland already has the Enabled box checked.
4. **Select the radio button under Default next to one of the themes.**

   For example, if you select the Chameleon theme (the second on the list), your site looks something like Figure 7-1.
5. **Scroll to the bottom of the page and click the Save Configuration button.**

You now see your site with the new default theme you selected.

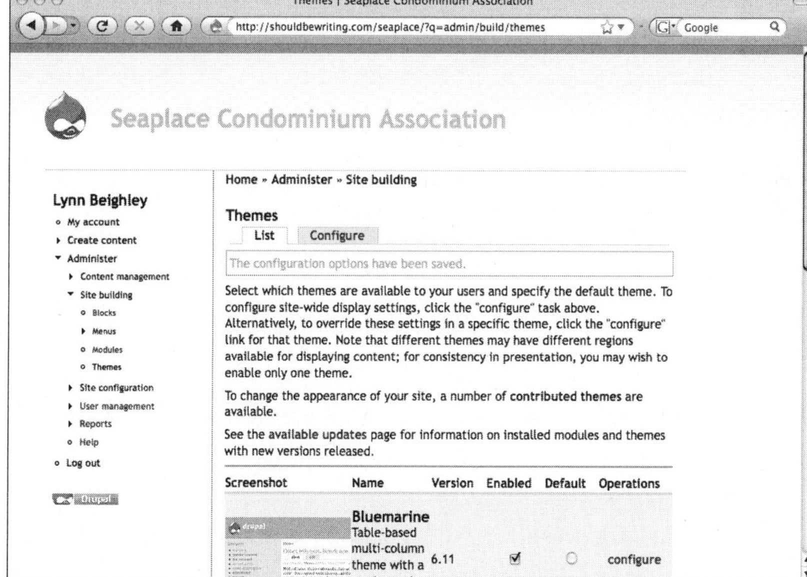

Figure 7-1: Your site with the Chameleon theme enabled and set as default.

Enabling a theme doesn't make it the active or current theme. Themes have to be *both*

- Enabled (the check box)
- Selected as default (the radio button under the Default column on the right)

Changing enabled themes

There are two ways themes on your site can be changed. The first is through the administrator interface. The second involves configuring Drupal to allow users to select from a list of enabled themes.

Changing the theme as administrator

While logged in as an administrator, you can change the current theme by following these steps:

1. **Navigate to the Site Building section under Themes.**
2. **Select the radio button under Default.**
3. **Press the Save Configuration button.**

Letting your user set his theme

You can allow any registered, or even unregistered, visitors to your site to select the enabled theme they wish.

Although giving your users the ability to change the site theme has its uses, in general you want them to see only the theme you have customized for your site. This feature is more useful for you to use as you test your site design. To turn this option on, follow these steps:

1. **Log in to your site with your administrator username and password.**
2. **In the left column, click on Administer⇨User Management⇨Permissions.**

   You are presented with a list of options (see Figure 7-2).
3. **Scroll down to the bottom of the page and locate the heading *system module*. Select the check box to the right of *select different theme* and press the Save permissions button.**

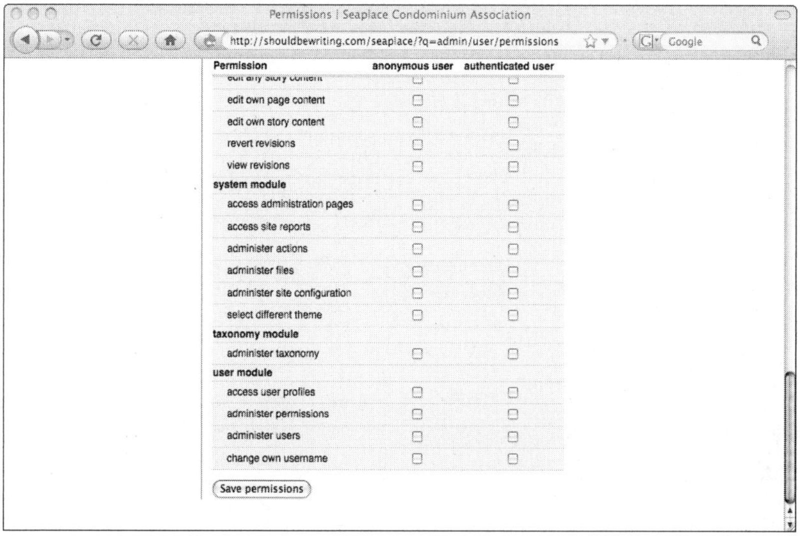

Figure 7-2: User Management Permissions.

By selecting that check box, you have now made a Theme selection option appear on every authenticated user's Edit page. To access it, follow these steps:

1. **Log in to your Drupal site with a non-administrator account.**
2. **In the left column, choose My Account.**
3. **On the right column, click the Edit tab. Scroll down on this page.**

   You see the Theme Configuration section (see Figure 7-3). This is a list of all of the themes you enabled. Your signed-in users can select any of these.

4. **Click on one of the Selected radio buttons to the right of the theme of your choice (see Figure 7-4). Then click the Save button at the bottom of the page.**

   This changes the active theme for just the user account you are currently logged in as.

By choosing a theme, your registered user always sees that theme when he visits your site. This theme selection overrides the default theme for the site.

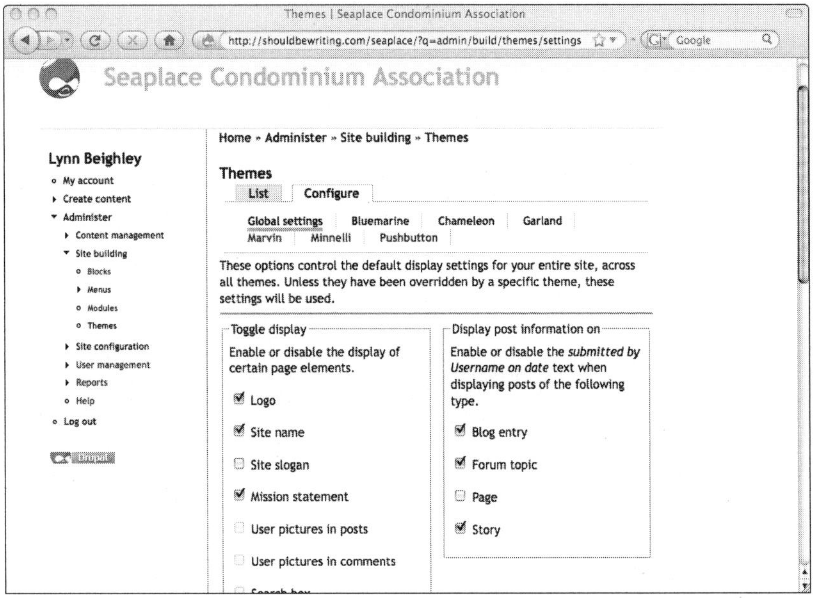

Figure 7-3: User theme editing options.

Setting an administration theme

While the theme you set as default is the active theme for the entire site, you can also set a different theme that appears only on the site administration pages when you are logged in as an administrator. This allows you to tinker with the site theme and layout and have the capability to reset the site theme should something go horribly wrong with the design.

To set a different theme for the site administrator pages, follow these steps:

1. **Log in to your site with your administrator username and password.**
2. **In the left column, click on Administer⇨Site configuration⇨Administration theme.**
3. **Choose your preferred theme from the drop-down list.**

   You can also enable this theme when you post or edit content by selecting the check box next to *Use administration theme for content editing.*
4. **Click the Save Configuration button.**

You now have a theme selected that only appears when you are logged in as the site administrator.

Configuring Themes

Themes have settings associated with them. You can change settings for all themes or manage individual themes. A custom theme may have special settings that only apply to it. The rest of this chapter shows you the general or global theme settings and common settings for individual themes.

Global theme settings

To get to the page with the global theme settings, log in as administrator and click Administer➪Site Building➪Themes. Locate and click the tab in the right column that says Configure (see Figure 7-4). Notice the list of themes, as well as the words Global Settings. These are all the currently enabled themes. Click on Global settings.

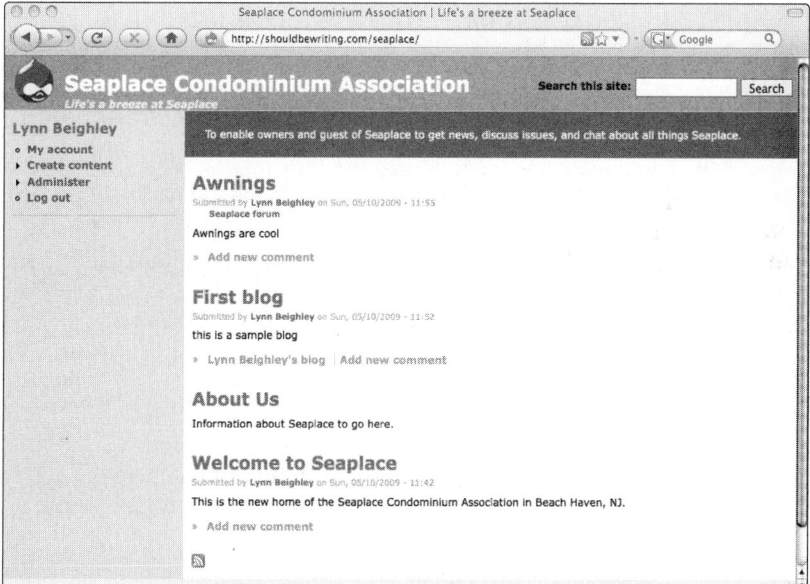

Figure 7-4: Global settings for themes.

The theme settings let you choose

- Elements that appear on the site
- User information that appears in various content sections

- Whether the default Drupal logo appears

  You can select an alternative logo here.

- A "favicon," that small shortcut icon that appears in the URL address bar in users' browsers when they visit your site.

  The default favicon is a tiny Drupal logo.

Toggle display settings

Of all the settings you can control, by far the most powerful are the appearance or absence of the elements. Here's what they do:

- **Logo:** Simply enough, this check box controls whether your site has a logo. By default, it is the Drupal logo, unless you specify another one in the logo image settings section farther down on this page.

- **Site name:** Check this if you want the site name to appear. In Figure 7-4, the site name is shown as *Seaplace Condominium Association.*

  To set your site name, log in as administrator and click on Administer➪Site configuration➪Site information. Whatever you type in the *Name* field appears as the site name.

- **Site slogan:** Also set on the site information page, this is an optional field that shows up on all pages of your site, typically under the site name, depending on the theme.

- **Mission statement:** Just under site slogan on the site information page, this is another optional field. Unlike Site slogan, some of the preinstalled themes don't display this field at all, even when it's checked on the Global settings.

- **User pictures in posts:** This controls whether the picture of the user who made a post appears in that post.

- **User pictures in comments:** If selected, the picture of each user appears next to any comments he makes. Both this setting and the preceding one depend on whether you have allowed users to have picture support.

- **Search box:** This displays a Search box that allows users to search through all the content on your site. It is disabled by default. To make the box functional, you need to turn on the Search module under Administer➪Site building➪Modules. Locate it in the Core modules list.

- **Shortcut Icon:** This check box controls whether visitors see a favicon in the address bar. By default, it is the Drupal logo, unless you specify another one in the shortcut icon settings section farther down on this page.

- **Primary Links:** Unchecking this causes your primary links to be hidden from the user. In general, you always leave this checked.
- **Secondary Links:** This is also one you typically leave checked. Unchecked, the secondary links don't appear.

Logo image settings

Just under the Toggle display section are the logo image settings. To use the logo that comes with the default theme you are using, just leave the check box selected.

If you want to use your own logo, uncheck the box, then either

- Type a URL for your logo image in the *Path to custom logo* text box (for example, `http://yourwebsite.com/images/yourlogo.jpg`).
- Click the Browse button next to the *Upload logo image* text box to locate the file on your local machine. This uploads the logo to the Web server where Drupal is located.

When you use a URL or path to your logo, you may not have control over that image. If, for example, you are using an image from a Web server you don't control, the owner can choose to delete that image at any time, leaving your site logo-less, and worse, with a broken image. If, however, the logo resides on the same Web server as your Drupal software, there's generally no reason why you shouldn't use a URL path.

Shortcut icon settings

Shortcut icons, also known as favicons, aren't the same as image files you may be familiar with. They are a specific type of image file that uses an `.ico` extension.

To create a shortcut or favicon, you need a special image editor. Most major image creation programs don't offer support for this file type.

If you have a favicon, these settings work the same way as the logo image settings described earlier. Uncheck the box and either enter a path to your favicon or upload it.

If you don't have an icon and don't wish to use the Drupal logo as your shortcut icon, uncheck the box. They aren't as popular as they once were, and many sites don't bother to use them at all.

Reset to defaults

Many administration pages have this wonderful button: Reset to defaults. As you first learn how to use Drupal, you may find yourself needing to back out of changes you made. The Reset to defaults button does just that, restoring the settings on the current page to the default settings Drupal uses when you first install it.

If you are happy with the changes you've made to the page, press Save configuration to see them. If you don't like them, you can reset to default settings.

Specific theme settings

If you aren't still on the global settings page, return there by clicking Administer➪Site Building➪Themes, and then click the tab in the right column that says Configure. Notice the other enabled themes listed after the *Global settings* link. Take a moment to click on these and notice the settings you can control.

When you are on one of these theme-specific settings pages, you can control those options for just that theme. For example, if you click on Bluemarine and deselect the Primary links check box, the primary links don't show up when Bluemarine is the default theme.

If you let users override the default theme, they see their chosen theme as you configure it here. Even if Bluemarine is not the default, for example, but they choose it, they see the Bluemarine theme, complete with your configuration settings for Bluemarine.

Chapter 8

Building Blocks and Managing Menus

In This Chapter

- Understanding regions
- Using blocks
- Creating and administering menus

Themes are customizable. A theme can be modified, for example, to put the primary menu on the left side of the Web page rather than across the top. In this chapter, I extend the discussion of themes and take a closer look at how they can be manipulated from their default appearances.

I also discuss menus in more detail. In this chapter, I look at secondary menus and custom menus. (Chapter 5 covers primary menus.) Finally, I discuss creating a dynamic menu that changes when you post new content.

Understanding Blocks, Regions, and Menus

You need to understand three Drupal terms before diving in to this chapter: menus, blocks, and regions.

- **Menu:** You probably have a pretty good idea of what a menu is. It's a set of links to Web pages. In Drupal, that basically describes a menu, but links can also point to Drupal nodes, such as stories and pages. When a link to a story or page node is clicked on from a menu, a Web page opens with the story or page node content presented as though it were an actual Web page.
- **Block:** A block is a container that holds a chunk of code. The menu you see on the left is in a single block. Drupal organizes menus and other

chunks of code into blocks. This makes it easier to move them around as you redesign the look of your site.

- **Region:** A region is a location on your Web page. For example, the Header region is located at the top of all your site pages. It usually contains a logo and the title of your site.

Think of it this way — menus are stored in blocks. Blocks are placed into specific regions on your Web site.

Using Regions

To see where regions are located, look at Figure 8-1. Look for the words Header, Left sidebar, and Right sidebar. These are regions.

The regions your site has depend on which theme you use. Figure 8-1 is using the Garland theme. In the Garland theme, a Header region is at the very top of each page of your Drupal site. The Left sidebar region is on the left and contains the administrative menu functions and the login. The Right sidebar is empty.

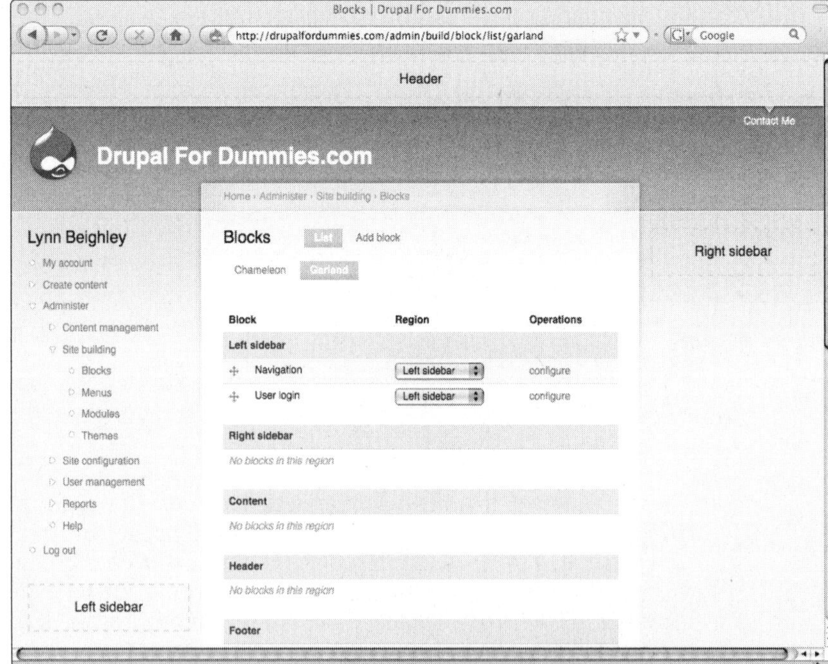

Figure 8-1: Header, Left, and Right sidebar regions of the Garland theme.

The Garland theme has two more regions (the Content region and the Footer region) visible when you scroll to the bottom of the Web page shown in Figure 8-1 (see Figure 8-2).

The Content region is where stories and pages appear. The Footer contains a default Drupal logo and any other footer content you add.

In Chapter 3, I configured the Site configuration⇨Site information page. The *Drupal For Dummies.com* name I set in the Site information page appears in the Header region in Figure 8-2.

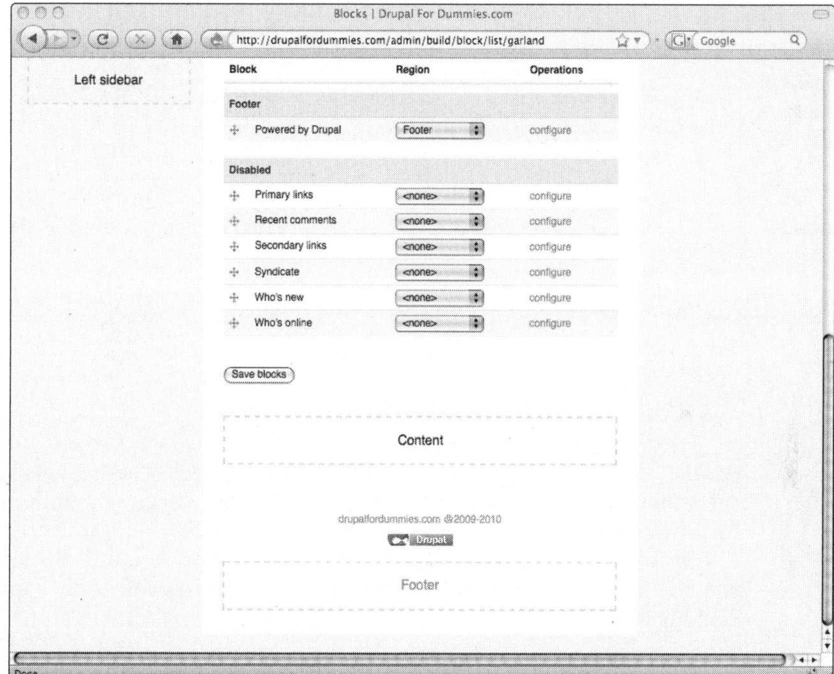

Figure 8-2: Content and Footer regions of the Garland theme.

Understanding how themes work with regions

The Garland theme has five regions: Header, Footer, Content, Left sidebar, and Right sidebar. Not all themes have the same regions. The theme I have been using so far in this book for most of the figures is the Chameleon. It only has two regions: the Left and Right sidebars. Figure 8-3 shows the two regions of the Chameleon theme.

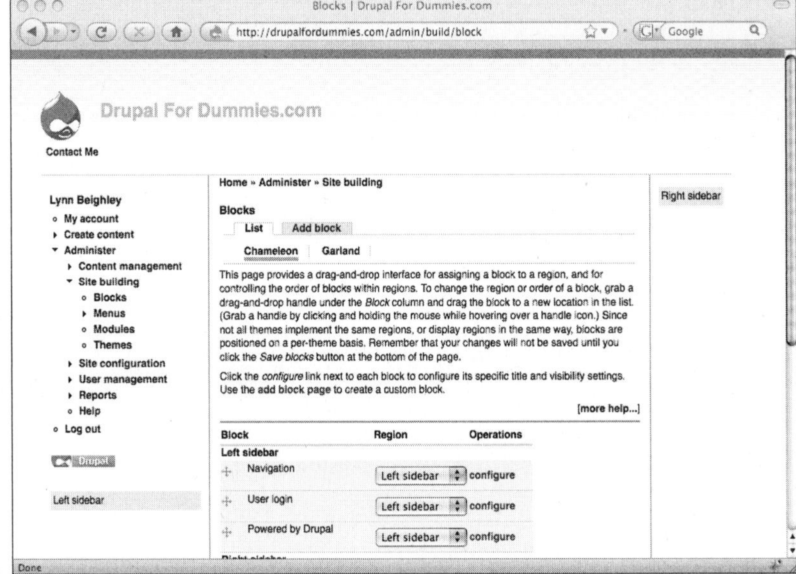

Figure 8-3: The Chameleon theme has two regions: Left and Right sidebar.

To see which regions your current theme has, follow these steps:

1. **Log in as administrator.**
2. **Click on Administer➪Site building➪Blocks.**

At this point, it's a good idea to enable a few different themes by clicking on Administer➪Site building➪Themes. Select the check box under Enabled and choose Save configuration. Now when you view the Administer➪Site building➪Blocks page, you will see links to all the enabled themes under the List tab. Clicking on any one of these theme links will show you all the regions it contains.

The preinstalled themes contain these regions:

- **Bluemarine:** Header, Footer, Content, Left and Right sidebars
- **Chameleon:** Left and Right sidebars
- **Garland:** Header, Footer, Content, Left and Right sidebars
- **Marvin:** Left and Right sidebars
- **Minnelli:** Header, Footer, Content, Left and Right sidebars
- **Pushbutton:** Header, Footer, Content, Left and Right sidebars

Programmers who build Drupal themes may create additional regions beyond those I cover here. If you add themes to your Drupal software (which I mention in Chapter 7), the regions may differ from these.

Exploring the regions

Each of the common theme regions controls a different section of each page of your site.

The following figures use the Minnelli theme because it contains all five regions.

Header

The Header, shown in Figure 8-4, contains the site logo and the site title.

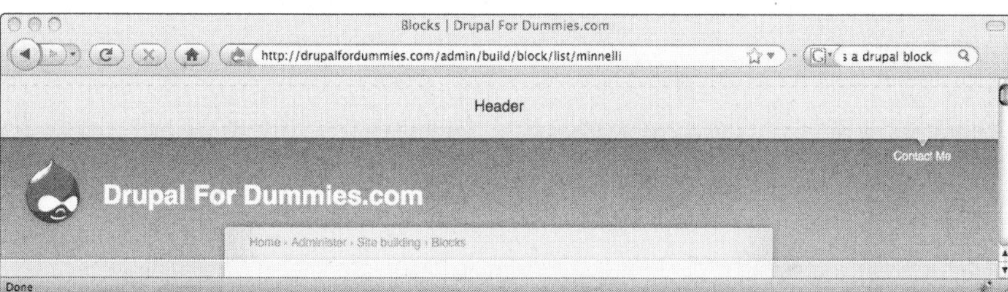

Figure 8-4: The Header region of the Minnelli theme.

This theme, Minnelli, also contains the primary menu. You can tell that the primary menu is in the Header because of the presence of the Contact Me link. Other themes may place the primary menu in a different region.

Content

The Content region is in the middle of the page, just below the Header (see Figure 8-5). It displays

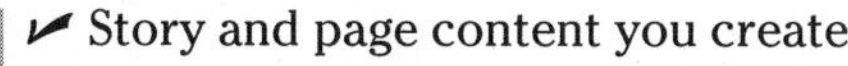

- Story and page content you create

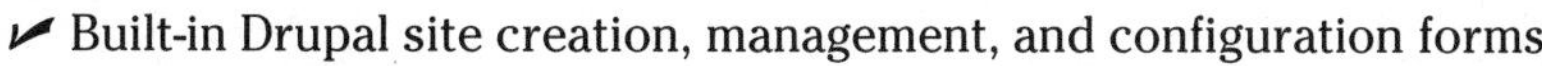

- Built-in Drupal site creation, management, and configuration forms

The most central region in a theme usually is Content. It contains the main content on each page of the site.

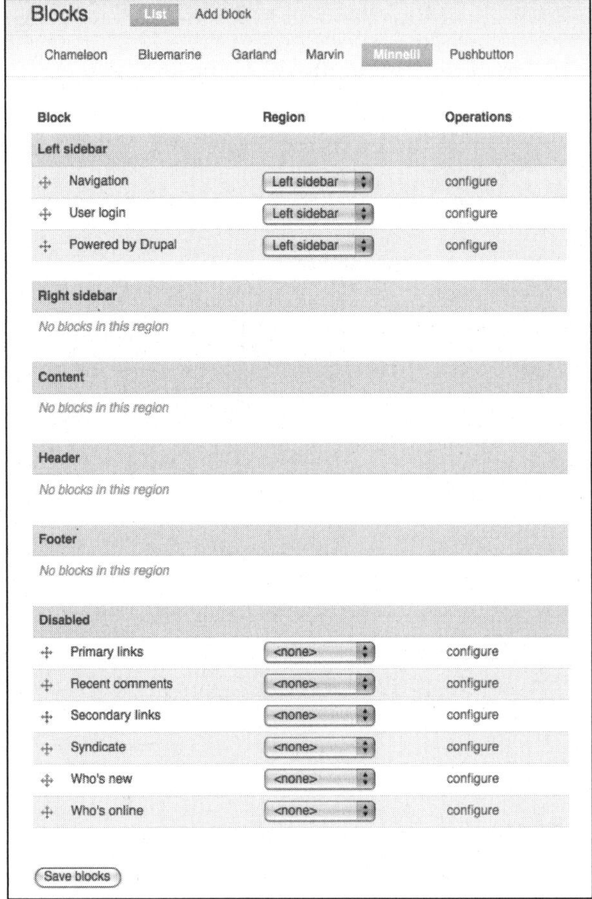

Figure 8-5: The Content region of the Minnelli theme.

Footer

The region at the very bottom of the Web site is the Footer (see Figure 8-6).

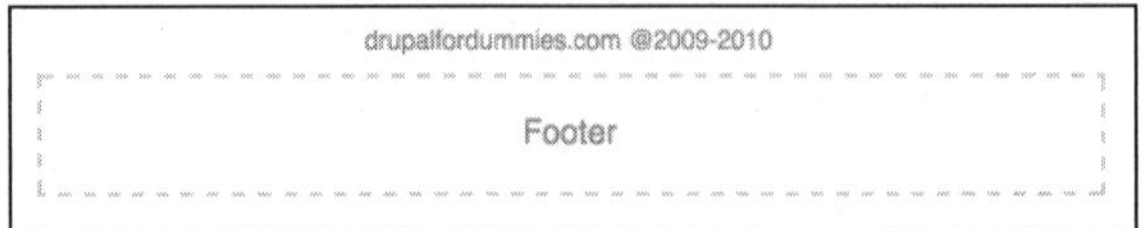

Figure 8-6: The Footer region of the Minnelli theme.

The Footer usually contains a copyright statement. Sometimes it will contain a small Drupal logo and RSS feed logo.

This is a great place to put company information links, which I explain how to do later.

Left sidebar

In this theme, all the administrative navigation occurs in the Left sidebar (see Figure 8-7).

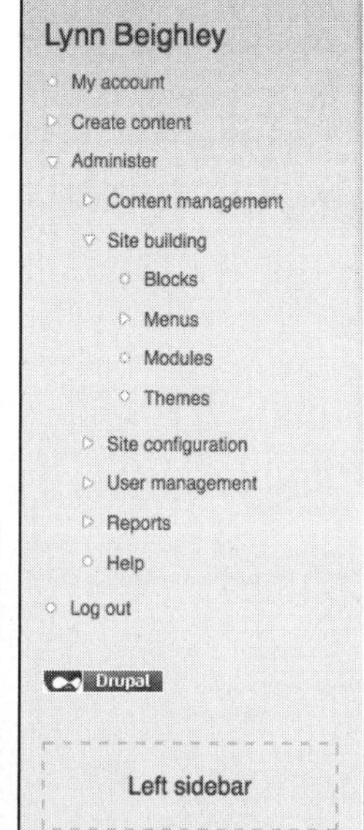

Figure 8-7: The Left sidebar region of the Minnelli theme.

The username of the logged-in user is displayed at the top of the Left sidebar region. If the site visitor isn't logged in, the log-in form is displayed in this region. In Minnelli, the small Drupal logo is here, but in other themes it's located in the Footer region.

Right sidebar

In Minelli, the Right sidebar is empty. It serves as a space between the Content region and the right side of the browser window.

Configuring regions

A useful feature of most Drupal themes is the capability to customize where various page elements (such as blocks containing navigation) appear on the page. For example, you can move the User login from the Left sidebar region to the Right sidebar region. To do this, follow these steps:

1. **Log in as Administrator.**
2. **Change to the Minnelli theme by clicking on Administer➪Site building➪Themes.**

   You will see the list of themes that come preinstalled with Drupal (see Figure 8-8).

3. **If Minelli is not enabled, click the Enabled check box. Select the Default radio button.**
4. **Choose Save Configuration.**
5. **Click on Administer➪Site building➪Blocks.**

   You will see the Block configuration page (see Figure 8-9).

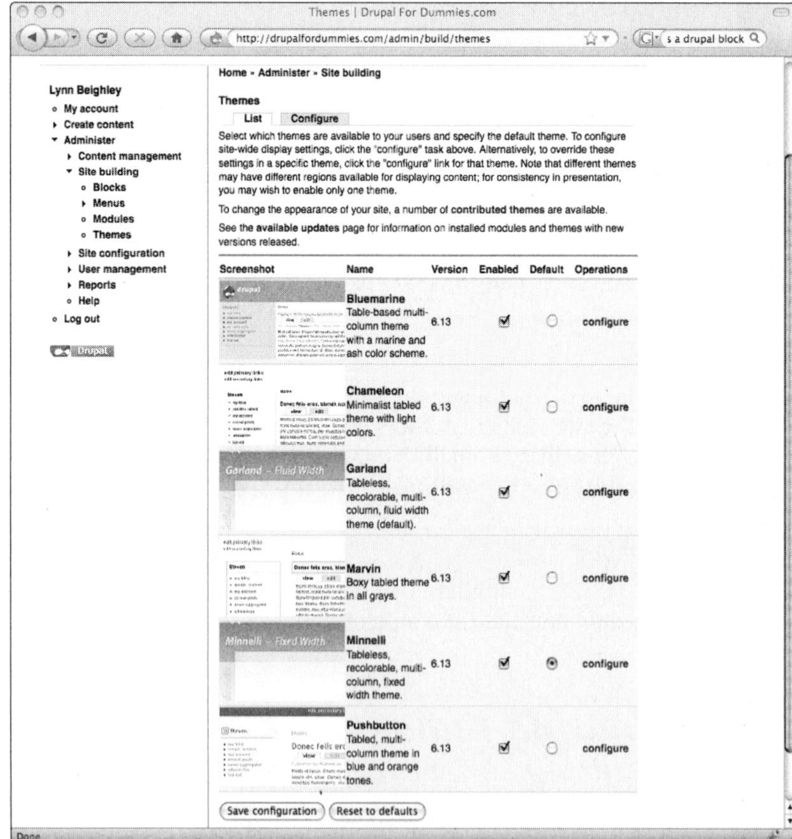

Figure 8-8: Theme selection with Minnelli set as default.

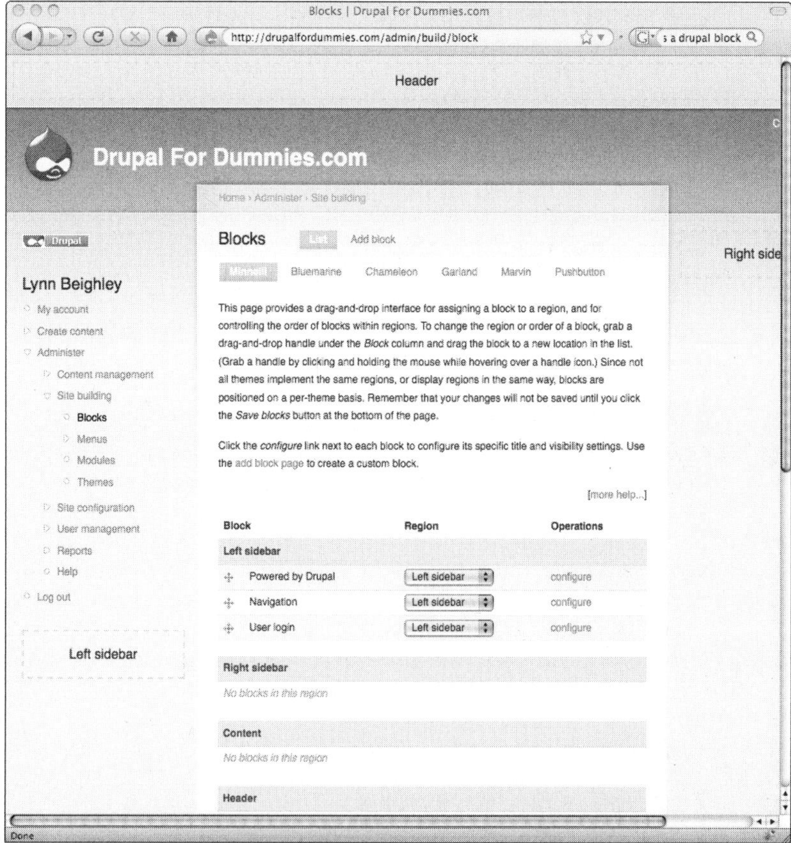

Figure 8-9: The Block configuration page for the Minnelli theme.

This page allows you to move blocks from one region to another. Since the User login form is contained in a block, when you move that particular block to another region, the User login form moves.

6. **Look at the table on this page and locate the User login Block. Click on the drop-down menu next to it and choose Right sidebar.**

   The User login label moves down to the Right sidebar section of the table.

   You can also simply grab and drag the cross icon down into the Right sidebar section of the table.

7. **Scroll down and click Save blocks.**

Your login form will now appear in the Right sidebar region. To see it, log out of the site and then browse to the home page. To change it back, log in as administrator, return to the Block configuration page, and drag the User login back up into the Left sidebar section.

See those links to your other enabled themes near the top of this page? If you click on one of the other themes and move blocks around, you will see those changes reflected on the Web site only when you make that theme the default. This means that you can change the block settings without changing themes. Because this page temporarily changes your theme when you click on a different theme, you can get a preview of how the page will look when you move blocks. This is why the Blocks configuration page displays the label for each region.

You move any of the built-in blocks between any of the regions in a given theme in the same way, by using the drop-down menu or dragging them into the region where you want them.

In the Block configuration page, the order of blocks matters. Suppose you have three blocks under the Left sidebar region. The order they are in will be the order they appear in all your Web pages. You can order the blocks within a region by dragging them above or below other blocks in the same region. For example, if you want the User login block to appear as the bottom item in the Right sidebar region, drag it under any other blocks in the list.

Administering Blocks

At this point, you have seen the User login block and moved it, but that isn't the only block you can move. All the preinstalled themes have the same nine other built-in blocks I describe below. Also, you can create your own blocks and move them to any region you wish. This can come in handy for posting images to the Right sidebar, for example.

Using the built-in blocks

There are nine built-in blocks in all of the preinstalled Drupal themes. You can see them in Figure 8-10, where I have selected the Bluemarine theme.

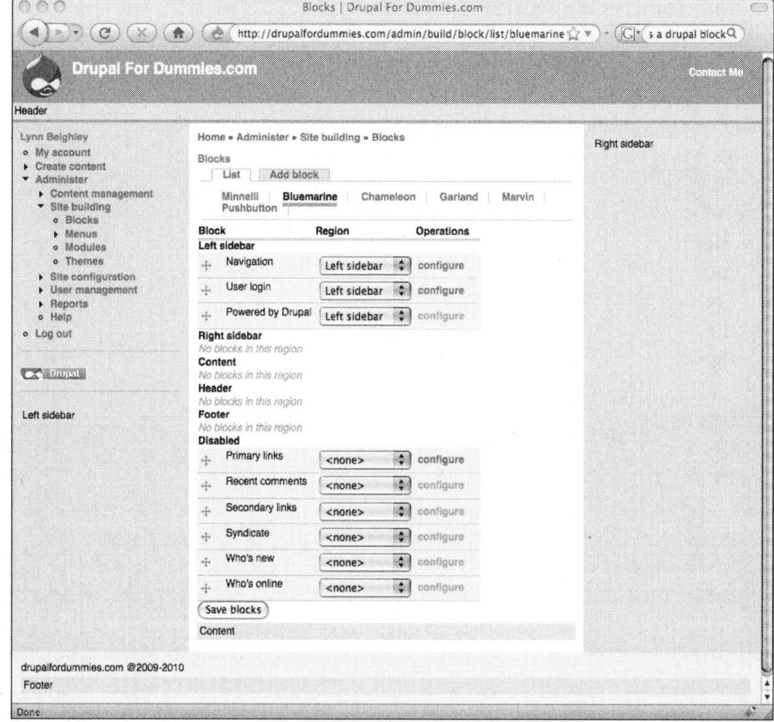

Figure 8-10: The nine built-in blocks shown with the Bluemarine theme.

The built-in blocks are:

- **Navigation:** The Navigation block contains the administrator links when you are logged in as administrator, and the My account and Log out links for logged-in users. It also displays the username (see Figure 8-11).

Lynn Beighley
- My account
- Create content
- Administer
  - Content management
  - Site building
    - Blocks
    - Menus
    - Modules
    - Themes
  - Site configuration
  - User management
  - Reports
  - Help
- Log out

Figure 8-11: The Navigation block.

- **User login:** This block contains the User login form. It's only visible when a visitor to the site has not yet logged in. If a visitor is logged in, the block is not visible. This block also contains Create new account and Request new password links (see Figure 8-12).

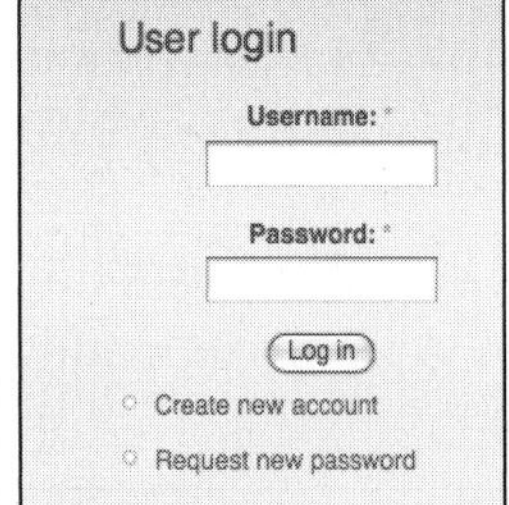

Figure 8-12: The User login block.

- **Powered by Drupal:** This little block, shown in Figure 8-13, contains a small logo and links to Drupal.org when you click on it.

Figure 8-13: Powered by Drupal block.

The following blocks are disabled by default.

- **Primary links:** Primary links are links such as the Contact Me that I created earlier. They link to important locations in your Web site. This block contains these links, but is disabled because Drupal also posts those links automatically in a location determined by the theme designer.

  Think of your primary links as being hardwired into your site.

  If you enable this block, you will have a duplicate set of these links. I recommend that you drag this block into the Right sidebar region and click Save blocks to see what it does. Don't forget to disable it when you are finished.

- **Recent comments:** This shows a list of the subject lines of up to ten of the most recent comments made anywhere on your site. It also includes a link to the comment (see Figure 8-14). It's a good candidate for the empty Right sidebar region.

Figure 8-14: Recent comments block.

- **Secondary links:** You haven't created any secondary links yet, so this block won't be visible. Think of the Secondary links as just another set of links that you can add to your site, links that aren't as important as the primary links. They are useful for pages you need to include, like legal information. In the next section, I show you how to add links to your Secondary links menu.
- **Syndicate:** This block adds a logo and a link to the XML version of your site pages, which allows users to grab and use the syndicated content from your site. I discuss this in detail later in the book.
- **Who's new:** Shown in Figure 8-15, this displays usernames and links to profiles of the newest registered users of the site.
- **Who's online:** Also in Figure 8-15, Who's online shows a summary of how many people are currently using the site, divided into registered users and people who aren't logged in. It also shows a list of the registered users and links to their profiles.

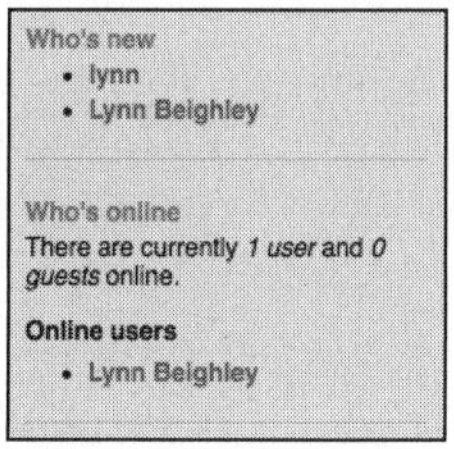

Figure 8-15: Who's new and Who's online blocks.

Creating custom blocks

You can create your own blocks and put content in them. In the last chapter, I created a story containing an image of me. I can create a block and take that same HTML code I pasted in the story and place it in a custom block instead. Here's how to create a custom block and add content to it:

1. **As administrator, click on Administer⇨Site building⇨Blocks.** You will see the Block configuration page, as shown in Figure 8-10.

2. **Locate and click on the Add block tab near the top of the page.** You will now see the Add block form (see Figure 8-16).

3. **Give your block a meaningful description.** For my image, I enter the description *My thumbnail photo.* Only you will see the description. It is used on the List tab of the Block configuration page where you drag your custom block to the region where you wish it to appear.

4. **Enter a title if you wish.** The Title will show up on all your pages just above whatever content you put in the body. I enter the title *Lynn Beighley.*

5. **Enter any content you wish for the body.** The same rules apply here as with other types of content, such as stories and pages. I enter the HTML code to display my image. If I wish, I can also enter text here.

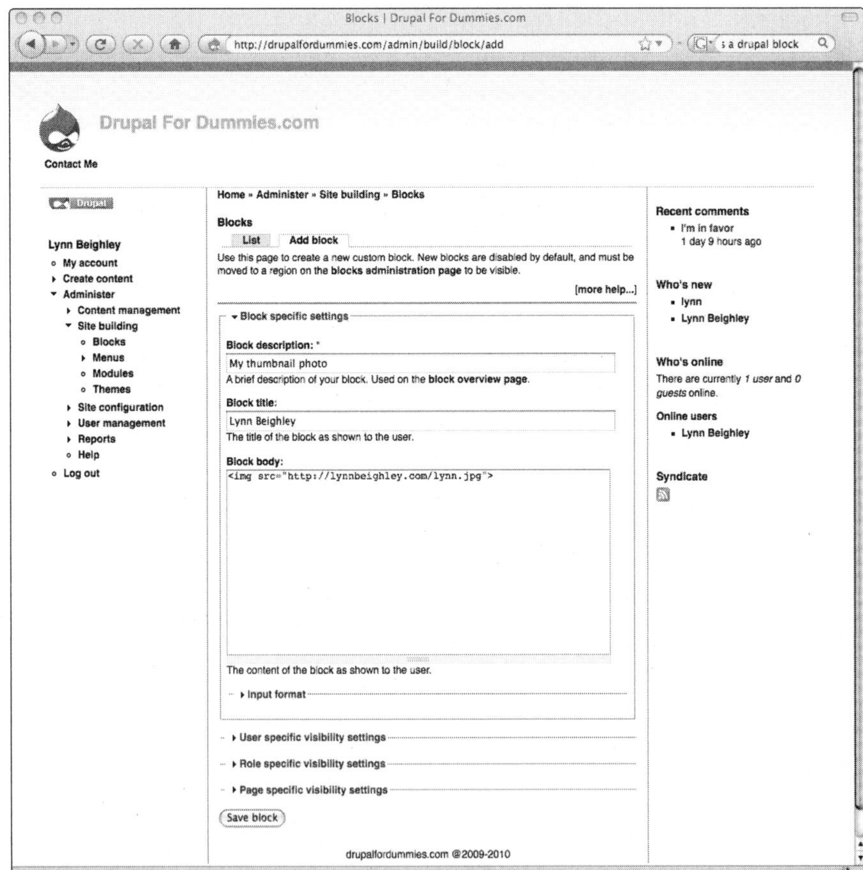

Figure 8-16: The Add block form.

6. **If you used any HTML code in your body content, click the Input format link and select the appropriate setting.** The `<IMG>` tag I used requires me to choose the Full HTML option.
7. **Click the Save block button.** Your new content block has been created, but it won't show up on your site until you drag it into the region where you wish it to appear.
8. **Click on the List tab at the top of the page. This returns you to the list of blocks.** Your new block should appear in this list under the Disabled section (see Figure 8-17).
9. **Drag your new block to the region of your choice and choose Save Blocks.**

Don't forget that the order of blocks in each region also matters.

Figure 8-17: Your new custom block now appears in the list of blocks.

Editing and deleting custom blocks

My new block is listed in the Block configuration page under the List tab, as shown in Figure 8-17. To edit a custom block, click on the Configure link next to your custom block description. This will open the same form as the Add block tab; only your content will be visible and editable.

If you want to delete your custom block, click on the Delete link next to it.

Changing block visibility settings

When you create a custom block, there are visibility settings at the bottom of the Add block form. These setting can also be applied to the pre-built blocks. To see them, click on the Configure link next to a block. You see three sections, as shown in Figure 8-18.

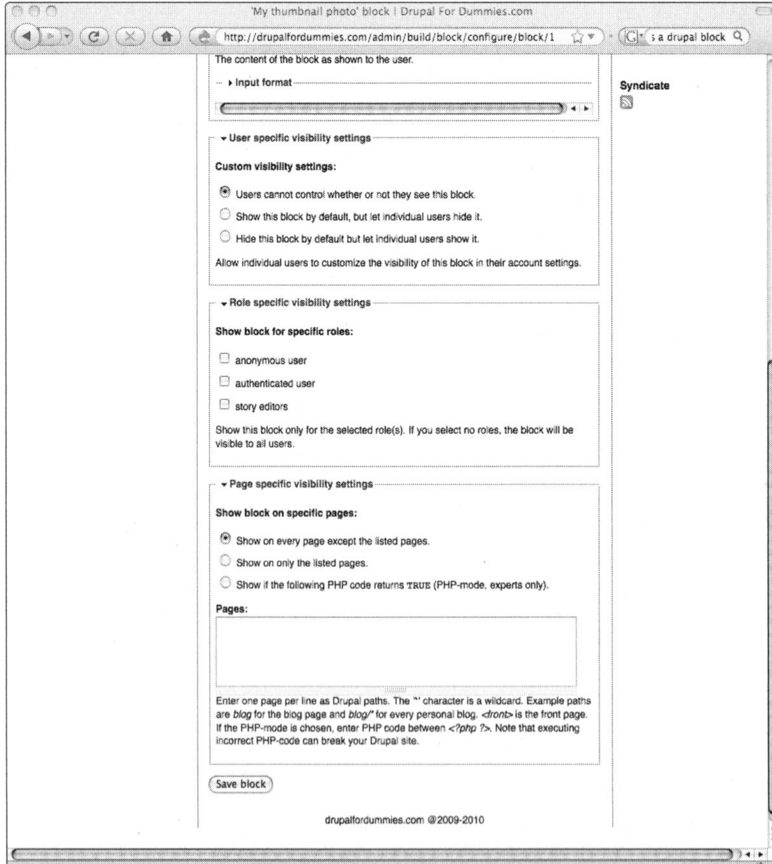

Figure 8-18: Block visibility settings.

The visibility sections are:

- **User specific visibility settings:** These settings control whether registered users can choose to hide a block from view when they visit pages on your site. The first option gives them no control. The second lets them hide the block, but it is visible at first. The third lets them hide the block but lets them show it if they wish. If you let them control the visibility, a check box with the block name will appear on their My account⇨Edit page.
- **Role specific visibility settings:** If you wish to allow only registered users to see your block, this is where you control that. Leave everything unchecked if you want both signed-in and guest users to see your block.
- **Page specific visibility settings:** This third option allows you to display your block on specific pages of your site. It requires you to enter the path to the pages on which you do or do not want the content to appear.

Before you can enter paths in here, you need more pages on your site. I will return to this setting later in the book.

Editing pre-built blocks

There aren't many things you can change about the nine pre-built blocks. If you click on the Configure link next to any of them, you will see a form that allows you to enter a title for the block. This will override any title the block currently uses. All of them also provide you with the visibility options.

Only three of the pre-built blocks have any other options:

- **Powered by Drupal:** This controls the color and size of the small Drupal logo. You don't have to include it. You can drag it to the disabled list, but I encourage you to leave it on your site. The block is shown in Figure 8-19.

'Powered by Drupal' block

The *Powered by Drupal* block is an optional link to the home page of the Drupal project. While there is absolutely no requirement that sites feature this link, it may be used to show support for Drupal.

▾ Block specific settings

Block title:

Override the default title for the block. Use *<none>* to display no title, or leave blank to use the default block title.

Badge color:

Blue

Badge size:

Small

Figure 8-19: Special configuration options for the Powered by Drupal block.

- **Who's new:** This option lets you control how many users are listed in the Who's new list (see Figure 8-20).

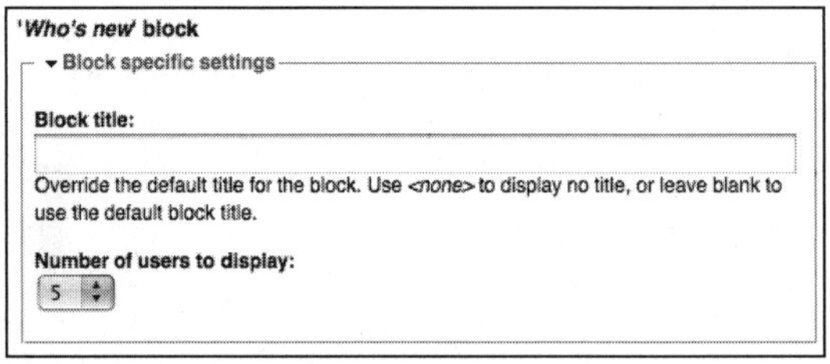

'*Who's new*' block

▾ Block specific settings

Block title:

Override the default title for the block. Use *<none>* to display no title, or leave blank to use the default block title.

Number of users to display:

5

Figure 8-20: Special configuration options for the Who's new block.

- **Who's online:** You can control which users this block lists based on how long it has been since they last clicked a link on your site. This also controls how many users to list (see Figure 8-21).

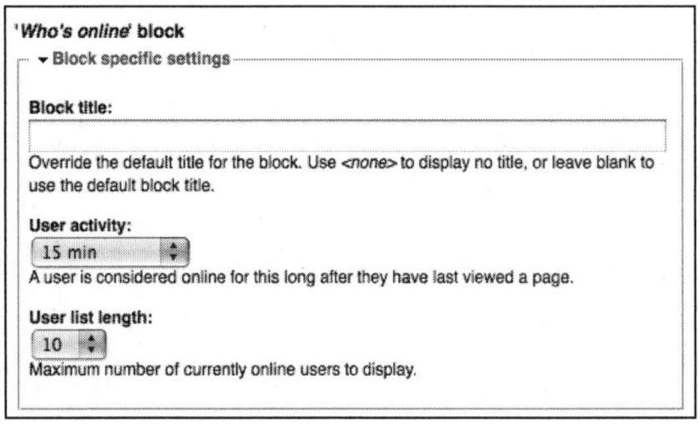

'*Who's online*' block

▾ Block specific settings

Block title:

Override the default title for the block. Use *<none>* to display no title, or leave blank to use the default block title.

User activity:

15 min

A user is considered online for this long after they have last viewed a page.

User list length:

10

Maximum number of currently online users to display.

Figure 8-21: Special configuration options for the Who's online block.

Managing Menus

Drupal has three menus that already exist. These are the Navigation menu, the Primary menu, and the Secondary menu (see Figure 8-22).

- **The Navigation menu:** This is the menu you use every time you log in as administrator and make changes to your site.
- **The Primary menu:** This is for important sections on your site. You might link to your company's Product page, a forum, or news about your business.
- **The Secondary menu:** These links are for less important pages, like legalese or partner sites.

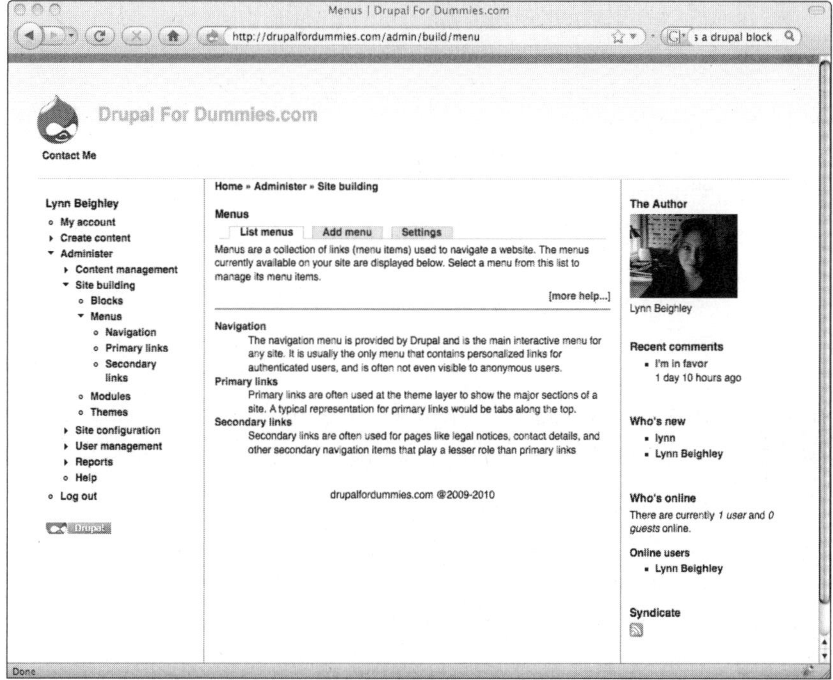
Menus | Drupal For Dummies.com
http://drupalfordummies.com/admin/build/menu
Drupal For Dummies.com
Contact Me
Lynn Beighley
My account
Create content
Administer
Content management
Site building
Blocks
Menus
Navigation
Primary links
Secondary links
Modules
Themes
Site configuration
User management
Reports
Help
Log out
Home » Administer » Site building
Menus
List menus
Add menu
Settings
Menus are a collection of links (menu items) used to navigate a website. The menus currently available on your site are displayed below. Select a menu from this list to manage its menu items.
[more help...]
Navigation
The navigation menu is provided by Drupal and is the main interactive menu for any site. It is usually the only menu that contains personalized links for authenticated users, and is often not even visible to anonymous users.
Primary links
Primary links are often used at the theme layer to show the major sections of a site. A typical representation for primary links would be tabs along the top.
Secondary links
Secondary links are often used for pages like legal notices, contact details, and other secondary navigation items that play a lesser role than primary links
drupalfordummies.com @2009-2010
The Author
Lynn Beighley
Recent comments
I'm in favor
1 day 10 hours ago
Who's new
lynn
Lynn Beighley
Who's online
There are currently 1 user and 0 guests online.
Online users
Lynn Beighley
Syndicate
Done

Figure 8-22: The three Drupal menus.

At this point, you know how to put a page node in the Primary menu when you create or edit it. My Contact Me page is in this menu, and a link to it appears on every page of my site. But instead of going through the process of editing a page to add it to the Primary menu, you can add additional links directly. To get to the Menus section, click on Administer➪Site building➪Menus. You will see the options shown in Figure 8-22. There are three tabs on this page: List menus, which lists all the menus; Add menu, where you can create a custom menu; and Settings, which controls the overall structure of your menus.

Setting primary and secondary links

WARNING!

It's best not to make any changes to the Navigation menu. It is used for the My account link, the Log out link, and all the administrative functions; if you change it, you run the risk of being unable to get to a particular administrative section of your site.

Adding an item to a menu

To add an item to a menu, follow these steps:

1. **Click on Administrator⇨Site building⇨Menus.**
2. **Click on the menu to which you wish to add an item.** In my case, I click on Primary links. You will see a list of links in the menu. In my case, I have only one, my Contact Me link (see Figure 8-23).
3. **Click on the Add item tab.** You see the Add item form (see Figure 8-24).
4. **Enter the URL or path to your page or story in the Path blank.** You can also use external links (for example, `http://fordummies.com`).

   TIP

   To get the correct URL for a page or story node, follow these steps:

   a. Open your site in another browser window.

   b. Click on Administer⇨Content management⇨Content.

   c. Locate the story or page to which you want to link and click on its title.

   d. Copy the URL to that page.

   The URL will look something like `http://drupalfordummies.com/node/10`. This is what you will paste in the Path blank.

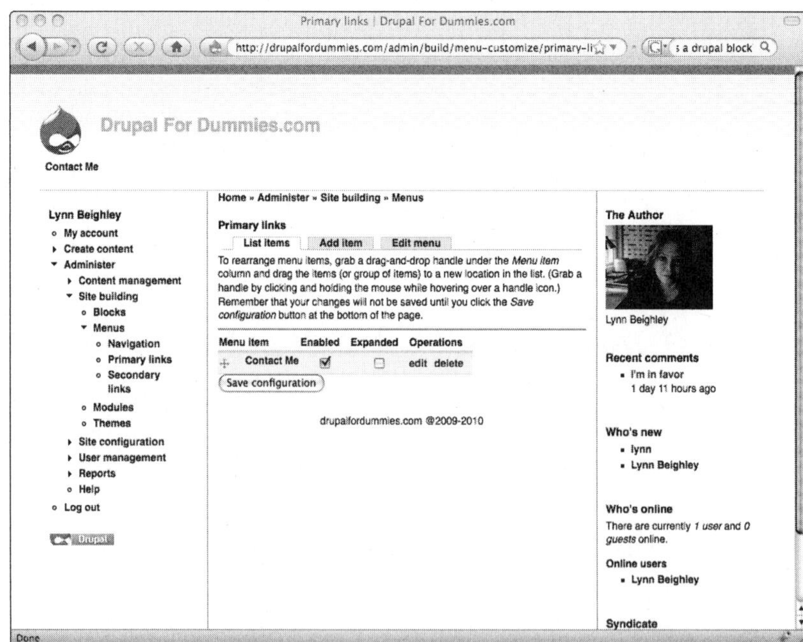

Figure 8-23: The list of links in the Primary menu.

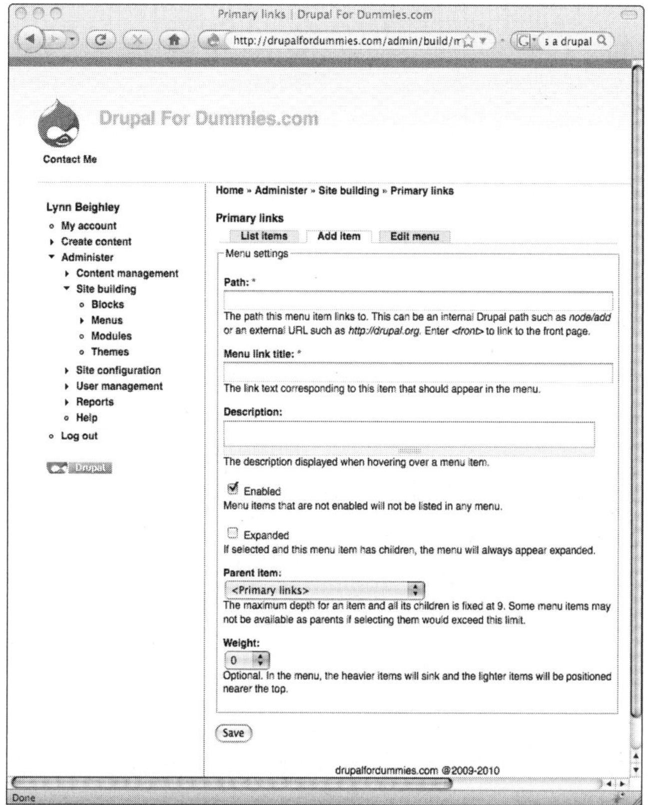

Figure 8-24: The Add item page to create a new menu link.

5. **In the Menu link title blank, enter the text you want used for the link.** This will be something like About Us or Products.

6. **(Optional) Enter a description of the page you are linking.** The description will appear when the mouse cursor passes over the link.

7. **If you wish to hide the link temporarily, uncheck the Enabled box.**

8. **For now, leave the Expanded, Parent item, and Weight settings as they are.** You will use these when you create child links, covered later in this book.

9. **Click Save.** You now return to the List items form.

TIP

You should already see your new Primary menu item on your pages.

You can change the order of the Primary menu items by dragging them up or down in the list on the List items page.

Editing and deleting links

Just as with the block menu, you have to delete links on the List items page to delete. To edit a link, click on the edit link. You are presented with the same form you used to create the link.

Adding a menu

Drupal allows you to create custom menus. They are automatically put in blocks and can be moved to various regions on the site in the same way as a custom block.

To create a new menu, follow these steps:

1. **Click on Administer➪Site Building➪Menus.**
2. **Click on the Add menu link.** You will see the form shown in Figure 8-25.
3. **Give your menu a name or identifier that can be used by the Web server.** Make it short, with no spaces or special characters, because it will become part of a URL. Something like *prodmenu* or even *p* is sufficient.

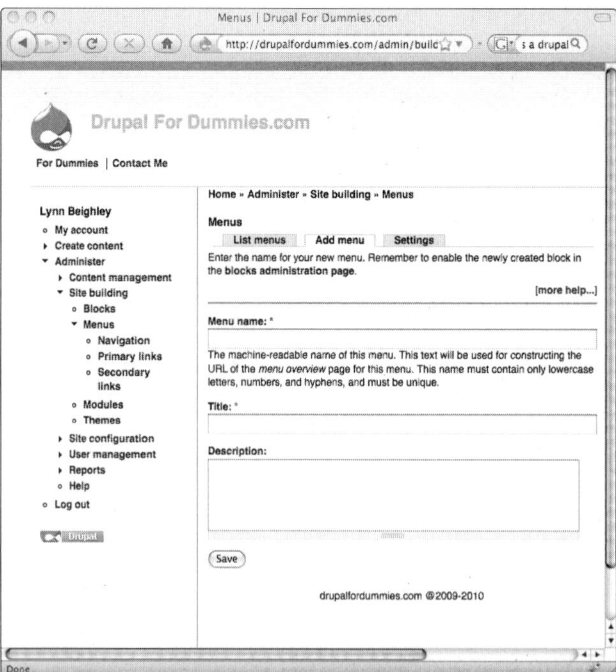

Figure 8-25: The Add menu form.

4. **Enter a title for your menu.** Something like *Product links* or *My links* is good. This will appear in the same listings with Primary links and Secondary links menus.
5. **(Optional) Enter a description of your menu.**
6. **Click Save.**

You add links to your menu in exactly the same way you added them to the Primary menu earlier.

With custom menus and block visibility settings, you can create a custom page that contains its own content and menu. Create as many custom blocks and menus as you need, put them in the Content region, and make them visible only on the necessary page. It's a bit of work, but it allows you increased control over your content and the ability to put more custom content than just a single story or page node can have.

Menu settings you shouldn't change

The Menu configuration page has a Settings tab that controls settings for the Drupal menuing system. To see this page, click Administer➪Site building➪Menus. Click the Settings tab (see Figure 8-26).

This form is extremely confusing. Here's what the options mean:

- **Default menu for content:** Remember the form you use to create a page or story? At the top of that form, there is a link, *Menu settings,* that allows you to put a link to your new page or story in a menu. Under Menu settings, there's a drop-down list box with all the menus in it. The default one is Primary links.

  There's generally no reason to change *Default menu for content.* This setting simply means, "Make the menu you choose here the one that shows up as the default menu in that drop-down list box."

- **Source for the primary links:** This option says, "Use the links from this menu as the one that show up as the primary links." If I change this to a different menu, the links in the new menu will show up instead of my Contact Me and For Dummies links that are currently in my Primary links menu.

  Again, it confuses things if you change the source for the primary links. It's rather like saying, "Don't use my primary links as my primary links; use these other links instead."

- **Source for the secondary links:** Same functions as the primary links, only affecting the secondary links. It's best to leave it alone.

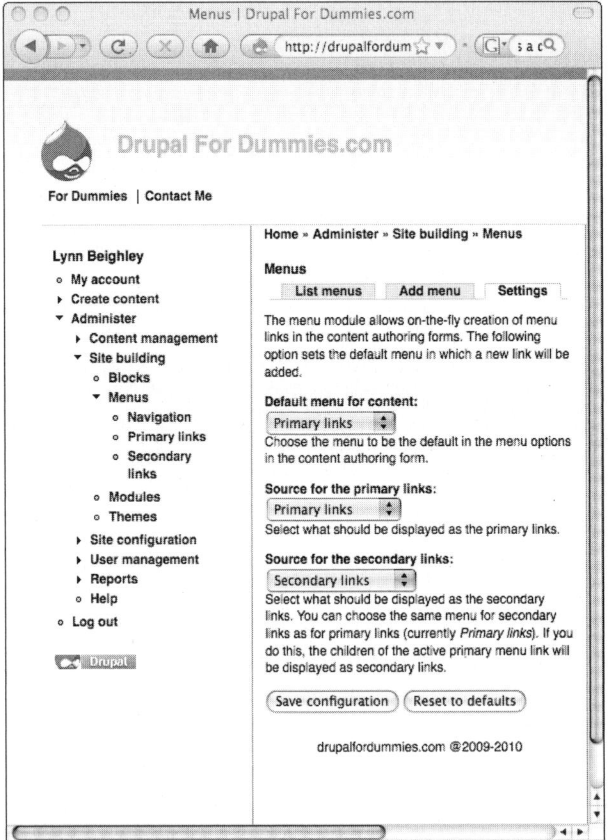

Figure 8-26: Menu settings.

Chapter 9

Using Modules: Create a Site with a Blog and Forum

In This Chapter

- Using modules
- Managing forums
- Building blogs
- Moderating comments

A Drupal module is a plug-in program that extends Drupal's core functionality. Think of a module like an add-on application that allows Drupal to do more things. In general, like themes, modules have to be downloaded, placed in a directory on your Web server, and then enabled. For example, the blog and forum I talk about in this chapter are modules. When you install Drupal, these modules aren't enabled, so you can't initially build a blog or forum. Enabling them adds this increased functionality to Drupal.

In this chapter, you take a close look at modules. You see how to build a site complete with a blog and a forum. Along the way, you discover how to upload and activate modules and where to find new ones.

Understanding Modules

You may not realize it, but you are already using modules. Drupal itself is composed of a set of modules, known as the *Core modules*. To see what I mean, choose Administer➪Site Building➪Modules (see Figure 9-1).

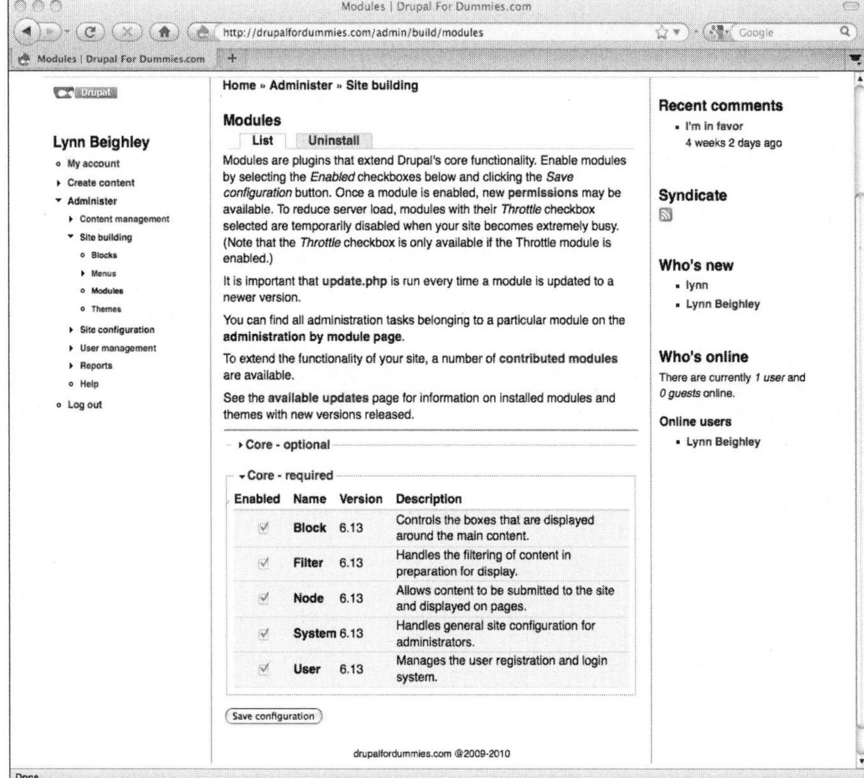

Figure 9-1: The Module menu displays all the pre-installed modules.

Modules preinstalled with Drupal are called Core modules. The two types of Core modules are

- **Optional:** These are modules you don't have to have enabled for Drupal to run, but they are some of the most useful ones. A few of them are enabled by default.
- **Required:** As you might guess, required modules have to be enabled for Drupal to run. These are the heart and soul of Drupal. You can't disable or delete them.

In Figure 9-1, the Core–optional menu is collapsed so you see the Core–required modules.

Understanding the required modules

Take a look back at Figure 9-1 and notice the required Core modules. There are five of them, and even though they have check boxes under *Enabled*, you can't uncheck them to disable them.

- **Block:** These are chunks of code that contain content and menus and can be placed in the regions around the main content area. In Chapter 8, you add and remove blocks from the various regions. The regions displayed in your site depend on the theme you are using and control where you can place blocks.
- **Filter:** Before Drupal displays content on your site, it removes and modifies certain kinds of code or content that could allow your site to be compromised by hackers. The Filter module scans and removes potentially harmful content. It also turns Web page addresses into clickable links.
- **Node:** Content types, such as a story, page, poll, or blog post, are organized into nodes, discrete units that can be viewed on a page by itself or on the same page as other nodes. This module is responsible for managing modes.
- **System:** This module manages all the important site configuration settings that you, as the administrator, control.
- **User:** If you couldn't log on to your website as the administrator to manage it, your site wouldn't be very useful. The User module contains the code that allows users to logon, the administrator to set up and manage accounts, and unregistered users to request accounts.

Each required module allows the administrator to modify specific settings.

Block module

In the preceding chapter, you used the Block module settings to control in which regions Drupal displays various content. It's worth taking another look at the Block module interface. There are three ways to access the Block module interface:

- **Choose Administer⇨Site building⇨Blocks.**
- **Choose Administer. Make sure you are on the By task tab. On the right side of the page, find Site building and locate and click on the Blocks link.**
- **Choose Administer. Click on the By module tab. Notice that under the box titled Block are three links, Configure permissions, Blocks, and Get help (see Figure 9-2). Click on the Blocks link.**

Under the Administer⇨By module tab, click on the Get help link under the box titled Block. This displays some useful rules that may come in handy when you are working with blocks. Also on the By module tab is a link to the Configure permissions page. On this page, the Block module has check boxes controlling which user roles can administer blocks and control where or if blocks appear on the site.

Modules currently enabled show up under the Administer⇨By module tab.

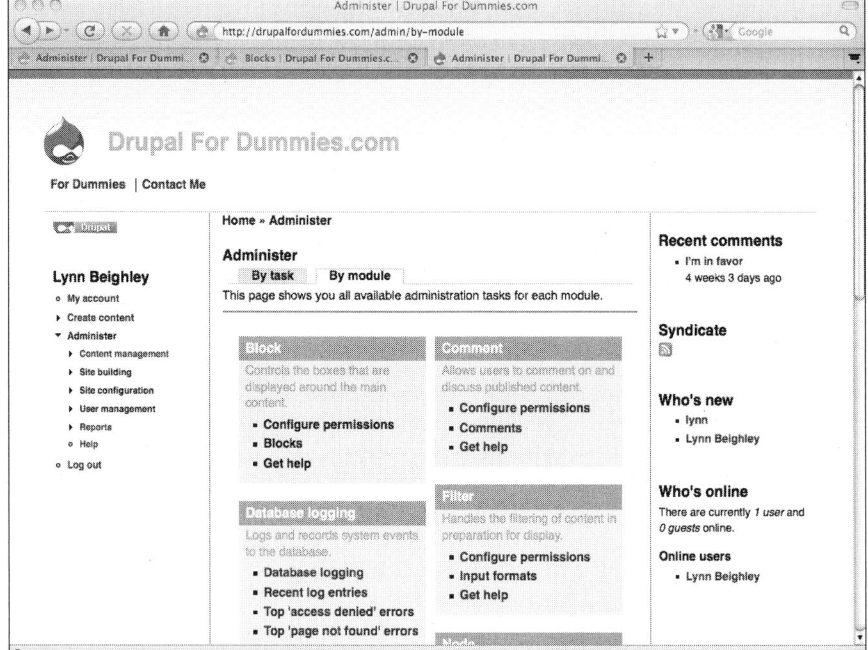

Figure 9-2: Three links pertain to blocks under the By module tab on the Administer page.

Filter module

The Filter module is responsible for four types of content filtering. These are

- **HTML corrector:** This filter attempts to find and correct faulty code. For example, if the HTML is missing a close table tag, </table>, this filter will add it. The HTML corrector applies only when HTML code is allowed.

- **HTML filter:** This filter removes HTML code when you choose to restrict certain HTML tags. You can also restrict all HTML tags and this filter will remove them.

  By default, Drupal filters out potentially harmful content. This includes JavaScript events, JavaScript URLs, and CSS styles. Even when you allow HTML, this kind of coding will be removed. Drupal also removes PHP scripts.

- **Line break converter:** This filter converts carriage returns and line feeds into HTML tags.

  Any time you create text content, Drupal scans it and looks for carriage returns or line breaks. When you type text into a text field to create a story or posting, the Filter module converts your carriage returns and line breaks into HTML style line breaks. Without this, when you publish your story, your carriage returns don't show up in a browser. This all happens behind the scenes, so you can type away without worrying about the HTML side of things.

- **URL filter:** When you are creating content and you type a URL (for example, `www.drupalfordummies.com`), after you publish it, Drupal turns it into a clickable link. This also applies to `mailto` links (for example, `<mailto://lynnbeighley@gmail.com>`).

Chapter 10 explains how to use any combination of these filters when you create content.

Node module

Because every bit of content is contained in a node, this module controls how content is created and submitted. The administration links for the Node module are used to manage content types, edit and delete submitted content, and manage how posts to the front page behave. The only settings you can change for the Node module itself are how the roles can interact with content. These settings are under the Permissions page at Administer⇨User management⇨Permissions. These are discussed in Chapter 4.

System module

The System module contains the code that runs Drupal. To get an idea of all the areas under the umbrella of this module, choose Administer⇨By module tab, and locate the section on the page titled System (see Figure 9-3).

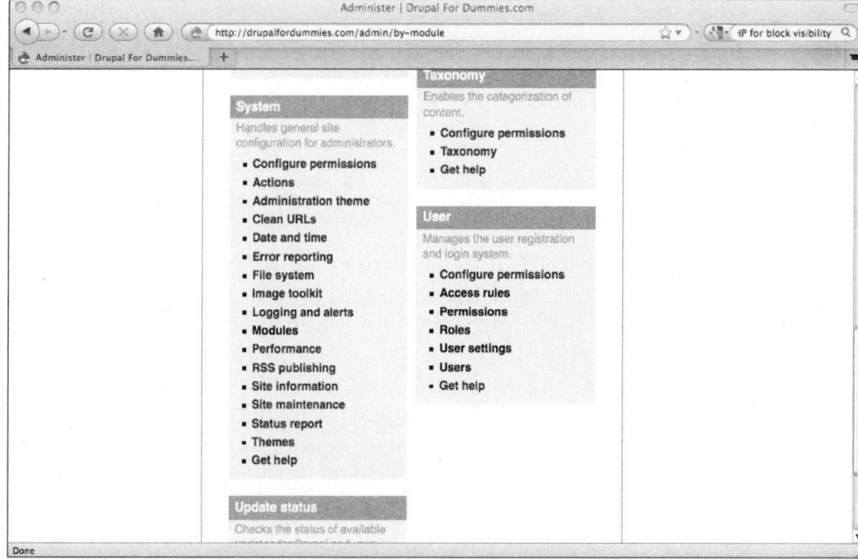

Figure 9-3: The System module section under the By module tab on the Administer page.

There are a number of settings here. Some you have seen already, and many are covered in detail in Chapter 10. To give you a sense of what the System module does, it controls, among other things:

- **Actions:** These are tasks that Drupal can do automatically when something happens. You can add custom actions, and I show you how in the next chapter.
- **Administration theme and Site Theme:** When you select a new theme, the System module manages the display of it.
- **Date and Time format**
- **Site maintenance:** This allows you to temporarily prevent your site from being viewed or logged on to by visitors while you work on it.
- **Site information:** These are settings for the entire site, such as site name, e-mail address for automated e-mails to users, and a site-wide footer (a bar across the bottom of all your pages that may contain copyright and contact information).

User module

If you take a look back at Figure 9-3 under the title User, you should recognize all the functions that that this module controls. The User module controls everything to do with roles, user accounts, and access rules and permissions.

You may have noticed that all the modules on the Administer⇨By module tab have a Configure permissions link and a Get help link. The Configure permissions link controls who can change the settings associated with each module. In general, unless you trust your authenticated users or story editors implicitly, you should never give anyone permission to control anything under the Core modules.

Looking at the optional modules

There are a number of optional modules installed with Drupal. Some of these are enabled by default; most are not. To see the list of optional modules, choose Administer⇨Site Building⇨Modules and expand the Core–optional section (see Figure 9-4).

If you want to learn more about any of the optional modules, click on the Enabled box next to them and choose Save configuration. Now when you browse to the Administer⇨By module tab, you will see them listed. Choose the Get help link for more information.

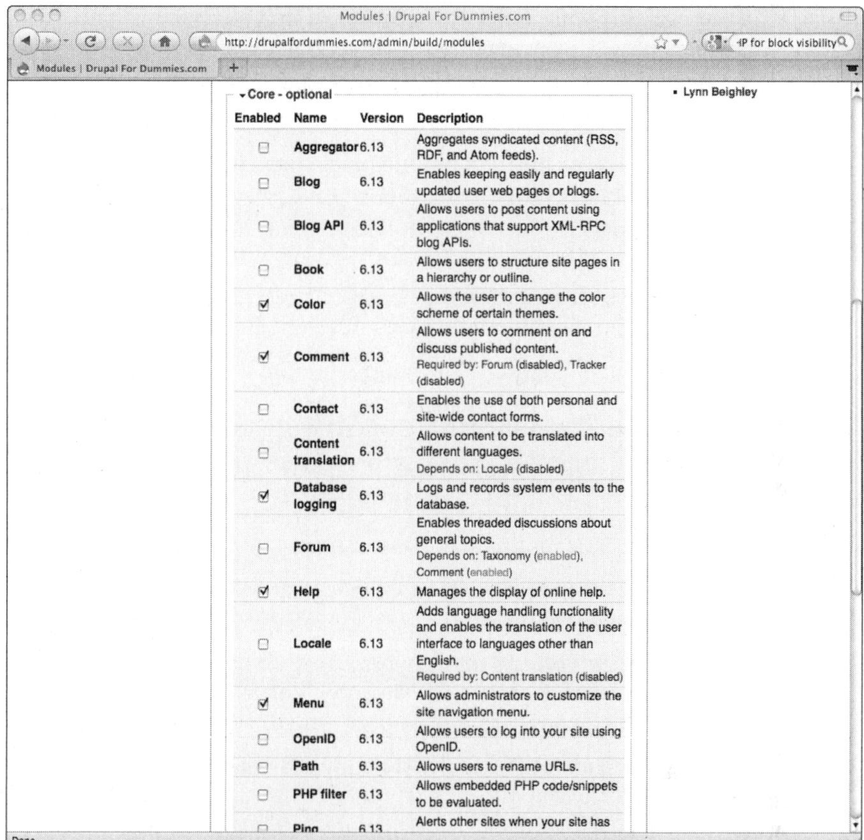

Figure 9-4: The Core–optional modules.

Here's a quick look at most of them.

- **Aggregator:** This module allows you to grab content from other sites and publish it on yours. You can add, edit, and delete RSS, Atom, and RDF feeds from other sites. I discuss this in more detail in Chapter 14.
- **Blog:** This is exactly what it sounds like, a module that allows you to create blog entries. This is the module you will use later in this chapter to create your own blogs.
- **Blog API:** This module lets you update your blog using a variety of other applications rather than having to log on to your Drupal site through a browser to post new blog entries.
- **Book:** A book in Drupal is an organized set of pages. They can be organized like a book table of contents and are useful if you want to publish anything structured, such a manual or user guide.

- **Color:** Some themes have settings that allow users to choose their own colors. This module has to be enabled for that option.
- **Comment:** This module is what allows registered users to comment on site content. It is enabled by default, and has to be enabled for forums to work.
- **Contact:** Rather than publishing a page with an e-mail address for your visitors to contact you, this module lets you create a contact form. Visitors can fill out and submit the form. You can have the information e-mailed to you, but you can also see it online and better keep track of it.
- **Content translation and Locale:** These two modules help you translate your published content into different languages.
- **Database logging:** This handy module keeps track of system events, such as user postings, people trying to browse to a nonexistent page on your site, and a record of when anything changes.
- **Forum:** Like a bulletin board, a forum allows registered users to post content and other users to respond.
- **Help:** This module controls online help documentation.
- **Menu:** With this enabled, administrators can add links to and edit the site navigation menu.
- **OpenID:** You can allow users to log on to your site with accounts from other service providers. They don't have to create a new account on your site. You can learn more about OpenIDs by visiting `www.openid.net/`.
- **Path:** The Path module lets you create simpler and shorter URLs for pages on your site.
- **PHP filter:** This allows PHP code to be included in content created for your site.
- **Ping:** Whenever you post new content, this module sends out a message to specific other sites to let them, and their users, know.
- **Poll:** Creates a question and a set of responses for your users to choose from.
- **Profile:** With this enabled, your users can create enhanced user profiles.
- **Search:** This module allows visitors to search through content posted on your site.
- **Statistics:** If you want to know more information about visitors to your site, this module can provide it. You can find out where your visitors are coming from and which pages they visit the most.
- **Tracker:** This creates a block displaying the newest content.
- **Update status:** It's always a good idea to keep your Drupal software, modules, and themes up to date. This module checks for available updates and keeps you posted.

Installing Your Blog

Blogs are incredibly popular, and it's no wonder. A blog is a relatively simple way of getting your message out to the interested public. People do read them, and a well-written blog may make the difference between a customer buying from you or going to your competitor.

As you probably figured out in the preceding section, setting up a blog in Drupal begins with enabling the Blog module.

Enabling your blog

To enable the Blog module, follow these steps:

1. **Choose Administer⇨Site building⇨Modules.**
2. **Scroll down to the Blog module listed under the Core–optional section (see Figure 9-5).**

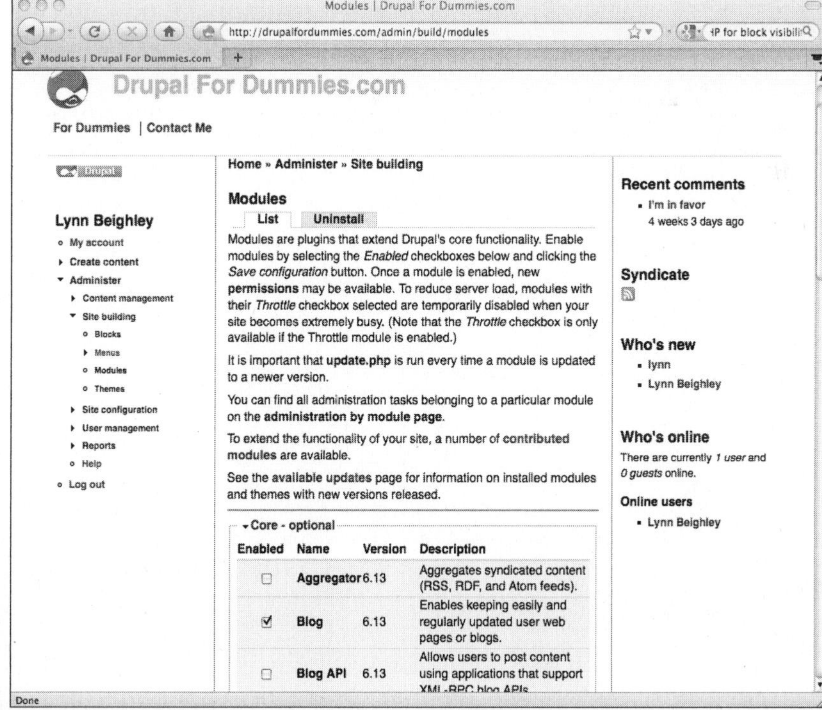

Figure 9-5: Enable the Blog module under the Core–optional section of the Modules page.

3. **Click the check box next to the Blog module.**
4. **Select Save configuration at the bottom of the page.**

The page will reload, and you will see the message "The configuration options have been saved."

Now that the Blog has been enabled, you have access to a new content type called Blog entry.

Creating your first blog entry

To create your first blog entry, follow these steps:

1. **Choose Create content.**

   A link for blog entry appears both on the site navigation menu and in the main content area. Both take you to the same Create Blog entry form.

2. **Click on the Blog entry link.**

   You see the form shown in Figure 9-6.

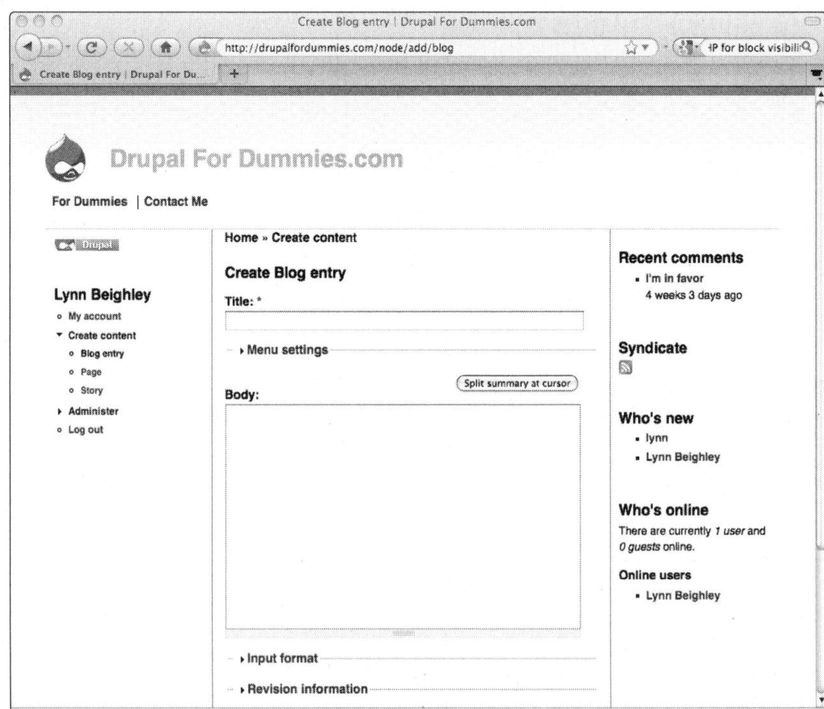

Figure 9-6: The Create Blog entry form.

3. **Enter a title and body for your first blog entry.**
4. **When you are done, click Preview.**
5. **You will see the preview of your post. If you are happy with it, press Save.**

By default, your blog posting is published to your site homepage. Browse to your homepage and take a look.

Changing blog entry settings

Creating your blog entry probably feels very familiar to you. It's very much the same as creating a story or page. If you scroll down the Create Blog entry form page, you see the same optional sections (see Figure 9-7).

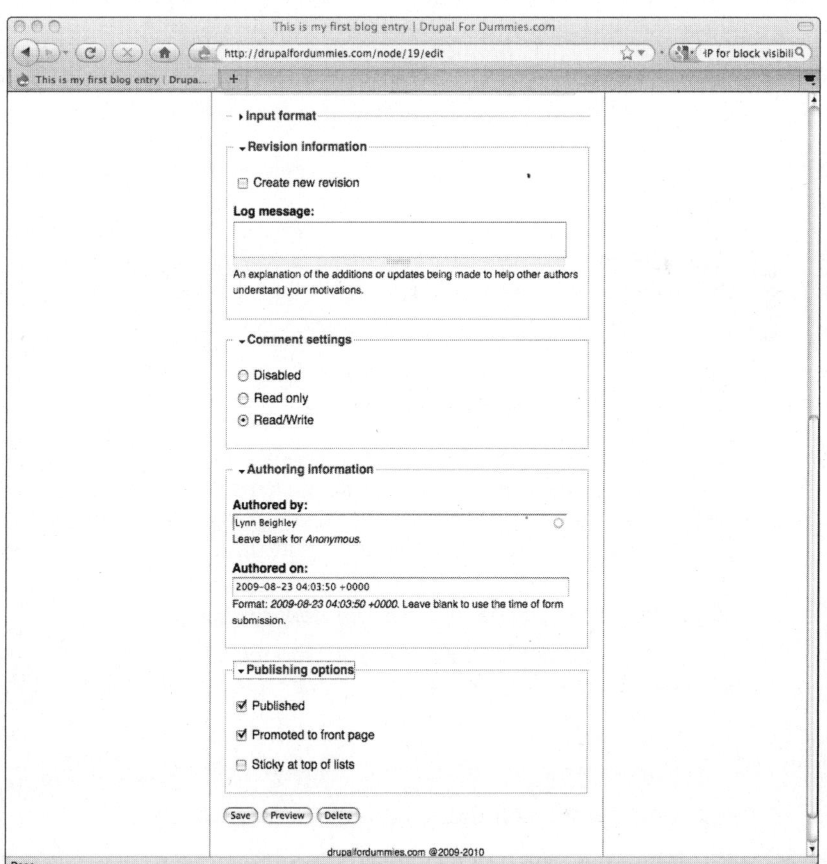

Figure 9-7: Settings on Create Blog entry form.

- **Menu settings:** In general, you should not change the Menu settings. The Blog module creates a specific area where all blogs are stored. Using the Menu link title and Parent item creates a link to just this specific blog entry, not to your entire blog.
- **Input format:** Decide whether to allow full or filtered HTML.
- **Revision information:** If you want to make changes just to this blog entry, but want to keep the old version, use Create new revision.
- **Comment settings:** Decide if you want to allow comments. This applies to just this blog entry, not all of them.
- **Authoring information:** Your name and the time and date are automatically populated. If you have several people contributing to the same blog, you can customize each entry here.
- **Publishing options:** This controls where this single blog entry will appear.

With the possible exception of Revision information, it's a bad idea to use these settings very often. Blog entries should be consistent, and when you change the settings for one, you will have an entry that no longer fits in with the others. Instead, you should change the overall configuration of your blog. In the next section, I show you how to apply some of these options to the entire blog, not just a single entry.

You can't change the Input format for your entire blog. You are stuck with managing it by blog entry. Since blog entries are best created by trusted people in administrator or story editor roles, you probably don't need to be restrictive in the content you allow, so the Full HTML setting is generally acceptable.

Configuring your blog

There are a number of other blog configuration tasks you should know about. Some accomplish the same things as the settings on the Create Blog entry page, only they apply to every entry in your blog. And some, like creating a link directly to your blog and adding it to a menu, help visitors locate your blog.

Removing blog postings from the home page

You may prefer not to clutter up your home page with blog entries, especially if you post frequently. To control where your blog postings show up, follow these steps:

1. **Choose Administer⇨Content management⇨Content types.**
2. **Click on the edit link on the Blog entry list item.**

   This takes you to a form that controls how your blog entries behave.
3. **Scroll down and expand the Workflow settings (see Figure 9-8).**

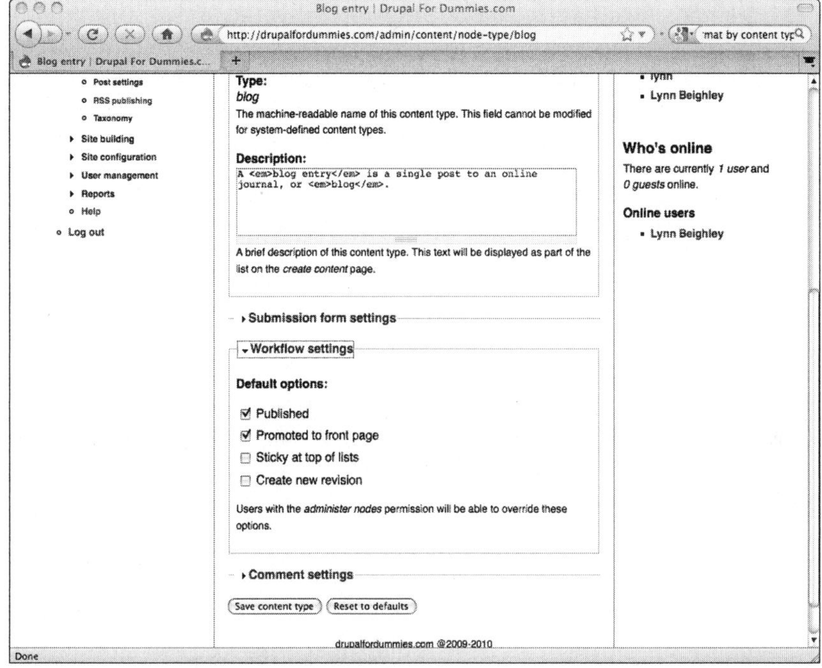

Figure 9-8: The Workflow section of the Blog entry settings form.

4. **To remove future blog postings from the front page, uncheck the Promoted to front page check box.**
5. **Press Save content type.**

Did you notice the Reset to defaults button at the bottom of the Blog entry settings form? If you ever make changes and you don't like them, but don't remember the original settings, click this to reset the form to the original settings. Don't be afraid to experiment with all the settings on this form as you set up your site; you can always reset them if you don't like the results.

Although you have made sure new blog postings won't make it to the front page, the blog entry you created earlier is still there. This is easy to fix. Follow these steps:

1. **Browse to the front page of your site. You will see your first blog post.**
2. **Click on the title of the entry.**
3. **Click on the Edit tab.**
4. **Scroll down to Publishing options and expand this section. Uncheck the Promoted to front page check box.**
5. **Click Save. Your blog post is no longer on the front page.**

Browsing directly to the blog

You have removed your post from the front page, but it still exists. As things stand now, though, you have no easy way to get to it. But Drupal puts all the blogs on your site in the same place, and it's easy to get to. The first blog you create is located under your site under the `directory/blog/1`. For example, mine is at `http://drupalfordummies.com/blog/1`.

You can also find your blog by choosing My account. You see your account settings and a link to View recent blog entries (see Figure 9-9). Clicking this link takes you to your main blog page. In my case, this is `http://drupalfordummies.com/blog/1`.

The Blog module creates one blog per authorized user with the appropriate permission settings. This means that you, as the administrator, can create a single blog with as many blog entries as you wish. Your blog is associated with your user name. Later in this chapter, I show you how to allow other authorized users to create blogs, but for now, I focus on the single blog I have created.

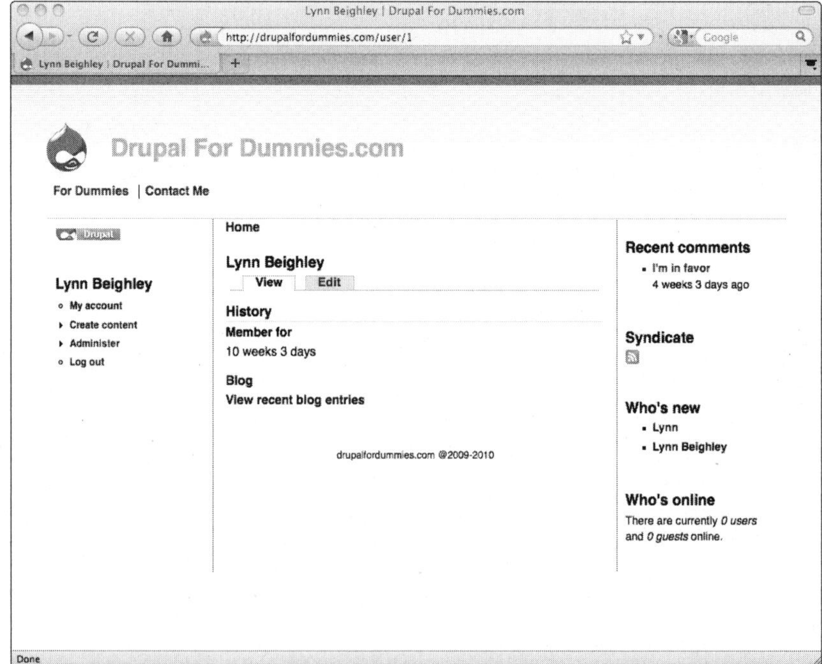

Figure 9-9: A link to your blog is under the My account link.

Creating a link to your blog

If you click on the link to your blog under your My account page, you are taken to the blog's main page. Copy the URL from your browser's navigation bar.

To add a link to your blog to the Primary links menu, follow these steps:

1. **Choose Administer⇨Site building⇨Menus.**
2. **Locate and click on the menu to which you want to add your blog.**

   In my case, I click on Primary links. You see a list of menu items already in the Primary links menu.
3. **Click on the Add item tab.**
4. **In the Path field, enter the URL of your blog.**

   In my case, it is `http://drupalfordummies.com/blog/1`.
5. **In the Menu link title, enter the text you want for your link.**

   In my case, I enter **Lynn's Drupal Blog**. The rest of the settings are optional and have been discussed earlier.

   Entering a description is a good idea. When visitors to your site move their mouse cursor over the link, they see this text. It also provides search engines a little more information about your site and can improve your ranking in search results. Every little bit helps!
6. **Click Save.**

   You are now back on the List items page.

Before you leave this page, drag your new link to your blog where you want it. I moved mine beside the Contact Me link, so that it appears to the left of Contact Me (see Figure 9-10).

In this figure, even though I have reordered by links, I have not yet pressed the Save configuration button, so the Primary links menu, shown across the top of the page, doesn't reflect the new order. Only after I press the Save configuration button will the Primary links menu will be in the new order:

- For Dummies
- Lynn's Drupal Blog
- Contact Me

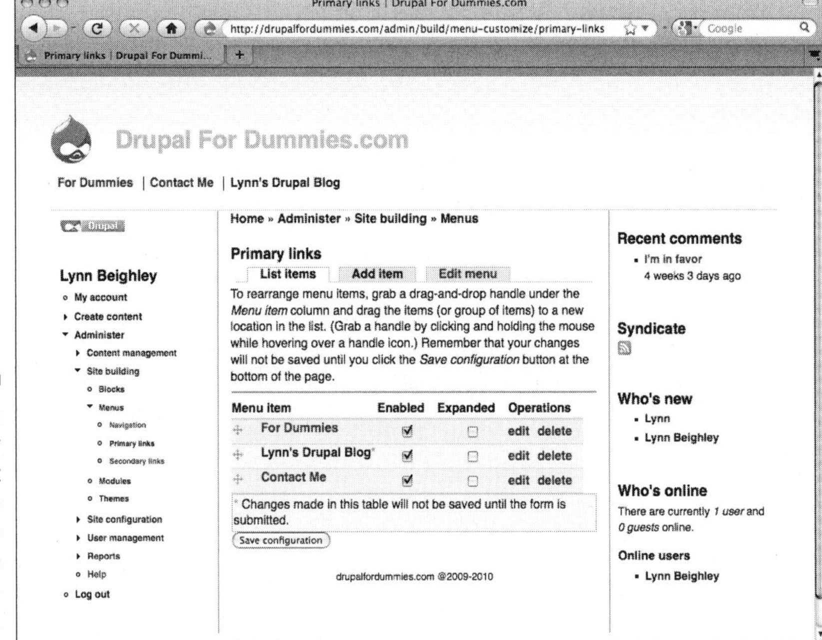

Figure 9-10: The Primary links List items tab before saving the configuration.

Adding more entries

There are two ways to add more entries to your blog. The first is the same technique you used above to create your first entry—that is, by choosing Create content⇨Blog entry.

The second is by clicking on the Post new blog entry link on your blog page. This link will be visible to you only when you are logged on and viewing your own blog.

Editing and deleting blog entries

Editing a blog entry is much the same as editing a story or page. When you are logged on and viewing one of your blog entries, you will see an Edit tab. Click on this and make your desired changes, and then press Preview or Save when you are satisfied with the changes.

To delete an entry, click on its Edit tab and choose the Delete button.

You can also edit and delete your blog entries by choosing Administer⇨Content management⇨Content and locating the entry you wish to change in the list. Don't forget to use the filtering options in the *Show only items where* section if you have a lot of content.

Creating multiple blogs

I mentioned that blogs are associated with user accounts; that is, one user can have one blog. By default, only the administrator can set up a blog. But if you want to allow a trusted group of users to create their own blogs, you can. Follow these steps to allow users in the story editors group to create blogs:

1. **Choose Administer⇨User management⇨Users.**

   Locate the user you wish to allow to create a blog in the list.

   Don't forget to use the filtering options in the *Show only users where* section if you have lots of users. You can also sort your user list by Username by clicking on the column heading Username. Click again to sort in reverse order.

2. **Click the Edit link next to the username.**

   This opens the My account page for that user.

3. **Click the Edit tab. Scroll down to the Roles section (see Figure 9-11).**
4. **Click the check box for story editors.**
5. **Scroll to the bottom of the page and click Save.**

   You still need to give all of your story editors permission to create blogs.

6. **Choose Administer⇨User management⇨Permissions.**
7. **Under the blog module heading, select the story editors check boxes for create blog entries, delete own blog entries, and edit own blog entries (see Figure 9-12).**
8. **Click Save permissions.**

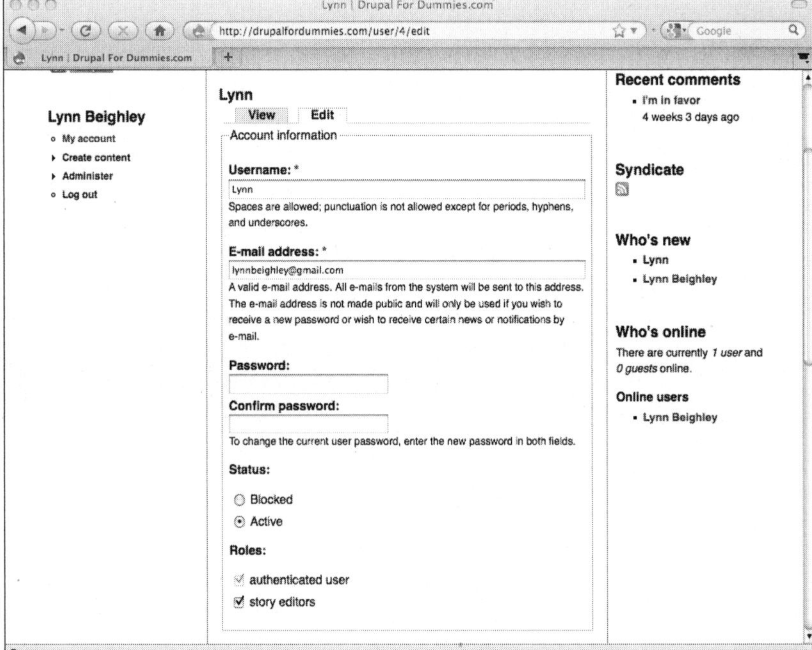

Figure 9-11: Assign the story editor role to a user.

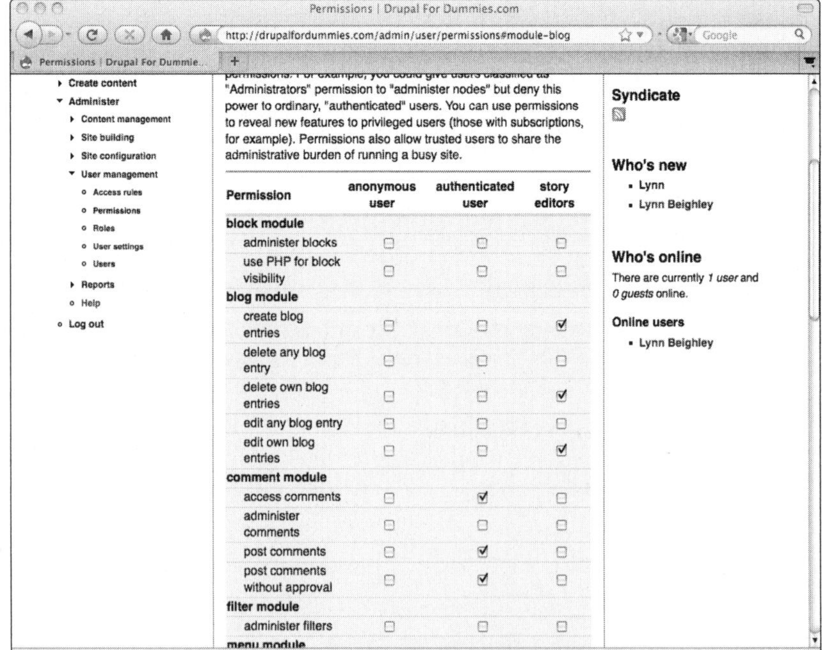

Figure 9-12: Permissions settings to allow story editors to create blogs.

Any user with the role of story editor can now create a blog. He will see the Create content link in the navigation menu.

The link to the new blog created by a story editor can be found under that user's My Account page. If you are logged on as the administrator, you can get to that page by choosing Administer⇨User management⇨Users. Locate the user in the list and click his username. You will see the link to his blog.

Installing the Forum Module

Forums are great for creating a user community. People can get help from others, provide you with feedback about your content, and simply socialize. Your forum can be as tightly or loosely controlled as you wish. You can control the categories allowed on your forum. To see an example of a forum, browse to `http://drupal.org/forum`.

Just like setting up a blog, creating a forum begins by enabling the Forum module.

Enabling your Forum module

To enable the Forum module, follow these steps:

1. **Choose Administer⇨Site building⇨Modules.**
2. **Scroll down to the Forum module listed under the Core–optional section (see Figure 9-13).**
3. **Click the check box next to the Forum module.**
4. **Make sure that the Comment module and Taxonomy module (near the bottom of the Core – optional section) are also enabled.**
5. **Select Save configuration at the bottom of the page.**

The page will reload and you will see the message "The configuration options have been saved."

You might notice that under the Create content link, there is a new link to create a Forum topic. You can't actually create forum content until you set up your forums.

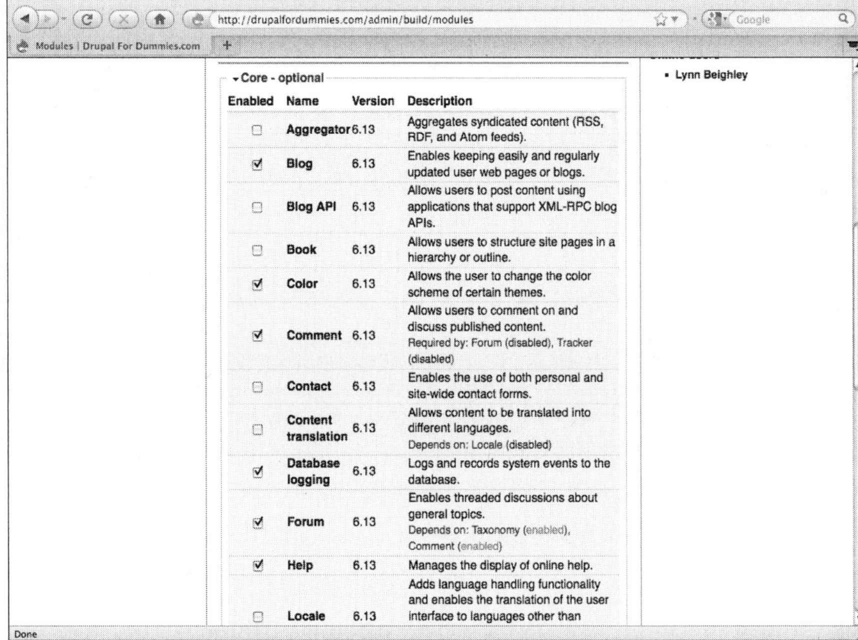

Figure 9-13: Enable the Forum module under the Core–optional section of the Modules page.

Organizing the Forum module

Take a look at a section of the drupal.org forum shown in Figure 9-14.

In this figure, there are three major headings: General, Services, and Newsletters. These groupings are called *containers.*

Inside each container are the actual *forums*. For example, under Services, the forums are *Hosting support* and *Paid Drupal services.*

If you click on one of these forums, you are presented with a list of *topics.*

So containers hold forums, and forums hold topics. But to confuse the issue, containers are optional. If you wish, you can create forums and not put them in containers at all. As an example, look at Figure 9-14 again. Imagine that all the containers (General, Services, and Newsletters) are missing. Instead, the page consists of a list of forums.

To help you decide whether you need containers, consider how many forum topics you want and whether they can be easily categorized. If you are creating only three topics, for instance, you probably don't need containers.

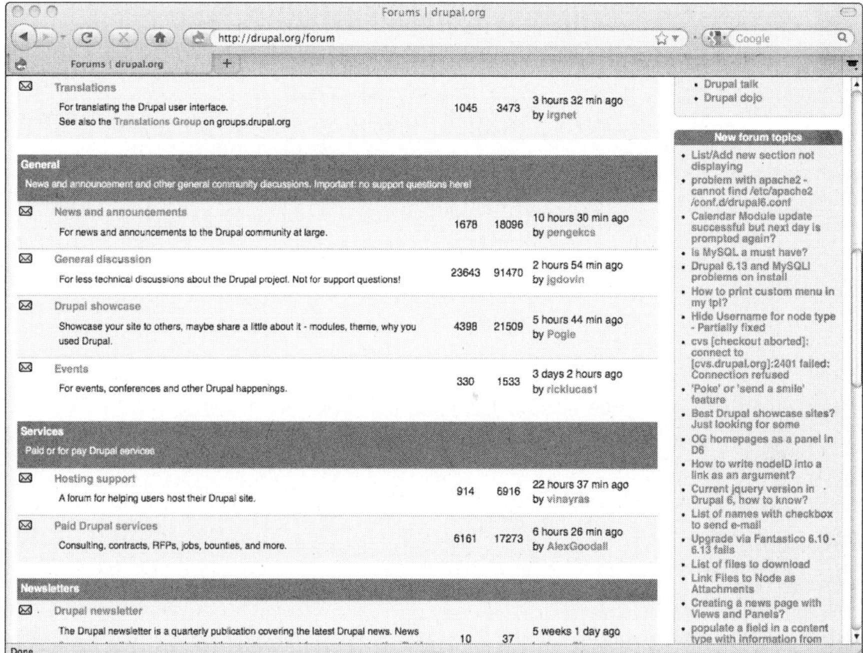

Figure 9-14: Part of the drupal.org forum.

Configuring your Forum module

In this section, I show you how to create containers and then how to create forums both with and without containers. Finally, I show you how to add existing forums to new containers, move forums to different containers, and remove containers.

Creating containers

To create a forum with containers, follow these steps:

1. **Choose Administer⇨Content management⇨Forums.**

   This opens the List tab of the Forum settings page. Because you don't yet have any containers or forums, you see the message "There are no existing containers or forums."

2. **Click on the Add container tab.**

   This opens the Add container form, shown in Figure 9-15.

3. **Enter a title for your first container.**

   In my case, I enter Drupal Help.

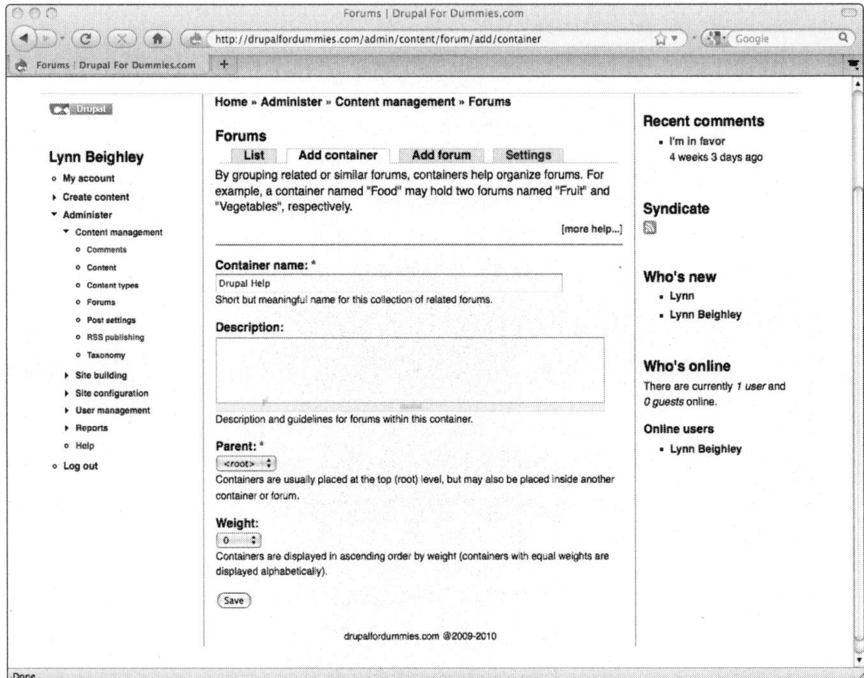

Figure 9-15: Add container form.

4. **Enter a description of this container.**

   This text will show up under the container title. Look back at Figure 9-14. One of the containers is named Services, and the description is the text under it, "Paid or for pay Drupal services." The description is optional.

5. **Click Save.**

6. **Add more containers by repeating Steps 2 through 5 until you have all the containers you need.**

   For this example, I created three containers: About the Book, Drupal Help, and Drupal Sites.

   When you finish, all your containers will show up under the Administer⇨Content management⇨Forums⇨List tab. From this page, you can:

   - Re-order your containers by dragging them in the list.
   - Edit container information by clicking Edit.
   - Delete a container by clicking Edit and then the Delete button.

Creating forums

To create a new forum, follow these steps:

1. **Choose Administer➪Content management➪Forums.**

   This opens the List tab of the Forum settings page.

2. **Click on the Add forum tab.**

   This opens the Add forum form, shown in Figure 9-16.

3. **Enter a title for your forum.**

   If you are using containers, the topic should fit under one of these. In my case, I create a forum called *Look at my site.* This will be a forum where visitors to my site can post the Drupal sites they build and get comments and praise.

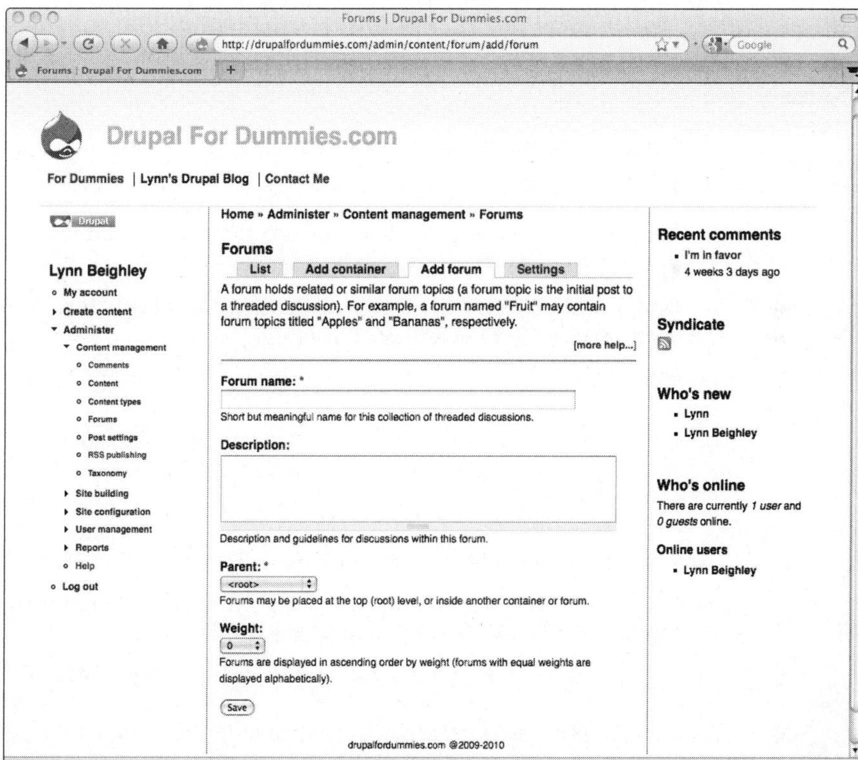

Figure 9-16: Add forum form.

4. **Enter a description of this forum.**

   This description will appear on the forum page. The description is optional, but it does help your visitors understand what should be posted in this forum.

5. **If you are using containers, choose the appropriate one from the Parent drop-down box. Leave this selection unchanged if you are not using containers.**

   In my case, I choose a container named *Drupal sites.*

6. **Click Save.**

7. **Add more forums by repeating Steps 2 through 7 until you have all the forums you need.**

Changing forum and container organization

After you create your forums (and optionally, your containers), you can move forums from one container to another or take them out of containers entirely. There are two ways to change the container a forum is in. To do it the first way, follow these steps:

1. **Choose Administer➪Content management➪Forums➪List tab.**

2. **Click on the edit link next to the forum you want to change.**

3. **Change the Parent drop-down box to the new container or select `<Root>` to leave the forum out of all containers.**

4. **If you wish, modify the name or description of this forum to be more appropriate for the new container.**

5. **Click Save.**

The second way of moving forums around is a bit easier but doesn't give you the chance to change the forum name or description. To use this method, follow these steps:

1. **Choose Administer➪Content management➪Forums➪List tab.**

2. **Click on the small cross icon to the left of the forum you want to change, and drag it under the new container.**

3. **If you want to take it out of all containers, drag it to the top of the list.**

When you remove a container with forums in it, they don't get deleted. Instead, they are located outside of any containers.

Viewing your forums

I imagine that you are ready to see the containers and forums you created. To view them, you need to create a forum topic. Follow these steps:

1. **Choose Create content⇨Forum topic.**

   This opens the Create Forum topic page (see Figure 9-17).

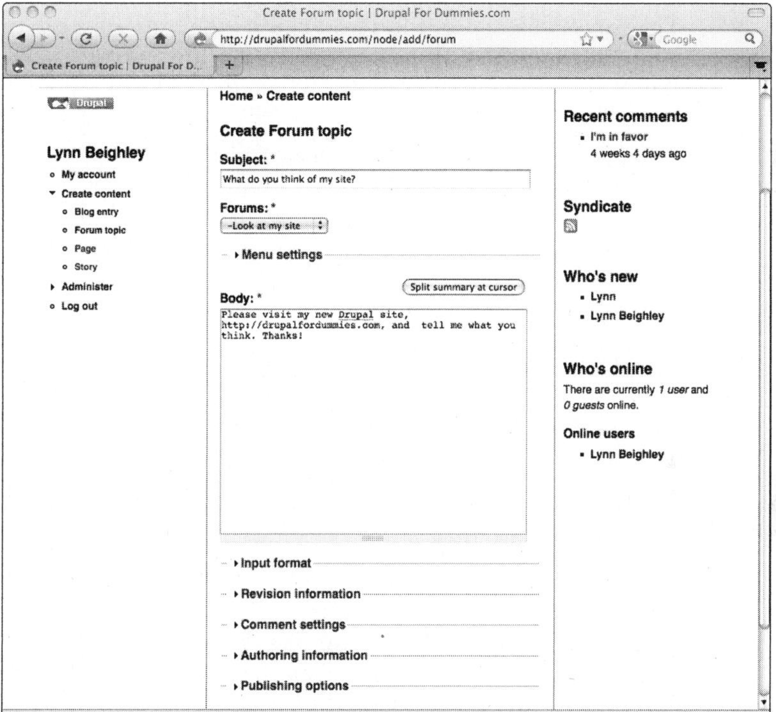

Figure 9-17: Create Forum topic page.

By now, this form should seem very familiar. With the exception of the Forums drop-down list, it's the same as the story, page, or blog content creation forms. The settings I discuss in earlier chapters (including Menu settings, Input format, and Publishing options) apply to this forum topic post as well.

2. **Create a subject and body that make sense for posting in one of the forums you created.**

   In my example, I create a post that shows off a new Drupal site.

3. **Choose the appropriate forum from the Forums drop-down list.**

   I chose *Look at my site.*

   You can tell the containers from the forums in this list. The forums all have a dash in front of their names to indicate they are underneath containers in the hierarchy.

   You can choose a container from this list rather than a forum, but then your post would be out of place. It would show up under a container but outside of a forum. You should test this out and see the results for yourself.

4. **When you are finished, press Save.**

To see your containers and forums, browse to `</forum>` under your domain name. In my case, it is `http://drupalfordummies.com/forum` (see Figure 9-18).

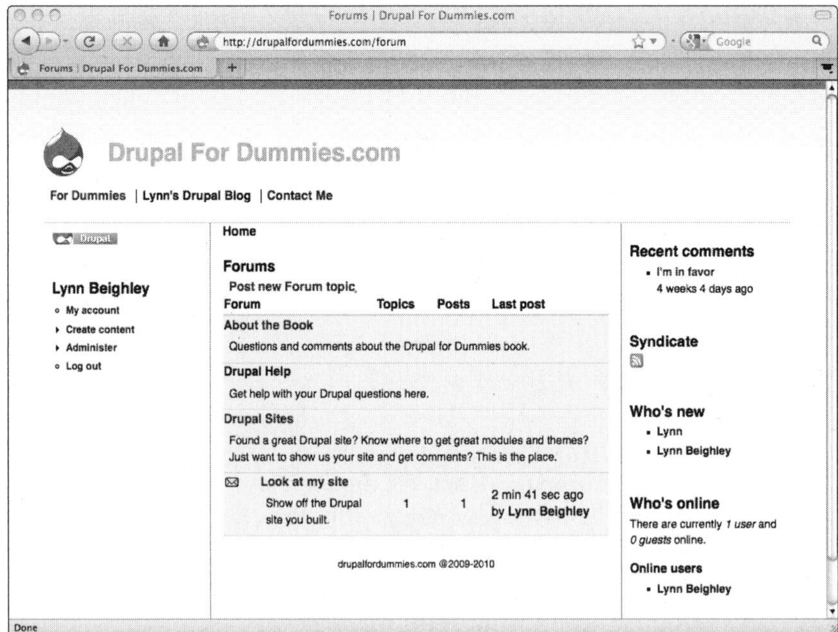

Figure 9-18: The forum page with containers and forums shown.

After you are on your main forum page, you can see posted forum topics by clicking on forums that contain posts. In Figure 9-18, you can see that a post exists under the forum *Look at my site.*

To see the individual forum topic posts, click on the forum title. In my case, when I click on the forum *Look at my site,* I end up on the forum topic list shown in Figure 9-19.

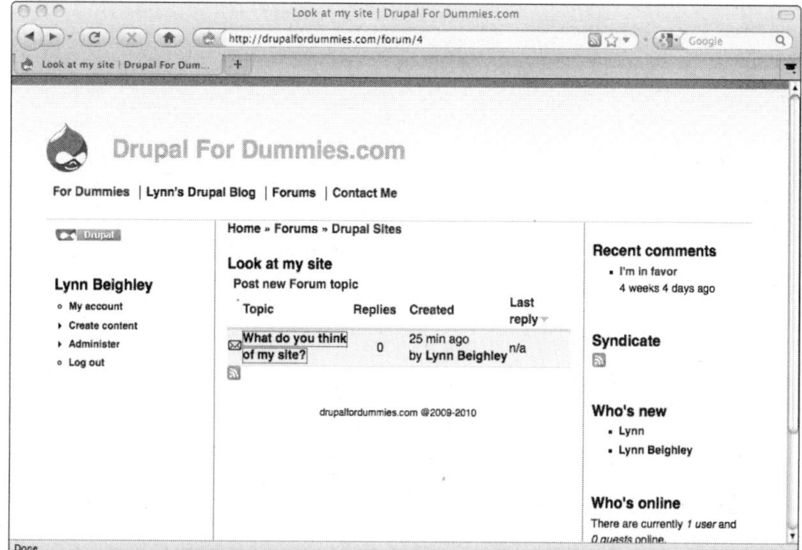

Figure 9-19: An individual forum topic.

Although I went to the trouble of creating this topic by choosing Create content➪Forum topic, the easy way to create new forum topics is to drill down into the forum and click the Post new forum topic link, shown in Figure 9-19.

Unlike containers and forums, forum topics exist to allow discussion. To view a forum topic and reply to it, click on the link to the topic. In Figure 9-19, clicking on the link *What do you think of my site* takes you to a page where you can comment on this topic.

By default, only the administrator can create containers and forums. Signed-in users can create forum topics and add a comment to a forum topic thread.

Linking to your Forum module

Just like with the blog I created earlier in this chapter, there is no main link to the Forum module. To add a link to your main Forum module page to the Primary links menu, follow these steps:

1. **Choose Administer⇨Site building⇨Menus.**
2. **Locate and click on the menu to which you want to add your forum link.**

   I chose Primary links menu.
3. **Click on the Add item tab.**
4. **In the Path field, enter the URL of your main forum page.**

   In my case, it is `http://drupalfordummies.com/forum`.
5. **In the Menu link title, enter the text you want for your link.**

   In my case, I enter *Forums.* Enter a description if you wish.
6. **Click Save.**

   You are now on the List items page.
7. **Arrange your links in the order you want them by dragging them in the list, and then click Save configuration.**

Changing forum topics settings

You have some control over the behavior of your forum topics. To access the forum topic settings, click the Administer⇨Content management ⇨Forums⇨ Settings tab (see Figure 9-20).

On this page, you can control the

- **Hot topic threshold:** When a topic reaches a certain number of postings, a small graphic is displayed, indicating that it is popular. This setting controls how many posts it takes to become a hot topic.
- **Topics per page:** You can limit the number of topics shown on a page here. If the total number of topics is greater, a Next link will appear.
- **Default order:** This is the order in which topics will appear on the page.

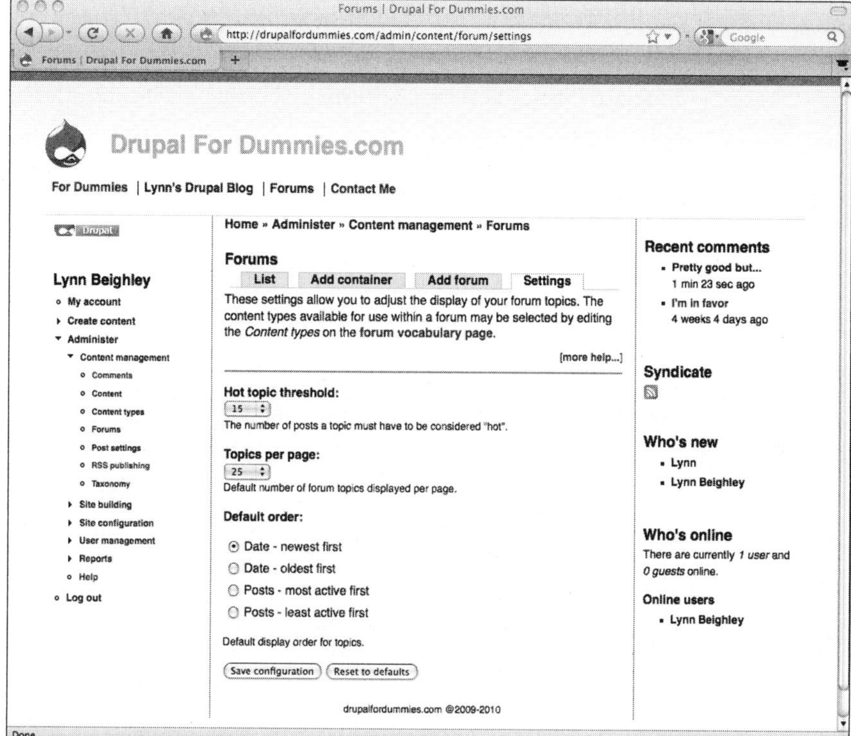

Figure 9-20: Settings for forum topics.

Managing forum permissions

Registered users can comment on forum topics. But right now, you are the only one who can post forum topics. Because the point of having a forum is to elicit discussion from visitors to your site, you may want to allow other people to post forum topics. This is controlled by the permissions settings for the Forum module. Open the Permissions page by choosing Administer⇨User management⇨Permissions. Scroll down to the Forum module settings. These are:

- **Administer forums:** Grants permission to create, edit, and delete containers and forums.
- **Create forum topics:** User is permitted to create new forum topic.
- **Delete any forum topic:** Grants permission to delete all forum topics, not just ones created by this user.

- **Delete own forum topics:** User can delete only forum topics he created.
- **Edit any forum topic:** User can edit all forum topics, not just his own.
- **Edit own forum topics:** User can edit only forum topics he has created.

If you trust your authenticated users not to abuse the privilege, allow them to create forum topics, delete own forum topics, and edit own forum topics.

Managing the Comments Module

The commenting system used by the Forum module and all the other content types is contained in another module, called the Comment module. As things stand, authenticated users can comment on any content on your site that allows comments.

Every time you create content, be it a page, story, blog entry, or forum post, you can select whether to allow comments. It's located on each content creation page in a section called Comment settings. There you can decide if no comments are allowed, new comments are allowed, or existing comments can be read, but no new ones added.

Moderating comments

Sometimes you might prefer to moderate comments. This means that comments people make aren't published. Instead, they are kept in a list for you to approve or delete. To turn on comment moderation, follow these steps:

1. **Choose Administer➪User management➪Permissions.**
2. **Under the Comment module section, uncheck the *post comments without approval* check box under *authenticated user.***
3. **Click Save permissions.**

Now each time a registered user posts a comment, she will see the message *Your comment has been queued for moderation by site administrators and will be published after approval.*

This comment will not be published until you approve it. To go through the list of comments waiting for you to moderate, follow these steps:

1. **Choose Administer➪Content management➪Comments➪ Approval queue (see Figure 9-21).**

Figure 9-21: Approval queue with comments to be moderated.

2. **Hold your cursor over the Subject line. The text of the comment will appear.**
3. **You can also click on the comment link. You can delete or edit this comment.**
4. **Click your browser's Back button to return to the Approval queue.**
5. **If you approve a comment, click the check box next to it.**
6. **Make sure Update options is set to *Publish the selected comments.***
7. **Click Update.**

You can also select multiple comments and delete them at the same time by clicking the check boxes for the comments you want to delete, setting the Update options drop-down to *Delete the selected comments,* and clicking Update.

Part III
Bending Drupal to Your Will

The 5th Wave By Rich Tennant

"We've got a machine over there that monitors our quality control. If it's not working, just give it a couple of kicks."

In this part . . .

There has to be more to Drupal than what you've seen so far. And there is. The chapters in this part take you deeper into Drupal administration. You dive into all those hidden but important nooks and crannies of the administration menus. You turn on more modules to help you keep tight control of your site. And you learn how to customize existing themes to make it truly yours.

Chapter 10

Advanced Administration

In This Chapter

- Getting new themes and modules
- Maintaining Drupal
- Monitoring your site
- Setting up a cron

Up to this point, if you've read the chapters in sequence, you have only touched the surface of administering your Drupal site. To make sure everything runs smoothly, you need to keep your software up to date. The Drupal community frequently comes out with updates. In this chapter, I show you how to keep your site protected by upgrading when necessary. Also, there are many administrative features you have not seen yet that extend your control over your site. You can monitor what visitors do when they come to your site, which can help you fine-tune your content.

Consider this chapter the next level in understanding how Drupal works.

Adding New Themes and Modules

Chapter 7 discusses how to change the default Drupal theme to a different one, also preinstalled. Chapter 9 shows how to add a blog and forum using modules that are also preinstalled.

One of the best things about Drupal is that developers are constantly contributing new themes and new modules. You can extend Drupal's functionality in incredible ways by adding new modules. You can create an incredibly professional-looking site in minutes by finding the right theme.

Follow these steps to add new contributed modules and themes to your site:

1. **Locate a new module or theme you want to use on your site.**
2. **Download the new module or theme to your local computer.**

   It will be a `.zip` or `.tar.gz` file.
3. **Upload the new module or theme to a specific folder on the Web server where Drupal is running.**
4. **Extract the new module or theme file.**
5. **Delete the original `.zip` or `.tar.gz` file.**
6. **Enable the new module or theme on your Drupal site.**
7. **Customize your new module or theme as desired.**

The first step in extending Drupal is to find new modules and themes.

Locating themes and modules

For new modules and themes, it's easy to head over to `drupal.org` and click on the Modules or Themes links on the topright corner of the page to browse around (see Figure 10-1).

Figure 10-1: Drupal.org has links to user-contributed modules and themes.

You can find especially popular modules and themes on `drupal.org` by clicking on the Usage statistics link under the Sort by block on the upper-right side of both the Modules and Themes pages. This lists the modules or themes in order of the most frequently downloaded to the least.

Chapters 16 and 17 contain links to some great sites to visit to find new modules and themes.

Downloading modules and themes

After you find a module or theme you want, look for a link to download it. Most of the time the module or theme will download as a single compressed, `.tar.gz` or `.zip` file. Save this file to a directory you will remember.

You should take a look at the documentation about the new module or theme. This documentation is generally available from the page with the download link and may contain detailed help to get the new theme or module up and running.

Installing modules and themes

Your module or theme comes as a single, compressed `.zip` file, but it actually consists of many files and folders. All of these files need to be located in a Web directory under your Drupal directory on your Web server.

You can upload the single `.zip` file to either the modules or themes directory under your Drupal installation on most ISPs. You can extract it after you have uploaded it to save you from having to upload a bunch of individual files.

In Chapter 2, when you install Drupal, I show you how to upload using a program called Fileman. Your ISP may have a different but similar program that handles file management. If you know how to use an FTP program, you may find that easier.

To upload the compressed file, follow these steps:

1. **Locate the e-mail from your ISP that has your username, password, and login information. Browse to the ISP's site and logon.**
2. **Find and click on the link to a file manager.**

   You need a file manager so that you can select the `.zip` file and put it in the correct directory on your ISP's site. After you click the file manager, you will see a screen that displays the files on your ISP's Web server.

3. **You should see a single folder or directory named `html`, *www*, or `htdocs`. Click on its name to open it.**

   There may be several directories, but the one for your Web site should be easy to spot. This is where all your Web pages belong and where you need to install Drupal.

4. **If you see a folder named Modules and one named Themes, click on the appropriate one.**

   This means that Drupal is installed in the root directory of your site.

5. **If you didn't see the Modules and Themes directories, look for a directory named Drupal. Click on it.**

   You should now see the Modules and Themes directories.

6. **If you downloaded a module, click on the Modules directory to enter it. If you downloaded a theme, click on the Themes directory.**

7. **Locate and click on the upload link on your file manager.**

   You should see an upload form with a Browse button.

8. **Click Browse and find the module or theme `.tar.gz` or `.zip` file you downloaded, then click Upload.**

   Your file is now on your site and in the correct folder. But you still need to extract it.

Extracting module or theme files

The file extensions `.zip` or `.tar.gz` indicate that many files are compressed into a single file. File managers can extract your compressed file for you. Following is an example of how it works. Your version may differ, so contact your ISP for help if you can't find the same functions on your file manager. Follow these steps to extract compressed files:

1. **Find the module or theme .tar.gz (or `.zip`) file you just uploaded to the Modules or Themes directory and select it. Click on the filename to open the file.**

   You will see a list of files that are stored inside your zip file. They will all be selected.

2. **You should see an option to uncompress your files. Leave the selection box set to uncompress All and click the Go button.**

   This will uncompress your single `.zip` file into a folder with the same name. You will now see both the compressed file (for example, supercoolmodule.tar.gz) and the uncompressed files in a new directory (for example, a folder named supercoolmodule).

3. **Select the original .tar.gz or .zip file on your Web server and delete it.**

   Be careful to delete only the new module or theme compressed file and nothing else.

Take a look inside the folder containing your new theme or module. If you see files named INSTALL.txt or README.txt, there may be more steps you have to follow for that specific module or theme. You need to read the instructions in that file. You may be able to view it through the file manager on your Web server. If not, the file manager can send a copy of the file to your desktop so that you can open it in Notepad (Windows) or TextEdit (Mac).

Enabling themes and modules

After you have uploaded and extracted your new theme or module, Drupal will see it and it will show up in your theme list or module list.

For example, I downloaded the Acquia Slate from a link on the drupal.org site under themes. I then uploaded it to my Web server under the directory /themes. I extracted it and deleted the original acquia_slate.tar.gz file.

Now I'm ready to enable it and use it on my site. To do this, I follow these steps:

1. **Browse to Administer⇨Site building⇨Themes.**

   The themes are in alphabetical order, so my new one, Acquia Slate, is at the top of the list (see Figure 10-2).

2. **Select the Enabled check box and select the Default radio button next to the new theme.**

3. **Choose Save configuration.**

   My new theme is now being used.

You can activate a new module in exactly the same way, except you browse to Administer⇨Site building⇨Modules. Since you can run multiple modules at once, there is no Default radio button. Select the Enabled check box next to your new module and then choose Save configuration.

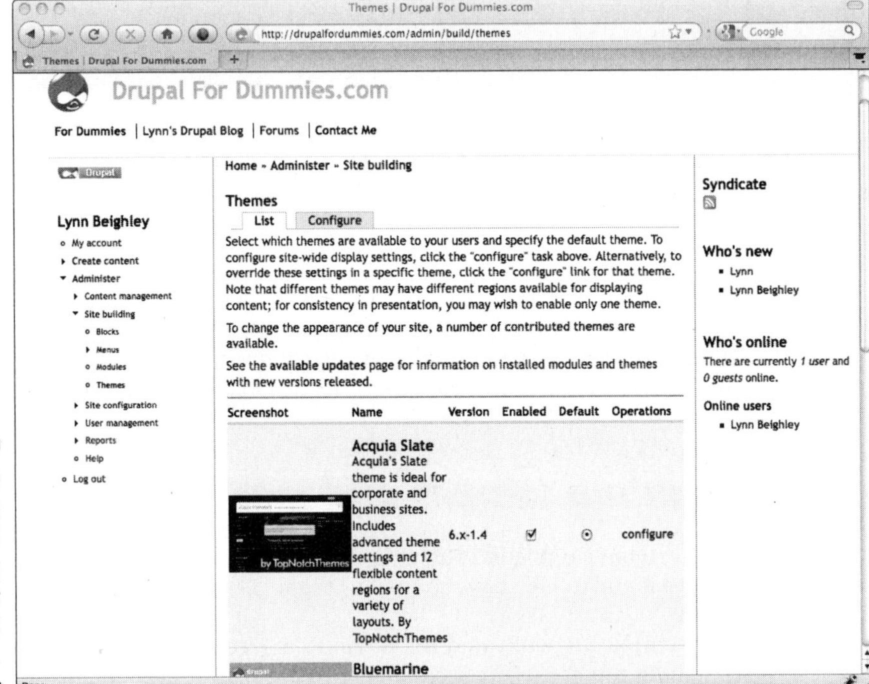

Figure 10-2: Enabling and activating a newly installed theme.

Disabling themes and modules

To disable a module or theme, you need only select the Enabled check box on the Administer➪Site building➪Modules or Administer➪Site building➪Themes page.

Keeping Drupal Up to Date

By now, you may be seeing a warning message on your site that says

No information is available about potential new releases for currently installed modules and themes. To check for updates, you may need to run cron or you can check manually. Please note that checking for available updates can take a long time, so please be patient.

Drupal is designed to automatically check for updates. You don't have to allow it, and by default, it may not be able to. You have two options. One is to click on the link in that warning message above that says *check manually.* This tells Drupal to check for updates for the main Drupal software as well as any updates to installed modules and themes.

You may decide to check manually, but Drupal is designed to check for updates frequently, because there are frequent updates you need to be aware of and install. To save yourself from checking manually, you can set up an automated process to check for you.

Drupal is designed to work with a small program or command called *cron* that exists on some Web servers running a UNIX operating system. You may have permission to access through your control panel your ISP provides you. In general, it may be easier to follow the instructions below and install a module called Poormanscron that emulates a cron command.

Setting up Poormanscron

Here's your chance to put your module installation skills to use. To install the Poormanscron module, follow these steps:

1. **Begin by getting the most recent version of Poormanscron from `http://drupal.org/project/poormanscron`.**
2. **Upload it to your Drupal modules directory.**
3. **Extract it.**
4. **Delete the `.tar.gz` file.**
5. **Choose Administer⇨Site building⇨Modules. Scroll to the bottom of the page and click the Enabled button.**
6. **Choose Save configuration.**

Now that you have installed and enabled Poormsanscron, you won't see the cron warning message. But you may want to tweak some of the settings for this module. Choose Administer⇨Site configuration⇨Poormanscron. You see the settings for this module (see Figure 10-3).

Drupal uses the cron for more than just checking for updated software. It is also for syndicating information from your site at specific times and retrieving syndicated RSS feeds from other sites or any process that has to happen at specific times. As you add new modules, some of them will use a cron to operate correctly. The settings for Poormanscron apply to any module that depends on a cron.

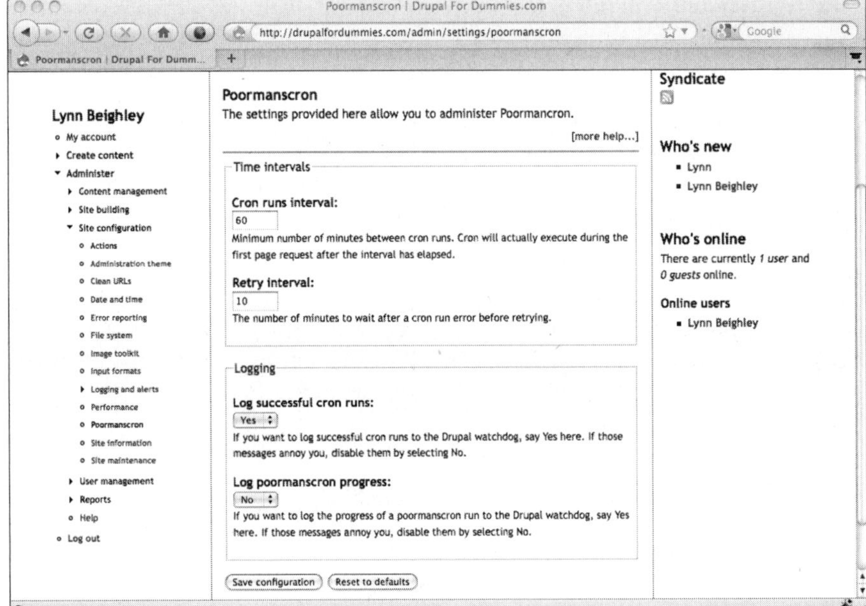

Figure 10-3: Settings for Poorman scron.

These settings are

- **Cron runs interval:** This is how often Drupal will run. It won't actually run every 60 minutes (the default setting), but after 60 minutes, the first time someone visits the site it will run.
- **Retry interval:** If for some reason a cron job fails, this is how many minutes until it should try again.
- **Log successful cron runs:** You can keep track of each time your cron runs successfully. To see the log, choose Administer⇨Reports⇨Recent log entries.
- **Log Poormanscron progress:** This will post more specific feedback about what the cron is actually doing when it runs to the report at Administer⇨Reports⇨Recent log entries.

Finding available updates

Drupal updates come out every 9 to 12 months. That applies to the main Drupal software, which includes the Core modules. But as you add more contributed modules and themes, the likelihood of needing to perform updates increases.

Updating a module or theme is an easier task than updating the Drupal software. Still, you need to know how to accomplish both. I start by showing you how to find out what you need to update, then show you how to update themes and module. Finally, I go through how to update the Drupal software itself.

It all begins by discovering what is out of date. Fortunately, that part is easy.

Choose Administer➪Reports➪Available updates. This page shows you the status of your Drupal software as well as individual listings for every extra module and theme you have installed (see Figure 10-4).

Even better, when your software is out of date, links to the newer versions appear on this page.

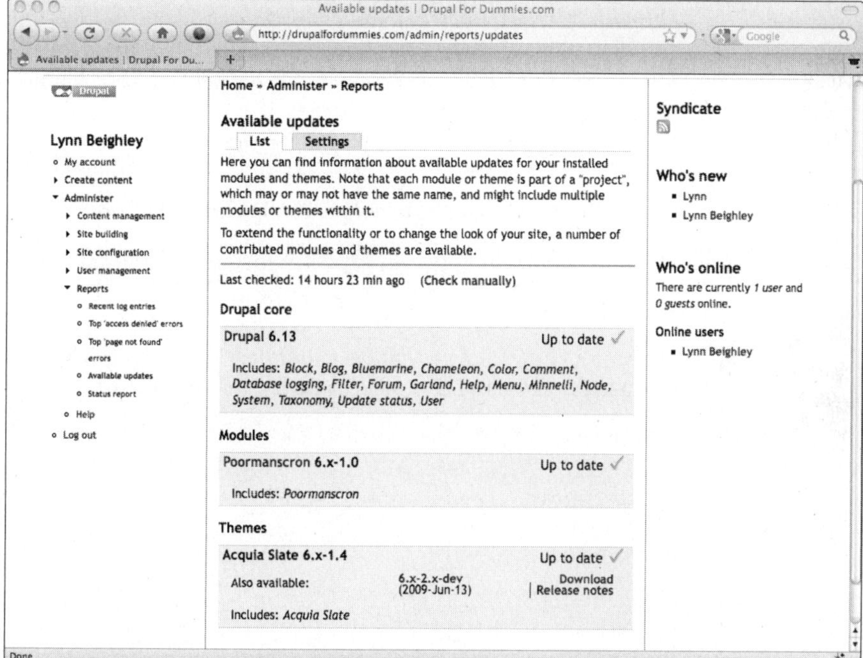

Figure 10-4: Status of all installed modules and themes.

Protecting Your Database

Before you update anything, you need to back up the database behind your Drupal site. By doing this, you safeguard all the work you have done on your site. Your database contains:

- **All content you have put on your site.**
- **Settings for everything you have customized.**
- **All user information, including logons and passwords.**

Updates are necessary but dangerous. Backing up your database is not difficult, and it's worth the few minutes it takes.

Backing up your database

To back up your database, follow these steps:

1. **Log on to your control panel, provided by your ISP.**
2. **Locate and click the phpMyAdmin icon.**

   You see the phpMyAdmin interface (see Figure 10-5).

   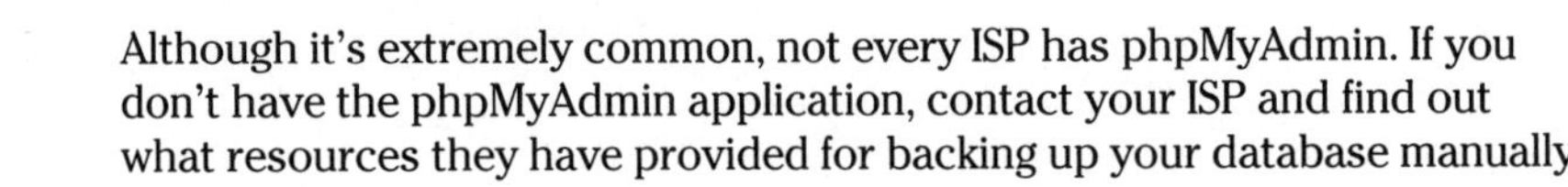

   Although it's extremely common, not every ISP has phpMyAdmin. If you don't have the phpMyAdmin application, contact your ISP and find out what resources they have provided for backing up your database manually.
3. **Click the Export link.**

   This opens the Export database screen shown in Figure 10-6.
4. **Under the Export section, select the Drupal database.**

   There may be two databases in your list. The Drupal database may be named with your username on your ISP site, or it may have Drupal in t he name.

   Chapter 2 shows how to create a database for Drupal. The database name you use for the database you create is the one to choose in this step.

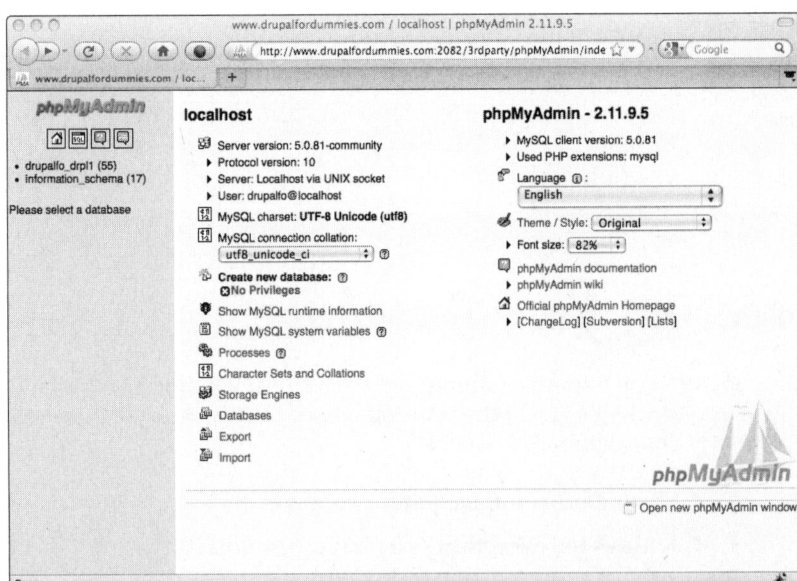

Figure 10-5: The phpMyAdmin interface.

Figure 10-6: The Export database screen of phpMy Admin.

5. **Under the database name, select the SQL radio button.**
6. **Under Options section, check these boxes: *Structure, Add IF NOT EXISTS, Add AUTO_INCREMENT value,* and *Enclose table and field names with backquotes.***
7. **Also under the Options section, check these boxes: *Data, Complete inserts, Extended inserts,* and *Use hexadecimal for BLOB Export type.***
8. **At the bottom of this page, select Save as File.**
9. **For compression, choose "zipped."**
10. **Click the Go button.**

    You may have to wait for a few minutes, but you will be prompted to save a file (see Figure 10-7). This file is your database backup file, which you will need if you ever have to restore your database.

By default, this file has a generic name, such as `localhost.sql.zip`. Rename this file so that later you will recognize what it is, and then save it in a location you will remember. You may want to use the date as part of the filename so you can always select the most recent backup if you do have to restore your database.

Opening localhost.sql.zip

You have chosen to open

localhost.sql.zip

which is a: PC ZIP Archive

from: http://www.drupalfordummies.com:2082

What should Firefox do with this file?

Open with StuffIt Expander (default)

Save File

Do this automatically for files like this from now on.

Cancel OK

Figure 10-7: Download your database backup file.

Restoring your database

Should you ever have to restore your database because you have lost your data, here are the basic steps for restoring it.

I highly recommend you consult your ISP's documentation for specific instructions on restoring a database. There's a good chance that you won't have the appropriate permissions, and the instructions below won't work for you. If you do have the appropriate permissions, follow these steps:

1. **Using the phpMyAdmin application, choose the Drupal database from the menu on the left.**
2. **Click the Operations tab.**
3. **Type a name into the Rename database to box and click Go.**

   Your new database will have the same name as your old one, so you need to save your old one with a new name. You will delete this old database when you are done.

   Your ISP may have restricted you from dropping databases. If this is the case, this step will fail. You need to contact your ISP and let them know that you need to restore your database and send them the backup file.

4. **Click the Operations tab.**
5. **Browse to the location of the database `.zip` file containing your Drupal database backup and select it. Click Go.**

   Your database should now be restored.

Updating Themes and Modules

Suppose I want to upgrade the module Author Pane I installed. The Available updates page in Figure 10-4 shows that it's out of date. I have the link to download the new version right there on that page. To upgrade, I need to follow these steps:

1. **Choose Administer⇨Site building⇨Modules (or Themes). Scroll to the bottom of the page and deselect the Enabled check box next to the module or theme to be updated. Choose Save configuration.**
2. **Find the old module or theme to be upgraded on the Web server using some kind of file manager program.**

   This may be through a control panel on your ISP's site. If you are comfortable using FTP, it will also work. In my case, it will be located under my Drupal directory at `/modules/authorpane`.
3. **Back up these old files.**

   The easiest way is to copy them to your desktop machine. The idea here is that you want to keep a copy just in case something goes wrong with your upgrade so you can restore the old files.
4. **After you make a copy of these files, delete the ones on your Web server.**

   Be *extremely careful* that you are deleting only the files inside the folder of the module or theme you are upgrading.
5. **Delete the now empty folder on your Web server.** In my case, I delete the `authorpane` folder.
6. **Copy the new `.tar.gz` for your module or theme to the appropriate folder as though you are installing it.**

   You are now following the steps you took when you installed your module in the first place.
7. **Extract the new `.tar.gz`.**
8. **Delete the `.tar.gz` file.**
9. **Choose Administer⇨Site building⇨Modules. Scroll to the bottom of the page and select the Enabled check box.**
10. **Choose Save configuration.**

There's one last step. You need to run the update.php file.

Run update.php

Anytime you upgrade a module, or update your Drupal software, you need to run a program called `update.php`. To do this, log on as administrator and browse to the `update.php` file on your Web site. It will be located at `http://yourwebsitenamehere.com/update.php`. For example, mine is at `http://drupalfordummies.com/update.php`. You will see a page listing steps you need to follow (see Figure 10-8).

There are three steps to follow before clicking that Continue button.

- **Back up your database.**

  See the section "Backing up your database," earlier in this chapter, for instructions.

- **Back up your code.**

  For this step, you make a copy of your entire Drupal directory on your Web server.

  You can copy the code using a file manager application on the control panel at your ISP's site. Or you can use an FTP program. The basic idea is to copy all of the Drupal code somewhere safe. Your best bet is to make a copy on your local computer that you can easily delete after you have confirmed that the update ran as expected.

- **Put your site in maintenance mode.**

  Choose Administer⇨Site Configuration⇨Site maintenance and select Off-line. Choose Save configuration.

Now you are ready to run update.php. Follow these steps:

1. **Browse to your site's `update.php`. Choose Continue.**
2. **Choose the Select versions menu to open it (see Figure 10-9).**

   This screen shows you any available updates for the current version of Drupal you are using.

3. **Choose Update.**

   Any updates you chose on the last screen will be made.

4. **Choose Administer⇨Site Configuration⇨Site maintenance and select Online. Choose Save configuration.**

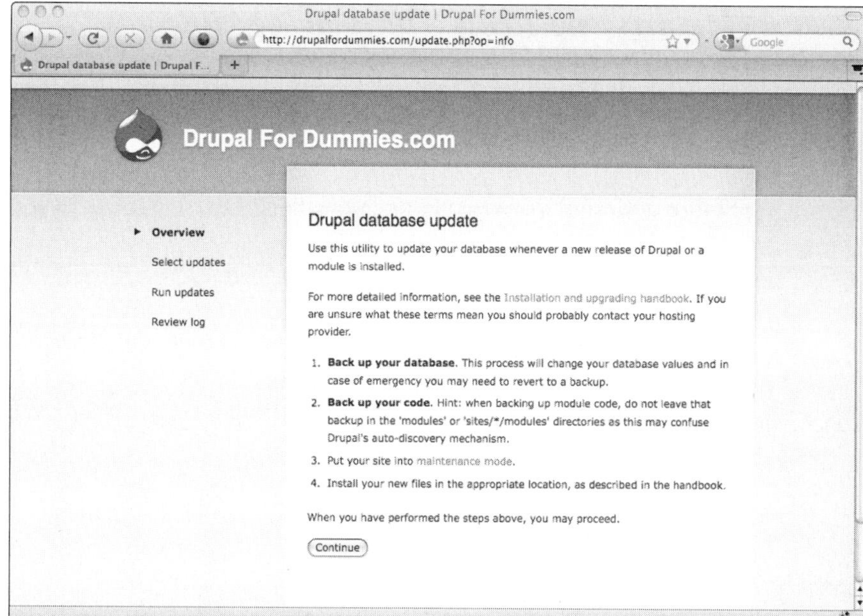

Drupal database update | Drupal For Dummies.com
http://drupalfordummies.com/update.php?op=info
Drupal For Dummies.com
Overview
Select updates
Run updates
Review log
Drupal database update
Use this utility to update your database whenever a new release of Drupal or a module is installed.
For more detailed information, see the Installation and upgrading handbook. If you are unsure what these terms mean you should probably contact your hosting provider.
1. Back up your database. This process will change your database values and in case of emergency you may need to revert to a backup.
2. Back up your code. Hint: when backing up module code, do not leave that backup in the 'modules' or 'sites/*/modules' directories as this may confuse Drupal's auto-discovery mechanism.
3. Put your site into maintenance mode.
4. Install your new files in the appropriate location, as described in the handbook.
When you have performed the steps above, you may proceed.
Continue

Figure 10-8: Steps to follow before running update.php.

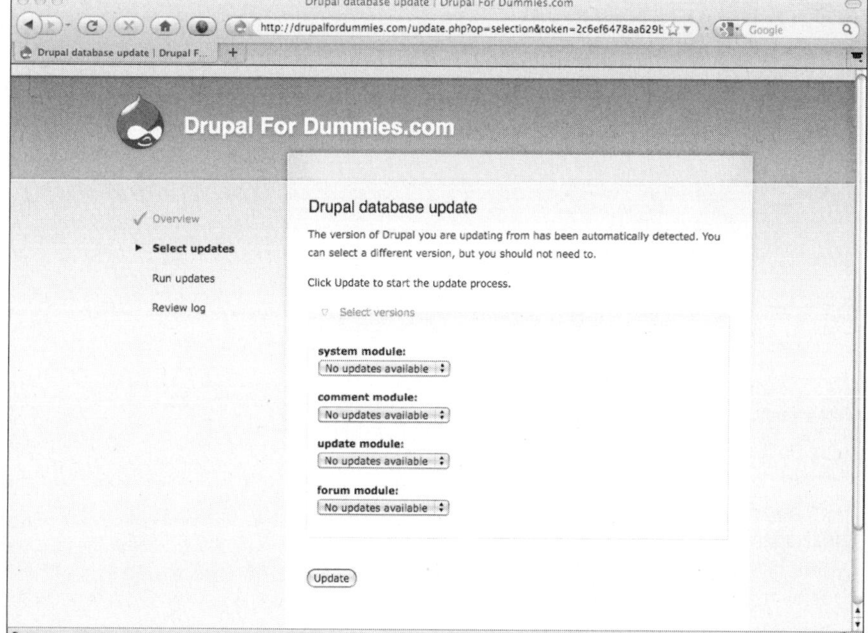

Figure 10-9: The update.php program finds available updates.

Updating your Drupal software

You already know two of the big pieces involved in updating your Drupal software: backing up your database and running `update.php`. In this section, I put it all together for you.

Before updating, you need to decide which of these applies to you:

- **You installed Drupal using Fantastico. You have not installed any contributed modules or themes.**
- **You installed Drupal using Fantastico. You have installed contributed modules or themes.**
- **You installed Drupal yourself by getting a copy from `drupal.org`.**

Installed Drupal with Fantastico, no additional modules or themes

This is the simplest scenario. Because you haven't installed any additional modules, Fantastico can easily update your site for you.

There is often a delay between when a new Drupal update comes out and when Fantastico can upgrade for you. You may have to wait a few days and periodically check.

To find out whether you can upgrade, visit the control panel on your ISP and click Fantastico. If you can update your Drupal installation, you will see a message to that effect (see Figure 10-10).

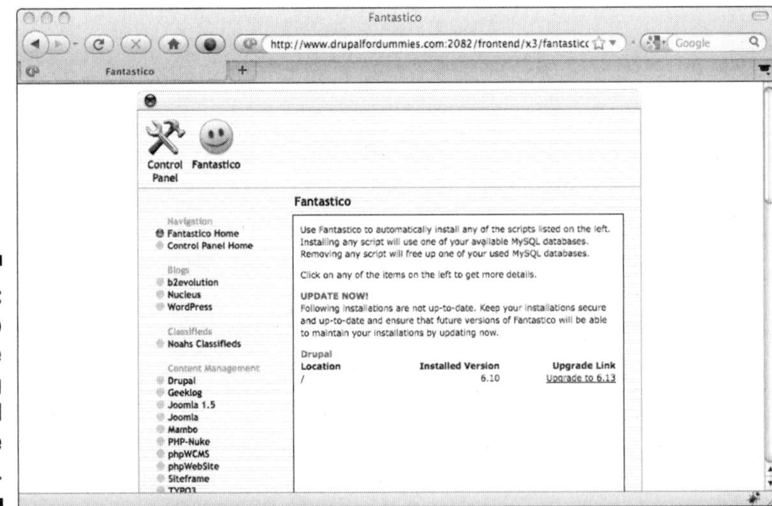

Figure 10-10: Fantastico message indicating Drupal software upgrade.

After you click on the Update link, you will see this message:

If you have modified the files, languages, themes or if you have added any third-party modifications to this installation of Drupal, it is possible that you may need to re-install your themes and/or reapply your custom changes after using Fantastico to upgrade. We take no responsibility for the integrity of custom modified installations after Fantastico upgrades them. We recommend that you make your own backup of your database and script directory before proceeding even though Fantastico will automatically make one before upgrading.

Fantastico works well if you haven't done much with your site. After you begin customizing things, however, Fantastico may not be able to restore the changes. For this reason, you need to back up your database.

Installed Drupal with Fantastico, added modules or themes

After you add additional modules or themes, Fantastico may no longer be able to adequately manage updates to your Drupal software. Instead, you need to begin managing your updates manually. Follow the directions under the next section, Installed Drupal by yourself.

Installed Drupal by yourself

To update Drupal, follow these steps:

1. **Back up your database** (see the section "Backing up your database, earlier in this chapter).
2. **Copy your entire Drupal site to another location.**

   Don't make a copy of your Drupal site and store it inside your Drupal site. Make sure it's outside of your entire Drupal directory, preferably not even on your Web server. You can always upload it back to the Web server later if you need to.
3. **Choose Administer⇨Site Configuration⇨Site maintenance and select Off-line. Choose Save configuration.**
4. **Choose Administer⇨Site Building⇨Modules and uncheck any contributed modules. Leave the Core module settings as they are.**
5. **Choose Administer⇨Site Building⇨Themes and choose one of the themes that was installed with Drupal originally, such as Garland.**
6. **Get the new version of Drupal from `drupal.org`.**
7. **Use a file manager or FTP program to copy the new files to your Drupal directory.**

   Transferring files is very much the same process you followed when you installed Drupal in the first place. Take a look at Chapter 2 for specific instructions on getting your files on your Web server.

If you browse to your site right now, you will see the original installation script I discuss in Chapter 2 when you install Drupal. **Do not run this program.** You are updating, not installing, and running this can destroy information stored in your database.

8. **Browse to the `update.php` on your Web site and click through the program.**
9. **Choose Administer➪Site Building➪Themes, and then choose your desired theme.**
10. **Choose Administer➪Site Building➪Modules and enable any contributed modules you wish to use. Leave the Core module settings as they are.**
11. **Browse to the `update.php` on your Web site and click through the program again.** It's important to run `update.php` every time you install a contributed module. Because this is the first time this new Drupal codebase is using the modules, it treats them like a new installation.
12. **Choose Administer➪Site Configuration➪Site maintenance and select Online. Choose Save configuration.**

Configuring Your Site

In previous chapters, I briefly mention many of the Drupal site configuration options. Now that you have the basic Drupal concepts down (you did read those other chapters, right?), many of these configuration options will make more sense. In this section, I take a closer look at a few of them.

Triggering actions

An *action* is some event that happens in response to something. For example, when a new user registers on your site, he is sent an e-mail. The sending of that e-mail is considered an action. The Actions section under Administer➪Site configuration shows you a list of available actions and allows you to create custom actions.

The missing piece here is a way to actually use these actions. Behind the scenes, Drupal has code built-in that *triggers* these actions; for example, in the code for new users registering is a trigger that fires off the e-mail action.

The way you can use actions without having to write programming to trigger them is to use the Trigger module. It is a Core–optional module that needs to be enabled to work.

Here's a basic example of how to create a trigger to display a custom message to a user who signs in. You must first create a custom action by following these steps:

1. **Choose Administer➪Site configuration➪Actions.**
2. **From the *Make a new advanced action available* section, choose *Display a message to the user* and select Create.**
3. **In the next screen (see Figure 10-11), type this in the message box:**

   Hi %username, it's good to see you. Let's do lunch sometime.

   The %username is a stand-in for the name of the user who just logged on. In other words, if a user with the username Elmer logs on, after you trigger this action, that user will see the message, *Hi Elmer, it's good to see you. Let's do lunch sometime.*

4. **Click Save.**

   The other half of this operation is to set up a trigger to fire off this action when a specific user logs on.

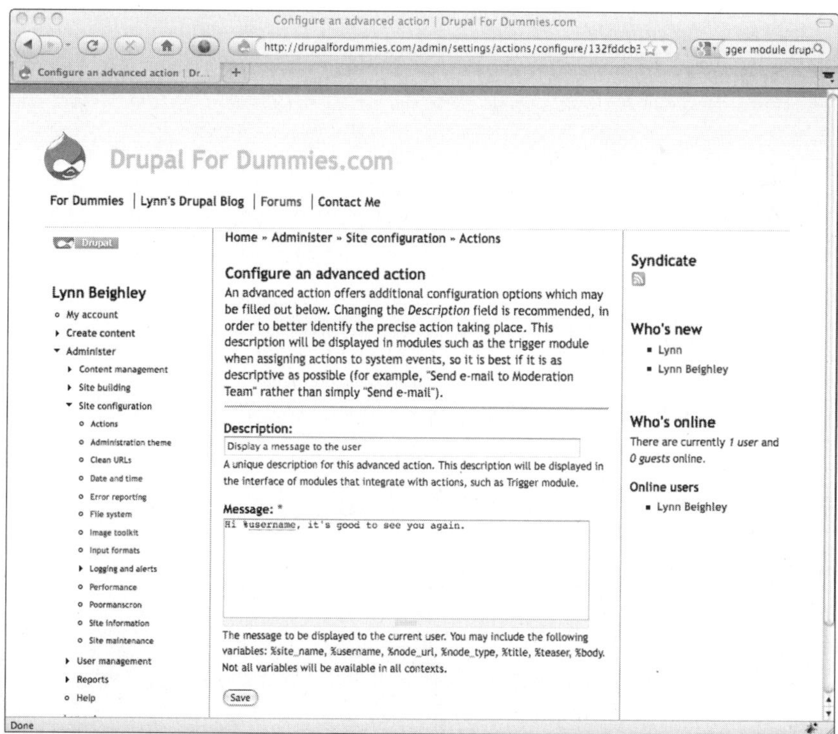

Figure 10-11: Configure an advanced action page.

5. **Enable the Trigger module from Administer➪Site building➪Modules.**
6. **Choose Administer➪Site building➪Triggers.**
7. **Click the Users tab.**

   The Triggers page has five tabs along the top. These correspond to the types of activities that happen on your site. Because you want something to happen when a user signs on, the trigger you want is under the Users tab (see Figure 10-12).
8. **Under the trigger *After a user has logged in,* select *Display a message to the user.***
9. **Click the Assign button next to this box.**

Now when a user logs on, he will see the message, with his username substituted for the %username you put in the action.

To delete a trigger, click the *unassign* link.

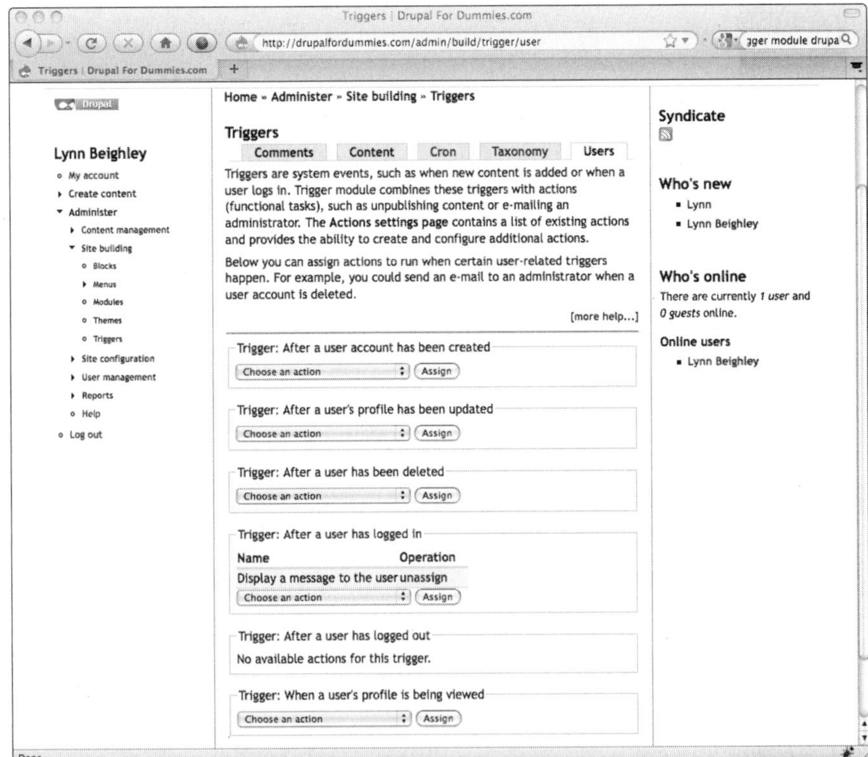

Figure 10-12: The Users tab of the Triggers module.

Setting an administration theme

As you customize the theme for your particular site, you may find it unsuitable for using when you administer your site. You can set a theme that will be used only when you log on as administrator. To do this, follow these steps:

1. **Choose Administer⇨Site configuration⇨Administration theme.**
2. **Choose a new theme from the drop-down menu.**
3. **Optionally, choose to use the administration theme when creating or editing content.** This means that when you choose Create content and create one of the content types, the administration theme is used.
4. **Click Save configuration.**

Creating clean URLs

Drupal automatically creates URLs for the content you add to the site. If this option is off, the URLs will be not be as simple and will contain `?` and `=` characters. For example, a URL without this setting might look like this:

```
http://drupalfordummies.com/?q=node/21
```

And with clean URLs, it looks like this:

```
http://drupalfordummies.com/node/21
```

Using error reporting

Sometimes visitors to your site will attempt to browse to a page that doesn't actually exist. This is known as a 404 error. Instead of displaying an ugly page that says Page Not Found, by default Drupal sends the visitor to the home page of your site.

If you have pages on your site that only logged-on users can see, and unregistered visitors try to go to one of those pages, Drupal redirects them to the home page of your site.

The settings that control this behavior are found at Administer⇨Site configuration⇨Error Reporting (see Figure 10-13).

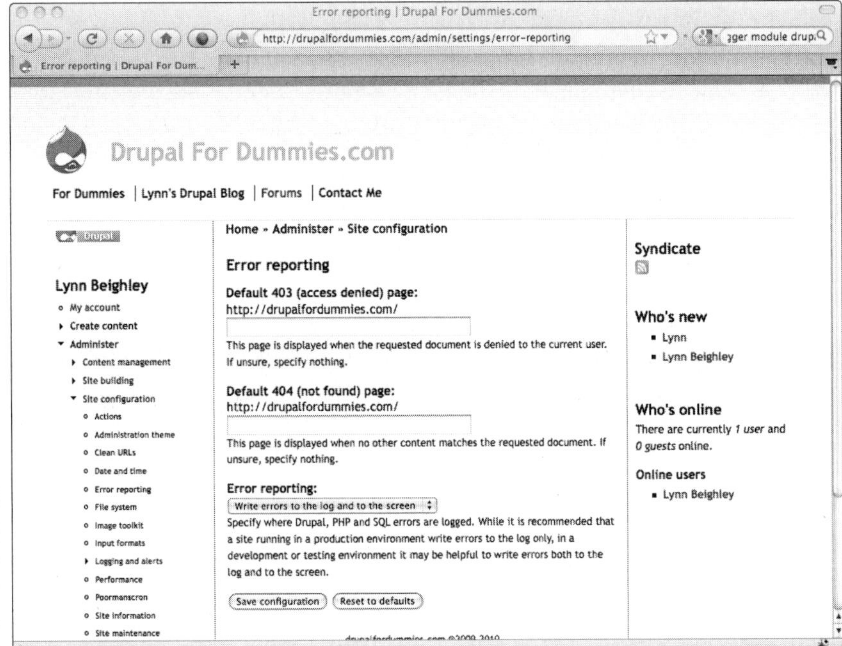

Figure 10-13: Error reporting settings.

On this form you can change what pages visitors are sent to in the two scenarios above.

The third setting on the page, Error reporting, controls where Drupal writes reports about errors that occur on the site. As you develop your site, it's fine to let the messages show up on the site, but once you start allowing users to register and move out of development, you should change this setting to *Write errors to the log.*

To see logged error messages, choose Administer➪Reports➪Recent log entries. Clicking on Filter log messages allows you to sort through the messages and locate precisely the ones you are interested in. On the left are the types of errors and on the right are the levels of severity.

Chapter 11

Customizing Themes

In This Chapter

- Understanding theme structure
- Modifying a theme
- Installing your theme
- Customizing your site appearance

In this chapter, I take you through the anatomy of a simple theme. I show you how to change things to make your site more distinctive. A single chapter on creating a custom Drupal theme can't possibly cover all the details, but you can make a surprising number of changes to a site by taking an existing theme and making a few relatively small changes to it.

If you are a bit familiar with CSS or HTML, you're in luck. Understanding a little PHP code would be great, but if you don't know any of these, you can still modify an existing theme and get great results.

Dissecting a Theme

Before you begin changing a theme, you need to know how a theme is structured. In this section, I show you the basic structure of a Drupal theme. I use the Bluemarine theme because it contains all of the essential parts of a theme.

To better follow the discussion, you need to enable the Bluemarine theme. You also need to activate the primary menu, which is not visible by default with this theme. Follow these steps:

1. **Choose Administer⇨Site building⇨Themes.**
2. **Check the Enabled box and select the Default radio button next to the Bluemarine theme.**
3. **Click Save configuration.**
4. **Choose Administer⇨Site building⇨Blocks.**

5. **Find the Primary links item in the list and drag it to the top of the Right sidebar section.**
6. **Click Save blocks.**

You can use FTP or your ISP's file manager to look in the themes directory under Drupal and see the files that make up each theme. Look at the bluemarine folder in the themes directory (see Figure 11-1).

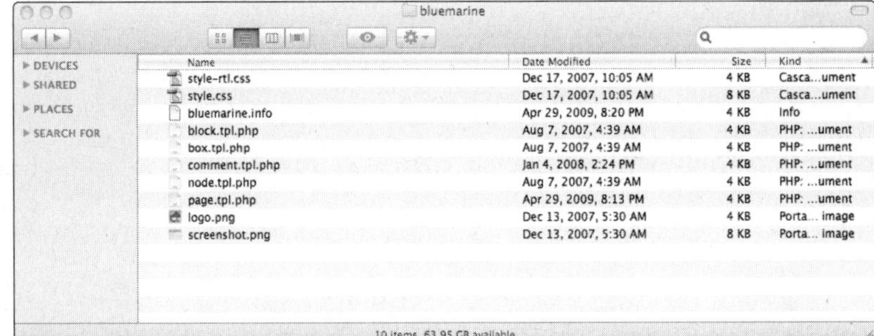

Figure 11-1: The Bluemarine theme files.

Theme file types

There are four types of files in the Bluemarine theme:

- **CSS:** Stands for Cascading Style Sheet. The information in these files controls all the colors, font sizes, font styles, margin widths, and much more.
- **INFO:** This is a very small text file containing module-specific information.
- **PHP:** These files contain lots of HTML code and some PHP code. They are responsible for displaying all the content that appears on the various content type pages like comments and blocks.
- **PNG:** These are image files.

Theme code files

This chapter focuses on showing you how to modify and customize an existing theme. To do that, you need to understand what each file in the theme controls. Bluemarine contains eight files containing code:

- **style-rtl.css:** Unless you are creating a site for a language that is read from right to left, you can ignore this file. This is used to help make right-to-left running languages more readable.

When you duplicate this set of files to make your own version, just copy this file as-is and include it with no changes.

- **style.css:** This is the file to which you have to pay the most attention. This controls practically everything to do with the appearance of your site.

  This chapter takes a close look at the contents of this file.

- **bluemarine.info:** This file contains the information Drupal needs about this theme. It's primarily used on the page at Administer➪Site building➪Themes. It will need a few simple tweaks to modify.
- **block.tpl.php:** This file controls all the content that appears in the blocks of the Bluemarine theme. You can see the blocks by choosing Administer➪Site building➪Blocks (see Figure 11-2). Bluemarine uses five blocks: header, left sidebar, right sidebar, content, and footer.
- **box.tpl.php:** This template places a box around a few elements of your site.

  You don't see boxes very often and won't need to change the appearance of boxes through this template.

- **comment.tpl.php:** The comment template pulls in and structures an individual comment. It can optionally include a user photo and signature block. Figure 11-3 shows comments in the Bluemarine theme.

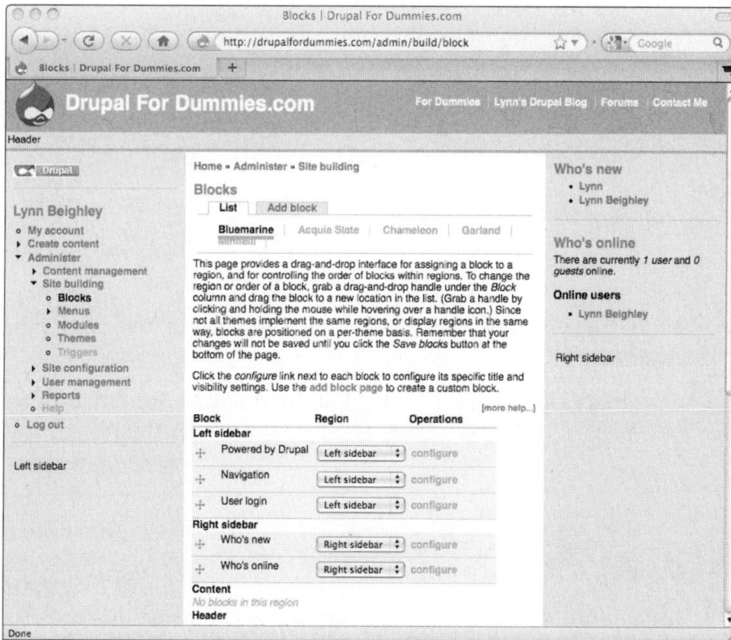

Figure 11-2: Blocks used in Bluemarine.

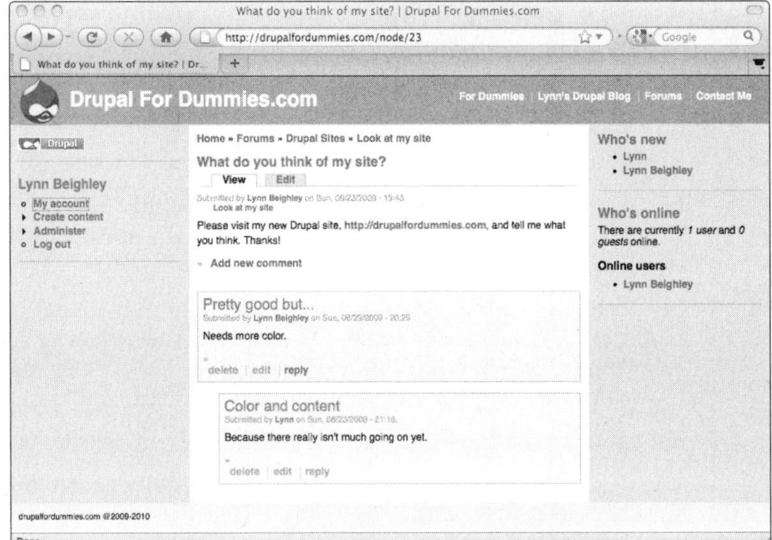

Figure 11-3: Comment layout in the Bluemarine theme.

- **node.tpl.php:** The node template controls the structure of content. All your stories and blog posts are contained in nodes, for example.
- **page.tpl.php:** The page template is the biggest one. It builds a complete page, including menus, all the blocks, and all the content. This defines where everything goes on the page. If, for example, you wanted the content in the left sidebar to shift to the right, this is the file you would change.

Theme image files

Bluemarine only has two image files:

- **logo.png**, which is the Drupal logo in the upper left-hand corner of this theme
- **screenshot.png**, which is used on the page at Administer➪Site building➪Themes to give you a preview of the theme

Creating Your First Theme

It's far easier to duplicate and rename the Bluemarine theme and use it to build your first theme than to build one from scratch. The first step is to make a copy of the Bluemarine directory on your computer.

To get a copy of Bluemarine, browse to `http://drupal.org/project/bluemarine` and download it. The actual file downloaded and used in this chapter is `bluemarine-7.x-1.x-dev.tar.gz`.

You can also get a copy of the Bluemarine theme by using FTP or your ISP's file manager. Navigate to the themes directory under Drupal and copy the entire Bluemarine directory to your desktop computer.

To edit the files in the Bluemarine theme, you need some sort of text editor:

- On Windows, you can use the NotePad application, a simple editor.
- On the Mac, TextEdit will work, although be sure to choose Format➪Make Plain Text.

You need to *extract* Bluemarine:

- Try double-clicking the `bluemarine tar.gz` file to expand it. This should create a folder named `bluemarine` containing all the theme files.
- If that doesn't work, you may need a program such as the free StuffIt expander to extract your files. You can find this program at `http://my.smithmicro.com`.

To create your own version, follow these steps:

1. **Rename the folder to a distinctive name you want to use for your theme.**

   I choose `drupalfordummies`.

2. **Open this folder and locate the `bluemarine.info` file. Rename this file with your new theme name.**

   In my case, I use `drupalfordummies.info`.

   Make sure you rename the info file. Don't copy it with a new name. You only want one info file in your theme directory, and the name needs to match the name of your theme.

3. **Open the info file in a text editor (see Figure 11-4).**

```
drupalfordummies.info
; $Id: bluemarine.info,v 1.2 2009/03/11 15:36:11 johnalbin Exp $
name = Bluemarine
description = Tableless theme with a marine and ash color scheme.
core = 7.x
engine = phptemplate

; Information added by drupal.org packaging script on 2009-03-11
version = "7.x-1.x-dev"
core = "7.x"
project = "bluemarine"
datestamp = "1236802317"
```

Figure 11-4: The contents of the `.info` file.

4. **Change the first line of this file from**

   ; $Id: bluemarine.info,v 1.2 2009/03/11 15:36:11 johnalbin Exp $

   to simply

   ;Id

5. **Change the name = Bluemarine line to use your theme name.**

   In my case, I change it to *name = Drupal For Dummies.*

   This will be the name that shows up on the module selection page. It can contain spaces.

6. **Change the description text to describe your theme.**

   I change mine to *description = Yellow and black theme.*

7. **The last two lines should read:**

```
core = 6.x
engine = phptemplate
```

8. **Delete the rest of the line of this file.**

   It should only contain the five lines mentioned earlier.

9. **Save this file.**

Installing Your Theme

You haven't made any actual changes to the appearance of the theme yet, but it would still be a good time to get your theme installed to make sure the info file is correctly configured. Use FTP or your ISP's file manager program to move the folder containing your new theme into the Drupal themes directory on your Web server. In my case, this means I copy the entire `drupalfordummies` folder with all my theme files into the themes directory.

You may find it easier to zip your theme folder, transfer it to your Web server's theme directory, extract it, and then delete the original zip file.

If you have correctly changed the theme folder name, the name of the info file, and the information inside the info file, you will see your theme in the list when you choose Administer⇨Site building⇨Themes (see Figure 11-5).

You see your theme, your themes description, and a thumbnail for your theme.

You should enable and set your theme as default. This will make it easier for you to see the changes to your theme as you make them.

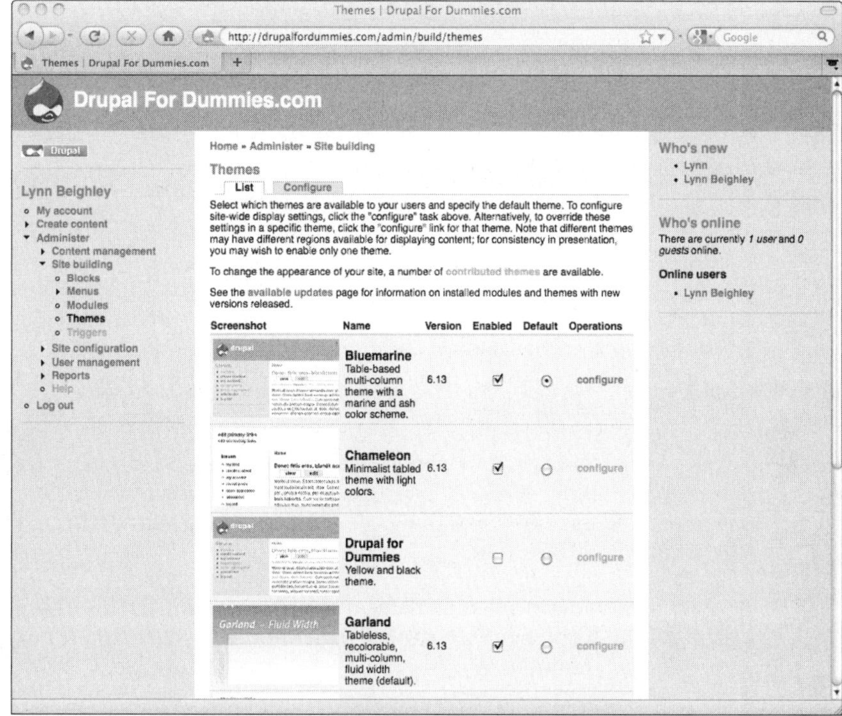

Figure 11-5: Your new theme shows up in the list of themes.

Because Bluemarine doesn't display the primary links menu by default, your theme doesn't either. To display your primary links, follow these steps:

1. **With your theme enabled and set as default, choose Administer➪Site building➪Blocks.**
2. **Find the Primary links item in the list and drag it to the top of the Right sidebar section.**
3. **Click Save blocks.**

Right now, your primary links are titled *Primary links* on your site. If you want to remove that title, choose Administer➪Site building➪Blocks. Click on the configure link next to Primary links. In the Block title field, type **<*none*>** and press Save block. That's it.

Changing Your Theme's Code

At this point, you can enable your new theme and set it as the default. It looks exactly like Bluemarine because you haven't changed anything yet. You can now make changes to your theme.

There's simply not room in this book to cover the ins and outs of CSS coding. The point of this chapter is to show you the possibilities and a few of the simpler, although still dramatic, changes you can make to customize your site.

Naming colors

To change the colors used by your theme, you need to understand how colors are used in CSS code.

Colors are described using numbers, rather than names. For example, the header block of the Bluemarine theme is a light blue color. But instead of saying "light blue" in the code (which you will see in a moment), the value #06090C is used instead.

This kind of number is known as an RGB value. RGB stands for Red-Green-Blue. The number #6699CC represents how much red (66), green (99), and blue (CC) to use. To make things even more complicated, these numbers are in hexadecimal notation.

Sometimes you will see only three digits, such as #69C. This one is the same as #6699CC. If you ever see a three-digit version, realize that it's simply leaving out duplicate numbers.

Don't let this throw you. You don't have to come up with these numbers; you can use a tool to help you. Here are some Web sites that show you colors and the numbers that correspond with them:

```
http://www.colorschemer.com/online.html
http://htmlhelp.com/cgi-bin/color.cgi
http://www.yellowpipe.com/yis/tools/hex-to-rgb/color-converter.php
```

Two colors you will see often are black (#000 or #000000) and white (#fff or #ffffff). Also, when you see letters, it doesn't matter if they are upper or lower case. So #fff is the same thing as #FFFFFF.

Changing colors

In my case, I want to begin with the colors used by my theme. To do this, I will open the `style.css` file on my desktop computer, make the changes, and then using FTP or the ISP's file manager, upload the altered `style.css` to my `Drupal/themes/drupalfordummies` folder on my Web server. This will write over the old version, and my changes will show up on my site. To begin, follow these steps:

1. **Open the version of `style.css` on your desktop with a text editor.**
2. **About halfway through the file, locate the lines:**

```
#header {
  padding: .2em;

  background-color: #69c;
}
```

3. **Change the value #69c to a different RGB value.**

   I'm using a yellow color, #FFFE01, so the background-color line now reads

   ```
   background-color: #FFFE01
   ```

4. **Save the `style.css` file.**
5. **Use the file manager or FTP to upload this file to your Web server under the right theme folder, the folder containing your new theme.**

   I put mine under my `Drupal themes/drupalfordummies` directory.

6. **You may get a warning that the file already exists. Go ahead and overwrite the existing `style.css` file.**
7. **Reload your Web site. You should see the new header color.**

If you don't see the change in the header color, make sure your theme is the currently selected default theme at Administer⇨Site building⇨Themes.

I now have a problem. The bright yellow color makes it difficult to read the header text on my site (see Figure 11-6). I want to change my header text to black so it's more readable.

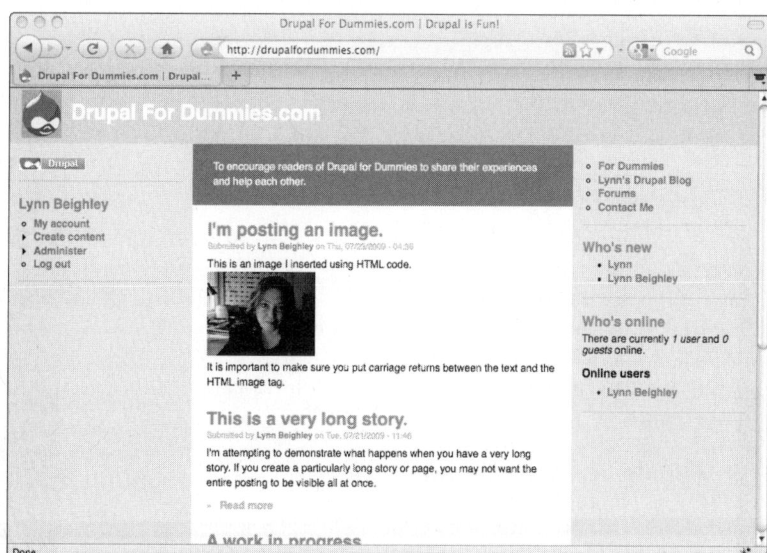

Figure 11-6: Web site with new header color.

To change the font color, I change the RGB value from white (which is #fff) to black (which is #000000) in the `style.css` file. The section I need to change is this:

```
.site-name a:link, .site-name a:visited {
  color: #fff;
}
```

I simply change the value #fff to #000000. Then, as in the preceding example, I save the `style.css` file and copy it over the version on my Web server in the `themes/drupalfordummies` directory.

Understanding the style.css file

By now, I hope you are getting the idea that the `style.css` file contains the values for all the colors on your site. The key to customizing your site's colors is to understand how this file is structured and to know what all the colors in this file stand for.

Everything in this file is divided into chunks of code. Each chunk consists of some names or labels, an open curly bracket, lines of code called rules, and a closing curly bracket. For example, the body section of the file looks like this:

```
body {
  margin: 0;
  padding: 0;
  color: #000;
  background-color: #fff;
}
```

For the moment, you only need to notice that this is the body section, and it has a background color defined in it, #fff.

Changing colors

Now that you know how to change `style.css` and upload it to your Web server, you can experiment. If you see a color setting and don't know what it controls, change it to a crazy color, such as hot pink (#FF00FF). When you reload your site, you will see what changes.

Here's a rundown of a few major color settings in this file that you may want to change:

- **body { background-color: #fff; }**

  Controls the color behind the main content area. Currently set to white.

- **a:link { color: #39c; }**

  This is the color of Web links on your site. It's a bluish color. For my site, I change it to #1F638A.

- **a:visited { color: #369; }**

  This is the color of a Web link a visitor sees after he has clicked on it. Mine is #1F638A, the same as the link color.

- **a:hover { color: #39c; }**

  The color of a link when a cursor is over it. I use #1F638A, the same as the link color.

- **body { background-color: #ddd; }**

  A second block that is setting the main background color. This sets it to a gray color (#DDDDDD).

  You may have noticed that there already was a bit of code labeled *main* with a background color. In CSS code, you may have multiple rules that set the same color for some part of your site. *The last one is the one that shows up on a page.* In this case, the second body tag has the color that actually shows up on the page.

- **#main { background-color: #fff; }**

  This controls the color behind your main content area.

- **#sidebar-left, #sidebar-right { background-color: #ddd; }**

  The left and right sidebars are set to a gray color.

- **#header { background-color: #FFFE01; }**

  This is the main header background color that I changed to a yellow color earlier.

- **.site-name a:link, .site-name a:visited { color: #000000; }**

  This is the site name in the header which I changed to a black color.

- **.site-name a:hover { color: #369; }**

  When a cursor is moved over the site name, it changes to this color. I change mine to match my link color, #1F638A.

- **#mission { background-color: #369; color: #fff; }**

  The mission statement appears just below the header and has two color settings. The first is for the background color; the second is the color of the text in it. I change mine to black for the background (#000000) and leave the text white.

- **#footer { background-color: #eee; }**

  This is the footer color. I change mine to the same yellow as the header, #FFFE01.

- **.title, .title a { color: #777; }**

  These are the titles above various sections of your site. In my case, this affects *Who's new* and *Who's online* in the right sidebar and the username in the left sidebar. I change mine to black.

Although it may be difficult to tell from a gray scale image in this book, my site is starting to look a bit more customized (see Figure 11-7).

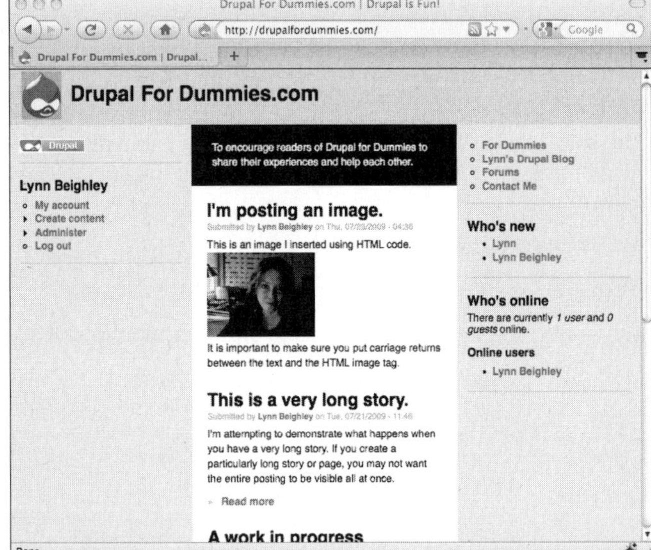

Figure 11-7: Changes to the site colors make the text stand out.

Changing fonts

The `style.css` file also contains the rules for the color, style, and size of fonts. Here's a rundown of some of the coding used to control the appearance of fonts that you see in `style.css`:

- **font:** This tag appears only once in `style.css` and specifies the font to use for the entire site.
- **font-size:** Controls how large or small the text is.
- **font-weight:** Used to set text to bold.
- **font-style:** Primarily used to set text to italic.

- **text-decoration:** Controls whether a link is underlined.
- **color:** Can sometimes set the color of text.

Here are a few major text settings in `style.css` that you may want to change:

- **body { color: #000; font: 76% Verdana, Arial, Helvetica, sans-serif; }**

  There are two things going on here. The first, color, controls the text color for the entire site, setting it black. If no other rules change it later in this file, it shows up as black on the site. This controls the color of all the content text all over the site.

  The font setting, 76% Verdana, Arial, Helvetica, sans-serif, is setting both the text size and font. If I want to use a different font and larger text, I can change this line to read:

  ```
  font: 100% Times New Roman, Georgia, Serif;
  ```

  This changes the font for the entire site, as you can see in Figure 11-8.

  The font is larger and is now Times New Roman instead of Verdana. I prefer the smaller font size and Verdana for the style, so after experimenting, I change this line back to:

  ```
  font: 76% Verdana, Arial, Helvetica, sans-serif;
  ```

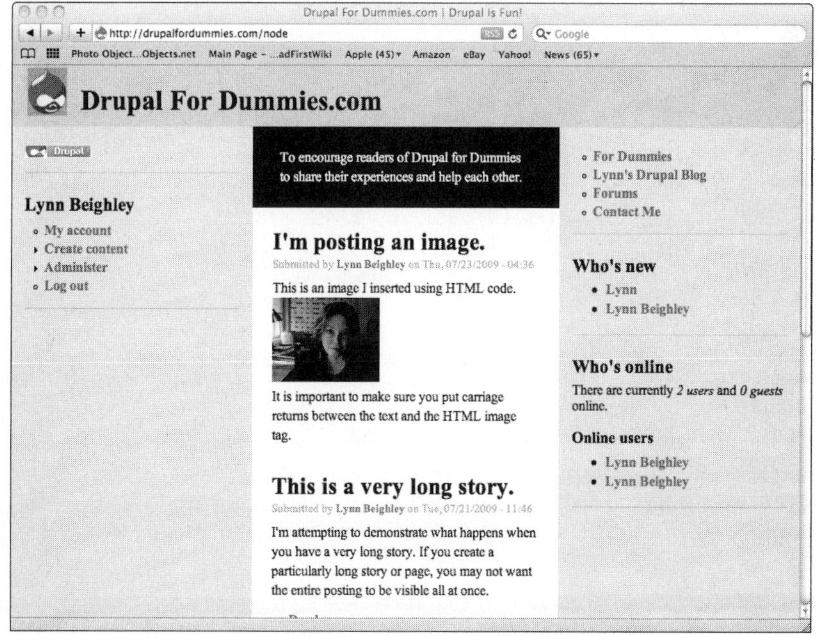

Figure 11-8: Using the Times New Roman, Georgia, Serif font family set to 100%.

- **a { text-decoration: none; font-weight: bold; }**

  The text-decoration controls whether links on your site are underlined. In this case, they are not. The font-weight makes the site links boldface.

- **a:hover { text-decoration: underline; }**

  When you move your mouse cursor over one of the links on the site, the underline appears. When you move your cursor off, it disappears. Any time you see *hover,* it's referring to the cursor being moved over something.

- **.site-name { font-size: 2em; }**

  An em is a unit of size, and this line is setting the size of the site name. If I change it to 6em, it becomes absurdly large (see Figure 11-9).

- **#mission { color: #fff; }**

  I changed the mission text to white and the background to black. But I also want to italicize the words. To do this, I add this line between the curly brackets:

  ```
  font-style: italic;
  ```

When changing CSS code, be careful to keep the punctuation marks exactly as they are. For example, each line in the block of code ends with a semicolon.

Figure 11-9: Site header text size set to 6em.

Using graphics

You should now be able to change any color on your site. But suppose you want to use an image as a background for one of the areas. For example, say you want to use a background image for the left and right sidebars. You still want the text on top, but instead of gray, you want faint, diagonal pinstripes.

Follow these steps:

1. **Use FTP or your ISP's file manager to copy your background image to your Web server. Put it in your theme's directory.**

   For example, I have a background image called `stripes.gif`. I upload it to my Drupal site under `themes/drupalfordummies`.

2. **Open a copy of `style.css` in a text editor.**
3. **Locate this section of code:**

   ```
   #sidebar-left, #sidebar-right {
     width: 16em;
     padding: 1em;
     margin-right: -18em; /* LTR */
     background-color: #ddd;
   }
   ```

4. **Add the following line inside the curly brackets:**

   ```
   background-image:url('stripes.gif');
   ```

5. **Save and upload your file.**

   Now when you look at the site, the stripes show up on the sidebars (see Figure 11-10).

   Unfortunately, the bottom parts of the sidebars don't have the background. Only the portions of the sidebars with actual content blocks are filled in. You need one more line of code.

6. **In the body section of `style.css`, add the same line of code:**

   ```
   background-image:url('stripes.gif');
   ```

7. **Save and upload your file.**

   Your background is now visible all the way to the bottom of the page.

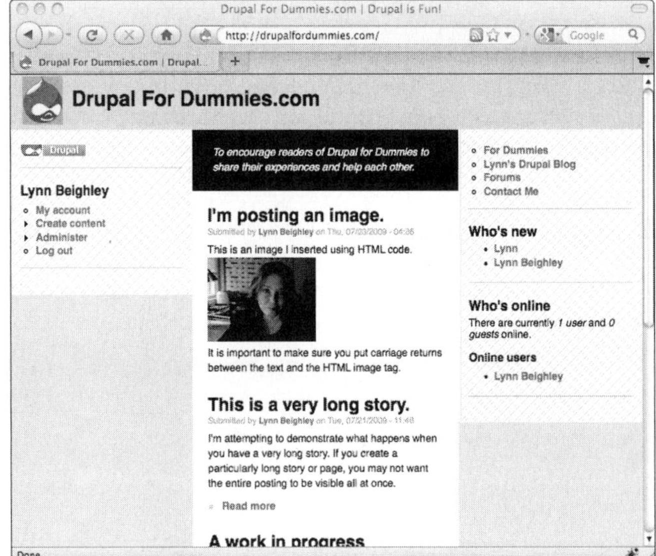

Figure 11-10: The stripe background fills up the top portion of the sidebars.

Changing the logo image

The logo on the site still leaves something to be desired. You can easily replace it with one that looks better. There's no coding involved. To change the logo, follow these steps:

1. **Choose Administer⇨Site building⇨Themes. Click on the configure link next to your theme.**
2. **Scroll down to the Logo image settings. Click Browse to select and upload your new logo.**
3. **Click Save configuration.**

   Your logo will now appear.

Editing templates

You can make lots of changes with `style.css`, but the template files allow you to change the structure and order of things. For example, this theme allows me to put my primary menu in the header block, but the layout isn't appealing (see Figure 11-11).

I really want my primary links to appear horizontally in the header. This theme doesn't allow me to do this using blocks, so I need to modify my page template and add code for the primary menu.

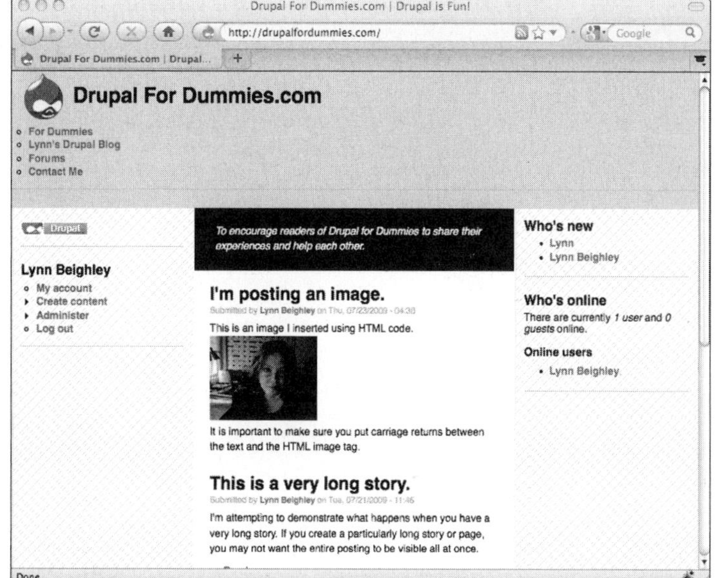

Figure 11-11: Primary links in the header block.

The code you are about to use may seem confusing, but don't panic. The point is that you are slightly altering and moving lines of code around, not really writing new code. Drupal handles the hard part; you just need to shuffle things around a bit.

Follow these steps:

1. **Open `page.tpl.php` in a text editor.**
2. **Locate this code near the beginning of the file:**

```
<?php if ($site_name) { ?><h1 class='site-name'><a
        href="<?php print $front_page ?>" title="<?php
        print t('Home') ?>"><?php print $site_name
        ?></a></h1><?php }; ?>

<?php if ($site_slogan) { ?><div class='site
        slogan'><?php print $site_slogan ?></div><?php
        } ?>
```

   I will add code between these two lines.

3. **Carefully type this line of code between the two preceding lines:**

```
<?php if (isset($primary_links)) { ?><?php print
        theme('links', $primary_links, array('class'
        => 'links', 'id' => 'navlist')) ?><?php } ?>
```

4. **Save and upload this file to the folder containing your theme on your Web server.**

5. **Reload your Web site.**

   The links are there, but unfortunately, they are difficult to read. I need to change the font color (see Figure 11-12).

   The link color is controlled in the `style.css` file so that file needs to be edited.

6. **Open the `style.css` file in a text editor.**

7. **Locate this block of code:**

```
#navlist a {
  font-weight: bold;
  color: #fff;
}
```

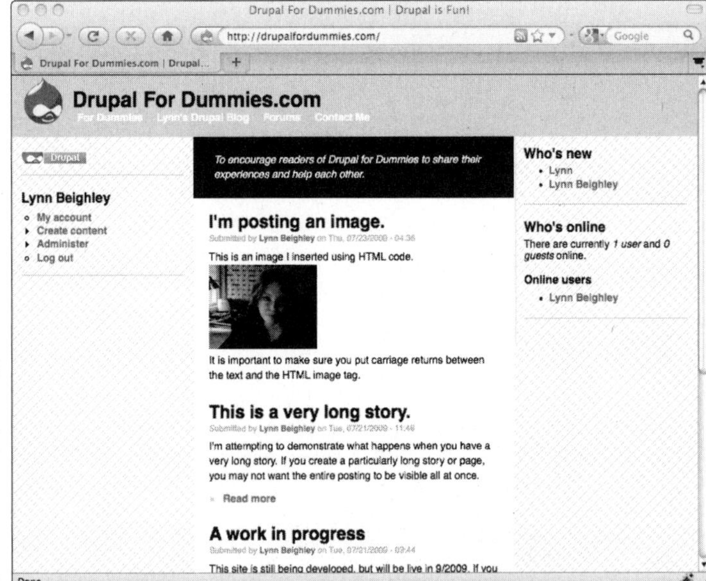

Figure 11-12: Primary links are difficult to read in the header.

8. **Change the color value from white (#fff) to black (#000).**

9. **Save and upload this file to the correct theme folder under your Drupal themes directory.**

Now your links appear in black in the header.

Trial-and-error is one way of figuring out what styles in the `style.css` belong to what elements on your site. But there's an easier way. I recommend you use the Firefox Web browser and install the add-in called Firebug. This opens a pane in the Web browser and shows you what styles are used by elements on your Web page. In Figure 11-13, you see which line in `style.css` is controlling the appearance of the primary links in the header. On the bottom right of the browser, you can see that the navlist block is responsible for the color. Learn more about Firebug at `http://getfirebug.com/`.

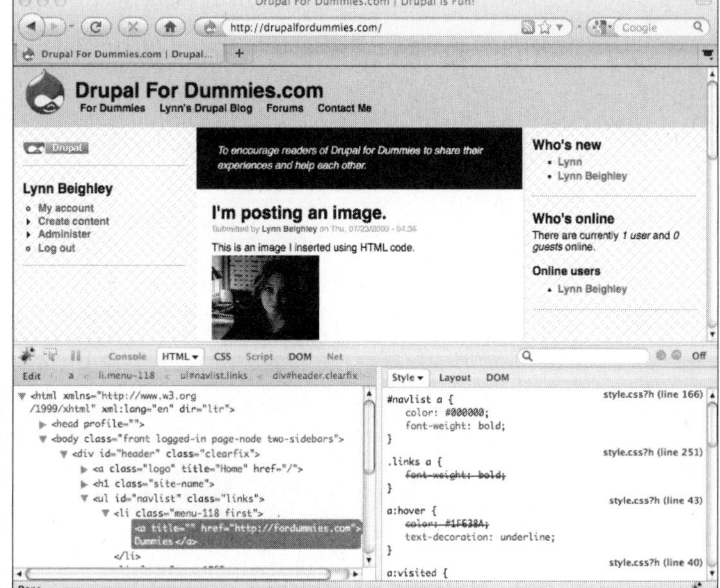

Figure 11-13: Firefox browser with Firebug.

Creating a Screen Shot

Now that you've customized your theme, you should take a screen shot that will show up on the Administer⇨Site building⇨Themes page. A screen shot is a small image that gives an idea of what your theme looks like. It needs to be 150 x 90 pixels in size.

There are lots of other details and modifications. `http://drupal.org/theme-guide` is an extremely thorough guide.

Part IV

Taking Drupal to the Next Level

"I've had a lot of experience running nonprofit organizations. Back in the '90's I ran several Internet start-up companies."

In this part . . .

Building a basic site in Drupal is child's play to you now. Blogs? Simple. Forums? A piece of cake. Controlling user permissions? Pshaw.

You yearn for more features. You want to do more. The chapters in this part show you how to set up an image gallery, build your own online storefront, and even display your Twitter and Facebook updates. And lots more.

Chapter 12

Creating a Robust Web Site

In This Chapter

- Determining the purpose of your site
- Adding user polls
- Enhancing user profiles
- Enabling visitors to search your site
- Adding a contact form

To create something more than a generic Web site, you must take a close look at what you want to accomplish and discover what specific modules and techniques suit your needs. This chapter will help you figure out the purpose of your site and show you some steps you can take to ensure that your site is effective and your message is getting across to your audience.

Planning Your Drupal Site

To figure out which Drupal modules features to add to your site, you need to have a clear idea of its purpose. Knowing this will help you pick the right features for your site.

Getting a clear picture of your site

Understanding the purpose of your site is the first step in creating it. Your site probably falls under one or more of these categories:

- **Blog:** Blogs allow you to share your view of the world or some particular topic. They're also good advertising tools for getting news out about a company. They're often one part of a larger site.

- **Brochure:** These sites are largely static advertisements or information about a business or service.

  An example of a brochure site can be seen at `www.thealamo.org`. While this site does have a calendar and gift shop, the main purpose is to serve as a brochure with rarely modified information (see Figure 12-1).

- **Community:** These sites exist to attract people with something in common. They typically encourage discussion of a topic with forums. `Drupalfordummies.com` falls under this category.

- **Image gallery:** Now that most people have digital cameras, photography has never been more popular. You may wish to build a site or portion of a site devoted to showcasing your images.

  Chapter 13 covers creation of an image gallery in depth.

- **Information or news:** You want to send out frequent news updates about a topic. You may also wish to aggregate information from other Web sites. Chapter 14 shows how to pull content from other Web sites with a technology called RSS.

- **Storefront:** You have a product to sell and need an online shopping cart system to allow site visitors to order your goods.

  Chapter 15 shows how to build a storefront using the Ubercart module.

Your site may fall under several of these categories. For example, you might want to sell things and also blog about your company to let your visitors know about sales or new products. Or you may want to create a community site that allows members to post images.

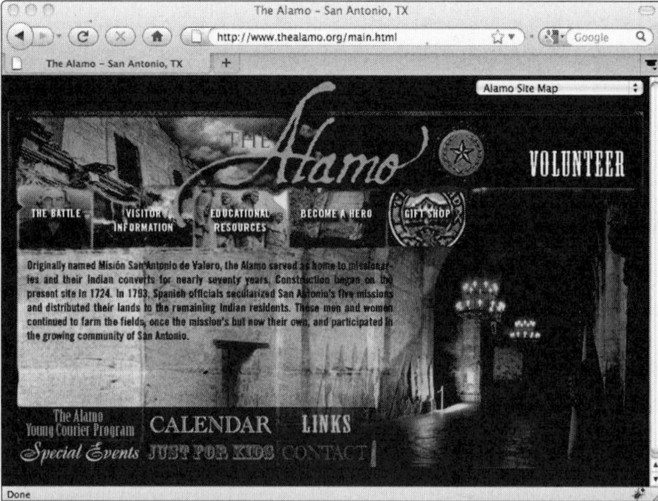

Figure 12-1: The Alamo Web site is primarily a brochure site.

Knowing your audience

As you create your site, keep your audience in mind. People visit Web sites for a variety of reasons, and the content of your site should be presented in a way to attract the visitors you want.

There are lots of good books about Web site interface design and designing for particular audiences. One book that provides a very quick and entertaining overview of the most important principles of site design and great insight into how visitors to a site will probably react to it is *Don't Make Me Think*, by Steve Krug.

Types of visitors to your site include:

- **The random visitor:** Some people will visit your Web site by accident. A compelling main page may draw them into your site, but in general these visitors won't be inclined to buy your products, join your community, or be interested in your services.
- **Researcher:** These folks found you by using a search engine. Your site was in their search results and may or may not be what they're looking for.

  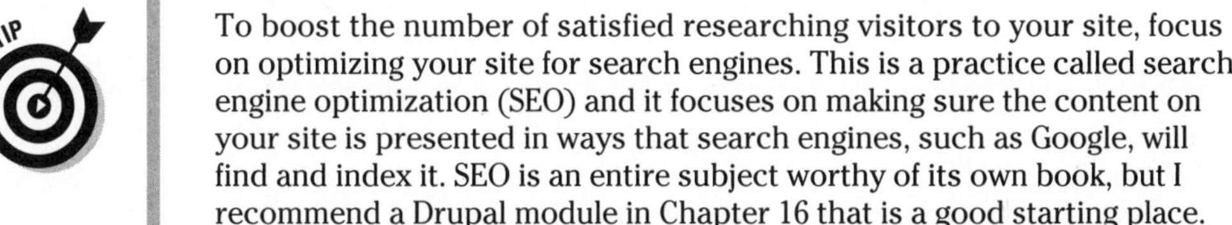

  To boost the number of satisfied researching visitors to your site, focus on optimizing your site for search engines. This is a practice called search engine optimization (SEO) and it focuses on making sure the content on your site is presented in ways that search engines, such as Google, will find and index it. SEO is an entire subject worthy of its own book, but I recommend a Drupal module in Chapter 16 that is a good starting place.
- **Direct user:** This is your main user base, visitors who arrive at your site knowing what they will find there. A friend or a link on another site may refer them to your site. These are the users you most want to please with your site layout. If your site is a community site, for example, you should make the link to your forums prominent on your main page. Or if you have a storefront, you might want to feature your most popular products on your main page.

You may also have to consider the technology your site visitors have available to them. For example, you may be creating a site that will be frequented by people with older computer equipment and slower connections. You may want to limit your use of Flash movies and large images to allow your site to load faster.

You should also consider the demographics of your audience. Perhaps you are trying to build a community for mothers, for example. That site would be very different from one built for video gamers.

Take your site design cues from sites that are successful. I'm not suggesting you steal designs from other sites, but you can definitely learn something by studying how they use their primary links, or how much, or little content they provide on their pages.

Choosing your features

Your choice of features depends on the purpose of your site, as well as your user base. Here's a sampling of site types and site features to consider:

- **Blog:** Obviously, if you have a blog site you need the Blog module. But you may want to provide a page about yourself, a contact form, and a page with archives of previous blogs.

Consider adding advertising blocks to your site as the number of visitors to your sites increases.

If your site consists of blogs about a set of topics, you might want to create a submenu with links to these topics. A good example (and also a site that sometimes offers Drupal tips) is `www.smashingmagazine.com` (see Figure 12-2).

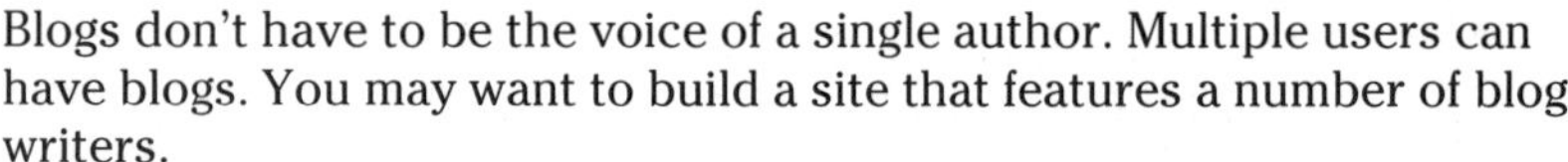

Blogs don't have to be the voice of a single author. Multiple users can have blogs. You may want to build a site that features a number of blog writers.

Figure 12-2: Smashing Magazine is an example of a blog site.

- **Brochure:** Brochure sites are largely informational, and the information on these sites doesn't change very often. Generally, they contain
  - A main page
  - A contact page
  - Directions
  - Sub pages containing more information

  A good example of a brochure site is the National Park Service's Grand Canyon site (`www.nps.gov/grca`). It almost looks like a printed brochure that has been turned into a site. Very little information on this site ever changes.
- **Community:** A Web site for which its members provide the content is considered a community site. Community sites are often sponsored by a company and used to advertise, while providing a valuable resource for users of a product or participants in some activity. Most community sites are part of a larger site and primarily consist of forums. You will often see advertisements and company branding, as well as links back to the other sections of the site, as shown on the community forums at Frommer's, a travel publishing company (see Figure 12-3).

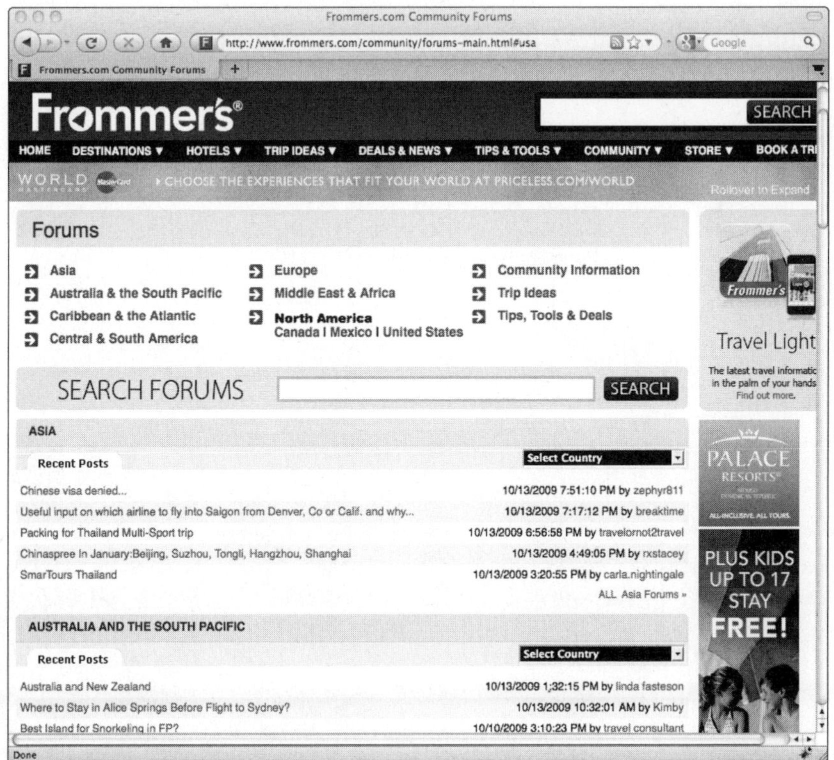

Figure 12-3: Frommer's community forums.

- **Image gallery:** Image galleries abound on the Web. They may contain images from a single source, or they can allow registered users of a site to contribute them. You've probably seen Flickr.com, a site that combines both image gallery and community Web site features. An image gallery can be extended to become a media gallery, offering videos, podcasts, or PDFs. The idea behind the site is to serve as a repository for files, allowing them to be previewed online, and under certain conditions, downloaded by visitors to the site. These sites need a form to allow files to be uploaded to the site.
- **Information or news:** These sites are almost the opposite of community sites because their content frequently changes. The focus is on publishing blurbs that visitors click on to read the full story. An example of this sort of site is `www.news.google.com`. Every time you visit the page, the news headlines have changed. News is acquired or aggregated from a variety of sources. News sites are typically very busy and don't have many other features beyond the headline links. New headlines may also be accompanied by thumbnail images.
- **Storefront:** From brick and mortar stores, like PetSmart and Target, to online-only retailers such as Amazon.com, storefront sites abound on the Web. Storefronts exist to sell, and usually focus on doing that. You don't see many bells and whistles on shopping sites. As you can see in Figure 12-4, they have links to the products prominently displayed, a link to a shopping cart, and often a search box to help visitors quickly find products they are seeking.

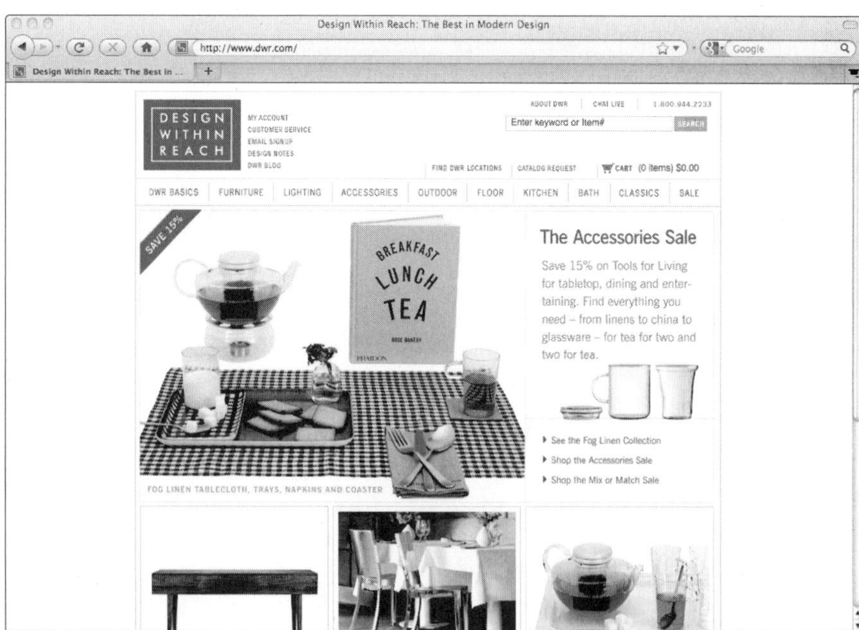

Figure 12-4: Storefront Web site for Design Within Reach.

Search boxes are great additions to most types of sites. They don't take up much room, and they save visitors to your site lots of frustration when they are looking for one particular subject, item, or article. Drupal has a preinstalled module for adding one to your site. I show how to enable and set it up in the next section.

Additional Modules to Install

Drupal comes with many preinstalled modules worth enabling. There are also many more contributed modules You can also download and add many more contributed modules to your Drupal program that extend the features of your site. First I show you a few more preinstalled modules, and then I take you through the process of locating and installing third-party modules.

More preinstalled modules

In this section, I take a closer look at four preinstalled modules that can add useful features to your site. The first is the OpenID module that allows people who already have accounts on other sites to log in to yours without registering. The second is the Poll module, which lets you set up questions for your registered users to vote on. The Profile module allows your users to have more robust profile pages, complete with images. Finally, the Search module allows you to place search boxes on pages of your site for visitors to easily locate content.

OpenID module

So many sites expect users to create accounts. The idea behind OpenID is to allow a user who has already registered on a major Web site (for example, google.com) to log in to your site using his google.com account information instead of creating a new account on your site. OpenID supports a number of major Web site logins. A user can also create a master login at `www.openid.net` that will allow him to log in at any site that allows OpenID.

If you turn on the OpenID module, you open your site up to users you haven't personally verified. This doesn't matter if your site is mainly informational or if you want a large user base. But if you allow your users lots of privileges, such as posting unmoderated content to message boards, you may not want to use this module.

To activate the OpenID module, follow these steps:

1. **Choose Administer⇨Site Building⇨Modules.**

2. **Check the box next to OpenID.**
3. **Scroll to the bottom of the page and click Save Configuration.**

The next time a visitor arrives at your home page, he will see the normal login form and a link to use an OpenID login. If he clicks that link, the login form changes to prompt for his OpenID (see Figure 12-5).

Poll module

Polls are great for community sites because they get people involved. You can also get valuable information if you use them to query your users about directions your site should take. To activate the Poll module and set up a poll, follow these steps:

1. **Choose Administer⇨Site Building⇨Modules.**
2. **Check the box next to OpenID.**
3. **Scroll to the bottom of the page and click Save Configuration.**
4. **Choose Create Content⇨Poll to set up a new poll.**

   Figure 12-6 shows the Create Poll form.

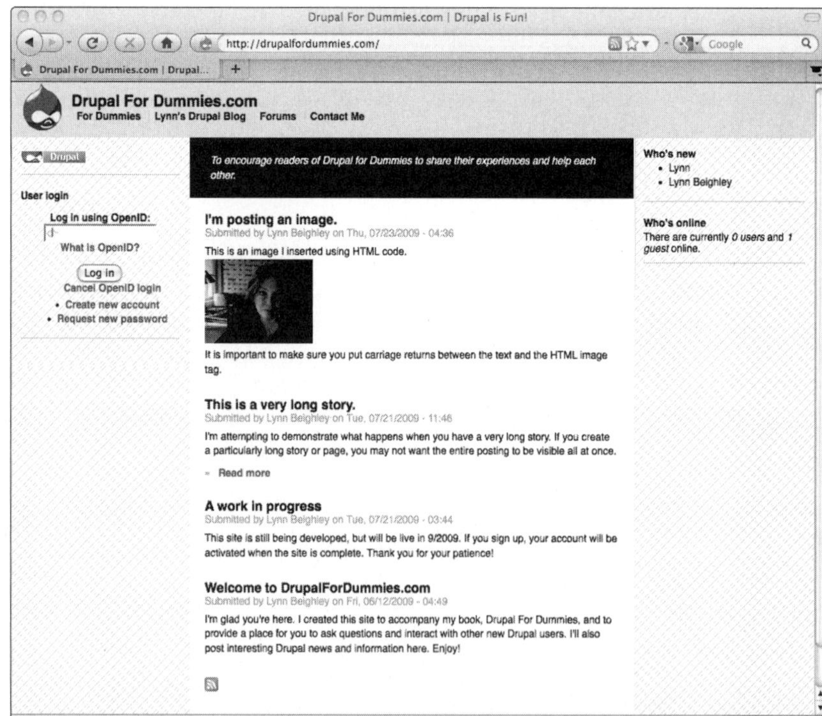

Figure 12-5: Login form with OpenID module enabled.

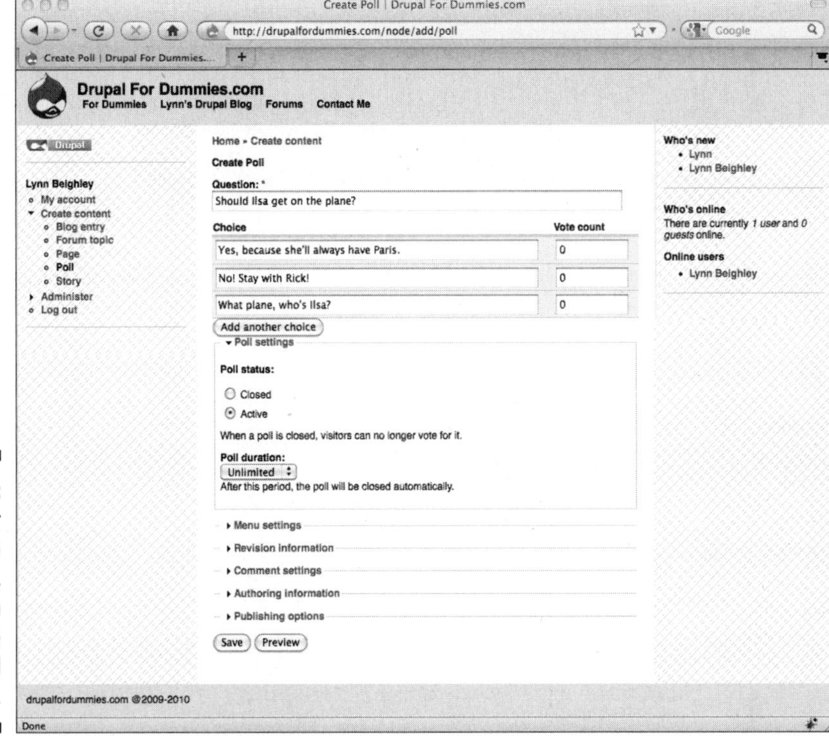

Figure 12-6: After enabling the Poll module, you can access the Create Poll form.

5. **Enter a poll question in the Question field.**
6. **Enter one of the possible answers in the first Choice field.**
7. **Enter another possible answer in the second Choice field.**
8. **If you want more than two choices, click the Add another choice button. Enter the new choice in the third Choice blank.**
9. **Make sure the Poll status is set to Active.**

   If this is set to Closed, the poll and the voting results will be visible, but no more voting will be allowed.
10. **Click Preview to see your question. When you are happy with it, click Save.**

The poll question will now be published on the front page of your site (see Figure 12-7).

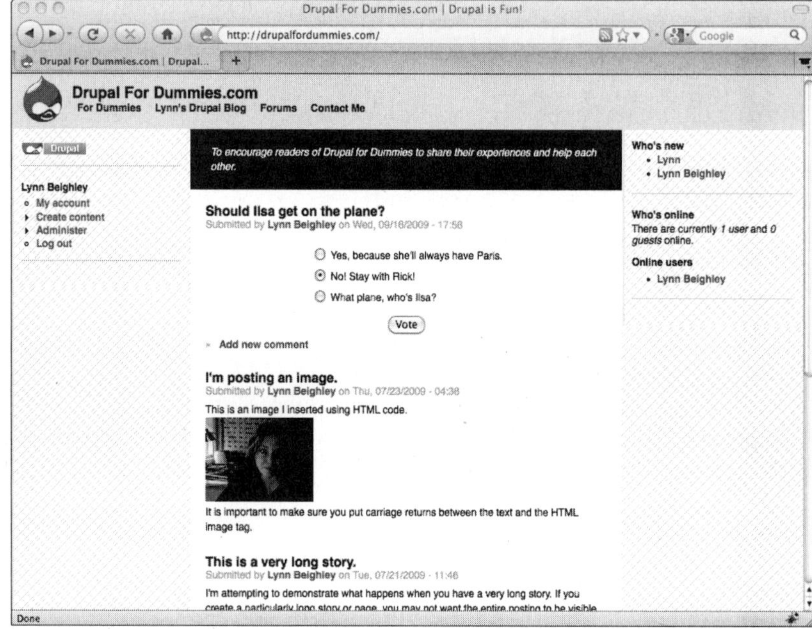

Figure 12-7: Poll published to the front page.

After a user clicks a choice, he sees the voting results. He can also cancel his vote if he chooses.

The Create Poll form (refer to 12-6) also controls a few other poll settings.

- **Poll publishing options:** As with a new post, your poll shows up as the top item on your home page. This can be changed for an individual post by changing the Publishing options section of the Create Poll page. Uncheck the Promoted to front page box.

  If you never want your poll to appear on the front page, you can control the behavior for all polls. Follow these steps:

  1. Choose Administer➪ Content Management➪Content types.
  2. Click the edit link next to the Poll type and uncheck the Published check box under Workflow settings.
  3. Click Save content type.

- **Comments about poll:** By default, your poll allows registered users to comment. You can change this by modifying the Comment settings section of the Create Poll page. Your choices are Disabled, Read only, and Read/Write.

- **Location of Poll:** You can control in which block your poll appears. Follow these steps:

  1. Choose Administer⇨Site building⇨Blocks.

     The item Most recent poll appears near the bottom of the page under the Disabled section.

  2. Change the drop-down box or drag it to the block of your choice.
  3. Click Save blocks.

Profile module

Another good choice for increasing the community feeling of a site is to enable the Profile module. This module allows a registered user to add additional information to his user profile. Enabling this module lets you configure the profile form to prompt the user for specific information. Figure 12-8 shows an example of a custom user profile form that users can fill out.

The information a user enters on this form will show up when anyone clicks on his username.

To set up the Profile module and create a form allowing registered users to add more information to their profile pages, follow these steps:

1. **Choose Administer⇨Site Building⇨Modules.**
2. **Check the box next to Profile.**

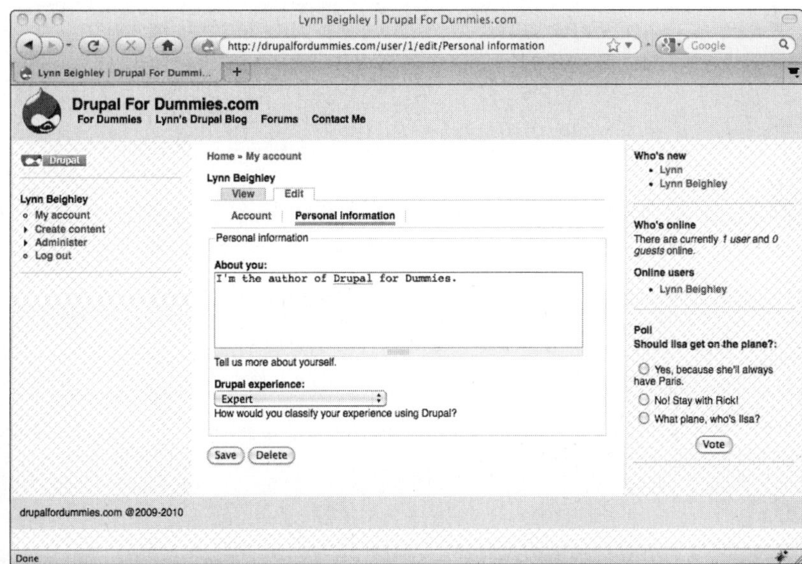

Figure 12-8: Profile form that asks for more user profile information.

3. **Scroll to the bottom of the page and click Save Configuration.**
4. **Choose Administer⇨User Management⇨Profiles to set up a form for users to fill out.**

   You have to create all the form fields that your users will answer.
5. **Click on the link multi-line text field under Add new field.**

   This opens a new form where you can name this text field and give your users instructions about what kind of information to enter. Figure 12-9 shows this form.
6. **For Category, enter a general description of the kind of question this is.**

   This allows you to ask several of the same type of questions. For example, in Figure 12-8, the two questions asked in that form are both in the category *Personal information.*
7. **For Title, enter the text you want the user to see next to the field.**

   This should tell the user what kind of information you want him to enter in this field.

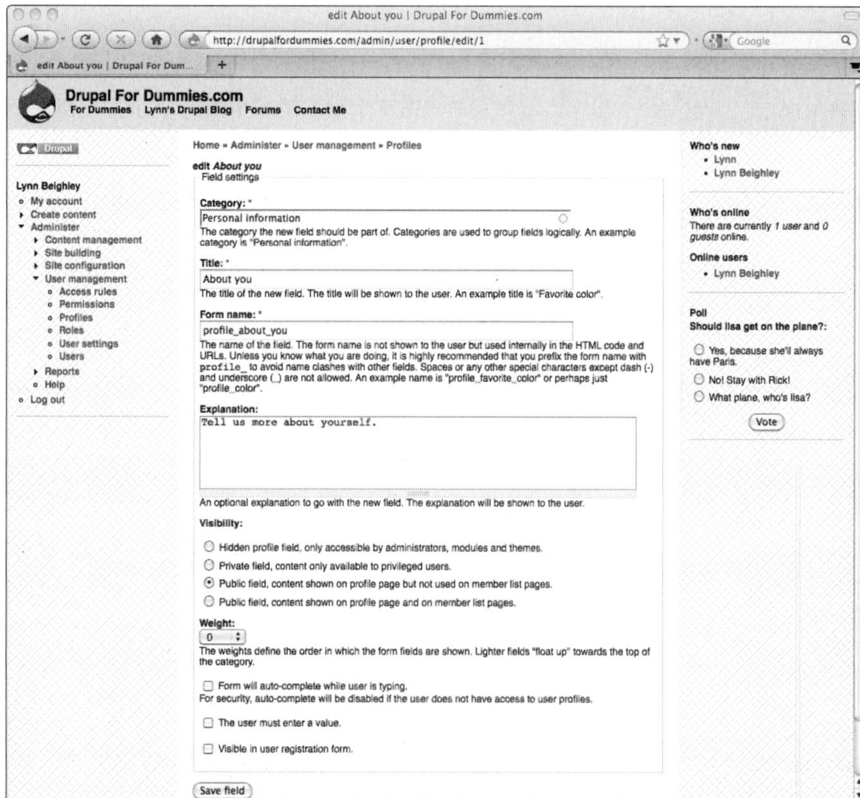

Figure 12-9: Form to create a multi-line text field for a user profile form.

8. **In the Form name field, add a distinctive name with underscores instead of spaces.**

   Drupal uses this to keep track of this field, but it will never be seen by you or the users filling out the form. I add the Title text to the word *profile* that was already in the blank and end up with *profile_about_you.*

9. **If the title of the field isn't clear enough, you can add more text to explain what sort of information to enter.**

10. **For Visibility, choose Public field, content shown on profile page but not used on member list pages.**

    The Visibility setting controls where and to whom the information the user fills in will show up on your site:

    - If you want to collect information from your users, but keep it private so only the administrator can see it, choose the first option, Hidden profile field.
    - If you want the information visible on pages that list all the users, check the last option, Public field, content shown on profile page and on member list pages.

    - Be careful with this option. If you're allowing the users to enter multiple lines of information, the list pages will be very cluttered.
    - The third option, Public field, content shown on profile page but not used on member list pages, is generally your best bet.

11. **Click Save field.**

When users sign up or click on the My account link, they will see the Personal information tab. Clicking that tab will display any form fields you created under the Personal information category.

Figure 12-8 also shows a drop-down list users can choose from under Drupal experience. To create this, follow these steps:

1. **Choose Administer➪User Management➪Profiles.**

2. **Click on the link list selection under Add new field.**

   Figure 12-10 shows the form that opens. It's very much like the form to create a multi-line text box, with the addition of a Selection options field.

3. **For Category, enter a general description of the kind of question this is.**

   If you enter the category *Personal information,* this question will show up in the same tab on the My account page (refer to Figure 12-8) as the About you field that I created in the last example.

4. **For Title, enter the text you want the user to see next to the field.**

   I enter *Drupal experience.*

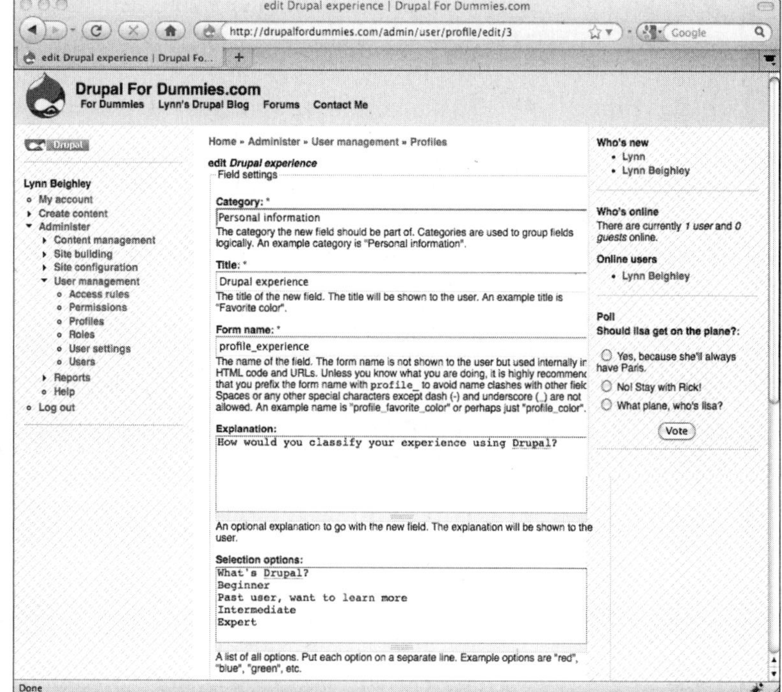

Figure 12-10: Form to create a list selection field for a user profile form.

5. **In the Form name field, add a distinctive name with underscores instead of spaces.**

   I enter *profile_experience.*

6. **If the title of the field isn't clear enough, you can add more text to explain what sort of information to enter.**
7. **For Visibility, choose Public field, content shown on profile page but not used on member list pages.**
8. **Click Save field.**

Now when a user browses to his My account page, he will see an Edit link with two options: Account and Personal information. Clicking on Personal information takes him to the form with the fields I just created.

By default, Drupal only allows administrators to see everyone's user profile. You need to allow registered users and, if you choose, anonymous users to see them by changing the permissions. To give registered users permission to view other people's user profiles, follow these steps:

1. **Choose Administer⇨User management⇨Permissions.**

2. **Scroll down to the bottom of the page and check the check boxes next to access user profiles.**

   You can choose to allow unregistered users to view them if you wish.

3. **Click Save permissions.**

Every username visible on your site will now link to that user's profile. Usernames show up in blog, comment, and forum postings. Figure 12-11 shows what an unregistered visitor to my site sees if he clicks on my username.

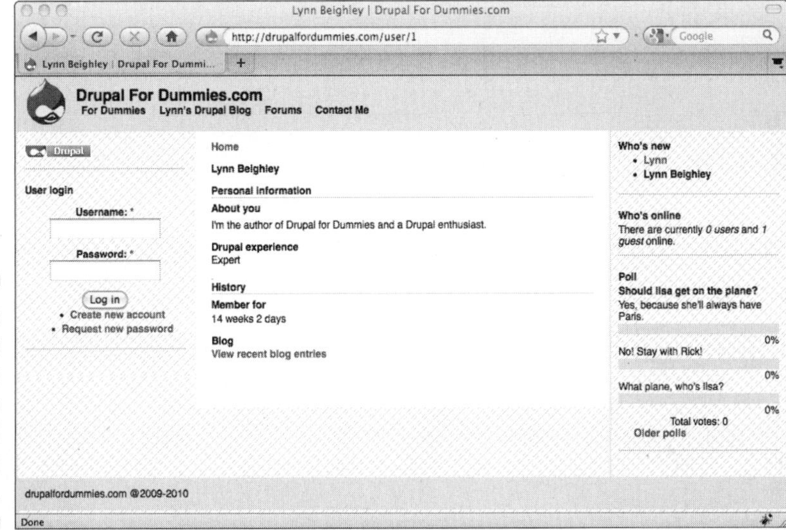

Figure 12-11: User profile page with custom Personal information fields.

Enhancing Profiles with user images

You can allow your registered users to upload an image that will show up on their profiles. To turn this on, follow these steps:

1. **Choose Administer➪User management➪User settings.**

2. **Scroll down to the Pictures section and select the Enabled radio button.**

   More options will appear (see Figure 12-12).

   You don't need to change any of these settings. The Picture image path controls where the user images will be stored under the Drupal directory on your Web server. The Picture maximum dimensions control the size of the profile image. It defaults to 85 pixels by 85 pixels. The Picture maximum file size defaults to 30k.

3. **Click Save configuration.**

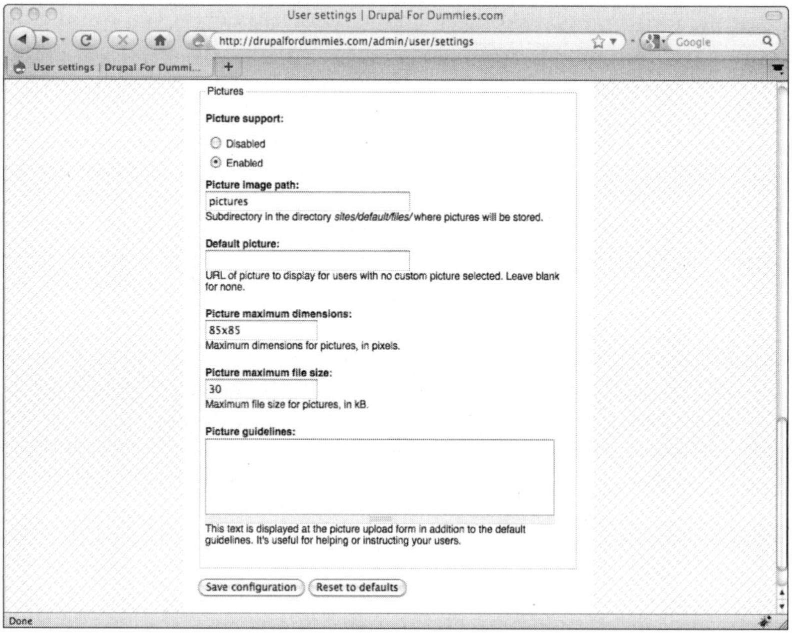

Figure 12-12: The Pictures settings to allow users to add profile pictures.

Now when a registered user chooses My Account➪Edit, he will see a Picture section on the Edit form where he can select a photo to upload. This photo will appear on his user profile.

Search module

As you and your registered users add more content to your site, be it blog entries, forum posting, or news posts, visitors to your site will want to be able to find content of interest. Drupal has a Search module that displays a search box and returns a list of links to content that matches the search terms entered in the box.

To set up the Search module, follow these steps:

1. **Choose Administer➪Site Building➪Modules.**
2. **Check the box next to OpenID.**
3. **Scroll to the bottom of the page and click Save Configuration.**
4. **Choose Administer➪Site Building➪Blocks.** The entry Search form now appears in this list under Disabled.

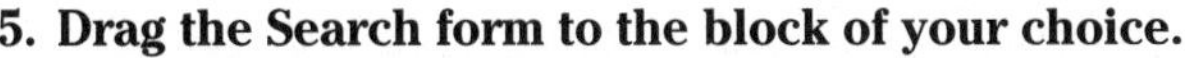

5. **Drag the Search form to the block of your choice.**

   You can drag the items in each block to control the order within the block. For example, you can drag the Search form item to the top of the Right sidebar section so it will appear near the top right of every page of your site.

6. **Click Save blocks.**

Your search form will now appear on your site. When users search for a word, links to content containing that word appear (see Figure 12-13).

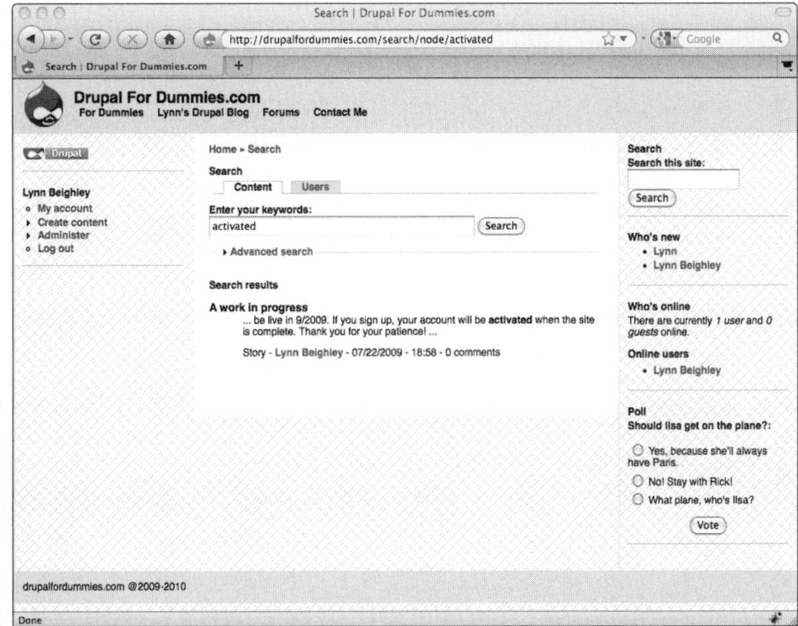

Figure 12-13: Search form in Right sidebar and search results.

By default, the search form appears with both *Search* and *Search this site* printed above it. To get rid of *Search*, follow these steps:

1. **Choose Administer⇨Site building⇨Blocks.**
2. **Click the configure link next to Search form.**
3. **In the blank Block title, enter the text** `<none>`**.**

   You need to include the angle brackets.

4. **Click Save block.**

You can use this same technique to remove the title from any block component. For example, the poll in Figure 12-13 has the word *Poll* as a title. Because it's fairly obvious that it's a poll, I remove the title by choosing Administer⇨Site building⇨Blocks, where I click the configure link next to Most recent poll, enter **<none>** for the title, and click Save block.

Adding a Contact Form

An important addition to most Web sites, especially ones offering products or services, is a contact form. This allows site visitors to ask for more information without having to locate an e-mail address on your site and send you a message.

Contact forms can also be constructed to allow certain types of messages to be sent to specific people on your staff. The contact form has a category drop-down box that allows visitors to select from a list of topics. For example, if you have a storefront and an employee in charge of shipping, you can create a contact form that, when submitted, sends the contents directly to the right person on your staff. The same contact form can be sent to your Web site administrator.

To create a contact form, follow these steps:

1. **Choose Administer⇨Site Building⇨Modules.**
2. **Check the box next to Contact.**
3. **Scroll to the bottom of the page and click Save Configuration.**
4. **Choose Administer⇨Site building⇨Contact form.**
5. **Click the Add category tab.**

   This opens the form, shown in Figure 12-14.
6. **For category, enter a subject that you think someone would like to contact you about.**

   I enter Website feedback. You'll have the chance to enter more categories later.
7. **For recipients, enter the e-mail addresses, separated by commas, of everyone you want to receive the results of this form when a user submits it.**
8. **If you want users to be sent a message after they submit the form, fill in the Auto-reply field.**
9. **If you think the category, or subject, of this form is the most common one users will choose, set Selected to Yes. Click Save.**

   You return to the Contact form list page.

To add more categories or subjects to your contact form, repeat Steps 1 through 9.

In my example, I add the category Product information.

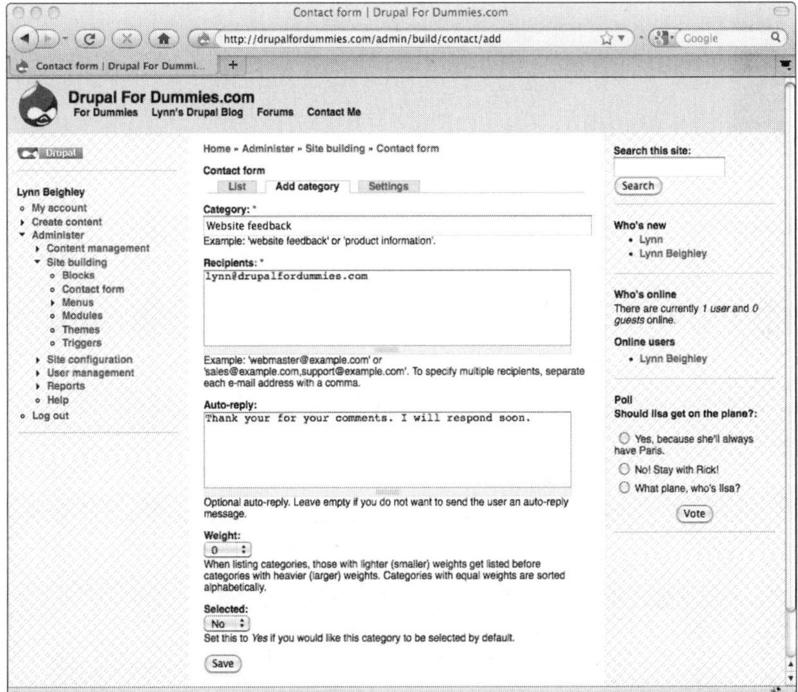

Figure 12-14: Adding a category to a contact form.

You now have a contact form (see Figure 12-15).

To view yours, go to `http://yourwebsitename.com/contact`. For example, mine is located at `http://drupalfordummies.com/contact`.

The last step is to provide visitors to your site with a link to this form. To add a link to your Primary menu, follow these steps:

1. **Choose Administer⇨Site building⇨Menus.**
2. **Click Primary links.**

   You will see a list of your current primary links. You need to add a new one for the contact form.
3. **Choose Add item.**

   This opens the form, as shown in Figure 12-16.

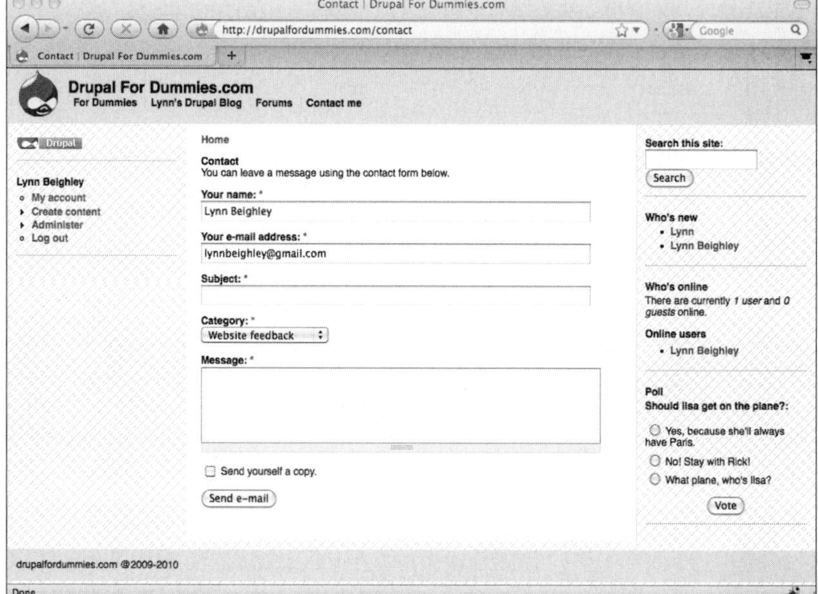

Figure 12-15: Contact form with Category drop-down box.

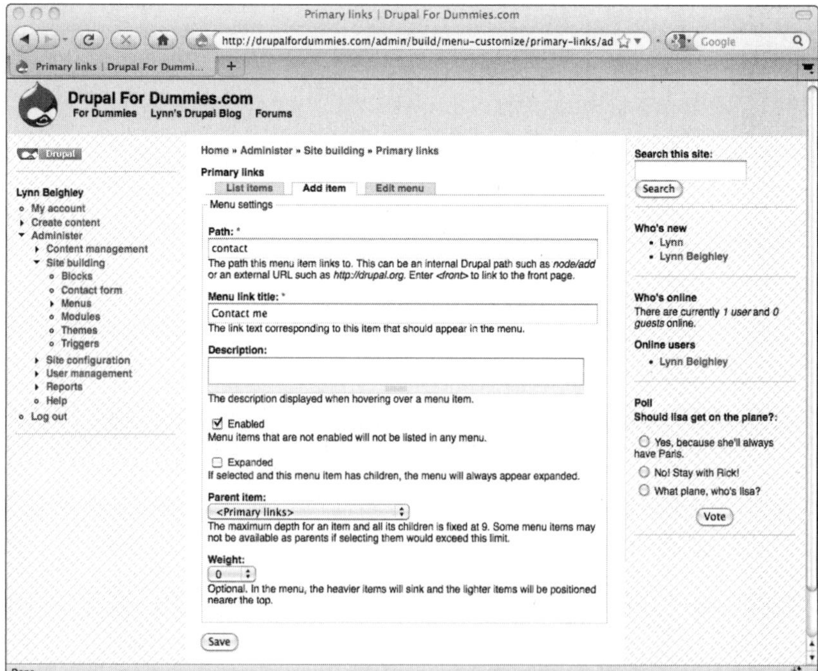

Figure 12-16: The Add item tab of the Primary menu settings.

4. **For Path, enter *contact*.**
5. **For Menu link title, enter the text you want to appear in your primary menu as the link to the contact form.**
6. **Click Save.**

Your contact form will now be available to registered users.

If you want to make your contact form available to both registered and unregistered users, you need to change the permissions:

1. **Choose Administer⇨User management⇨Permissions.**
2. **Locate the contact module and check the box next to *access site-wide contact form* under *anonymous user*.**
3. **Click Save permissions.**

Chapter 13

Developing an Image Gallery

In This Chapter

- Using the Image module
- Creating image galleries
- Attaching images to nodes
- Adding multiple images
- Creating gallery moderators

These days almost everyone is taking digital photos. Having an online image gallery, a place where you can showcase your photos, is a great way to share your personal experiences. You may wish to create a gallery as an archive just for yourself. Fortunately, you can create a gallery using the contributed Image module rather easily.

This chapter shows what a Drupal image gallery looks like, how to install the Image module, how to manage the gallery settings, how to allow others to help you manage your galleries, and how to create your own gallery or set of galleries.

Understanding Image Galleries

An image gallery is generally a set of images organized into some sort of collection and displayed as a set of small previews or thumbnails that link to individual larger images. Figure 13-1 shows the thumbnail view of an image gallery in Drupal.

In the thumbnail view, photos are represented by smaller versions. Each page of the album holds six thumbnails. If there are more than six images in the album, page numbers and next and previous links appear underneath.

Clicking on one of the thumbnails opens the larger version of that image (see Figure 13-2).

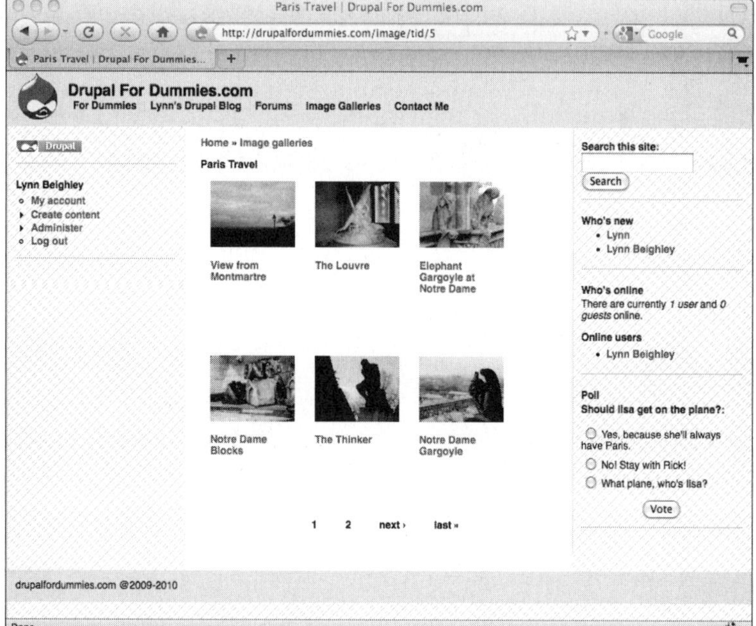

Figure 13-1: Thumbnail view of an image gallery.

Figure 13-2: Full size view of gallery image.

The full-size image displays the title of the image, which is set when the image is added to the gallery. It also shows the time and date the image was added as well as who added it. A link to allow users to add comments about the image is underneath.

The Image module discussed in this chapter allows GIF, JPG, and PNG file types.

Getting the Image and Image Gallery Modules

Unlike most of the modules previously covered in this book, the Image and Image Gallery modules aren't part of the default Drupal installation. The Image Gallery module is included as part of the contributed Image module. It needs to be downloaded to your computer, uploaded to your Web server, extracted, enabled, and configured. The first step is downloading it.

Installing the Image module

The Image module is available on the drupal.org Web site. To download this file, follow these steps:

1. **Browse to `http://drupal.org/project/image`. Scroll down the page to find the download links (see Figure 13-3).**
2. **Locate the link to download this module and click it. Save this file to a directory you will remember.**

   This module will download as a single compressed `.tar.gz` file.

   As of this writing, the most current version for Drupal 6 is 6.x-1.0-beta3. Feel free to download more recent compatible versions.
3. **Log in to your control panel on your ISP's Web site.**

   If you are comfortable using FTP software, you connect directly to your Web server with the FTP login and password provided by your ISP. If you go this route, extract the module on your local computer and FTP the extracted Images directory directly to your Web server's module directory under your Drupal installation.

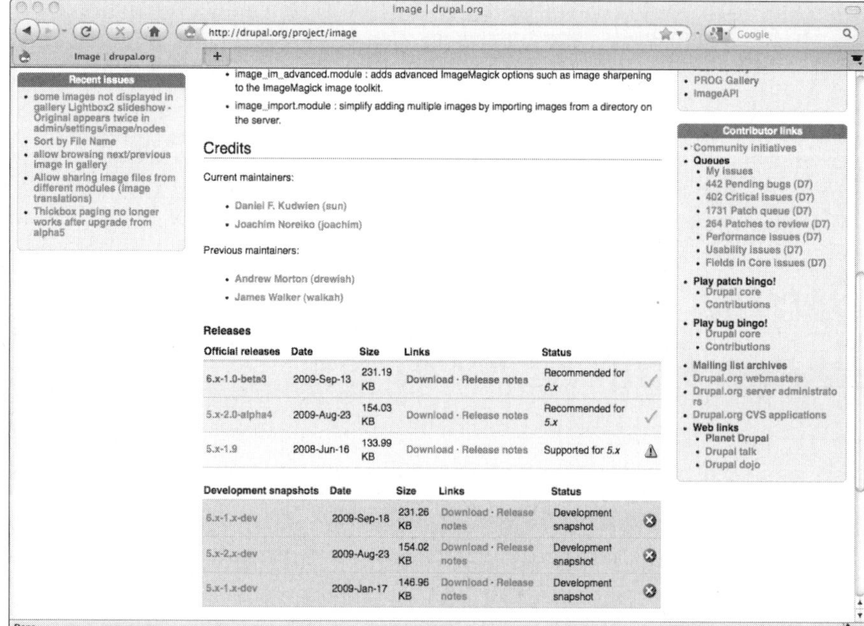

Figure 13-3: The Image module download page.

4. **Find and click the link to a file manager.**

   You need a file manager so that you can select the `.tar.gz` file and put it in the module directory on your Web server. After you click the file manager, you will see a screen that displays the files on your Web server.

5. **You should see a single folder or directory named "html," "www," or "htdocs." Click on its name to open it.**

   There may be several directories, but the one for your Web site should be easy to spot. This is where all your Web pages belong and where you need to install Drupal.

6. **Locate the folder named modules and click on it.**

7. **Locate and click the upload link on your file manager.**

   You should see an upload form with a Browse button.

8. **Click Browse and find the Image module `.tar.gz` file you downloaded. Click Upload.**

   The compressed Image module file is now on your site in the correct folder and ready to be extracted.

9. **Click on the Image module `.tar.gz` to select the file.**

   You see a list of files that are stored inside your compressed file, all selected. You should see an option to uncompress the files. Leave the selection box set to uncompress "All."

10. **Click the Go button.**
11. **Select the original Image module `.tar.gz` file on your Web server and delete it.**

Enabling the Image and Image Gallery modules

After you have uploaded and extracted the Image module, Drupal will see it and it will show up in the module list. To enable it, follow these steps:

1. **Browse to Administer⇨Site building⇨Modules.** The Image module is made up of several modules and they all appear on this page (see Figure 13-4).
2. **Click the Enabled check box next to both the Image module and the Image Gallery module.**
3. **Click Save configuration.**

   The new modules are now activated.

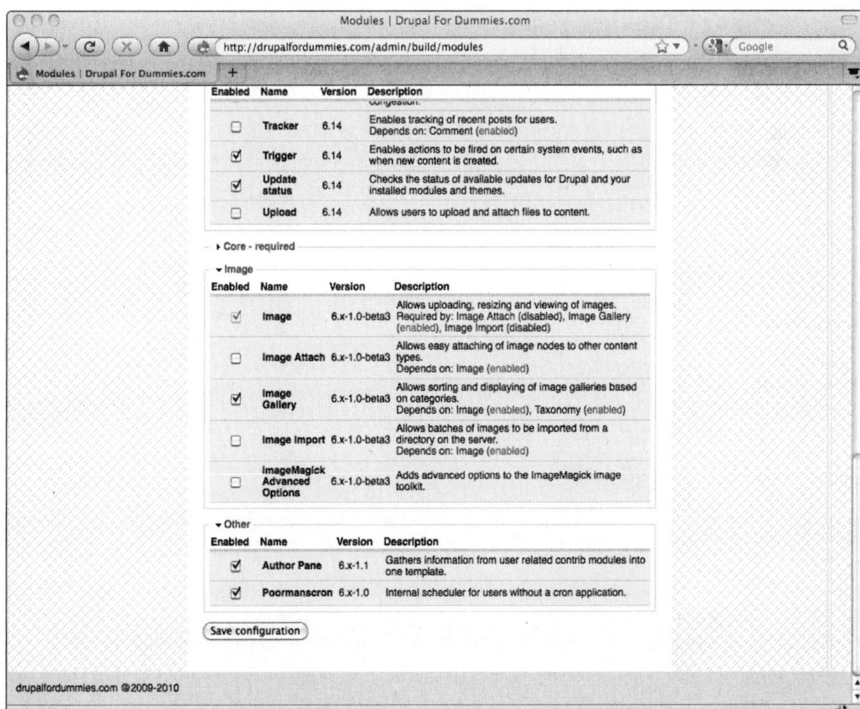

Figure 13-4: The new Image module contains five modules.

Configuring image galleries

Before you can put an image into an image gallery, you need to create your first image gallery. Follow these steps:

1. **Browse to Administer⇨Content management⇨Image galleries.**
2. **Click the Add gallery tab.**

   This opens the Add gallery form (see Figure 13-5).
3. **For Gallery name, enter a short, descriptive title.**
4. **For Description, enter a few sentences that describe the images you will store in this gallery.**
5. **Click Save.**

The Image Gallery module allows you to create as many galleries as you want. Simply repeat the preceding steps to add additional galleries.

Figure 13-5: Add gallery form to create a new image gallery.

Adding images to your gallery

Now that you've created your galleries, you can add images to them. Adding images to a gallery is similar to adding other content types, like posts or blogs.

For each image to add to a gallery, follow these steps:

1. **Choose Create content➪Create image.**

   This opens the Create image form (see Figure 13-6).

2. **Enter a title for you image in the Title field.**
3. **Choose one of the galleries you created in the preceding section from the Image Galleries drop-down box.**
4. **Click the Image text box or the Browse button to locate the file you wish to upload.**
5. **If you want to add more information about this image, type it in the Body field.**
6. **Click Save.**

Your image has now been placed in your image gallery.

To view your new image galleries, go to `http://yourwebsitename.com/image`. For example, mine is located at `http://drupalfordummies.com/image`.

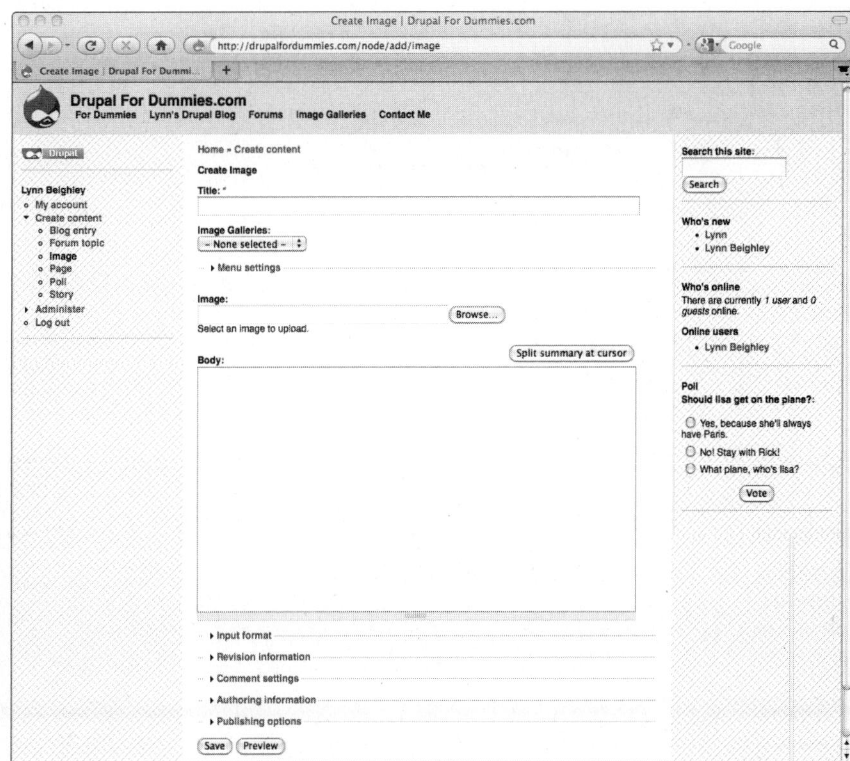

Figure 13-6: Add an image to your gallery with the Create Image form.

Linking to your gallery

The last step is to make your galleries more visible by providing a link to them. To add a link to your image galleries in your Primary menu, follow these steps:

1. **Choose Administer➪Site building➪Menus.**
2. **Click Primary links.**

   You will see a list of your current primary links. You need to add a new one for the image galleries.
3. **Choose Add item.**

   This opens the form shown in Figure 13-7.
4. **For Path, enter *image*.**
5. **For Menu link title, enter the text you want to appear in your primary menu as the link to your image galleries.**
6. **Click Save.**

Your image galleries will now be available to site visitors.

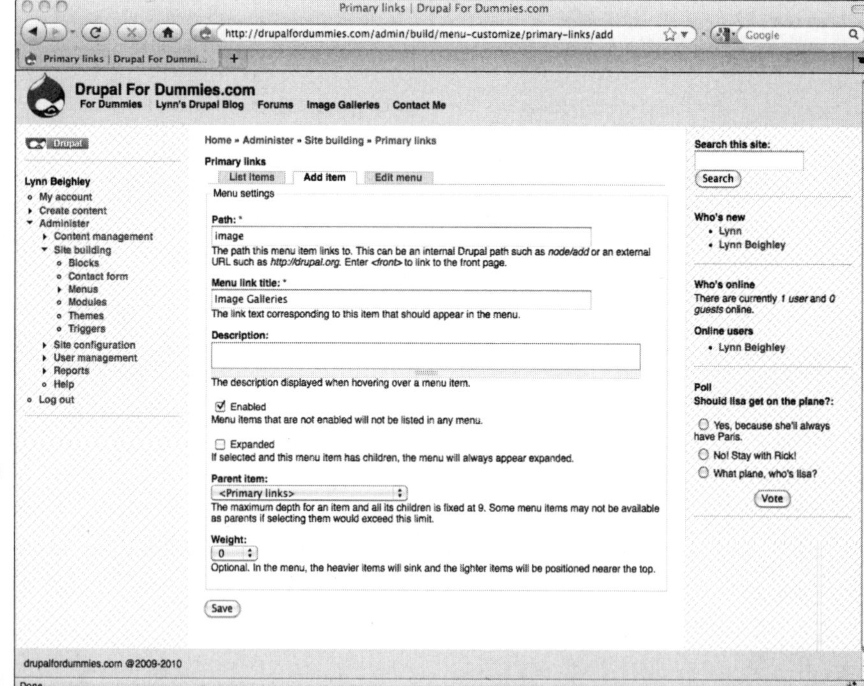

Figure 13-7: The Add item tab of the Primary menu settings.

Controlling gallery options

When you view your main image gallery page, you see a list of galleries, each with a representative thumbnail from that gallery. The thumbnail displayed is always the most recent added to the gallery. When you click a link to a gallery, you see a set of thumbnails of images in that gallery. By default, gallery listings contain six images per page.

You can change the number of images displayed on each gallery listing page and modify the order in which image thumbnails are displayed. Follow these steps:

1. **Choose Administer➪Site configuration➪Images.**
2. **If you see several tabs, click the Image gallery tab.**

   This opens the Gallery settings form (see Figure 13-8).
3. **Change the Images per page setting to control how many thumbnail images show up on each gallery thumbnail page.**
4. **If you wish to display the name of the person who uploaded an image, check the Display node info box.**

   This only matters if you allow other people to post images to your galleries.

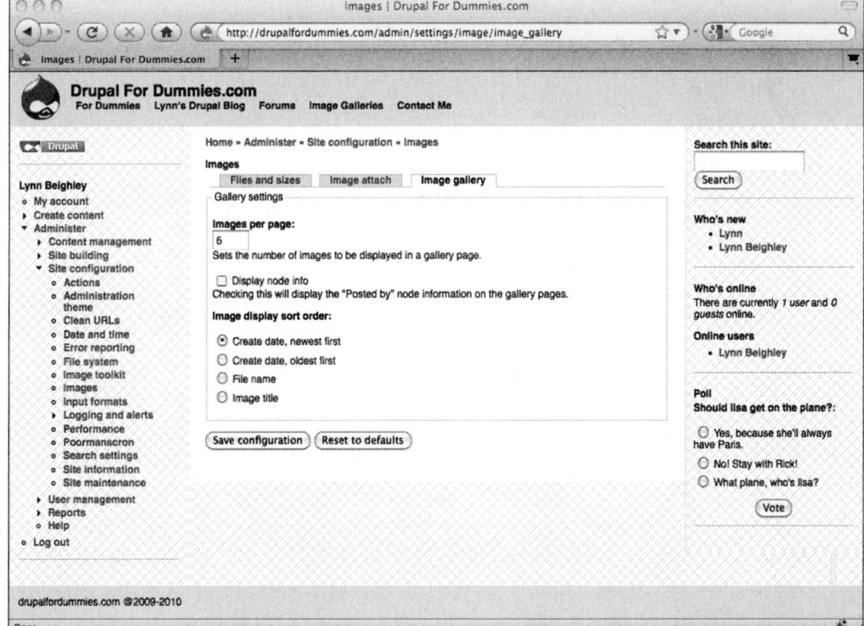

Figure 13-8: The Gallery settings form allows you to modify gallery settings.

5. **You can change the order in which the thumbnails are displayed in your gallery listings using the Image display sort order options.**

   By default, the most recently added images appear first and the oldest ones last.

6. **Click Save configuration.**

Controlling image options

The Image module has more options that control the size of the thumbnails it creates from your images, the size of images you can upload, and several other settings. You can modify the default image settings by accessing the Images configuration options. Follow these steps:

1. **Choose Administer⇨Site configuration⇨Images.**
2. **If you see several tabs, click the Image tab.**

   This opens the Image file settings form (see Figure 13-9).

3. **Leave the Default image path set to image.**

   The Default image path is a folder under the Drupal directory on your Web server that controls where all the images you add are saved.

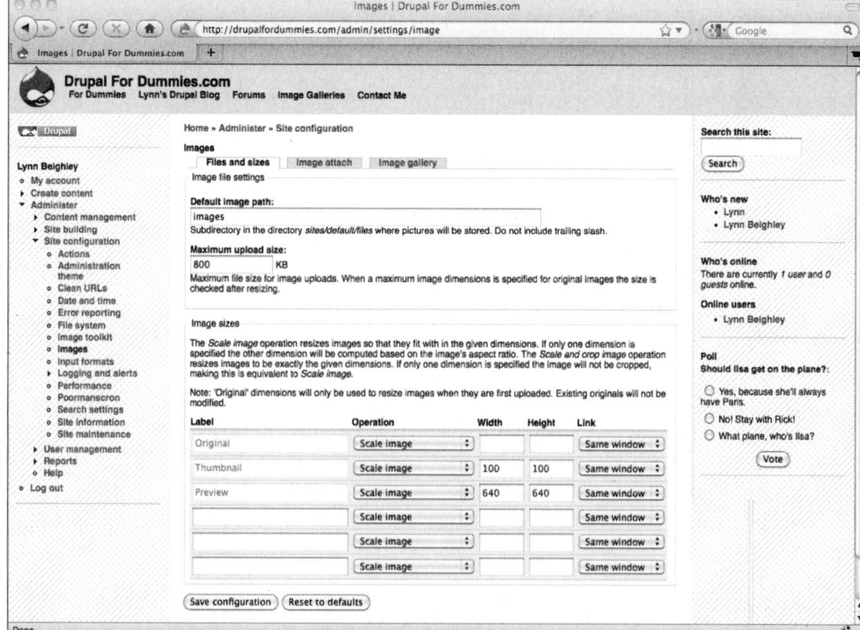

Figure 13-9: The Image file settings form allows you to modify image settings.

4. **If you will be adding images larger than 800KB to your image gallery, increase the maximum size.**

   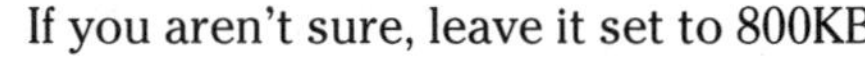

   If you aren't sure, leave it set to 800KB.

   If you try to add an image that is larger than 800KB, you will get a message that your file is too large. You can then change the Maximum upload size setting appropriately.

5. **To change the size of the thumbnail images, change the Width and Height boxes next to the Preview row under the Image sizes section.**

   If you have images with differing dimensions in your collection, you might want to use only a width setting and leave the height setting blank.

   If you wish, you can make full-size images open in a new browser window when a thumbnail is clicked. To do this, change the Link setting drop-down box to New window next to the Preview row under the Image sizes section.

6. **Click Save configuration.**

Additional Image Modules

When you install the Image module, you also receive a few other modules. These are Image Attach, Image Import, and ImageMagick Advanced Options.

Before you can use these modules, you need to enable them:

1. **Choose Administer⇨Site building⇨Modules.**
2. **Click the Enabled check boxes.**
3. **Click Save configuration.**

Image Attach

Image Attach allows you to easily add images to all your content types. Using this module, you don't need to use HTML code, as I did when I added my profile photo in Chapter 6. Instead, you can use the same form to add an image to a post, forum response, or blog entry that you used to add photos to the gallery.

To add the capability to attach images to your content types, follow these steps:

1. **Choose Administer⇨Content management⇨Content types.**

   You will see a list of the current content types set up on your site.

2. **Click the edit link next to the content type to which you want to be able to attach images.**

   In my case, I choose Blog entry. The Blog entry settings page opens (see Figure 13-10).

3. **Scroll down to the Image attach settings section and expand it.**
4. **Change Attach images to Enabled.**
5. **Leave the Teaser image size set to Thumbnail.**

   The Teaser image size controls what size image is actually posted. If you want a thumbnail-sized image to accompany your content, leave this set to Thumbnail. You can also display the image at its full size by changing this setting to Original.

6. **Click Save content type.**

Now every time I create a blog entry, a new section named Attached images appears on my content creation page. I can either attach an image I've already added to my gallery or add an entirely new image.

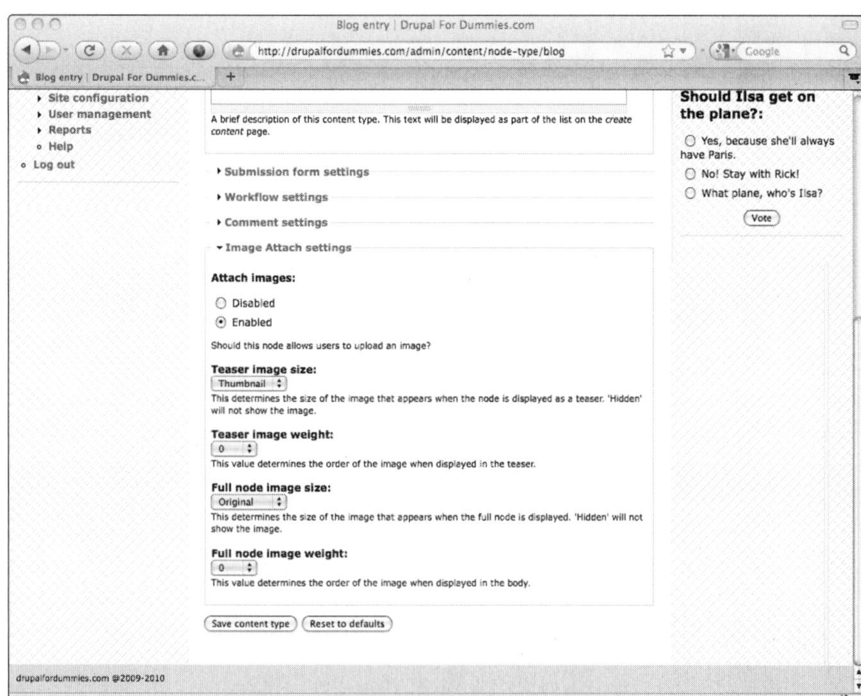

Figure 13-10: Blog entry settings page.

To attach an image to a node, in this case a blog entry, follow these steps:

1. **Choose Create content ➪ Blog entry.**

   This opens a Create Blog entry page.

2. **After you finish writing your blog entry, scroll down and expand the Attached images section (see Figure 13-11).**

   You will see a list of all the images you have already added.

3. **Either choose an image from the list, or upload a new one by clicking on the Browse button and selecting one.**

4. **If you upload a new image, give it a title and click Attach.**

5. **Click Save.**

Your latest blog entry will now have a thumbnail image in it. When the thumbnail is clicked, the full size view of the image will appear (refer to Figure 13-2).

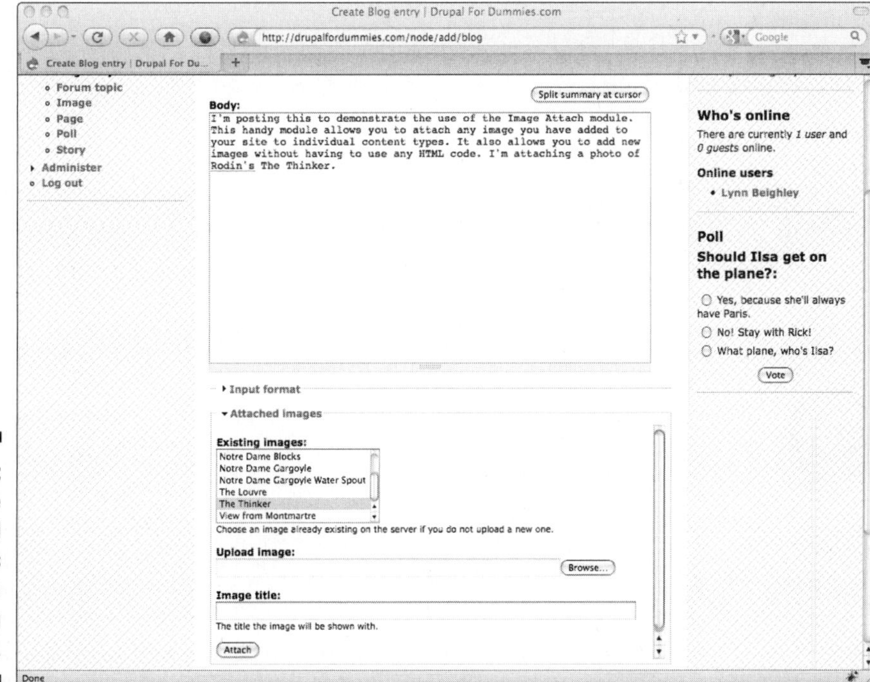

Figure 13-11: The Attached images section of a Create Blog entry page.

Using the Image Import module

The Image Import module allows you to import a large number of images into Drupal.

Unlike using the Image module to upload a single image, the Image Import module requires you to use a file manager or FTP program to copy all of your image files to your Web server before it will pull them into Drupal.

To add multiple images to Drupal with the Image import module, follow these steps:

1. **Log in to your control panel on your ISP's Web site.**
2. **Find and click the link to a file manager.**
3. **You should see a single folder or directory named "html," "www," or "htdocs." Click on its name to open it.**
4. **Create a new folder on your Web server. Name it *tempimages* or a name you will remember.**

   This is the folder where you will temporarily store your images until you add them to Drupal.
5. **Locate and click the upload link on your file manager.**

   You should see an upload form with a Browse button.
6. **Click Browse and find the images you wish to upload. Copy them to the tempimages directory.**
7. **Choose Administer⇨Site configuration⇨Images. Click the Image import tab.**
8. **Type the path to your new folder in the box labeled *Import path* (see Figure 13-12).**

   The path will be either */tempimages* or *tempimages*, depending on where Drupal is installed:

   - If you installed Drupal right under the main Web directory and don't have a Drupal folder on your Web server, use *tempimages.*
   - If you created a folder under the Drupal directory, use */tempimages.*
9. **Click Save configuration.**

   Drupal knows where your images are, but they still haven't been added to galleries or the image system on Drupal. You need to tell Drupal which images to add, and if you wish, give them titles.
10. **Choose Administrator⇨Content management⇨Image import.**

    This displays a list of all the images you have placed in the tempimages directory (see Figure 13-13).

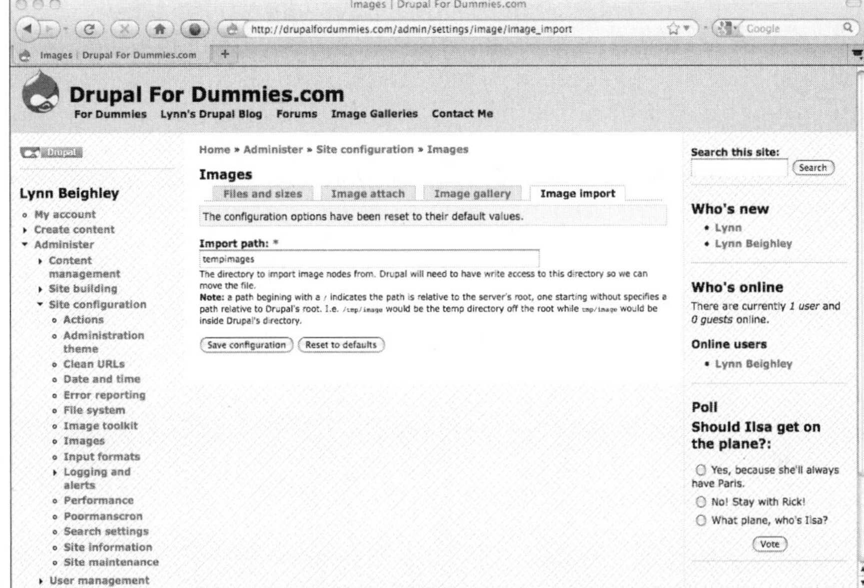

Figure 13-12: Setting Image path for the Image Import module.

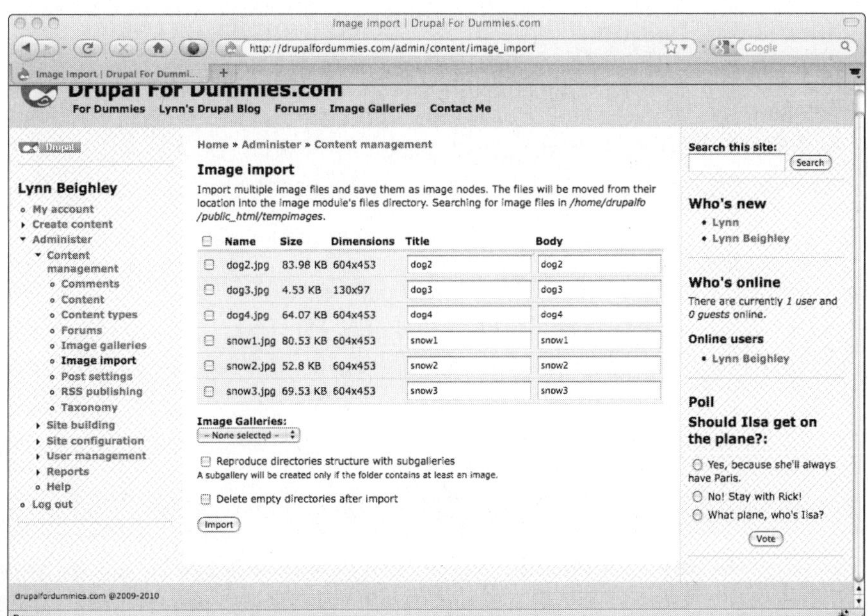

Figure 13-13: Images in the tempimages directory.

11. **Change the title and body text, or make them blank.**

    Drupal fills in the blanks with the first part of each filename. Chances are you don't want that to appear as the title and body text under your images, so replace or remove it.

12. **Click the check box next to each file you wish to import and choose the image gallery where you want it to appear. Click Import.**

You don't have to move all the files at once, and you don't have to put them in galleries. Any files you don't select by clicking the check box will still be on this page when you come back after choosing Import.

Files that you select will be deleted from the tempimages directory after they are added to Drupal.

Finding images in Drupal

When you add an image to a gallery, it's pretty easy to find by viewing the gallery and locating the thumbnail. But as you add more images, and when you add images that aren't in a gallery, locating them can be tricky. Here are two ways to find your images:

- Use the Search module.

  This isn't the best method (you may see results in your list that are not images), but it's the quickest. Type in a word from the title of an image to see that image included in the search results.

- Follow these steps to generate a list of images:
  1. Choose Administer⇨Content management⇨Content.
  2. Select the type radio button and change the drop-down to Image.
  3. Choose Filter.

     You will see a list of all your images and can click on the name of the one you are looking for.

Modifying or deleting images

As with any content type, you can modify or delete images by browsing to them and clicking the Edit tab. There you can make changes or press Delete if you no longer want the image on your site.

Allowing Others to Contribute Images

As your site grows, you might want to allow trusted users to add images to the site galleries. You can create a new user role with the correct permissions and then assign specific users to that roll.

Create a photo editor role

The first step is to create a new role. Users in this role will have the same permission as any authenticated user, except they will have the additional permission to add images and delete images they have added.

1. **Choose Administer➪User management➪Roles.**
2. **Type** photo editors **in the blank and click Add role.**

The photo editors role has been created but can't actually do anything more than any other authenticated user at this point. You need to add permissions.

Add permissions to photo editor

To add permissions to the photo editors role, follow these steps:

1. **Choose Administer➪User management ➪Permissions.**

   This opens the Permissions page (see Figure 13-14).

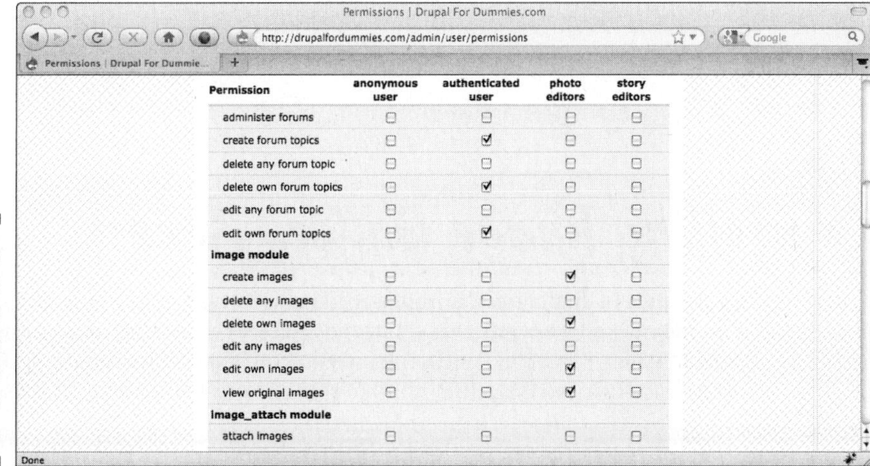

Figure 13-14: Image module section of the Permissions page.

If you are still on the Roles screen, you can click the edit permissions link next to the newly created photo editors role.

2. **Scroll down to the image module section.**
3. **Under the photo editors column, check the following: create images, delete own images, edit own images, view original images.**
4. **Click Save permissions.**

Assign photo editors role to user

To allow a trusted user to add and delete his own images, he needs to be added to the photo editors role. Follow these steps:

1. **Choose Administer➪User management➪Users.**
2. **Locate the user you wish to add to the photo editors role and click the edit link to the right of his name.**
3. **Click the Edit tab.**
4. **Under the Roles section, check the photo editors box.**
5. **Click Save.**

When this user logs in, he will now see a link called *Image* under the Create content section of the navigation menu. He will be able to add an image using the form shown in Figure 13-6.

Users with the photo editor role will not be able to create new galleries. If you wish to allow them that permission, follow these steps:

1. **Choose Administer➪User management➪Permissions and scroll down to the image_gallery module section.**
2. **Check the box under photo editors.**
3. **Click Save permissions.**

Controlling Image Gallery Access

By default, Drupal allows unregistered users to view your image galleries. You may wish to only allow registered users to see them, or you might want certain galleries visible, and other ones protected. Unfortunately, there are no permissions settings that control this. You need the Image Gallery Access module.

Installing the Image Gallery Access module

To control access to your image galleries, follow these steps:

1. **Download the latest version of the Image Gallery Access module, located at `http://drupal.org/project/image_gallery_access`.**
2. **Download the ACL module, located at `http://drupal.org/project/acl`.**

   The Access Control List (ACL) module works behind the scenes with the Image Gallery Access module. By itself, the ACL module doesn't add any new features, but the Image Gallery Access requires the ACL module to operate correctly.
3. **Install both the Image Gallery Access module and the ACL module.**

   Follow the steps shown in the earlier section "Installing the Image module."
4. **Choose Administer➪Site building➪Modules and enable both the ACL and Image Gallery Access modules. Click Save configuration.**
5. **At this point, you may see the error message *The content access permissions need to be rebuilt. Please visit this page* (see Figure 13-15). Click the link.**
6. **Choose Rebuild permissions.**

   The new modules now function.

Using the Image Gallery Access module

You can now use the Image Gallery Access module to restrict access to individual galleries. Follow these steps:

1. **Choose Administer➪Content management➪Image galleries.**

   You are on the List tab of the Image galleries section.
2. **Click the edit link next to the gallery you wish to modify.**

   This opens the gallery settings form with a new Access control section (see Figure 13-16).

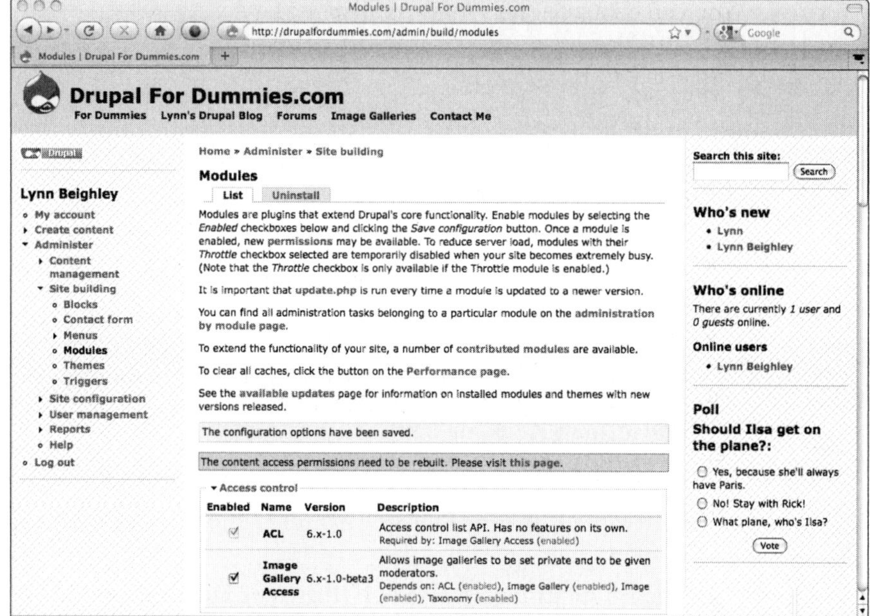

Figure 13-15: Error link when installing the ACL module.

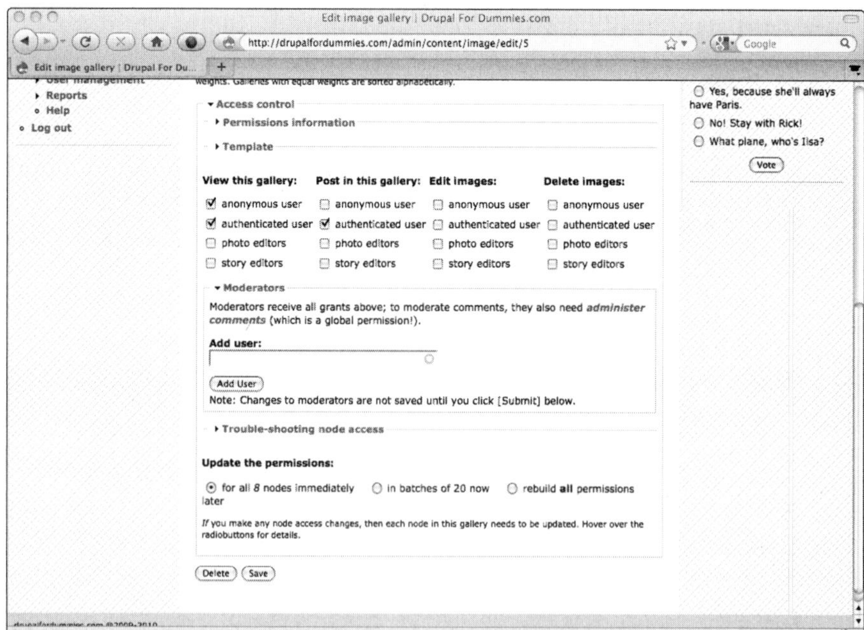

Figure 13-16: Image Gallery Control module options.

You can control access to the current gallery with the four columns:

- **View this gallery:** Allows designated roles to view images in this gallery.

  Allowing only authenticated users to view this gallery is how you make a gallery private.
- **Post in this gallery:** Allows designated roles to post new images into this gallery.
- **Edit images:** Allows designated roles to change the title and body text for an image.
- **Delete images:** Allows designated roles to delete an image from this gallery.

On this form, as well as the Permissions page, if you give anonymous users permission to do something, you should also give authenticated users the same permission. The two groups are mutually exclusive. They are either anonymous or registered. If you give permission only to the anonymous group, authenticated users will not have it.

Adding moderators

A moderator is a user with the capability to add, edit, and delete images. The Image Gallery Control module grants moderators all four capabilities: view, post, edit, and delete. Moderators can edit and delete images added by everyone, not just their own.

Making someone a moderator has the same end result as creating a role and assigning a user to it. The advantage of using the moderator feature of the Image Gallery Control is that it doesn't clutter up your Permissions page with yet another role. It's simpler to assign a moderator than to create an entire role and assign a user to that role.

To add a moderator to a gallery, follow these steps:

1. **Choose Administer⇨Content management⇨Image galleries.**
2. **Click the edit link next to the gallery you wish to modify.**
3. **If it isn't visible, expand the Moderators section under the Access control section.**
4. **In the Add user field, type in the username of the person you wish to have moderator status.**
5. **Choose Add user.**

   You will see the username with a check box (see Figure 13-17).
6. **Click Save to save the new moderator information.**

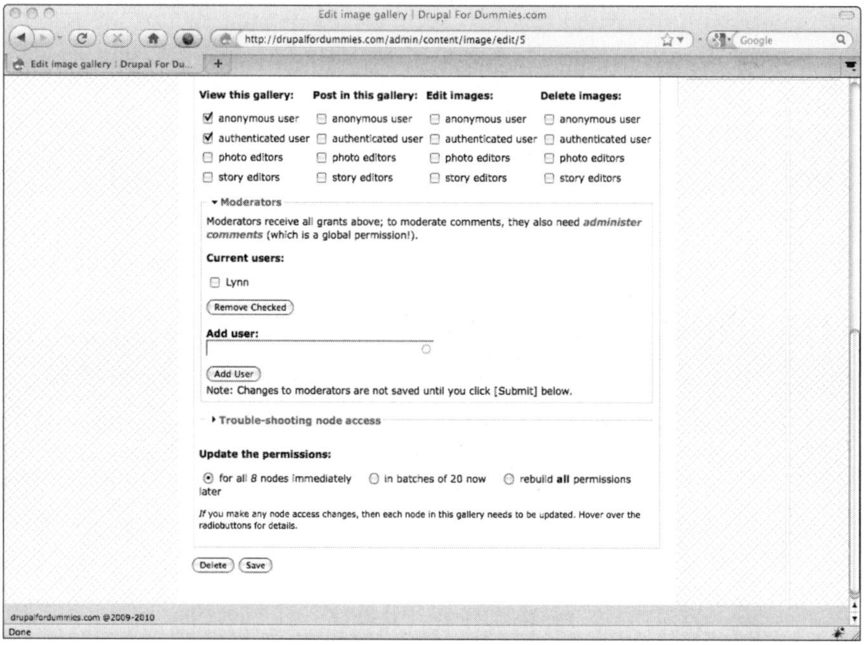

Figure 13-17: The Moderator feature of the Image Gallery Access module.

Removing moderators

If you want to remove a moderator, follow these steps:

1. **Choose Administer⇨Content management⇨Image galleries.**
2. **Click the edit link next to the gallery from which you want to remove a moderator.**
3. **Check the box next to the username you wish to remove, and click Remove Checked.**
4. **Click Save.**

Chapter 14

Interacting with Other Sites

In This Chapter

- Pulling in Twitter and Facebook statuses
- Displaying YouTube videos
- Aggregating RSS feeds
- Sharing a feed from your site

It's all about Web 2.0. You're developing a Web site for your users with interactive features and timely information. But until now, all the content on your site has come from you, with a little help from your users.

Your site doesn't have to exist in a vacuum. There are lots of modules for Drupal that let you pull in information from other sites and push out content from your site. In this chapter, I take a look at a few nifty modules that let you tie in content from other sites, including such favorites as Twitter, Facebook, YouTube, and Amazon.

Working with Activity Stream

Activity Stream is a Drupal module that lets you publish your social media content on your own Web site. With Activity Stream, every time you twitter, post a link on Digg, or receive a Facebook notification, you can view that information on your Drupal site. There are many add-on modules for popular social media sites and services that extend the Activity Stream module. Here are a few of them:

- **Facebook:** The current front-runner in the social media wars.
- **YouTube:** Post video streams directly from YouTube.
- **Qik:** Allows you to share live video from your mobile phone.
- **Identi.ca:** A Twitter-like status update site with a few more features.

- **Blogger:** Online blogging service.
- **Goodreads:** A place to research and compare notes on books.
- **IMDB:** All about movies and entertainment information.

Each registered user on your site can have his own set of activity streams. By default, they appear under the user profile section. Later in this chapter, I show you how to put your activity stream in a block and place it in the Right sidebar.

Installing Activity Stream

The Activity Stream module is available on the drupal.org Web site. To download this file, follow these steps:

1. **Browse to `http://drupal.org/project/activitystream`. Scroll down the page to find the download links (see Figure 14-1).**

2. **Locate the link to download this module and click it. Save this file to a directory you will remember.**

   This module will download as a single compressed `.tar.gz` file. As of this writing, the most current version for Drupal 6 is 6.x-1.0-rc2.

3. **Log in to your control panel on your ISP's Web site or use an FTP client.**

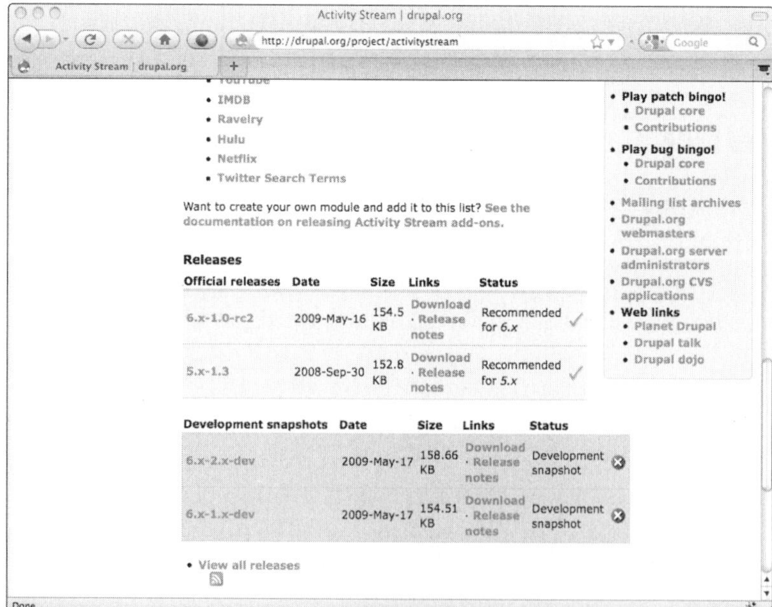

Figure 14-1: The Activity Stream module download page.

4. **Find and click the link to a file manager.**

   After you click the file manager, you will see a screen that displays the files on your Web server.

5. **You should see a single folder or directory named *html, www,* or *htdocs.* Click on its name to open it.**

   There may be several directories, but the one for your Web site should be easy to spot.

6. **If you see the Drupal directory, click on it, and then the modules directory. If not, locate the modules directory and click on it.**

7. **Locate and click the upload link on your file manager.**

   You should see an upload form with a Browse button.

8. **Click Browse and find the Activity Stream module `.tar.gz` file you downloaded. Click Upload.**

   The compressed Activity Stream module file is now on your site in the correct folder and ready to be extracted.

9. **Click on the Activity Stream module `.tar.gz` to select the file.**

   You see a list of files that are stored inside your compressed file, all selected.

10. **You should see an option to uncompress the files. Leave the selection box set to uncompress "All" and click the Go button.**

11. **Select the original Activity Stream module `.tar.gz` file on your Web server and delete it.**

Installing additional modules

Depending on which services you use, you can download and install some additional modules. The Activity Stream page at `http://drupal.org/project/activitystream` has a list of links to add-ons.

Follow the steps you used to install the Activity Stream module. The additional modules I installed are:

- **Activity Stream for Facebook:** `http://drupal.org/project/activitystream_facebook`
- **Activity Stream for YouTube:** `http://drupal.org/project/activitystream_youtube`
- **Twitter Search Feeds:** `http://drupal.org/project/twitter_search_feeds`

Enabling Activity Stream modules

Your new modules will now appear in the module list (see Figure 14-2).

To enable them, follow these steps:

1. **Browse to Administer➪Site building➪Modules.**

   The new modules are located in the Activity Stream section.

2. **Select the Enabled check box next to all the modules in the Activity Stream section.**

3. **Click Save configuration.**

   The new modules are now enabled.

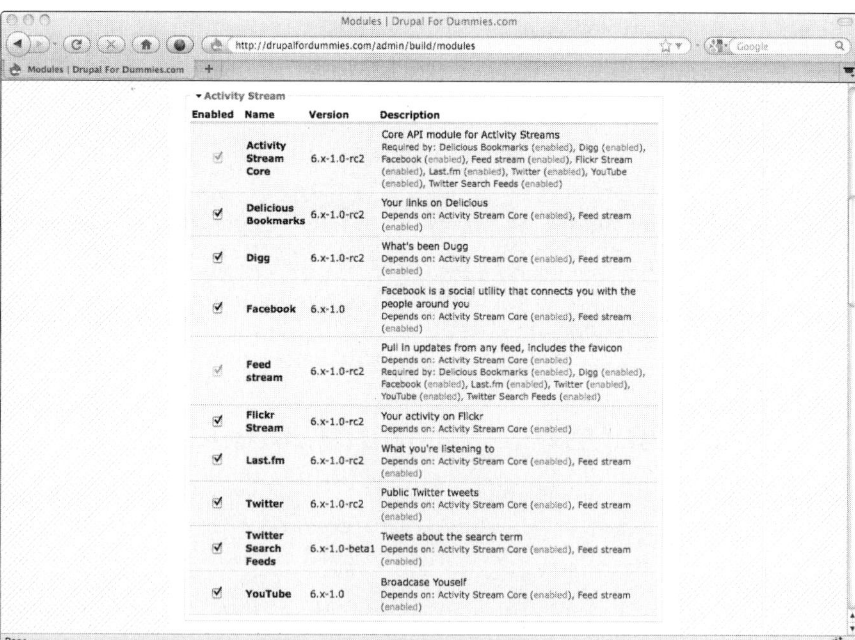

Figure 14-2: The Activity Stream modules.

Pulling in social media

After the Activity Stream and related modules are enabled, you can begin pulling in content from other sites. Activity Stream is based on an individual user. To set it up for use with a particular user, follow these steps:

1. **Choose Administer➪User management➪Users.**

2. **Locate the user you want to have an activity stream. Click the Edit link to the right of the user's name.**

   In my case, I add it to my own account.

   If you are adding the Activity Stream to the user account you are currently using, you can choose My account ➪Edit➪Activity Stream.

3. **Click the Activity Stream link under the Edit tab.**

   This opens the Activity Stream setup page (see Figure 14-3).

   This form has blanks for specific Web sites and a large box for Rich Site Summary (RSS) feeds. (I discuss RSS feeds later in this chapter.) With the exception of the Facebook field, the fields on this page are simple to fill out. Del.icio.us, lastfm, Digg, Twitter, Flickr, and YouTube simply need your username on those sites.

4. **Enter your username for the particular Web site you wish to include in your Activity Stream output and click Save.**

   Your streams will update automatically at intervals, but to make it update immediately so you can see the new data, you need to run your cron program to make Drupal go out and get your information from the Web sites.

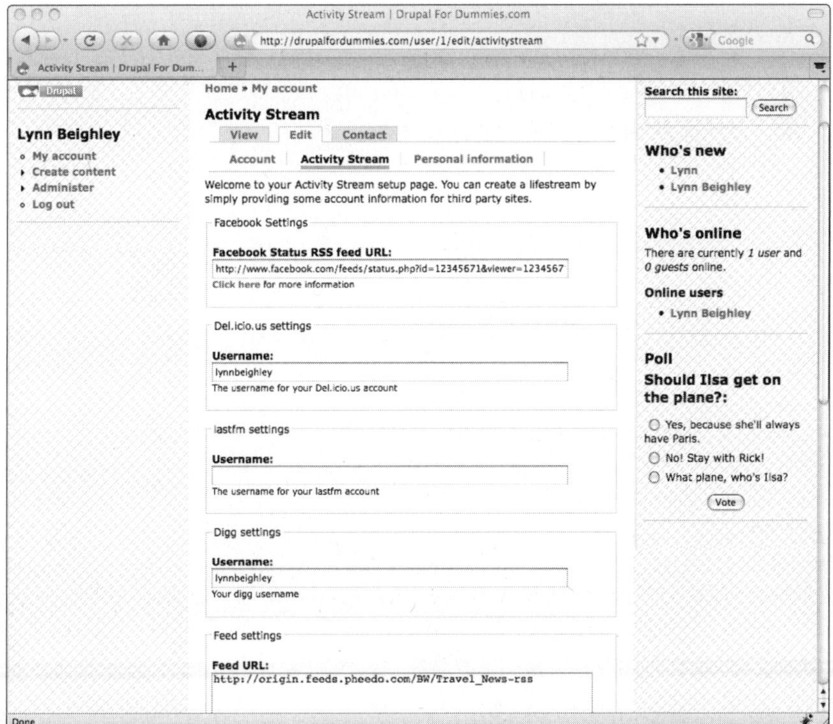

Figure 14-3: Activity Stream settings page.

5. **Choose Administer➪Reports➪Status Report.**
6. **Under the listing Cron maintenance tasks, click the link *run cron automatically*.**

You can now view your Activity Stream page by choosing the View tab of the user's profile. In my case, I choose My account. The Activity Stream appears on the View tab (see Figure 14-4).

To activate your Facebook feed is a little trickier. Facebook requires a URL that you have to dig around a bit to find. Follow these steps:

1. **Log in to your FaceBook account.**
2. **Navigate to `http://www.facebook.com/notifications.php`.**

   This opens a page with a list of your notifications (see Figure 14-5).
3. **Click the Your Notifications link at the bottom of the gray right-hand column.**

   This opens a page with a URL similar to:

```
http://www.facebook.com/feeds/notifications.php?id=1234567
        89&viewer=123456789&key=74074ea623&format=rss20
```

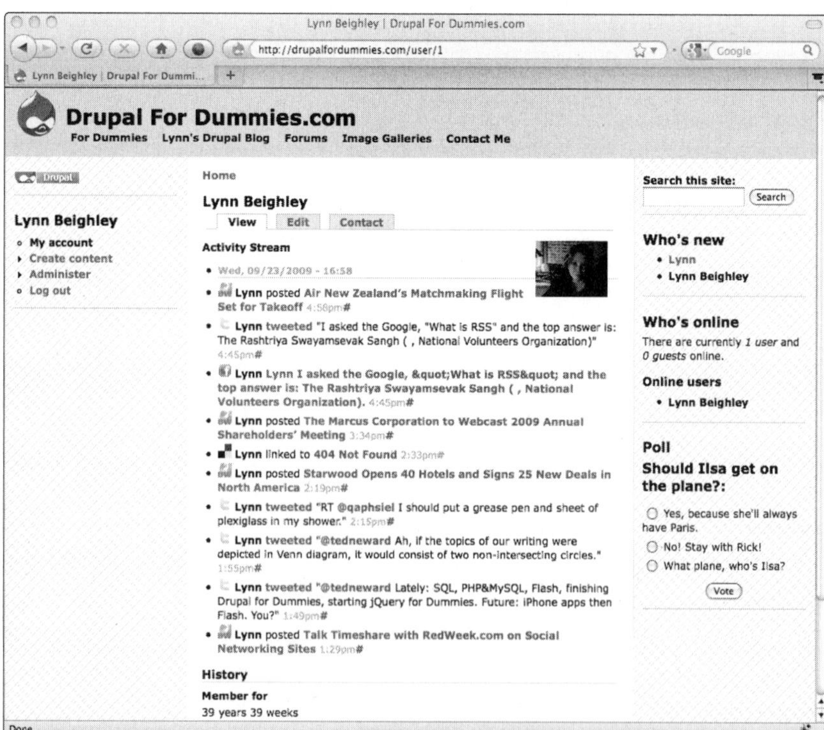

Figure 14-4: Activity Stream output on the profile page.

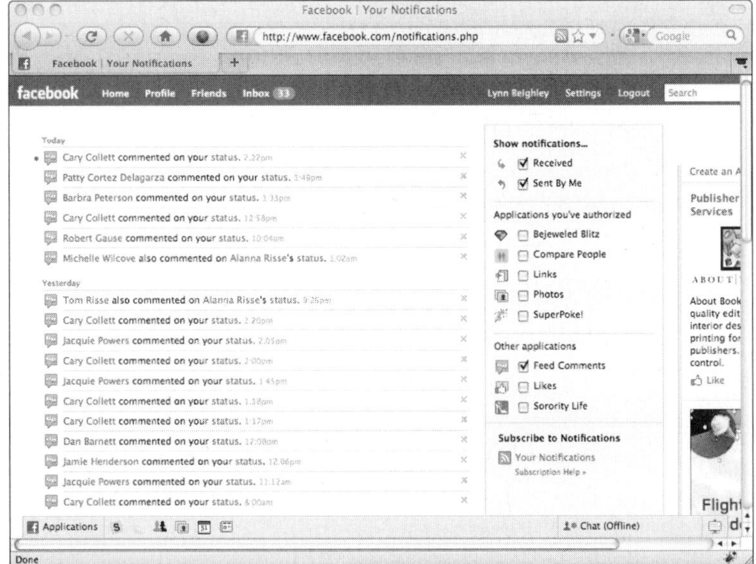

Figure 14-5: FaceBook notifications page.

4. **Copy this URL to a notepad or word processor.**
5. **In your copy of the URL, change the word *notifications* to *status.***

   This is the URL you will paste into the FaceBook blank on your Activity Stream setup form.
6. **Choose Administer⇨User management⇨Users.**
7. **Click the Edit link to the right of the username.**
8. **Click the Activity Stream link under the Edit tab.**
9. **Paste the URL in the blank titled Facebook Status RSS feed URL.**
10. **Click Save.**

To see the FaceBook feed immediately, you need to run your cron program. Otherwise, it may take an hour or more to appear on your user profile page.

The Activity Stream module only has one setting you can change, the title. By default, the title is *Activity Stream.* This will appear above your pulled in content. To change it, choose Administer⇨Site Configuration⇨Activity Stream. Change the text in the Title box and click Save configuration.

As things stand, unregistered users can see your Activity Stream. The Activity Stream module doesn't permit you to allow only registered viewers to see it.

Posting your streams in a block

By default, Activity Stream shows up only in your profile. If your stream contains content of interest to your customers or site visitors, you may want to post it to one of the blocks on your site. Follow these steps:

1. **Choose Administer➪Site building➪Blocks.**
2. **Locate Activity Stream in the list.**

   It will be near the bottom in the Disabled section.
3. **Drag or use the Region drop-down to move it to the block of your choice.**

   I move mine to the Right sidebar.
4. **Drag it to the position within the block where you want it to appear.**

   I want mine at the bottom of the Right sidebar block, so I drag it to the bottom of that section (see Figure 14-6).
5. **Click Save blocks.**

My Activity Stream now appears in the right column.

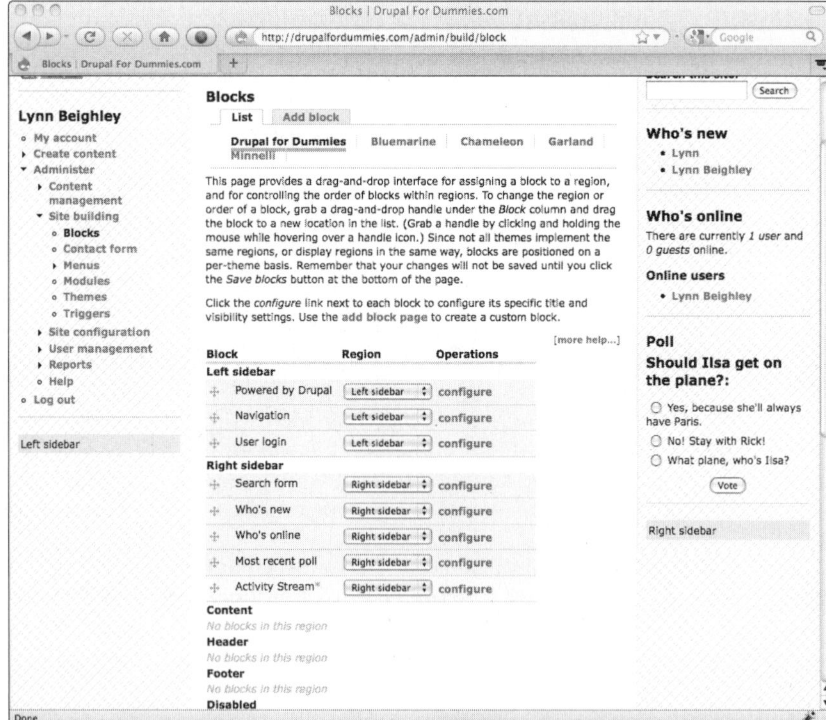

Figure 14-6: Blocks page with Activity Stream moved to bottom of Right sidebar section.

Posting YouTube Videos

Activity Stream for YouTube posts messages about videos you have made favorites along with links to them on the YouTube site, but it doesn't post the actual videos on your site. You can post YouTube videos to any content type, be it story, blog post, or page, by first visiting YouTube to gather information about the video and then posting it on your site. Here's how it works:

1. **Locate the video you want to post on the YouTube site. Open its page.**

   I open a video located at `http://www.youtube.com/watch?v=7EYAUazLI9k` (see Figure 14-7).

2. **Locate the box on the upper right of the page with two text fields named *URL* and *Embed*.**

3. **Click on the text in the Embed text box. Select all of it and copy it.**

4. **On your Drupal site, choose Create content and pick the content type where you want to post this video.**

   I choose Blog.

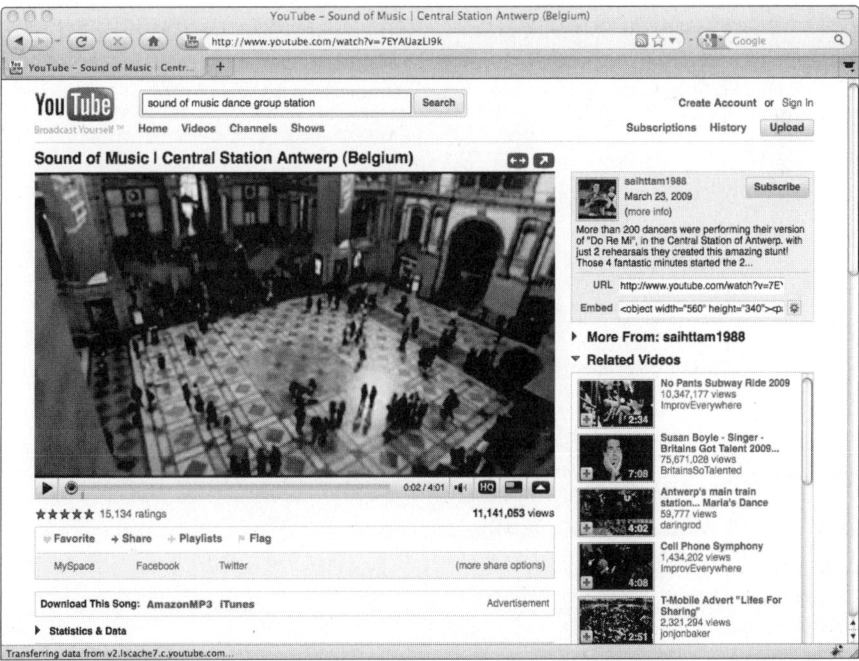

Figure 14-7: Individual video page on YouTube.

5. **Paste the code you copied from the YouTube embed text box into the Body box on your Drupal Create content form.**

   • You can put text above or below video if you wish. Type any text you want above or below the section of code you just pasted into the Create content form Body field.

   • Don't forget to give your posting a title by entering text in the Title field of the Create content form.

6. **Click on the Input format section to open it.**
7. **Select the Full HTML radio button.**

   This is what allows the code you pasted in the Body field to be interpreted correctly by the Drupal software. If you don't do this, Drupal will simply ignore the code and your video won't show up.

8. **Click Save.**

   Your video will now be published.

Using Apture to Link and Embed Content

Go to any major news or article based Web site today, and you'll probably see links on specific words in the articles. Clicking these links opens small boxes with lists of additional resources based on the highlighted words (see Figure 14-8).

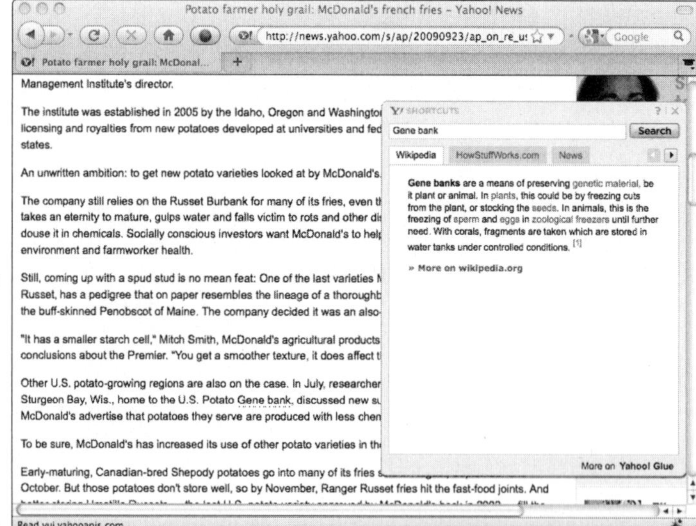

Figure 14-8: Yahoo.com article with keywords that open an information box.

Apture is an extremely robust module that allows you to link terms in your content to external sources. For example, say I write a blog entry about a restaurant in my neighborhood. I can use Apture to create a link on the restaurant's name. When the link is moused over, a box pops up containing the map to the restaurant.

I can also put news links, images, or embedded videos about my topic in the box. Apture also lets you easily embed third-party content in your pages.

Installing Apture

The Activity Stream module is available on the drupal.org Web site. To download this file, follow these steps:

1. **Browse to `http://drupal.org/project/apture`. Scroll down the page to find the download links.**
2. **Locate the link to download this module and click it. Save this file to a directory you will remember.**
3. **Log in to your control panel on your ISP's Web site or use an FTP client.**
4. **Find and click the link to a file manager.**
5. **You should see a single folder or directory named *html, www,* or *htdocs.* Click on its name to open it.**
6. **If you see the Drupal directory, click on it, and then the modules directory. If not, locate the modules directory and click on it.**
7. **Locate and click the upload link on your file manager.**
8. **Click Browse and find the Apture module `.tar.gz` file you downloaded. Click Upload.**
9. **Click on the Apture module `.tar.gz` to select the file.**
10. **You should see an option to uncompress the files. Leave the selection box set to uncompress "All" and click the Go button.**
11. **Select the original Apture module `.tar.gz` file on your Web server and delete it.**

Enabling the Apture module

To enable Apture, follow these steps:

1. **Browse to Administer⇨Site building⇨Modules.**

2. **Select the Enabled check box next to the Apture module, located in the *Other* section.**

3. **Click Save configuration.**

   Apture is now enabled.

Setting up Apture

Setting up Apture is a little tedious, but you only have to do it once. To set it up, follow these steps:

1. **Choose Create content and click on a content type.**

   I choose Blog. This opens the Apture First Time Setup form (see Figure 14-9).

   It doesn't matter which content type you pick; your Apture setup will apply to all of them.

2. **Enter your e-mail address, full name, and a password.**

3. **Type your password again to confirm.**

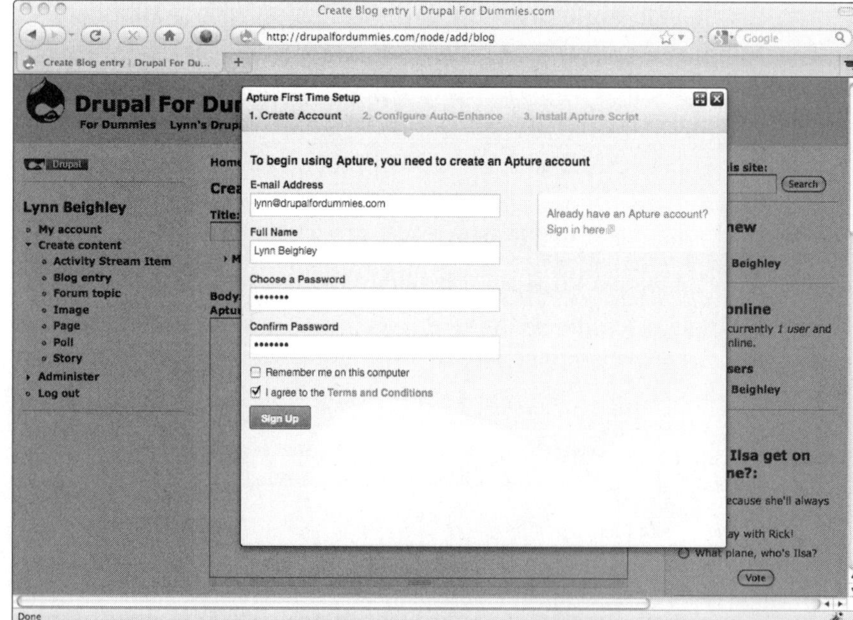

Figure 14-9: Create Account page of Apture First Time Setup form.

4. **Select the check box next to *I agree to the Terms and Conditions* and click Sign Up.**

   This opens the Configure Auto-Enhance screen. The settings here tell Apture to scour your site for existing links and modify them to open in Apture windows rather than new browsers.

5. **You can choose to let Apture modify specific types of existing links or turn off this option by unchecking the box next to *Auto enhance existing links with Apture.***

   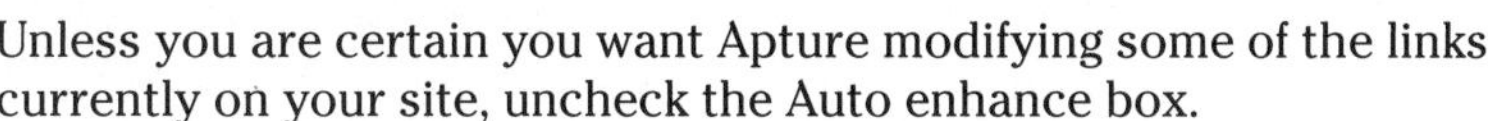

   Unless you are certain you want Apture modifying some of the links currently on your site, uncheck the Auto enhance box.

6. **On the Install Apture Script page, click** Install Token.
7. **Click** Start Using Apture.
8. **Check the e-mail for the account you entered in Step 2. Click the link in the e-mail to confirm.**

   Now Apture is ready to be used.

Creating Apture links

You now see the Apture toolbar above the Body field on all your Create content forms (see Figure 14-10).

There are only two functions in this toolbar:

- The *Add Apture Link* button on the left creates Apture links that open small windows with content from other sites.
- The *Add Apture Embed* button embeds third-party content that you choose into the content you are creating. Figure 14-11 shows a blog entry with an Apture link and an image embedded using the Apture tool.

To create an Apture link, follow these steps:

1. **Choose Create content and select the content type of your choice.**

   I choose Blog.

2. **Enter a title. Type some content in the Body field. Include some terms you want to turn into links.**
3. **Hold down the mouse button and highlight the word or words you want to make into a link.**

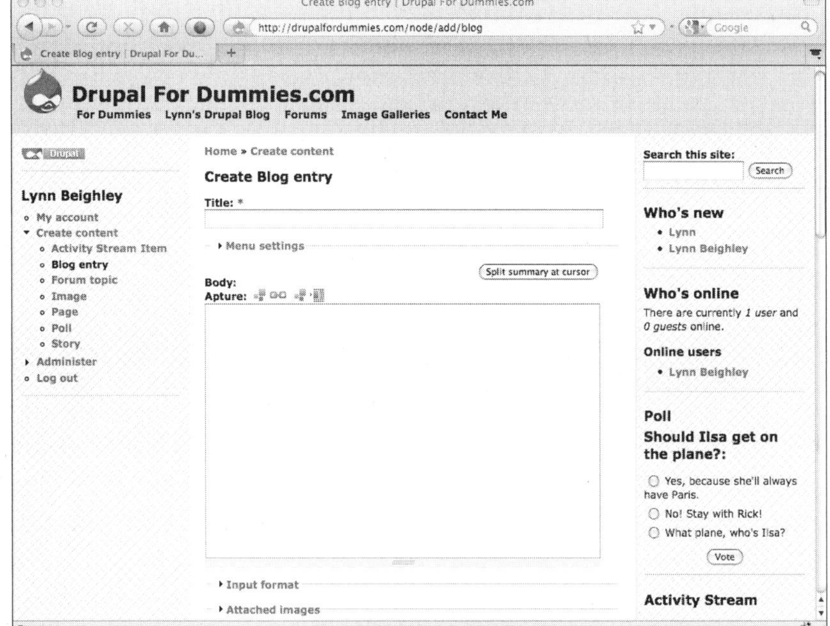

Figure 14-10: The Apture toolbar appears above the Body field on a Create content form.

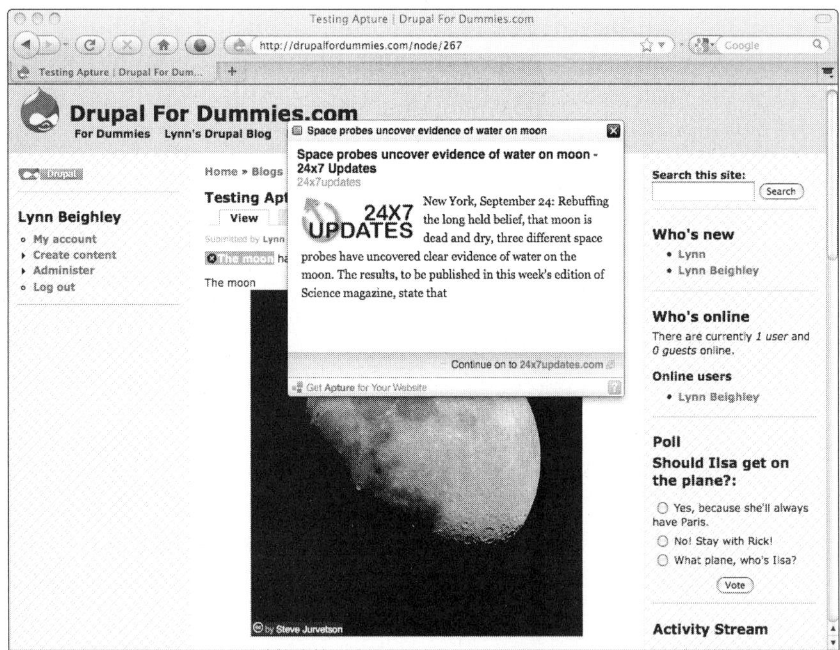

Figure 14-11: Apture link and Apture embedded image content in a blog entry.

4. **Click the left button in the Apture toolbar, the Add Apture Link button.**

   This opens the Add Apture Link window (see Figure 14-12).

   This is where you select the content you want to appear when users mouse over your link.

5. **Click the type of content you want to pop up for your link from the options along the top of this box.**

   In my example, I'm looking for news articles about the moon. I click on the arrow to the right of Document to see more options and find the News Article icon.

6. **Click the blue Go button to the right of your link term.**

   This opens a list of related content.

7. **Scroll down and find the best match for your term. Click it.**

8. **You can include a thumbnail image by checking the Show Image Thumbnail box and clicking the arrows to the right to find the best image for your article.**

9. **If you want to add additional items, click Add Related Items. This takes you to the list of content again.**

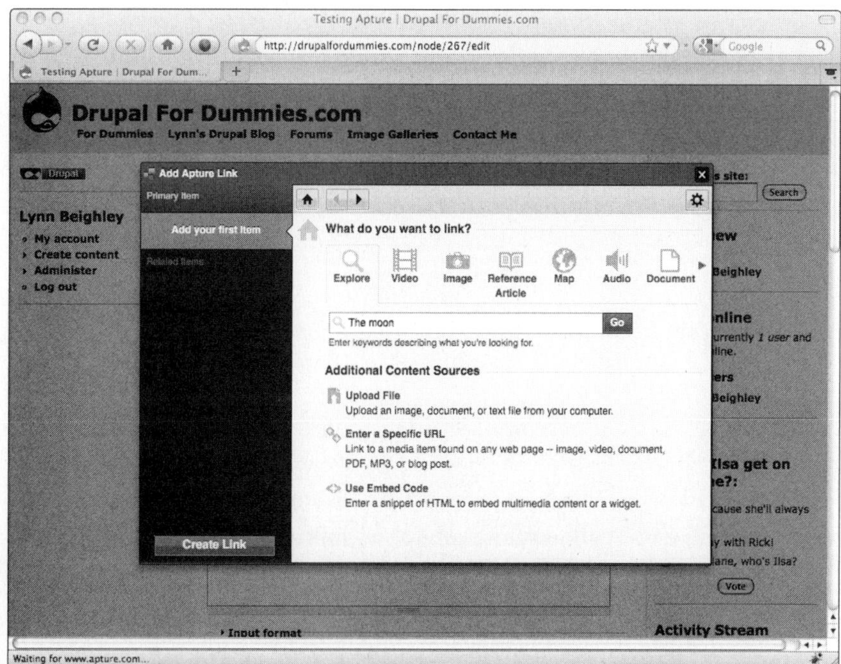

Figure 14-12: Add Apture Link.

10. **When you are finished, click Create Link.**

    This returns you to the Create content form (see Figure 14-13).

    Apture adds HTML code to your content. It can be daunting to look at, but when you publish your content, the HTML code turns into links and embedded content.

11. **Click Input format at select Full HTML.**

    If you don't do this, Drupal won't correctly render the HTML code Apture added.

12. **Click Save.**

Because the code Apture adds can be dense and confusing, add your Apture links at the very end after you've created all your text.

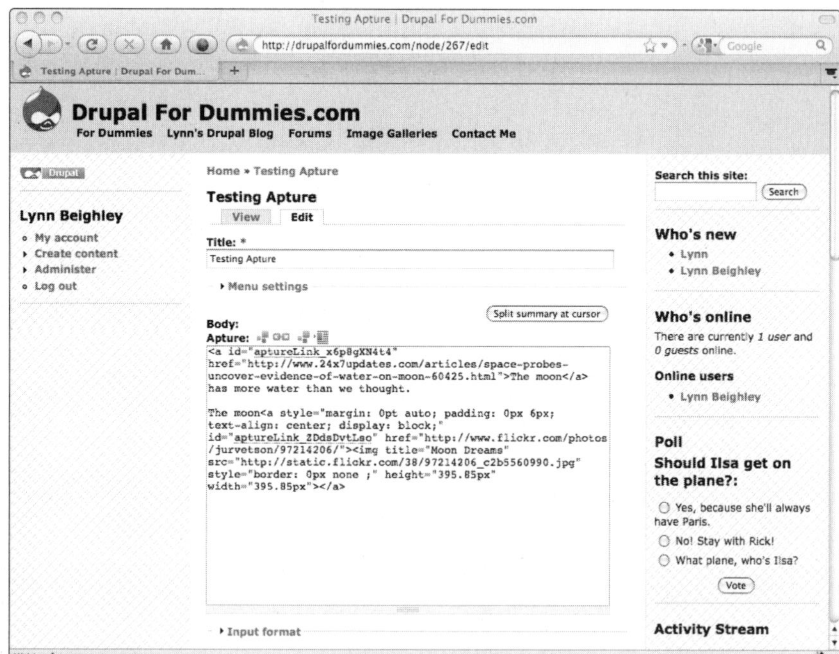

Figure 14-13: Blog entry with Apture link and Apture embed code.

Figure 14-11 shows both an Apture link and a photo of the moon, which is embedded content created by Apture. To create your own embedded content, follow these steps:

1. **In a Create content form, place your cursor in the Body field where you want the content to appear.**
2. **Click the Add Apture Embed button.**

3. **Select the type of content you want to embed from the icons at the top of the window.**
4. **Type a search term for the type of content you are seeking in the search box and click Go.**

   You can add an embedded map to your content by typing an address in the search box and choosing Map from the content types.
5. **Click Create Embed to finish.**

Make sure you change the Input type of your content to Full HTML before you preview or publish it.

You can set the Input type to automatically default to Full HTML by choosing Administer ➪ Site configuration ➪ Input formats. Select Full HTML and click Set default format. Keep in mind that this allows registered users to also use all HTML tags in their content.

By default, anyone who can create content on your site can use the Apture toolbar. There are no permissions settings to prevent site users from creating Apture links and embeds. Your only recourse is to not allow them to use Full HTML. This will cause Apture links to not be interpreted by Drupal on content they create.

Sharing Content with RSS

RSS, or *Really Simple Syndication,* is a specific format for content that can be read by Web applications written for that purpose. Sites with frequently updating content, like news, often provide versions of their content in an RSS format.

If your browser understands how to interpret RSS formatted content, and most modern browsers do, you can preview RSS feeds by browsing to them. These feeds use Web addresses, so you can paste them into your browser to preview them. For example, you can see a feed by browsing to `http://drupal.org/node/feed`. This is a dynamic list of items from drupal.org.

Just as you added your tweets, FaceBook status, and YouTube videos earlier, you can add a set of feeds to your Web site. But you have to find good ones first.

Finding feeds can be tricky. Most major Web sites with content that frequently changes provide feeds. Lots of blog sites have feeds as well. If you want a feed from a specific site, hunting around and looking for a link to a feed is your best bet. The easiest way I know to find feeds is to use Google Reader to get the address of feeds of interest to you.

Finding feeds with Google Reader

You can find feeds about particular topics by using a feature of Google Reader. Follow these steps:

You need to have a Google account to be able to use Google Reader and find feeds with it.

1. **Log in to Google and browse to `http://www.google.com/reader`.**
2. **Click on *Add a subscription* on the upper left.**

   This opens a small search box.
3. **Type a search term and click Add.**

   I search for the word *dogs.* A list of feeds appears on the right (see Figure 14-14).

   Each item in the list has the URL of the feed printed in green beneath the description.
4. **Copy a feed you want to use and paste it in the address bar of a browser window to preview the content.**

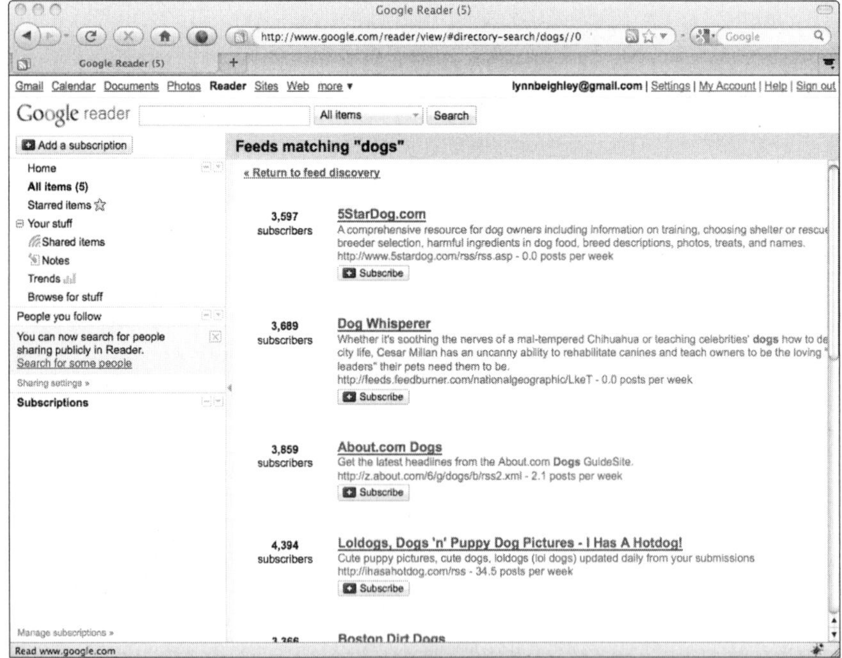

Figure 14-14: Google Reader list of feeds about dogs.

This is a roundabout way to find feeds, but it works fairly well. You can use the Add a subscription button again and again, refining your search terms, until you find feeds on the subjects you want.

Using the Aggregator Module

You can use your feeds with the Activity Stream module by pasting them, one per line, in the Feed URL box (refer to Figure 14-3). But if you're already using that to publish content from your social media sites, you may want the content from the feeds to go somewhere else on your site.

A simpler solution is to use the included Core module, Feed Aggregator. To enable and use the Aggregator module, follow these steps:

1. **Choose Administer➪Site building➪Modules.**
2. **Click the Enabled module next to the Aggregator module under the Core section. Click Save configuration.**

   The Aggregator is now active and a new link to Feed Aggregator appears in the Navigation menu. This will be where all your feed content appears.
3. **To add a feed, choose Administer➪Content management➪Feed aggregator.**
4. **Click the Add feed tab.**

   This opens the Add feed form (see Figure 14-15).
5. **Give your feed a title.**

   For example, I use a feed from the drupal.org site and call this Drupal.org.
6. **Paste or type the URL of the feed in the URL field. Click Save.**

Your feed will update every 15 minutes. To get the feed to appear immediately, run cron by choosing Administer➪Reports➪Status report. Choose *run cron manually* next to Cron maintenance tasks on the right.

You can view your new feed by choosing the Feed aggregator link in the Navigation menu.

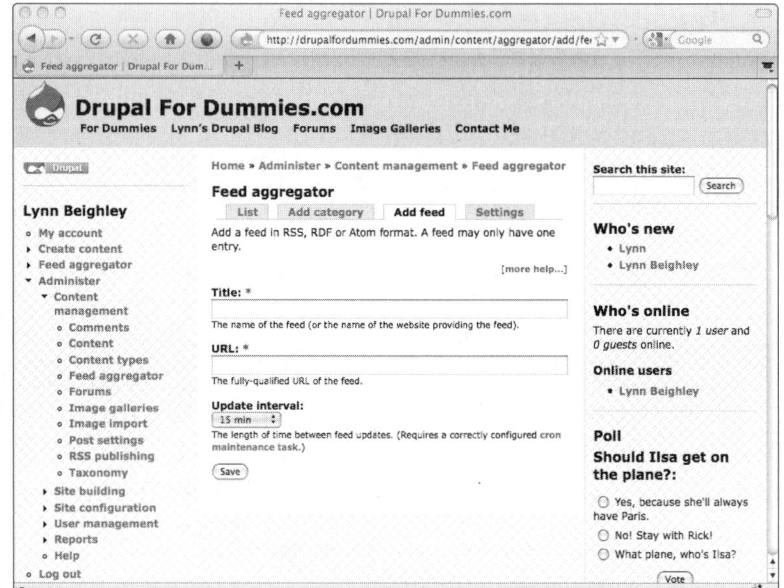

Figure 14-15: The Feed aggregator Add feed form.

To move the Feed aggregator from the Navigation menu, and to give it a different Link title, follow these steps:

1. **Choose Administer⇨Site building⇨Menus.**
2. **Click Navigation.**
3. **Locate Feed aggregator in the list and click edit.**
4. **If you wish, change the Link title.**

   Mine will be used to aggregate feeds about Drupal, so I change my title to Drupal News.
5. **Change the menu by clicking on the Parent item drop-down and choosing a different menu.**

   I select `<Primary links>`.
6. **Click Save.**

   The Drupal News link is now the last link in my Primary menu. I want it to come before my Contact Me link. I'm already on the right page to do it, the List items under the Primary menu.
7. **To move the position of the link, click and drag it to the new position.**
8. **Click Save configuration.**

Creating a feed for your site

Not only can you pull in RSS feed content from other sites, but you also can create your own RSS feed for other sites to pull content from you. Behind the scenes, Drupal has already created a feed; you simply need to give your site visitors a link to it. Follow these steps:

1. **Choose Administer⇨Site building⇨Blocks.**
2. **Find Syndicate in the list under the Disabled section. Move it to the location you wish.**

   I drag mine to the bottom of the Left sidebar.
3. **Click Save blocks.**

   You now have a Syndicate block on your site, with a small logo (see Figure 14-16).

   This logo is used all over the Web to represent RSS feeds. You can click on it on a site with a feed you want to use, copy the URL from the address bar of the page that opens, and use it with Feed aggregator.

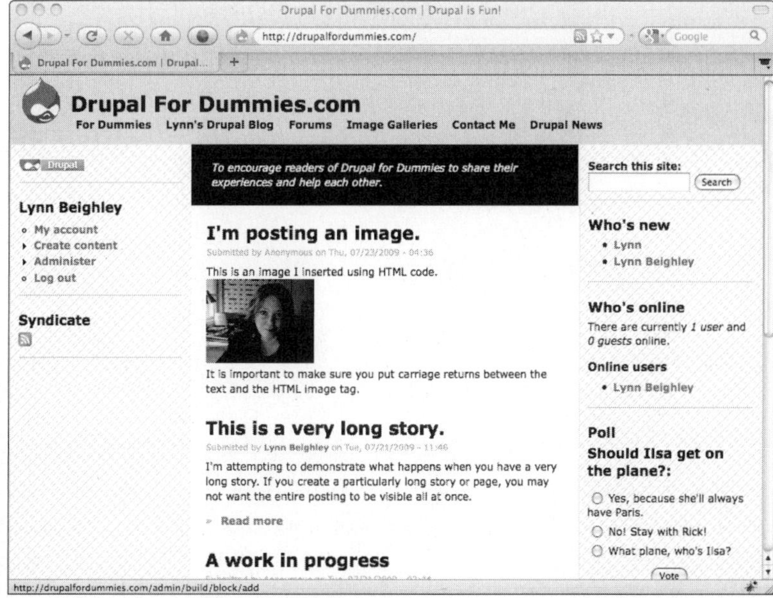

Figure 14-16: The Syndicate block and RSS feed logo in the Left sidebar.

4. **You can remove or change the title of the Syndicate block by clicking the configure link next to it on the Blocks page.**

5. **Type a new title, or if you don't want a title, type** `<none>`**. Click Save block.**

   Clicking on this logo opens your feed page. In my case, it is `http://drupalfordummies.com/rss.xml`.

Chapter 15

Building a Storefront

In This Chapter

- Creating product listings
- Organizing products into catalogs
- Accepting online payments
- Keeping track of orders

If you need to sell products online, the Ubercart module is an easy-to-use, robust option. You can have your items online in minutes, complete with a shopping cart and an online order form that collects the necessary customer information. Additional modules allow you to add more robust product listings, automatically figure sales tax, and of course, accept credit cards.

In this chapter, I discuss the parts of an online storefront. You learn about Ubercart and how to install it. Then I show you how to build and customize your own storefront, fetch order information, enhance your product listings, and finally how to accept payments.

Understanding Storefronts

At their most basic, storefronts are made up of products for sale, a shopping cart, and some form for a customer to provide information and purchase items in his cart:

- **Product listings:** An individual page with product information and a button for the shopper to click to add an item to his cart.
- **Shopping cart:** A form that displays all the products a user has clicked on to purchase.
- **Order form:** A form the shopper fills out to finish making his order. It collects information and saves it for processing.

Figure 15-1 shows a basic storefront with product listings.

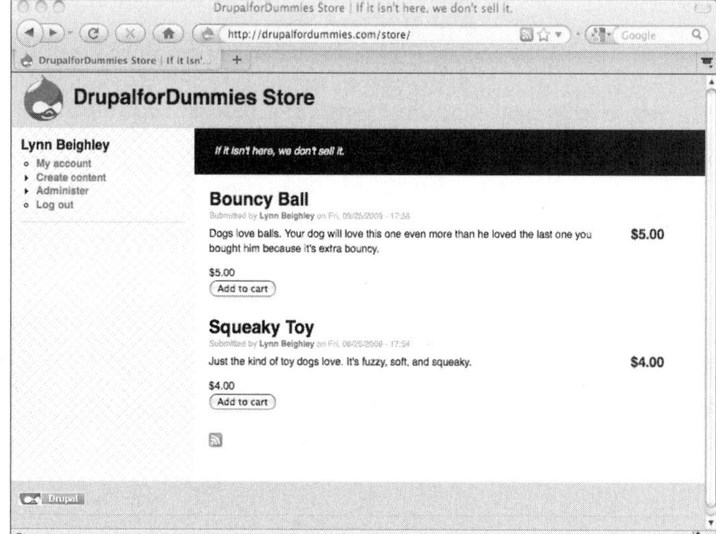

Figure 15-1: Basic Drupal product listings.

Storefronts can have lots of other features. Take a look at the Amazon.com Web site (see Figure 15-2).

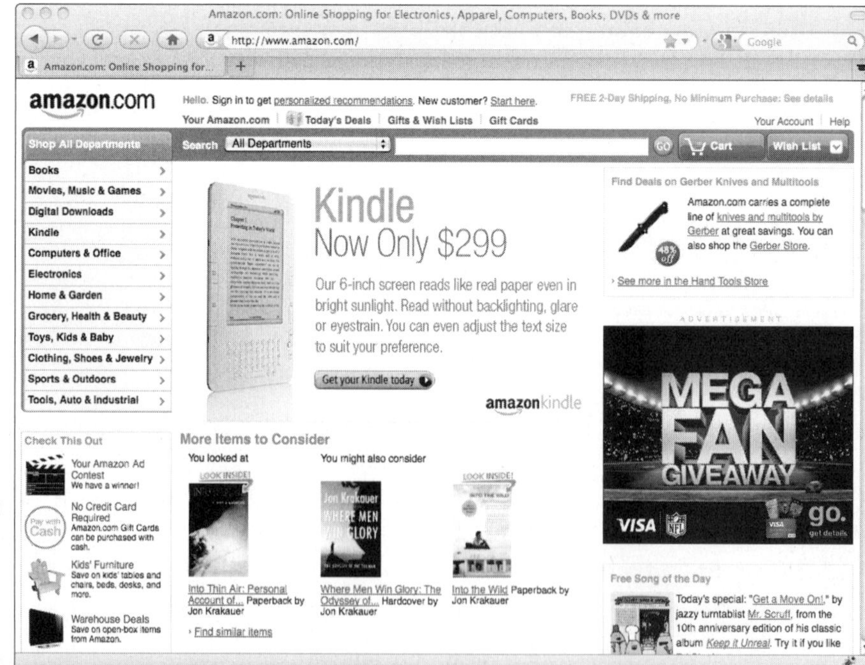

Figure 15-2: Amazon.com storefront.

Amazon.com includes these additional e-commerce features:

- **User accounts:** To buy something from Amazon, you can set up an account. Amazon saves your shipping information and you don't need to provide it each time you buy something.
- **Order tracking:** Along with having an account, you can log in to view the status of orders you have placed.
- **Wish lists:** If you want to hang on to an item listing so you can find it again later but not purchase it right away, you can save it in a wish list.
- **Product catalogs:** This is a collection of product listings grouped into categories.

The Ubercart module allows you to easily implement all these functionalities, with the exception of wish lists.

Getting Started with Ubercart

Ubercart is a single download composed of a number of modules. Ubercart also depends on several other modules that need to be downloaded and installed. In this section, I go through the steps to download and install Ubercart and the other modules it requires.

Ubercart works best when users can register for your site automatically. Also, you can choose to post a link to a shopping cart for your users in a block on your site. For these reasons, you may wish to devote an entire Drupal site to being a store rather than adding Ubercart to your existing site. In my case, I created a new Drupal installation at `http://drupalfordummies.com/store`. I then created a link on the main site to the store, and vice versa, making the Primary navigation match both sites. I also used the same theme on both.

Getting Ubercart and additional modules

You can install just the minimum necessary modules, or the complete system.

I recommend you download and install all the modules for the full system. Even if you don't want to use all the features, you can have them available for future enhancements.

If you want a minimal install, you need just the module Ubercart and Token modules (see below for download locations). For the full install, navigate and download each of the following `.tar.gz` files:

- **Ubercart:** `http://drupal.org/project/ubercart`
- **Token:** `http://drupal.org/project/token`
- **CCK:** `http://drupal.org/project/cck`
- **FileField:** `http://drupal.org/project/filefield`
- **ImageAPI:** `http://drupal.org/project/imageapi`
- **ImageCache:** `http://drupal.org/project/imagecache`
- **ImageField:** `http://drupal.org/project/imagefield`
- **Thickbox:** `http://drupal.org/project/thickbox`
- **Google Analytics:** `http://drupal.org/project/google_analytics`

Save all these files in the same directory so you can easily locate them later.

Installing Ubercart and additional modules

You need to install the modules you have downloaded. For each module, complete the following steps:

1. **Browse to the module x page (listed in the preceding section). Scroll down the page to find the download links.**
2. **Locate the link to download this module and click on it. Save this file to a directory you will remember.**

   This module will download as a single compressed `.tar.gz` file.
3. **Log in to your control panel on your ISP's Web site or use an FTP client.**
4. **Find and click the link to a file manager.**

   After you click on the file manager, you will see a screen that displays the files on your Web server.
5. **You should see a single folder or directory named "html," "www," or "htdocs." Click on its name to open it.**

   There may be several directories, but the one for your Web site should be easy to spot.
6. **If you see the Drupal directory, click on it, and then the modules directory. If not, locate the modules directory and click on it.**

7. **Locate and click on the upload link on your file manager.**

   You should see an upload form with a Browse button.

8. **Click Browse and find the module `.tar.gz` file you downloaded. Click Upload.**

   The compressed module file is now on your site in the correct folder and ready to be extracted.

9. **Click on the module `.tar.gz` to select the file.**

   You see a list of files that are stored inside your compressed file, all selected.

10. **You should see an option to uncompress the files. Leave the selection box set to uncompress "All" and click the Go button.**

11. **Select the original module `.tar.gz` file on your Web server and delete it.**

Your new modules will now appear on the Modules administration page on your site.

Enabling the basic Ubercart installation

In this section, I walk you through enabling the appropriate modules to create a basic storefront Web site.

Don't enable all the new modules at once. There's a specific order that Ubercart recommends.

To enable a basic storefront, follow these steps:

1. **Choose Administer➪Site building➪Modules.**
2. **Under the Core section, select the box next to the Path module.**
3. **Under the Other section, select the box next to Token.**
4. **Under the Ubercart – core section, select the box next to all modules: Cart, Conditional Actions, Order, Product, and Store.**
5. **Click Save configuration.**

Your site has now been configured to allow you to create product listings and take orders.

Creating Your First Storefront

You are now ready to add product listings to your site and test the ordering process.

Creating product listings

With Ubercart, product listings are a type of content. To create your first product, follow these steps:

1. **Choose Create content⇨Product.**

   This opens the form shown in Figure 15-3.

2. **Enter a name for your product in the Name field.**

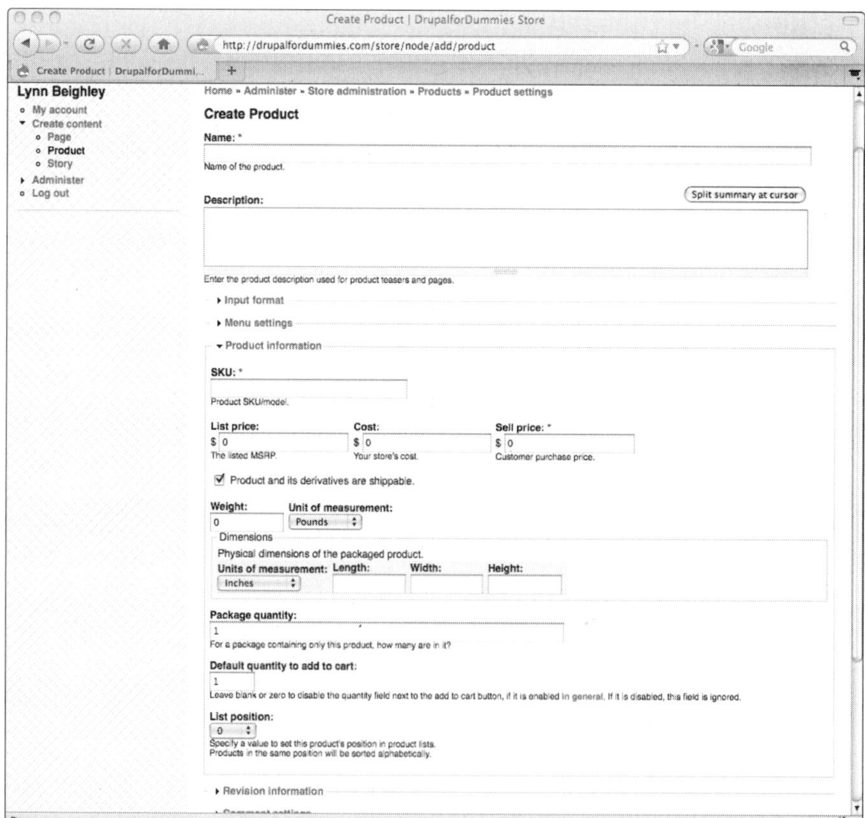

Figure 15-3: The Create Product form.

3. **Enter a description of your product in the Description field.**
4. **In the Product section, enter an SKU number or unique description for your product.**

SKU stands for stockkeeping unit. It is a unique number or combination of numbers and letters that represents a particular product. The SKU allows a product be tracked for inventory. An SKU is associated with a particular item in a store or catalog. For example, a dog toy of a particular style and size might have an SKU of 1234-M, meaning Style 1234, size medium.

5. **In the List price field, you can optionally enter the manufacturer's suggested list price.**
6. **In the Cost field, you can optionally enter the cost you paid for the item.**
7. **In the Sell price field, enter the cost of the item for shoppers to purchase it.**
8. **If you need to know the weight of an item to figure shipping costs, enter the weight of the item in the Weight field. You can modify the value in the Unit of measurement drop-down as needed.**
9. **Enter the dimensions of the item in the Length, Width, and Height fields. Change the Unit of measurement drop-down as needed.**
10. **If this is a product that comes in multiples, enter the number in one order here.**

    For example, if you were selling a 6-pack of soda, you enter 6 here.
11. **If necessary, change the Default quantity to add to cart.**

    In general, this will always be 1.
12. **Change the List position to control how high or low this item will show up in a list of items.**
13. **The rest of the options are the same as used in any content item. Change them if you wish.**
14. **Click Save.**

Your first product has been created. By default, it is posted on the main page of your site. Repeat this process to add more products. Figure 15-1 shows a listing of two products added to a storefront.

If you don't want your products to appear on the main page of your site by default, modify the Publishing options setting to uncheck *Promoted to the front page.*

Clicking on the name of a product opens the product information page (see Figure 15-4).

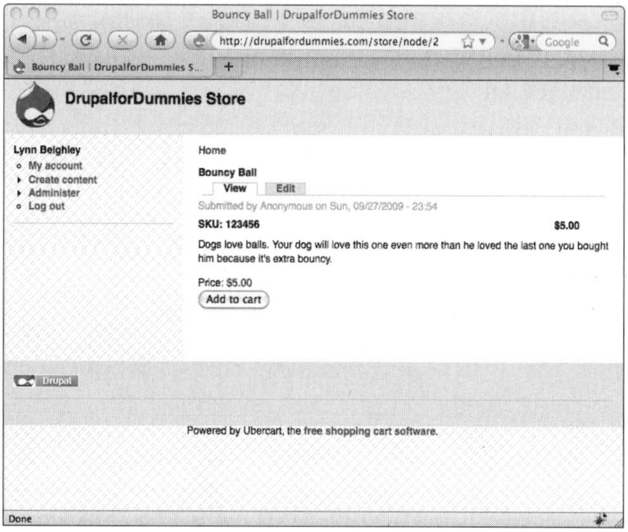

Figure 15-4: Individual product listing.

Testing the ordering process

To see how your storefront works, you should test it. At this point, you have no payment mechanism tied into your store. When someone adds products to her cart and checks out, she is presented with a form to gather information. When she finishes, she is sent a confirmation e-mail, you are sent an e-mail notifying you of the order, and the order information is saved on an administration page on your Drupal site. To test it for yourself, follow these steps:

1. **Log out as Administrator by clicking the Log out link.**

   You should now see any products you added on the main page of your site.

2. **Click on the Add to cart button for one of the products.**

   This opens the Shopping cart form (see Figure 15-5).

   The shopping cart lists all the items a shopper has added and the total cost. This form also allows him to update or remove items.

3. **Click Checkout.**

   This opens the Checkout form (see Figure 15-6).

4. **Fill in a valid e-mail address in the E-mail address field.**

   This is where the order confirmation will be sent after a shopper completes this form.

5. **Fill out the required information First name, Last name, Street address, City, Country, State/Province, and Postal code under the Delivery information section.**

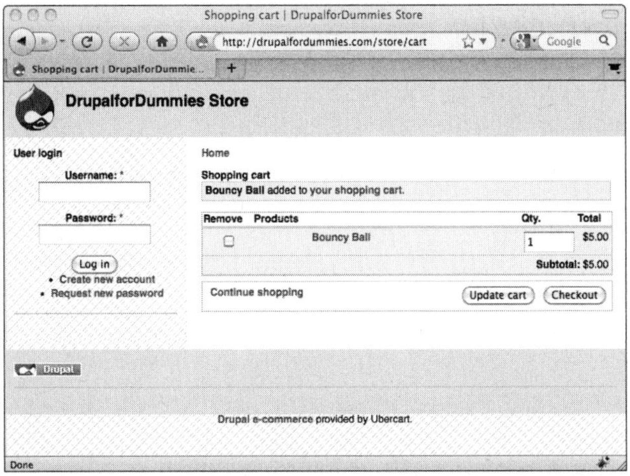

Figure 15-5: The Shopping cart with a product added to it.

6. **Select the box next to *My billing information is the same as my delivery information.***

   This handy box automatically pulls the information from the Delivery information and enters it into the Billing information fields.

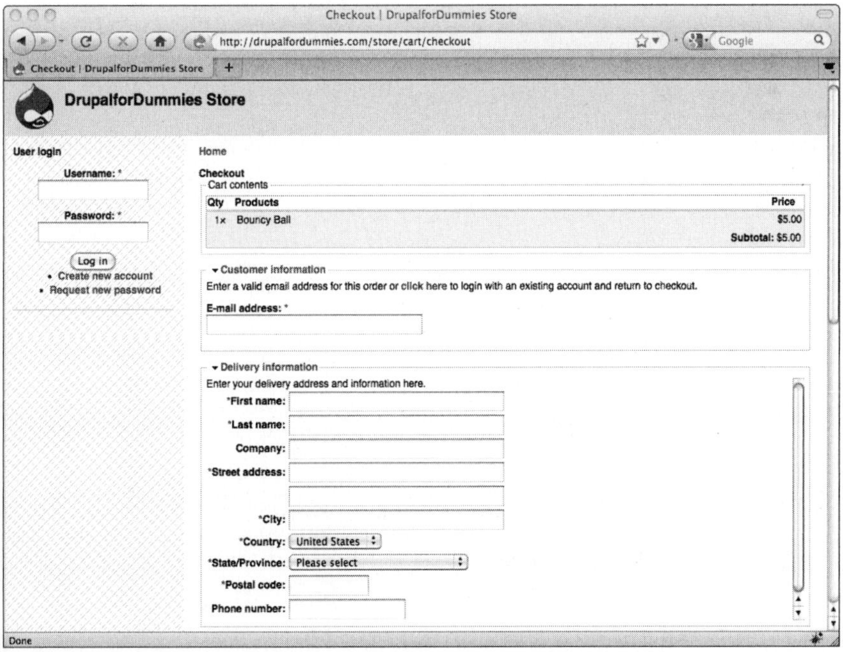

Figure 15-6: The top part of the Checkout form.

7. **Click Review order.**

   This opens a confirmation page with the information the shopper has entered. At this point, shoppers can click Back to change their order, or Submit order to finalize it (see Figure 15-7).

8. **Click Submit order.**

   An Order complete message appears.

If the user had no account on your site, a new one is automatically created for him.

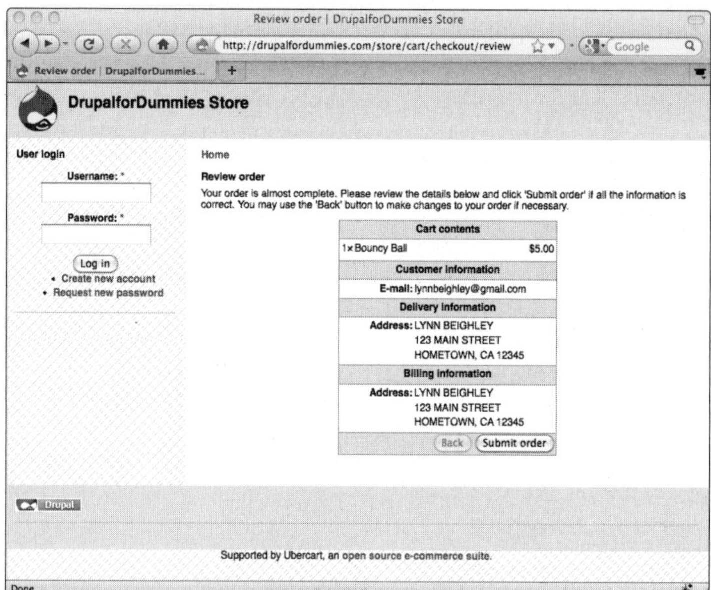

Figure 15-7: Review order page.

Managing orders

An e-mail is automatically sent to you when a new order is made. You can see all the orders made on your site. To review orders, follow these steps:

1. **Choose Administer⇨Store administration⇨Orders.**

   This opens a list of orders that have been placed on your site (see Figure 15-8).

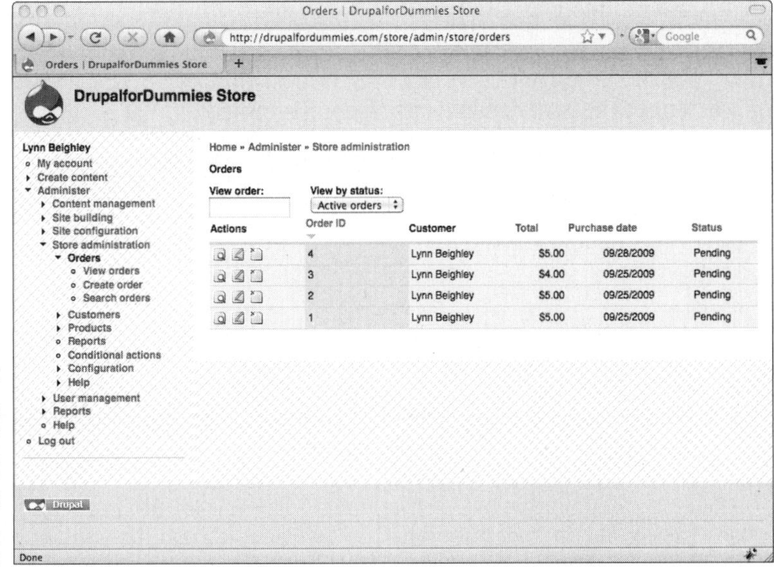

Figure 15-8: List of orders and current statuses.

2. **Click on the View order icon next to one of the orders.**

   Each order has icons on the left of the order id:

   - *View* allows you to see the order details.
   - *Edit* allows you to make changes to the order and send an invoice to the customer.
   - *Delete* deletes the order.

   Each order has a status that indicates whether the order has been fulfilled. As you get more orders, you may need to filter them by status. For example, if you only want to see Completed orders, change the View by status drop-down box to Completed.

3. **You can change the Order status for an individual order at the bottom of the order View screen.**

   Currently, the status is Pending. As you go through each stage of handling an order, you can change the status to Processing, Completed, Canceled, or In checkout.

In addition to changing the status of an order, you can modify an existing order. Follow these steps:

1. **Click the Edit button next to the order you wish to change.**
2. **Make sure the Edit tab is clicked.**

3. **Make any desired changes on this form.**

   You can modify any information the shopper entered; add, edit, or delete the products that were ordered; and add private Admin contents about the order that the shopper never sees.

4. **When you are finished, choose Submit changes.**

You can use the Orders section of your site to send out invoices by e-mail or create a printable invoice that can be mailed to your customer. Follow these steps:

1. **Click the Edit button next to the order you wish to change.**
2. **Click the Invoice tab.**
3. **You can view, print, or e-mail an invoice by choosing the appropriate link at the top of the Invoice page.**

As you make changes to the customer's order, such as changing the status or e-mailing an invoice, Ubercart keeps track of them for you automatically. Click the Edit button next to an order, and then click on the Log tab to see activities related to that order.

At this point, you aren't set up to take credit cards. Before you can accept credit cards, you need to

- Make sure your site is hosted on a secure server, which protects the credit card information you users enter on an order form.
- Activate additional modules.
- Sign up for an account with a company that can process your credit card orders for you.

Configuring Your Storefront

While Ubercart is practically ready to work after you add products, there are a number of customizations you can make to your site.

Adding a shopping cart block

Most major storefronts give shoppers a link to their shopping carts. This way, they can easily check what they've already purchased. To add a link to the shopping cart on your site, follow these steps:

1. **Choose Administer⇨Site building⇨Blocks.**

2. **Locate the Shopping cart block under the Disabled section.**
3. **Drag this block to the location you want it to appear.**

   I move mine to the top of the Right sidebar.
4. **Click Save blocks.**

   Not only is the Ubercart Shopping cart block a link to the cart, but it also keeps a running total of the cost of items added to it.

Using the Configuration settings

There are more than 100 configuration options under the Administer⇨Store administration⇨Configuration menus. In this section, I highlight some of the most important ones to know.

Cart settings

The *Cart settings* control how the shopping cart behaves. To modify them, choose Administer⇨Store administration⇨Configuration⇨Cart settings under the Edit tab. Here are the ones you are most likely to change:

- **Minimum order subtotal:** Use this to set a minimum order amount a shopper must meet before the order can be submitted.
- **Anonymous cart duration:** If a shopper adds items to his shopping cart, but isn't signed in on your site, this duration controls how long the items in his cart will remain. If he browses to a different site but returns within four hours, his items will still be in the cart.
- **Authenticated cart duration:** If a shopper adds items to his shopping cart, and is logged in, items in his cart will remain for a year. Each time he logs in, he can click on the shopping cart link and see them.

Checkout settings

The *Checkout settings* control the checkout process. To modify them, choose Administer⇨Store administration⇨Configuration⇨Checkout settings under the Edit tab.

- **Enable checkout:** Located on the Checkout settings screen. If you eventually use a third-party vendor to manage the transaction, you need to deselect this option.
- **Checkout instructions, review, and completion messages:** Under Checkout messages, you can customize the text of a number of different messages the shopper sees during the checkout process.
- **Address fields:** You can modify the Title of any of the fields in the address section of the checkout form. You can also specify whether they're required.

Country settings

The *Country settings* allow you to set up the checkout form for other countries. To modify them, choose Administer➪Store administration➪Configuration➪Country settings under the Edit tab. You can import countries into your list.

When a shopper reaches the Contact form, he chooses a country from a drop-down box. The Country settings control which countries appear in that box. Also, after he changes the country, the values in the State/Province drop-down list change accordingly.

Order settings

The *Order settings* control what happens to the order after the checkout is completed. To modify them, choose Administer➪Store administration➪Configuration➪Order settings under the Edit tab.

- **Number of orders on overview screen:** Controls the number of orders you see when you choose Administer➪Store administration➪Orders.
- **Order statuses:** Under Order workflow, you can customize the text of the order statuses. You can also add custom ones.

Product settings

The *Product settings* control the appearance of the information on product listings pages. To modify these settings, choose Administer➪Store administration➪Configuration➪Product settings under the Edit tab.

- **Display an optional quantity field in the *Add to Cart* form:** This places a quantity field on the product listing pages. I recommend checking this box.
- **Product fields:** You control which fields show up on the product listing pages. If the products you sell should display their dimensions or weight, here's the place to add them. Select the appropriate check box and choose Save configuration.

Store settings

The *Store settings* control many of the overall store settings. To modify these settings, choose Administer➪Store administration➪Configuration➪Store settings (see Figure 15-9).

- **Contact settings:** There are a number of fields you should enter data into on this form. If possible, provide contact info for your store here.
- **Footer message for store pages:** Under Display settings. You can remove the Ubercart messages, although if you don't have to, it's nice to leave them at the bottom of your site.

- **Format settings:** This form allows you to change the default currency. You can also change the units of measurement for weight and length, and the date format.

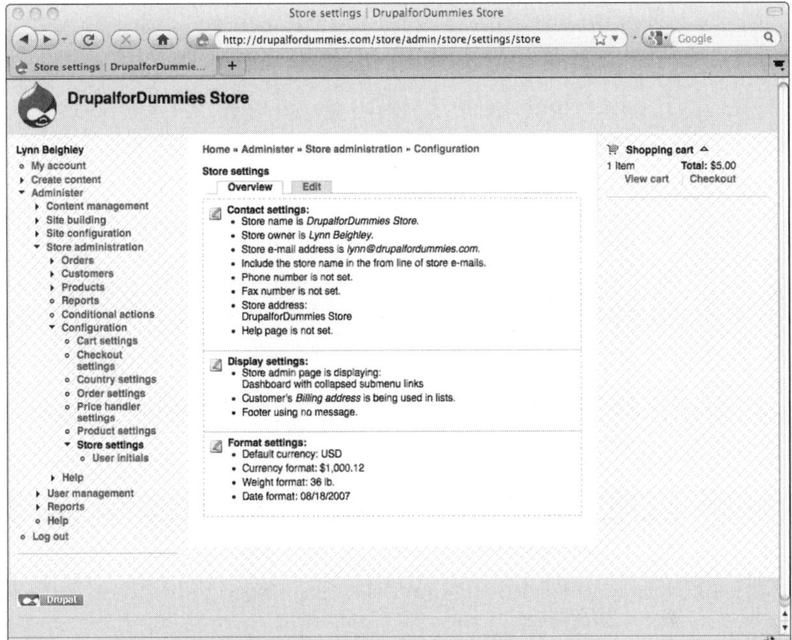

Figure 15-9: Store settings Overview page.

Enhancing Product Listings

The basic product listing from Ubercart doesn't include a field for photos. The product listings also aren't organized into catalogs. These are important features that will make your site more professional, and they are worth spending a few minutes to add.

Using images

To add images to your product listings, you need to enable some modules, and create an image field as part of the Product content type. Then you can freely upload images when you are creating products. Follow these steps:

1. **Choose Administer➪Site building➪Modules.**

2. **Under the CCK section, select the boxes next to Content, FileField, and ImageField.**

   If you don't see this section, you may need to download and install the CCK module. See the instructions in the first part of this chapter.

3. **Click Save configuration.**

   Now you are ready to create an image field for the Product content type.

4. **Choose Administer➪Content management➪Content types.**
5. **On the List tab, click the edit link for Product.**
6. **Click on the Manage fields tab.**

   This opens the Manage fields form shown in Figure 15-10.

7. **In the New field section at the bottom of the form, type the word *Photo* for the Label, and *photo* for the Field name.**
8. **For *Type of data to store,* select File from the drop-down box.**
9. **For *Form element to edit the data,* select Image from the drop-down box.**
10. **Click Save.**
11. **To add an image to a product, create a new product by either choosing Create content➪Product or clicking on the Edit tab of an existing product listing.**
12. **Scroll down the page and find the Photo field. Click Browse to find your image and Upload to save it.**

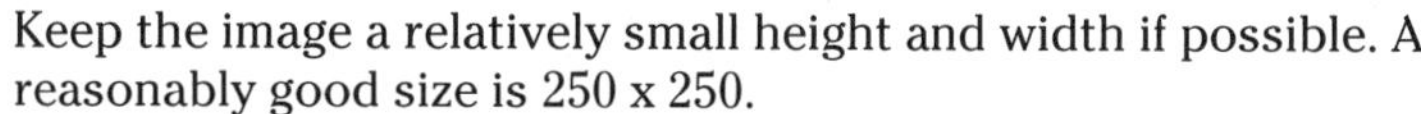

   Keep the image a relatively small height and width if possible. A reasonably good size is 250 x 250.

13. **Click Save.**

Adding a catalog

To add catalog pages and organize your products by type, follow these steps:

1. **Choose Administer➪Site building➪Modules.**
2. **Under the Ubercart – optional section, select the box next to the Catalog.**
3. **Click Save configuration.**

   Now you are ready to create an image field for the Product content type.

4. **Choose Administer➪Content management➪Taxonomy.**
5. **Click on *add terms* next to Catalog.**

   This opens the Add term form (see Figure 15-11).

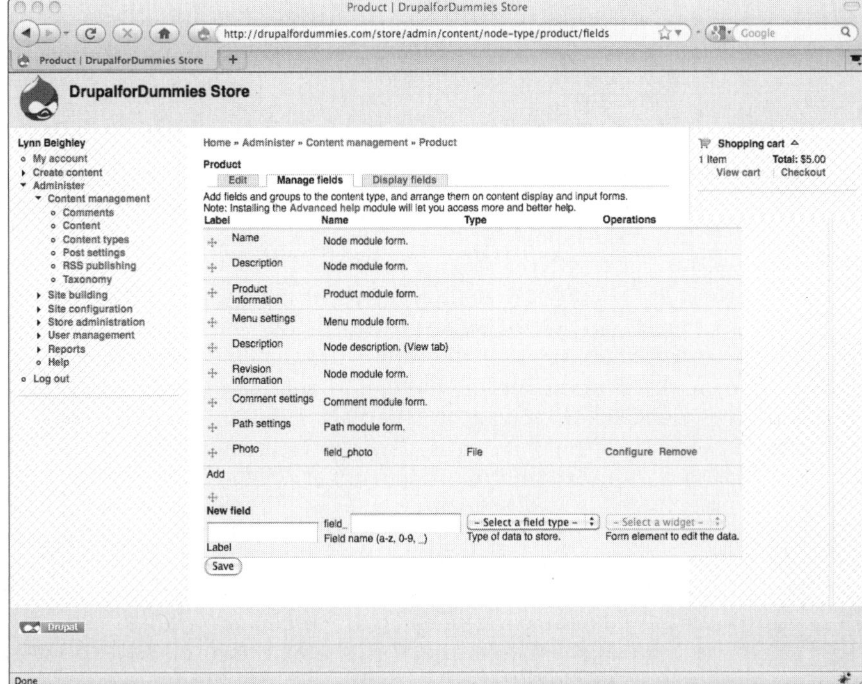

Figure 15-10: Manage fields form for Product content type.

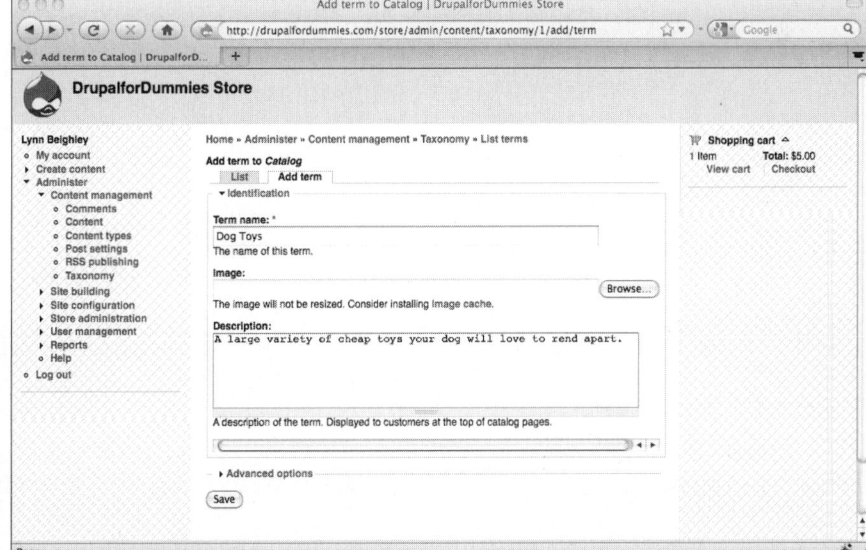

Figure 15-11: The Add term form is used to create categories for your catalog.

6. **Enter a product category in the Term name field.**

   For example, if you had an online pet store, you might use Dog Toys or Cat Food for a Term name.

7. **Add a small image and description if you wish.**
8. **Click Save.**
9. **Repeat Steps 6 through 8 until you have created all the categories you need.**

Now you are ready to add products to your catalog. You will now see a box on your Content Product forms with all of the product categories you just created. Simply choose the appropriate one for the product you are adding. You can also put a product into more than one category by pressing the Ctrl key while selecting categories.

To see your catalog, browse to /catalog on your site. For example, `http://`*`yourdrupalsitehere`*`.com/catalog`. Mine is shown in Figure 15-12.

You can add a description to your catalog. Choose Administer➪Content management➪Taxonomy. Click on *edit vocabulary* next to Catalog. Enter a description in the Description field. You can also change the name of your catalog by changing the Vocabulary name on this form. For example, you might want to call it Our Products.

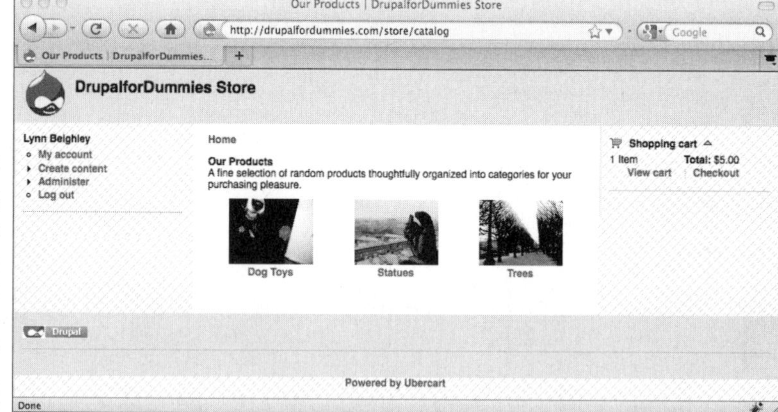

Figure 15-12: A simple catalog page with a description and three categories.

You can create a Primary navigation link so shoppers can find your product catalog. Follow these steps:

1. **If you haven't done so, move your Primary links to a block on your site by choosing Administer➪Site building➪Blocks.**

2. **Move your Primary links to the block of your choice.**

   I choose the Header block.

3. **Click Save blocks.**
4. **Choose Administer⇨Site building⇨Menu.**
5. **Click on Primary links.**
6. **Click on the Add item tab.**
7. **For Path, enter catalog. For Menu link title, enter Catalog.**
8. **Click Save.**

Getting Paid

You have a number of options for third-party merchant services you can use to handle the credit card transactions on your site. In this section, I discuss activating the modules that allow interaction with these sites and let you accept payment. I focus on Google Checkout specifically, but other companies operate in a similar fashion.

Setting up a Google Checkout account

Before adding the modules to accept payment, you should create an account with the service you intend to use. Some of your options are:

- **2Checkout:** `http://2checkout.com`
- **Authorize.net:** `http://authorize.net`
- **PayPal:** `http://paypal.com`
- **Google Checkout:** `http://checkout.google.com/sell`

All these services take a small fee for each transaction they process. Check with the specific company for details.

To give you an idea of the process involved in setting up one of these accounts, the steps below walk through setting up a Google Checkout account. Unfortunately, sites and processes change all the time, so your best bet is to visit the site and read the documentation for the correct processes to follow.

To set up a Google Checkout account, follow these steps:

1. **Browse to `http://checkout.google.com/sell`. If you don't already have a Google account, you need to create one.**

2. **You will fill out a form to gather business information for your account (see Figure 15-13).**

3. **After you complete the form, click the Settings tab to get the Merchant ID you will need for your site.**

   It's in the section Private contact information next to Merchant ID.

4. **On your site, choose Administer➪Store administration➪Configuration➪ Google Checkout settings. Click the Account tab.**

5. **In the instructions, copy the URL it tells you to enter on the Google Checkout Merchant Center site (see Figure 15-14).**

6. **In another window, browse to `http://checkout.google.com/sell` and log in if necessary.**

7. **Click on the Settings tab. Click on the Integration link on the left.**

8. **Copy and paste the Google merchant ID number and Google merchant key to the form on your site at Administer➪Store administration➪ Configuration➪Google Checkout settings under the Account tab.**

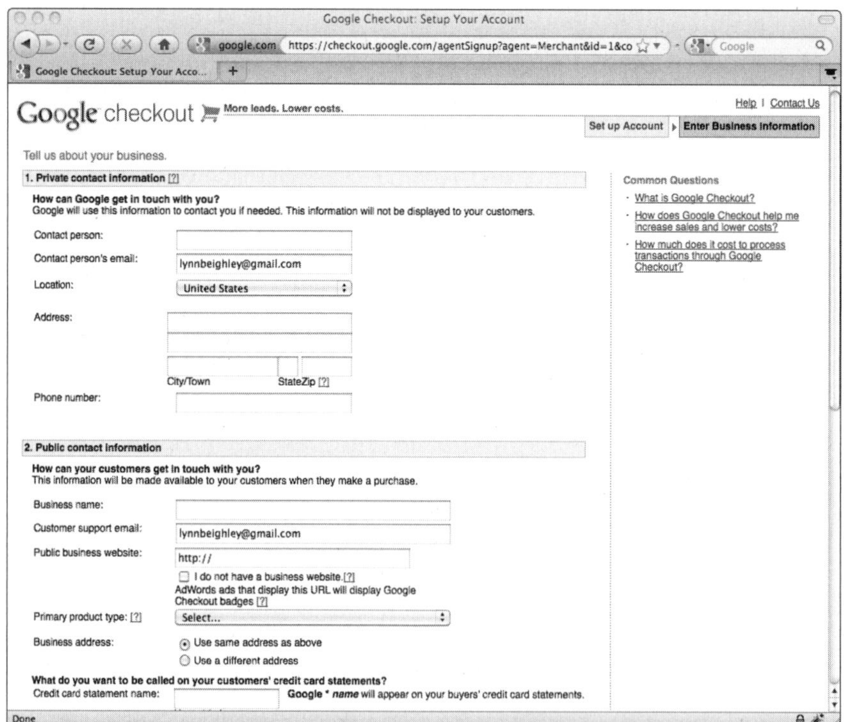

Figure 15-13: Google Checkout new merchant form.

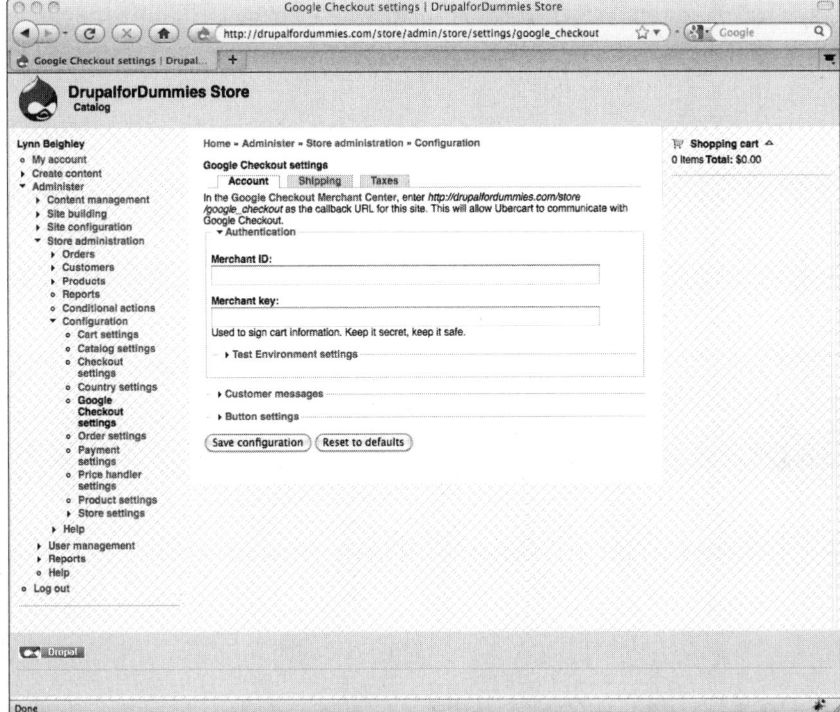

Figure 15-14: Google Checkout settings.

Turning on payment

Once you've chosen a company to work with to process your transactions, you need to enable the correct modules and set your site to process payments with that merchant. To set Ubercart to accept payment, follow these steps:

1. **Choose Administer➪Site building➪Modules.**
2. **Under the Ubercart➪2nd core (optional) section, select the box next to Payment.**
3. **Under the Ubercart – payment section, select the box next to Google Checkout or your particular vendor.**

   Most of the options under the Ubercart – payment section are additional options you can use with different terms and conditions.

4. **Click Save configuration.**

All of the configuration options for setting up payment are found under Administer⇨Store administration⇨Configuration⇨Payment settings. To set Ubercart to use your payment method of choice, follow these steps:

1. **Choose Administer⇨Store administration⇨Configuration⇨Payment settings.**
2. **Click on Payment methods.**

   You see the list of Payment methods you enabled (see Figure 15-15).
3. **To use a particular method, select the Enabled box next to it.**
4. **Click Save configuration.**

Enhancing Your Store

When you installed all the Ubercart and related modules at the beginning of this chapter, you added in lots of functionality you haven't yet turned on. This section is a quick look at the best of the other parts of Ubercart you haven't yet seen.

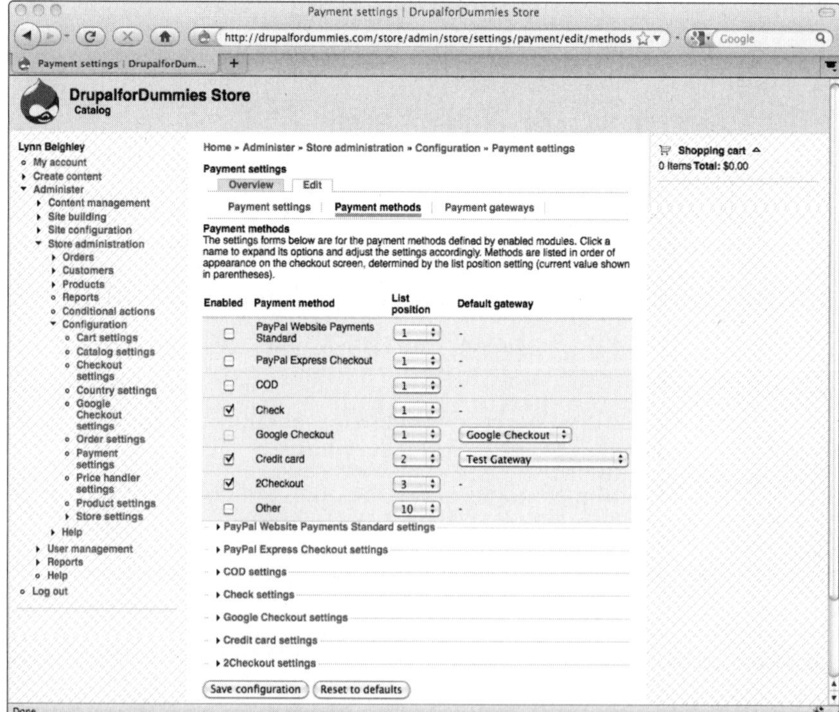

Figure 15-15: Enabling Payment methods for Ubercart.

Using the fulfillment modules

Not only does Ubercart manage the products, catalog, shopping cart, and order form for you, but it also has the capability to handle shipping cost calculations. To use the fulfillment modules, follow these steps:

1. **Choose Administer➪Site building➪Modules.**
2. **Under the Ubercart – core (optional) section, select the box next to Shipping Quotes.**
3. **Under the Ubercart – fulfillment section, select all four boxes.**
4. **Click Save configuration.**

   Now you are ready to create an image field for the Product content type.
5. **Choose Administer➪Store administration➪Configuration➪Shipping quote settings.**
6. **Click on the Quote methods tab, and then the General settings link (see Figure 15-16).**

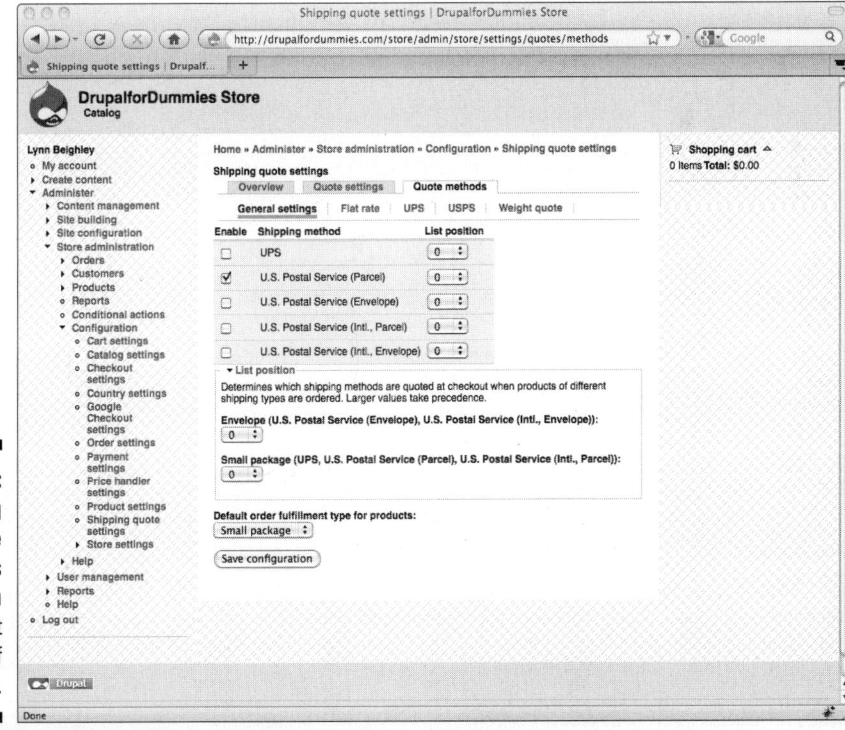

Figure 15-16: Shipping quote settings allows you to select types of shipping.

On this page, you select the shipping type you use. Depending on which type, clicking on the appropriate link gives you more options for providing account information you may have with that service.

Taxing your customers

It's not a fun thing to think about, but it's necessary for many online merchants to collect tax on the goods they sell. Three modules can help. Follow these steps:

1. **Choose Administer➪Site building➪Modules.**
2. **Under the Ubercart – core (optional) section, select the boxes next to Reports, Tax Report, and Taxes.**
3. **Click Save configuration.**
4. **Choose Administer➪Store administration➪Configuration➪ Tax rates and settings.**
5. **Click on the Add a tax rate tab (see Figure 15-17).**

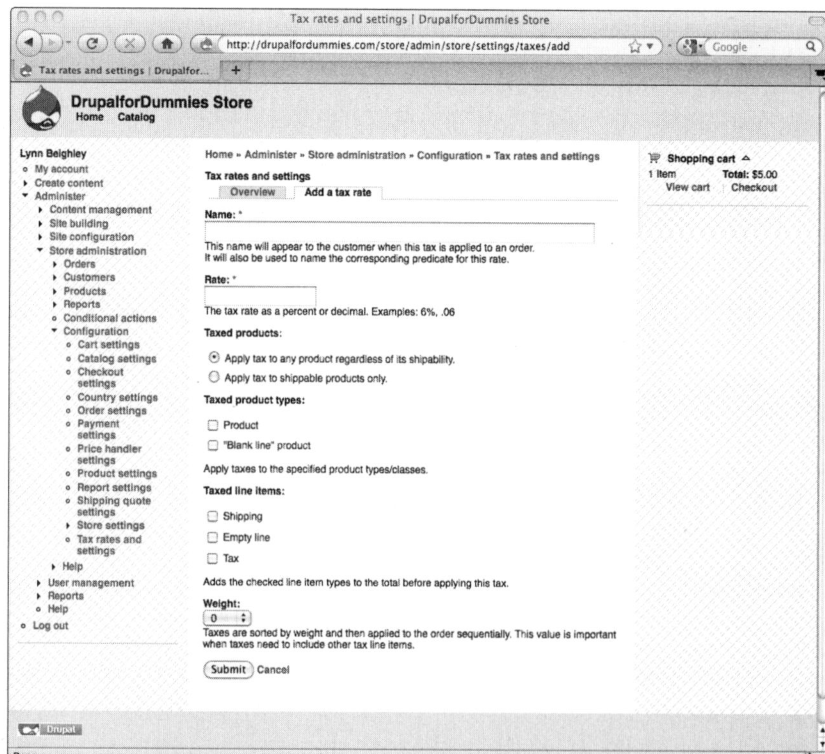

Figure 15-17: Add a tax rate form sets up automatic taxation of purchases.

On this page, you select the tax rate and give it a name that will appear on the customer's checkout form.

When you installed the Reports module, you gained access to a Sales tax report, located at Administer⇨Store administration⇨Reports⇨Sales tax report. There are a number of other valuable reports in this same area of your site:

- **Customer reports:** Presents the total orders, products, sales, and average order totals for each customer.
- **Product reports:** Shows every product listed in the store, how many have sold, how many times it has been viewed, revenue, and gross profit.
- **Sales reports:** Displays sale summaries for the last two days, average monthly sales, and projected sales.
- **Sales tax report:** A handy report that shows you the sales tax you have collected for a particular period.

Part V
The Part of Tens

In this part . . .

You've built a tremendous Web site, but you want more. More modules, more themes. These two chapters each consist of ten nuggets — ten more modules for Drupal and ten Websites that let you connect with other users to garner even more knowledge about Drupal. Because now that you've built one site using Drupal, there's no reason not to build more.

Chapter 16

Ten Must-Have Drupal Modules

In This Chapter

- Adding Web forms
- Ensuring search engine optimization
- Preventing spam
- Generating a site map

Drupal sites can be extended with hundreds of additional modules available for free download. In this chapter, I point out ten interesting ones.

CAPTCHA

A *CAPTCHA* is a random question that site visitors are prompted to answer. Most often, a CAPTCHA is a small graphic image that contains a printed word. The word in the image has to be typed into a form before a user can complete some action on a site. CAPTCHAS can also be basic math questions (for example, your visitor has to type in the answer to **10+8**). Finally, it can consist of a string of text about which the visitor is asked a question (for example, "What is the first word in the phrase *ofomom isulul iki udev uquse*?") Using a CAPTCHA keeps spammers from being able to use programs to spam your site with lots of fake comments that are actually advertisements for prescription drugs, online casinos, or other questionable services.

While using a CAPTCHA is a good idea, it doesn't stop humans from posting spam. It only prevents automated spamming, programs that locate Drupal sites and root through them looking for places to add spammy comments. I highly recommend you moderate all comments in addition to using the CAPTCHA plug-in. This may seem like overkill, but CAPTCHA limits the amount of spam you have to wade through so you have a manageable number of comments to moderate.

After you have uploaded and activated the module, you can configure where CAPTCHAS appear in your site by choosing Administer⇨User Management⇨Captcha (see Figure 16-1).

You will see a list of form types on your site and a drop-down menu that allows you to select which of the three CAPTCHA types — text, image, or math — that must be answered before a form can be successfully submitted.

The Image CAPTCHA tab gives you some options to control the image CAPTCHA. You can specify font size, which font to use, what characters should be used, and what colors to use. The Distortion and noise section lets you control the appearance of the text by adding noise and distorting the letters. If you do distort the text in your image CAPTCHA, make sure you test it a few times to ensure that it is still readable.

Hacker techniques grow increasingly sophisticated all the time. Image CAPTCHAS work best when they are a little difficult to read. Optical character recognition programs, the same algorithms used to allow scanned documents to be output as text, can easily scan CAPTCHA images and extract the text, so adding a bit of noise or distortion can help foil them.

The Text CAPTCHA tab allows you to create and use your own phrase for visitors to answer rather than the random gibberish it produces.

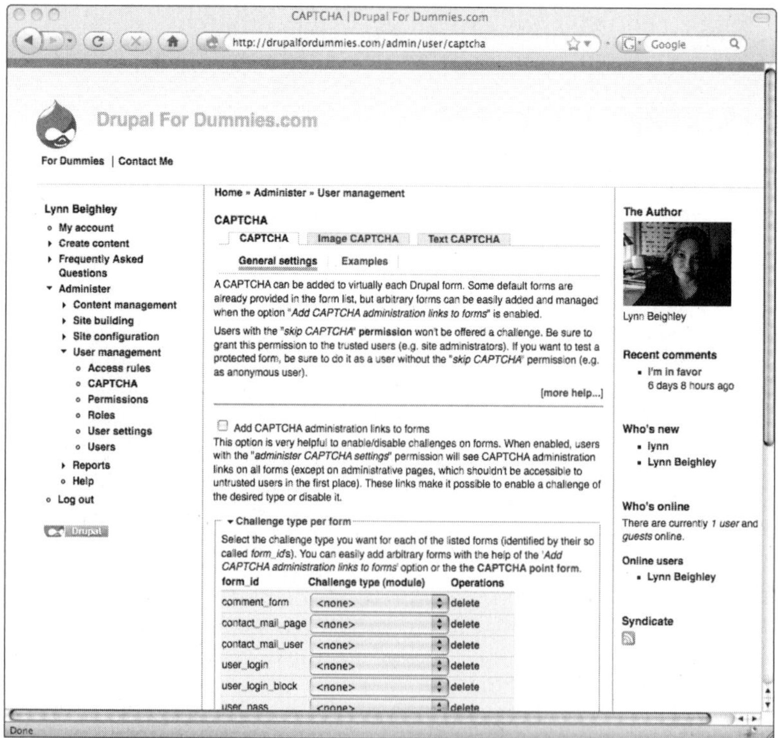

Figure 16-1: CAPTCHA interface.

FAQ

Many Web sites benefit by having a Frequently Asked Questions (FAQ) page where you can answer questions about the purpose and function of your site. The FAQ module allows you to easily create one without having to worry about formatting a page for it.

As soon as you add this module, a link appears in the Navigation menu (see Figure 16-2).

You probably will want Frequently Asked Questions to appear as a link in the Primary menu. To do this, follow these steps:

1. **Choose Administer⇨Site building⇨Menus⇨Navigation. Find the Menu item *Frequently Asked Questions* and click the Edit link to the right.**
2. **Find the Parent item drop-down, and scroll down to choose the `<Primary links>` option.**
3. **Click Save.**

The Frequently Asked Questions link will now appear in your Primary menu.

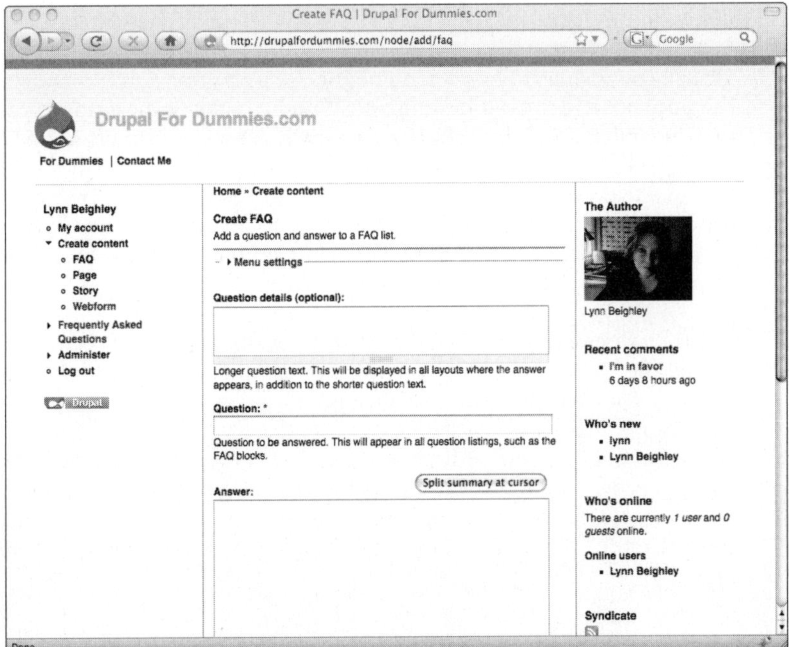

Figure 16-2: FAQ configuration.

To add questions to your FAQ page, choose Create Content⇨FAQ. Enter a question in the Question blank and an answer in the Answer block, and then click Save. To add more questions, simply choose this link again.

Enter the comments in the *reverse* of the order you want them to show up on the page. The last question you enter is first in the list.

You can also control the order by changing the weight of each question. To do this, either

- Enter the desired weight when you create the question
- Choose Administer⇨Content Management⇨Content and click Edit next to the question you wish to change or to add weight.

This is also where you delete the questions.

FCKeditor – WYSIWYG HTML Editor

Despite its risqué name, the FCKeditor module allows you and your users to easily create formatted content, much like a word processor produces. It places a framework of formatting commands on top of any large text entry fields (see Figure 16-3).

To use the formatting panel, highlight the text you wish to change. Then click the appropriate button in the panel. Finally, when you're done typing and formatting, click the Submit button. You will see your formatted text.

Unlike a true word processor, this panel formats text with HTML code behind the scenes. In the case of fonts, this means you have a limited set available through this panel. The font you use on a Web page will show up only for your users who also have that same font on their computers.

Not only does FCKeditor modify your text, but it also allows you an easy way to include images and Flash movies in your posts. You can also control the color of your text and the background color behind your post.

While having this extra editing functionality is great, sometimes you simply want to type plain text. Every time the FCKeditor appears, a link that says *Switch to plain text editor* appears under the editing block. Click this to hide the FCKeditor panel. To change back, click the *Switch to rich text editor* link.

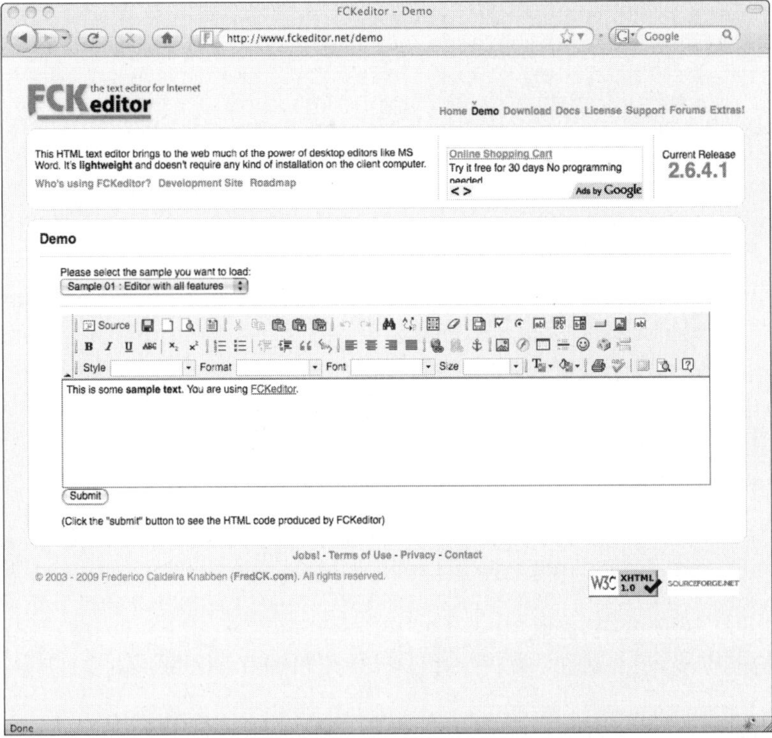

Figure 16-3: FCKeditor embedded in Drupal site.

Once you've installed FCKeditor, you need to change the permissions to allow at least one of your roles to use it. To do this, choose Administer➪User Management➪Permissions. FCKeditor is in the list. You have several configuration options to choose from:

- *Access fckeditor* causes the FCKeditor interface to appear whenever a user in that role attempts to create any new content.
- *Administer fckeditor* allows this role to control the settings for FCKeditor.
- *Allow fckeditor file uploads* allows files to be uploaded to your Web site through the FCKeditor interface.

Although software creators do their best to ensure the security of their applications, malicious people constantly work hard to exploit weaknesses. In general, when using a module that allows users to upload files, or customize content, be cautious. I recommend that you only allow people in highly trusted roles access to this, and any other modules involved in content creation.

Mollom

If you find that, in spite of using the CAPTCHA module, you still have spam, Mollom is your best bet. Mollom is more than a module; it's also Web service. Mollom.com knows how to detect spam from a variety of sources. When a new comment is entered on your site, Mollom.com checks it to see if it's spam. If Mollom thinks it may be, the user who entered it is shown a CAPTCHA.

Fortunately, you don't have to do anything. Your Drupal software, thanks to the Mollom module, automatically sends the user information to the Mollom.com server, checks for spam, and then, if the CAPTCHA challenge is not passed, the comment never even reaches your Web site. It's estimated that Mollom blocks up to 99.7% of all spam messages.

One of the great things about Mollom is that users don't see the CAPTCHA unless they are suspected of creating spam. This means that most legitimate users don't have to go through the trouble of answering a CAPTCHA. A recent study showed that a significant number of users will not bother filling out a CAPTCHA, and they don't end up writing their comments on your site.

For all its sophistication, Mollom is relatively simple:

1. **Browse to mollom.com and set up an account there.**

   You are walked through a process in which a Public key and Private key are created for your site.

2. **Enter the Public and Private keys in the Mollom settings by choosing Administer⇨Site Configuration⇨Mollom.**
3. **Enter the keys from the mollom.com site in the corresponding blanks on this form.**
4. **Click Save configuration** (see Figure 16-4).

That's all there is to it. Each time you browse back to Administer⇨Site Configuration⇨Mollom, you see a report of spam that Mollom has stopped.

Mollom has another nifty feature. Suppose you have a spammy comment on your site. With Mollom installed, every time you delete content, you are presented with a form that asks you if you want to report the content to Mollom as spam. This is part of how Mollom keeps its data up to date and is able to detect new types of spam. You can even classify what kind of spam it is (for example, violent content, taunting, or simply unsolicited advertising). Reporting the content is optional, which is good because sometimes you delete comments that are not spam.

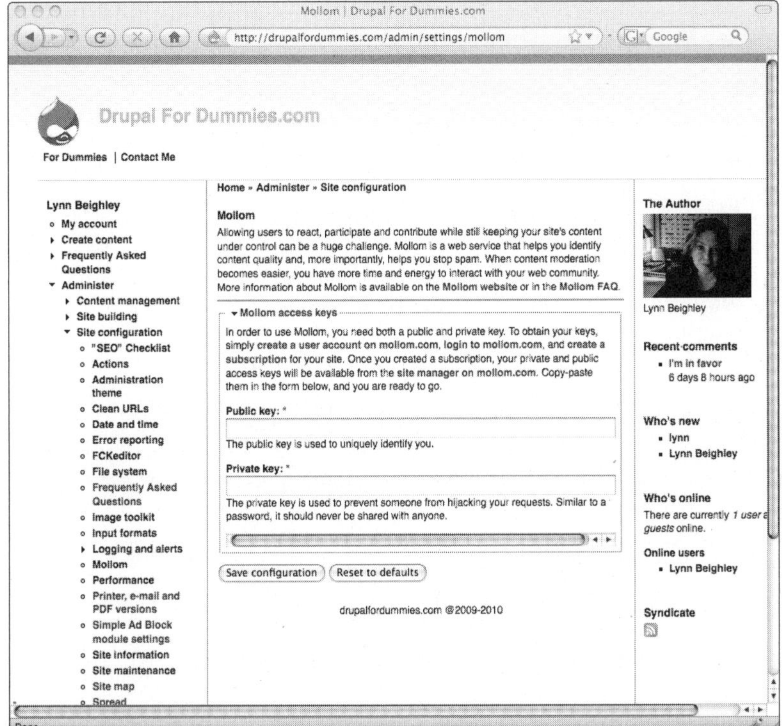

Figure 16-4: Mollom configuration.

Printer, E-mail, and PDF Versions

This module allows your visitors to print, e-mail, and create PDF versions of your content.

To control the settings, choose Administer⇨Site configuration⇨Printer, e-mail, and PDF versions. There are four tabs: Web page, which controls the printer version settings; e-mail; PDF; and Settings, which controls module-wide settings.

This module gives you nearly complete control over the appearance and behavior of this module. For example, you can specify the text or logo to be used to produce the print, e-mail, or PDF output. With the e-mail output, among many other options, you can control how many e-mails a user can send out in an hour.

By default, no pages or stories on your site will have the print, e-mail, or PDF links. You have to activate them. After you install the module, each time you create content, you will see a *Printer, e-mail and PDF versions* menu on the content creation page (see Figure 16-5). This controls whether this content can be output, and in what fashion.

When you publish your content, links to print, e-mail to a friend, or create a PDF will appear. By default, they show up after the Add new comment link at the end of the content.

Sometimes it's easier to set an entire content type to have these output links. For example, you might have a news section that you always want visitors to be able to e-mail, print, or create a PDF out of. To set an entire content type with the same output settings, follow these steps:

1. **Choose Administer⇨Content management⇨Content types.**
2. **Click on the Edit link to the right of the content type you wish to modify.**

   You will see the same Printer, e-mail and PDF versions menu on this page.
3. **Choose your settings and click Save content type.**

   From now on, anytime you create content of that type, the output options you selected will be visible.

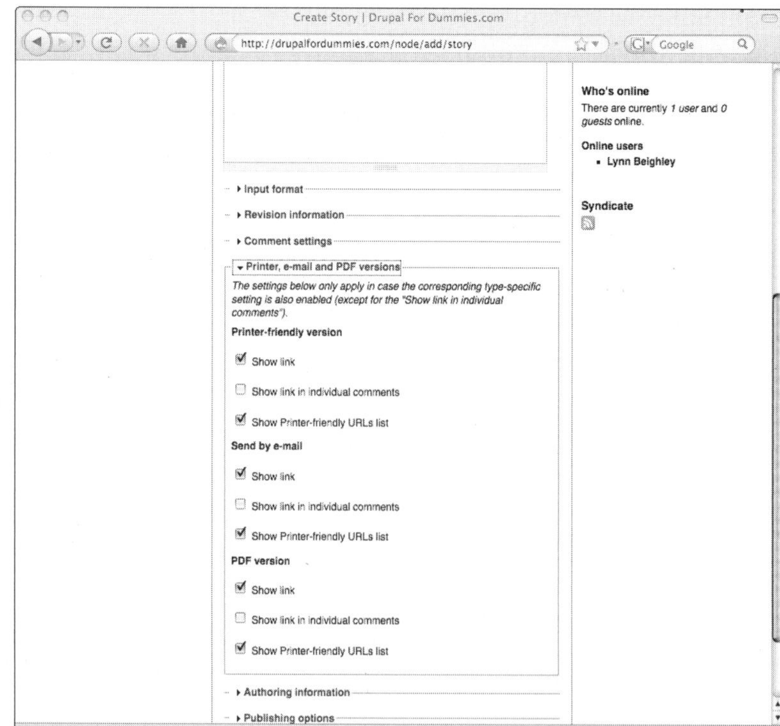

Figure 16-5: Printer, e-mail, and PDF versions settings in story content creation form.

SEO Checklist

This handy module creates a page that recommends other modules and techniques to make your site more visible to search engines. This means that when someone is searching for a service your site provides or information on your site, it will appear closer to the top of the list in search engines. This makes it more likely that the person searching for information will click on the link to your site. The practice of making your site more search-engine friendly is known as *search engine optimization (SEO).*

When you activate the SEO check list module, it creates a check list with suggestions for modules you can add to optimize your site for search engines. To get to the check list, choose Administer➪Site configuration➪SEO Checklist. You see a list of check boxes (see Figure 16-6).

As you check off each one, you click the Save button to keep track of what you have finished from the list. Most involve the installation of additional modules.

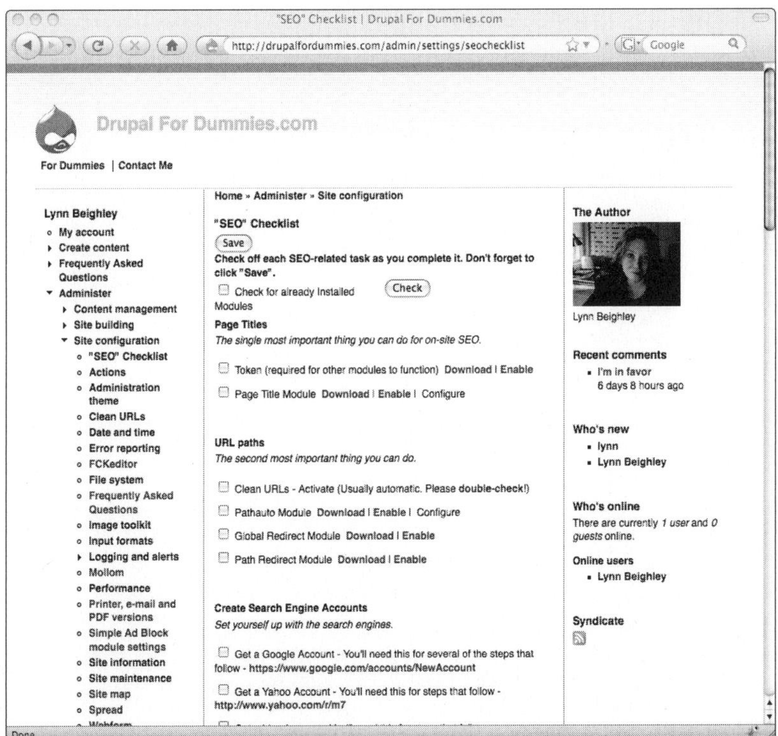

Figure 16-6: "SEO" checklist.

Chances are it's too time consuming to work through the entire list in one sitting, so you can save the form. The next time you choose Administer➪Site configuration➪SEO Checklist, the items you have finished will still be checked off.

A few of the modules I mention in this chapter are on this list, so when you finish you can check off Sitemap, both Mollom check boxes, and CAPTCHA.

Simple Ad Block

This is a simple module that lets you enter text from a third-party advertising service or your own advertising content and posts it for you in the Left or Right sidebar.

To create the advertisement, choose Administer➪Site configuration➪Simple Ad Block. This opens the Simple Ad Block module settings form, where you can paste or create your ad (see Figure 16-7).

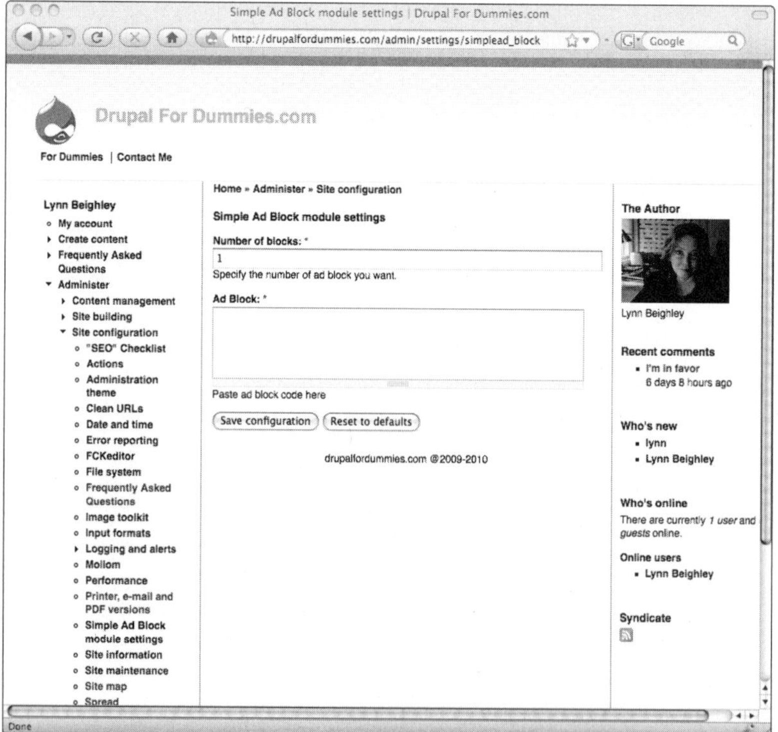

Figure 16-7: Simple Ad Block configuration.

To display your ad on your site, follow these steps:

1. **Choose Administer⇨Site building⇨Blocks.** You will see tabs for each enabled theme.
2. **Click on the current site theme and locate the Simple Ad Block in the list.**
3. **Use the drop-down menu to select the Left or Right sidebar.**
4. **Click Save blocks.**

You can change the location of the ad block in your sidebar by dragging it above or below other content in the same sidebar on the Administer⇨Site building⇨Blocks settings.

Your ad will now appear on all pages of your site in the designated sidebar. If you want more than one ad block, change the number of blocks in the Simple Ad Block module settings form (refer to Figure 16-7). Click Save configuration and more ad blocks will appear.

Site Map

As your site grows, it's important that visitors be able to find the information they are seeking. Creating a site map can help, and the Site map module automatically creates one for you. To create one, choose Administer⇨Site configuration⇨Site map. This opens the Site map form, shown in Figure 16-8.

The form allows you to enter text to appear at the top of the page. You can specifically include menus and front page content if you wish. Click Save configuration to generate your site map.

You have to activate the site map by changing the Permissions. To do this, follow these steps:

1. **Choose Administer⇨User management⇨Permissions.**
2. **Scroll down to site_map module and click in the check boxes to the right for the roles you wish to see the site map.**
3. **Click Save permissions.**

The newly created site map is located on your site under `yourdomainname.com/sitemap`. For example, mine is at `http://drupalfordummies.com/sitemap`. You can link to the site map as you would any other page by adding a link in one of your menus.

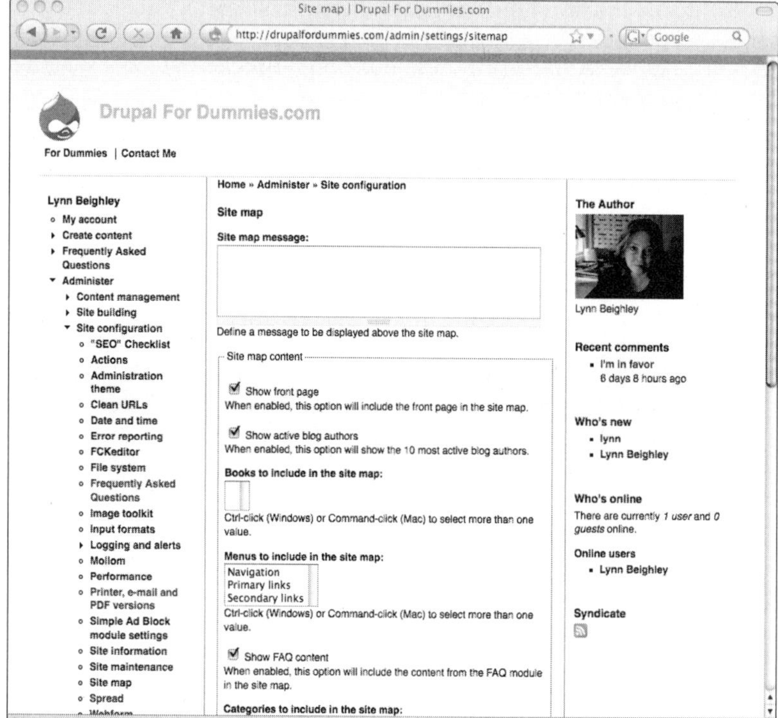

Figure 16-8: Site map configuration.

Spread

The Spread module creates a small form that allows site visitors to send the URL of a page of your site to a friend. The form shows up in a sidebar.

This form is a bit nicer than the Send to a friend link that the Printer, e-mail, and PDF versions module creates:

- The visitor never leaves the page he is on when he uses or submits the form.
- The form is a bit more visible than the link.
- The form is persistent. Any page on your site can be sent.

The downside is that the form takes up screen real-estate on your site that might be better served with different content.

Use *either* the Send to a friend link or the Spread module, not both. While behaviors are not quite the same, having both on your site is a bit redundant and clutters things up more than necessary.

To use the Spread module, follow these steps:

1. **Choose Administer⇨Site configuration⇨Spread.** This opens the Spread module settings form (see Figure 16-9).
2. **Check Enable Mollom integration.** This will be an option if you have added the Mollom module I mention earlier in this chapter.

   Selecting Mollom integration means that anonymous users of the Spread form will have to go through CAPTCHA verification. This prevents your form from being abused. For example, a malicious automated program can't submit the form again and again, which could result in your site being overloaded with traffic and crashing, or e-mails from your site being placed on various spammer lists.

3. **Customize the Thank you message, Subject, and Body fields with your own content.**
4. **Change the number of e-mail fields to 1.** In general, most people will only send the information to one address. Also, it's very easy for users to send the form again and again since it doesn't reload the Web page it's on. Changing e-mail fields to 1 reduces the clutter.
5. **Click Save configuration.**

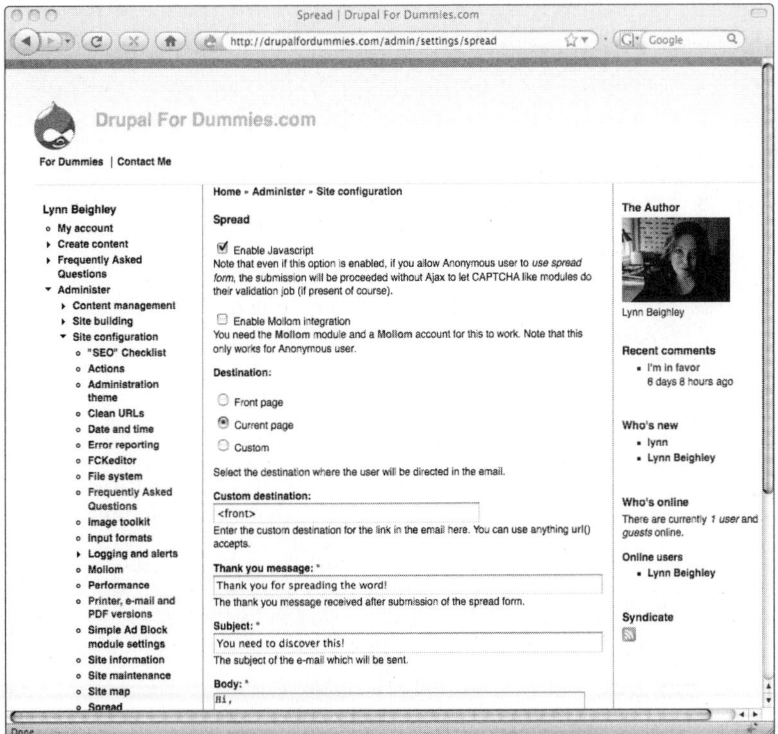

Figure 16-9: Spread configuration.

You still need to make the Spread form visible by placing it in one of the sidebars. To do this, follow these steps:

1. **Choose Administer⇨Site building⇨Blocks.** You will see tabs for each enabled theme.
2. **Click on the current site theme and locate the Spread form in the list.**
3. **Use the drop-down menu to select the Left or Right sidebar.**
4. **Click Save blocks.**

Webform

Webform lets you create forms and questionnaires for your Web site without having to use HTML code to create the form or any other programming language to gather and send the submitted form data to you.

This section is an introduction to this module. For more information about this robust module, I recommend the documentation at `http://drupal.org/handbook/modules/webform`.

To create a Webform, follow these steps:

1. **Choose Create content⇨Webform.** This opens the Create Webform form (see Figure 16-10). This is the Configuration tab, the first of two tabs you click in order to create your Web form.
2. **Fill in a Title for your form.** The Description is optional.
3. **Enter text in the Confirmation message or redirect URL box.** After your visitor fills out the form, this is the text he will see. If you prefer taking him to a Web page, enter the URL here instead of text.
4. **Scroll down to Webform mail settings to specify an e-mail where the results of the form submission will be mailed.**

   You don't have to specify an e-mail here to get the results of your form being submitted. After your form is set up, you can see the collected results of visitors submitting your form:

   Choose Administer⇨Content management⇨Webforms. Click on the edit link next to the form you are interested in. Finally, click the Results tab to see a table of all the form submissions. Click on one to see the answers that user gave to the form questions.
5. **Click Save.** You are now on the Form components setup page. This is where you add all the questions to your form. You can create text boxes, radio buttons, drop-down lists, and other standard form elements.

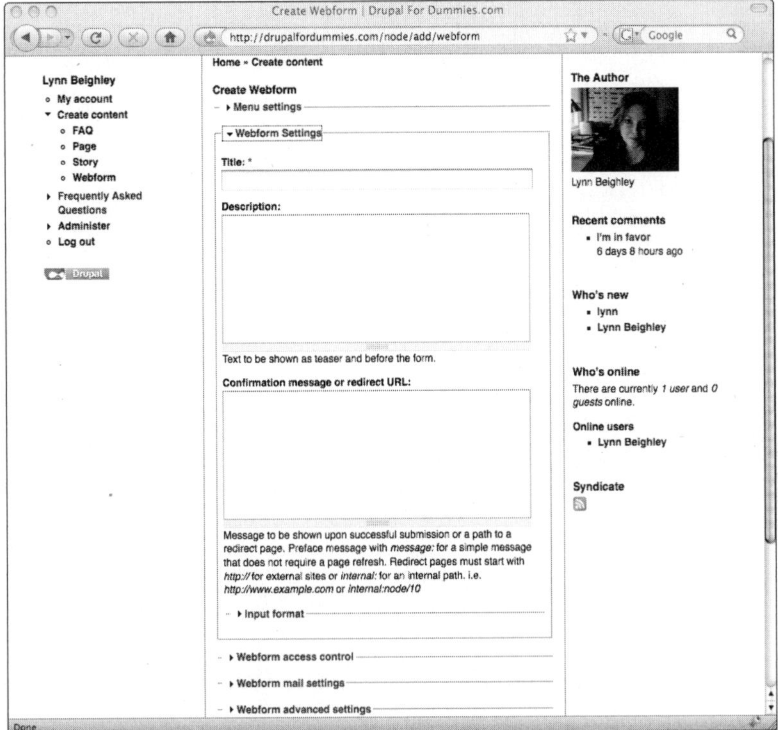

Figure 16-10: Webform configuration.

6. **Add a text box by typing a name for the field (for example, Last Name). Choose Textfield for type. Click the Add button.**
7. **Add a drop-down box by typing a name for the field (for example, Favorite Color). Choose Select for Type. Click Add. Enter your choices, one per line, in the Options text box (for example, Red, Blue, Green). Click Submit.**
8. **Click Publish to create your form.**
9. **To view your new form, click on the View tab.**

You still need to make your form available to people visiting your site. The easiest way to accomplish this is to edit your form and change the settings under the Menu setting. Select the menu where you want your form to appear, give it a title, and click Save.

Chapter 17

Ten Places to Help You Do More with Drupal

In This Chapter

- Getting more help
- Changing themes
- Meeting other Drupal users

There are many great resources where you can get help, download new themes, and meet other Drupal users. This chapter contains ten great resources to help you get the most from Drupal.

Getting More Help

The following six resources are great for getting help and advice from experienced Drupal developers.

Drupal.org forum

When in doubt, go to the source. The Drupal.org Web site has a great user forum (see Figure 17-1).

To access the forum, browse to

```
http://drupal.org/forum
```

You don't need an account on the Drupal.org site to read the forum, but if you want to post your own questions, you will. Having an account also enables you to receive notifications when your questions get responses, as well as other news about Drupal.

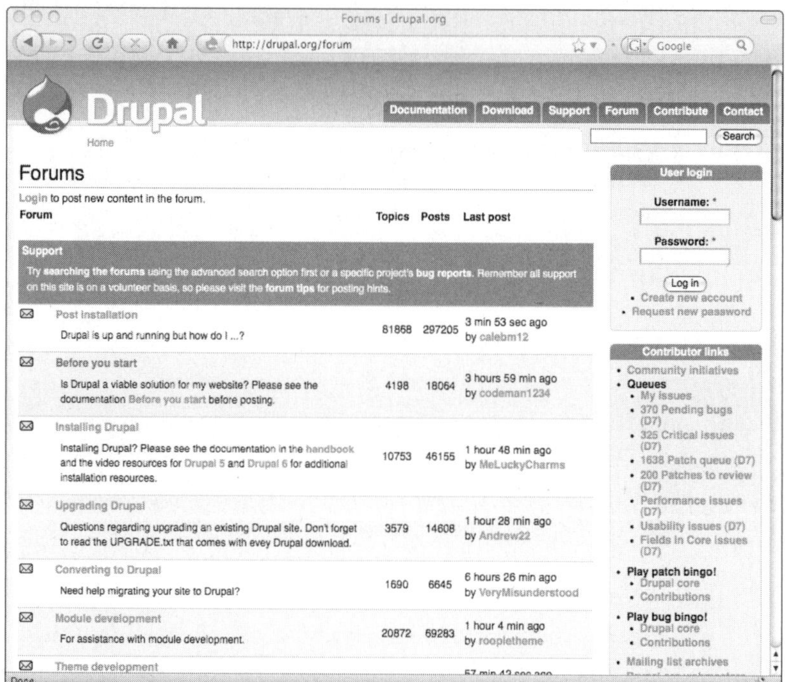

Figure 17-1: Drupal.org user forum.

Twitter

Twitter may seem an unlikely source for Drupal help and information, but it's worth a bit of attention. You can screen for tweets about Drupal topics by typing **#drupal** in the search box located on the right side of the twitter.com home page (see Figure 17-2).

Many of the resulting tweets point you at new themes, Drupal sites, and Drupal developments.

Facebook

Facebook may seem like another unlikely resource, but the Facebook Drupal group is a great place to get help and ideas (see Figure 17-3).

To join the group, you need a Facebook account (`http://facebook.com`). After you have an account, click the small groups icon on the bottom right of the screen. You can also browse directly to

```
http://www.facebook.com/group.php?gid=2218157342
```

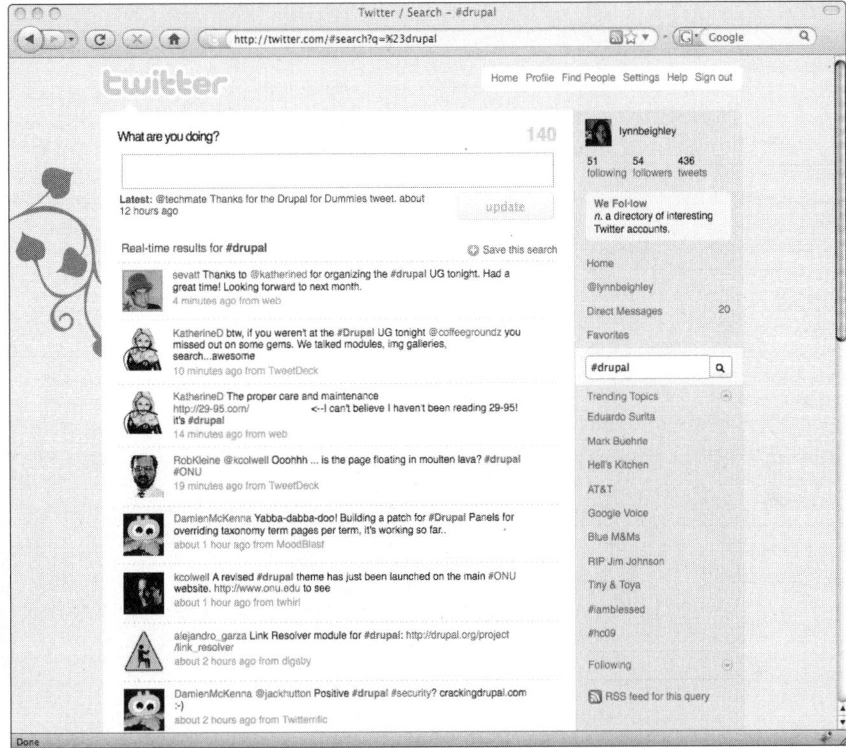

Figure 17-2: Twitter search of #drupal.

Figure 17-3: Facebook Drupal group.

Learn By The Drop

If you like video demonstrations, a good site to visit is Learn By The Drop (`http://learnbythedrop.com`), shown in Figure 17-4. This site contains a number of video and written tutorials.

GotDrupal.com

Another tutorial site with videos is GotDrupal.com (see Figure 17-5). The videos are created as the site is being developed, and it's a bit like watching a house being built.

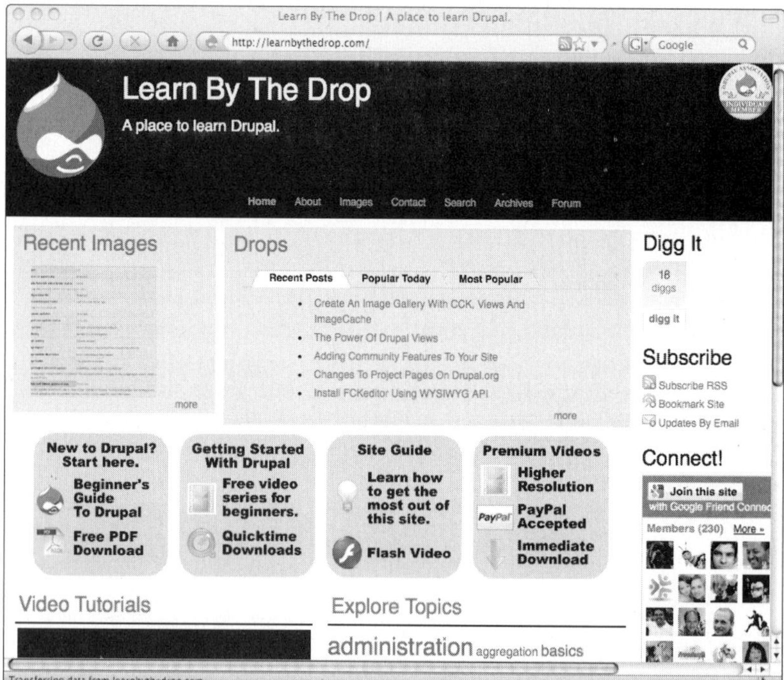

Figure 17-4: Learn By The Drop is a Drupal tutorial site.

Figure 17-5: GotDrupal.com contains videos about Drupal site construction.

Drupal.org mailing lists

It's a good idea to stay informed of Drupal news. The Drupal.org site offers a number of mailing lists (see Figure 17-6). These are located at

```
http://drupal.org/mailing-lists
```

I recommend these lists:

- **Support:** A list for support questions
- **Development:** A list for Drupal developers
- **Consulting:** A list for Drupal consultants and Drupal service/hosting providers

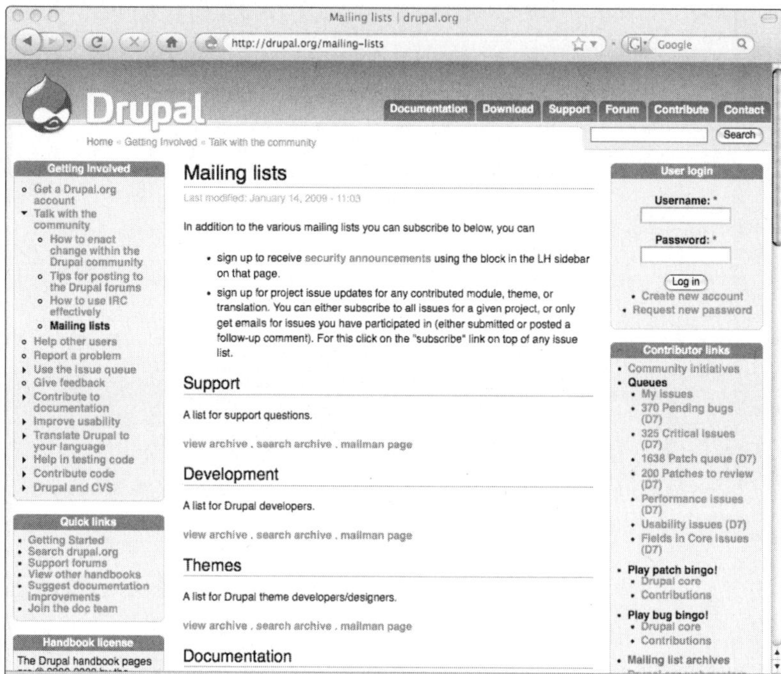

Figure 17-6: Drupal.org mailing lists.

Getting New Themes

New Drupal themes are constantly being developed. Here are two sites to get new ones.

Drupal.org themes

Once again, the Drupal.org site is a great place to turn and has links to newly developed themes (see Figure 17-7).

You can find them at

```
http://drupal.org/project/themes
```

Drupal2U.com

Another site with great new themes is Drupal2U.com (see Figure 17-8).

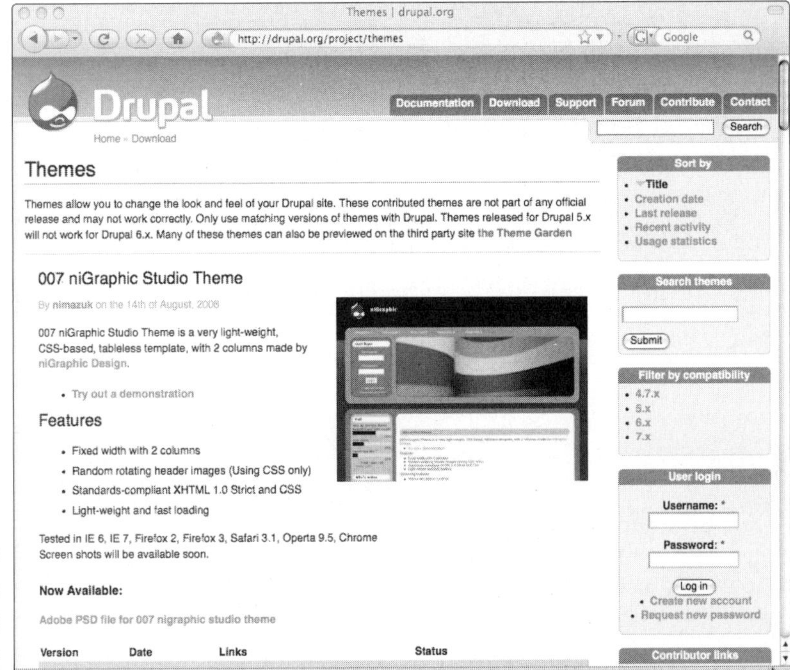

Figure 17-7: Drupal.org themes.

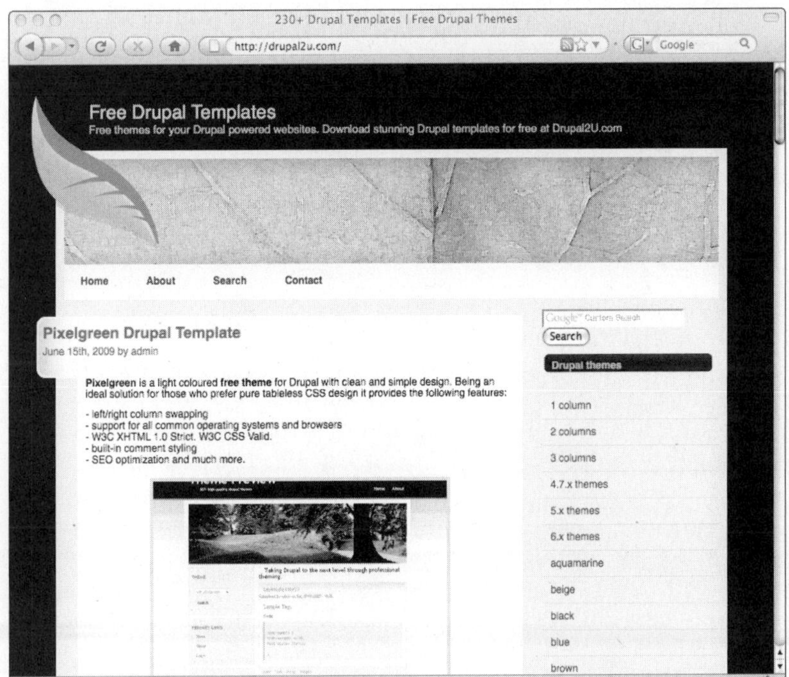

Figure 17-8: Drupal2U.com contains additional Drupal themes.

Meeting Other Drupal Users

A great way to extend your knowledge of Drupal is to get to know other Drupal users. Here are two sites where you can find local users of Drupal.

Drupal.org user groups

The Drupal.org site keeps a list of local Drupal user groups (see Figure 17-9).

To access the directory of groups, visit

```
http://groups.drupal.org/groups
```

Meetup.com

Meetup.com is a great place to find other people in your area who are building Drupal sites (see Figure 17-10).

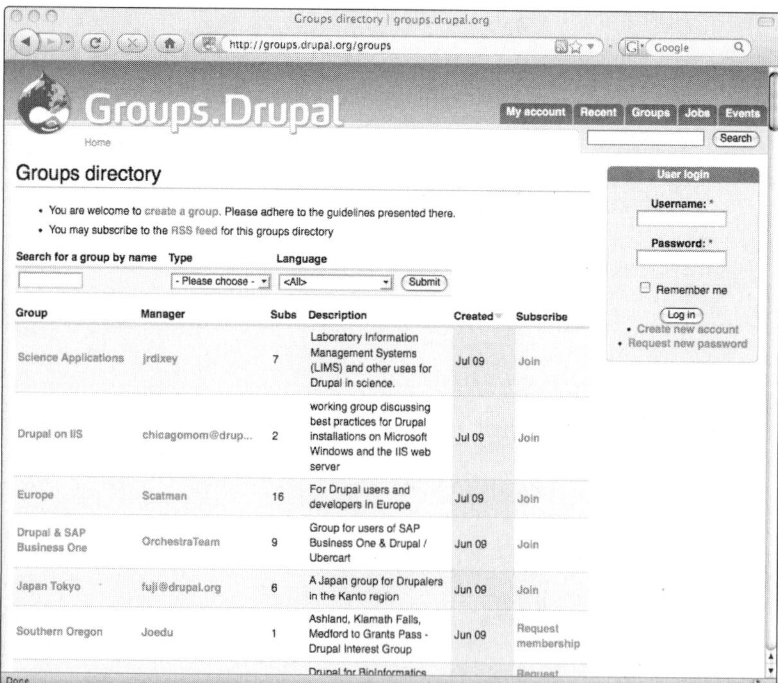

Figure 17-9: Drupal.org list of user groups.

To find a local Drupal Meetup group, visit

```
http://drupal.meetup.com
```

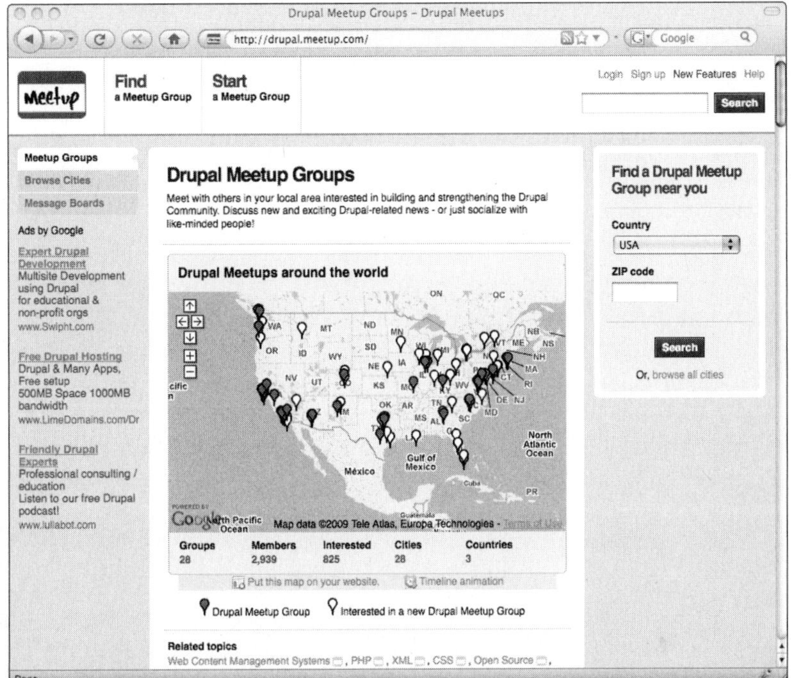

Figure 17-10: Meetup.com map of local Drupal user groups.

Index

Symbols and Numerics

• A •

• D •

• E •

• N •

• O •

• P •

• Q •

• R •

• S •

• T •

• Z •

Internet
Blogging For Dummies, 2nd Edition
978-0-470-23017-6

eBay For Dummies, 6th Edition
978-0-470-49741-8

Facebook For Dummies
978-0-470-26273-3

Google Blogger For Dummies
978-0-470-40742-4

Web Marketing For Dummies, 2nd Edition
978-0-470-37181-7

WordPress For Dummies, 2nd Edition
978-0-470-40296-2

Language & Foreign Language
French For Dummies
978-0-7645-5193-2

Italian Phrases For Dummies
978-0-7645-7203-6

Spanish For Dummies
978-0-7645-5194-9

Spanish For Dummies, Audio Set
978-0-470-09585-0

Macintosh
Mac OS X Snow Leopard For Dummies
978-0-470-43543-4

Math & Science
Algebra I For Dummies
978-0-7645-5325-7

Biology For Dummies
978-0-7645-5326-4

Calculus For Dummies
978-0-7645-2498-1

Chemistry For Dummies
978-0-7645-5430-8

Microsoft Office
Excel 2007 For Dummies
978-0-470-03737-9

Office 2007 All-in-One Desk Reference For Dummies
978-0-471-78279-7

Music
Guitar For Dummies, 2nd Edition
978-0-7645-9904-0

iPod & iTunes For Dummies, 6th Edition
978-0-470-39062-7

Piano Exercises For Dummies
978-0-470-38765-8

Parenting & Education
Parenting For Dummies, 2nd Edition
978-0-7645-5418-6

Type 1 Diabetes For Dummies
978-0-470-17811-9

Pets
Cats For Dummies, 2nd Edition
978-0-7645-5275-5

Dog Training For Dummies, 2nd Edition
978-0-7645-8418-3

Puppies For Dummies, 2nd Edition
978-0-470-03717-1

Religion & Inspiration
The Bible For Dummies
978-0-7645-5296-0

Catholicism For Dummies
978-0-7645-5391-2

Women in the Bible For Dummies
978-0-7645-8475-6

Self-Help & Relationship
Anger Management For Dummies
978-0-470-03715-7

Overcoming Anxiety For Dummies
978-0-7645-5447-6

Sports
Baseball For Dummies, 3rd Edition
978-0-7645-7537-2

Basketball For Dummies, 2nd Edition
978-0-7645-5248-9

Golf For Dummies, 3rd Edition
978-0-471-76871-5

Web Development
Web Design All-in-One For Dummies
978-0-470-41796-6

Windows Vista
Windows Vista For Dummies
978-0-471-75421-3

Available wherever books are sold. For more information or to order direct: U.S. customers visit www.dummies.com or call 1-877-762-2974. U.K. customers visit www.wileyeurope.com or call (0) 1243 843291. Canadian customers visit www.wiley.ca or call 1-800-567-4797.

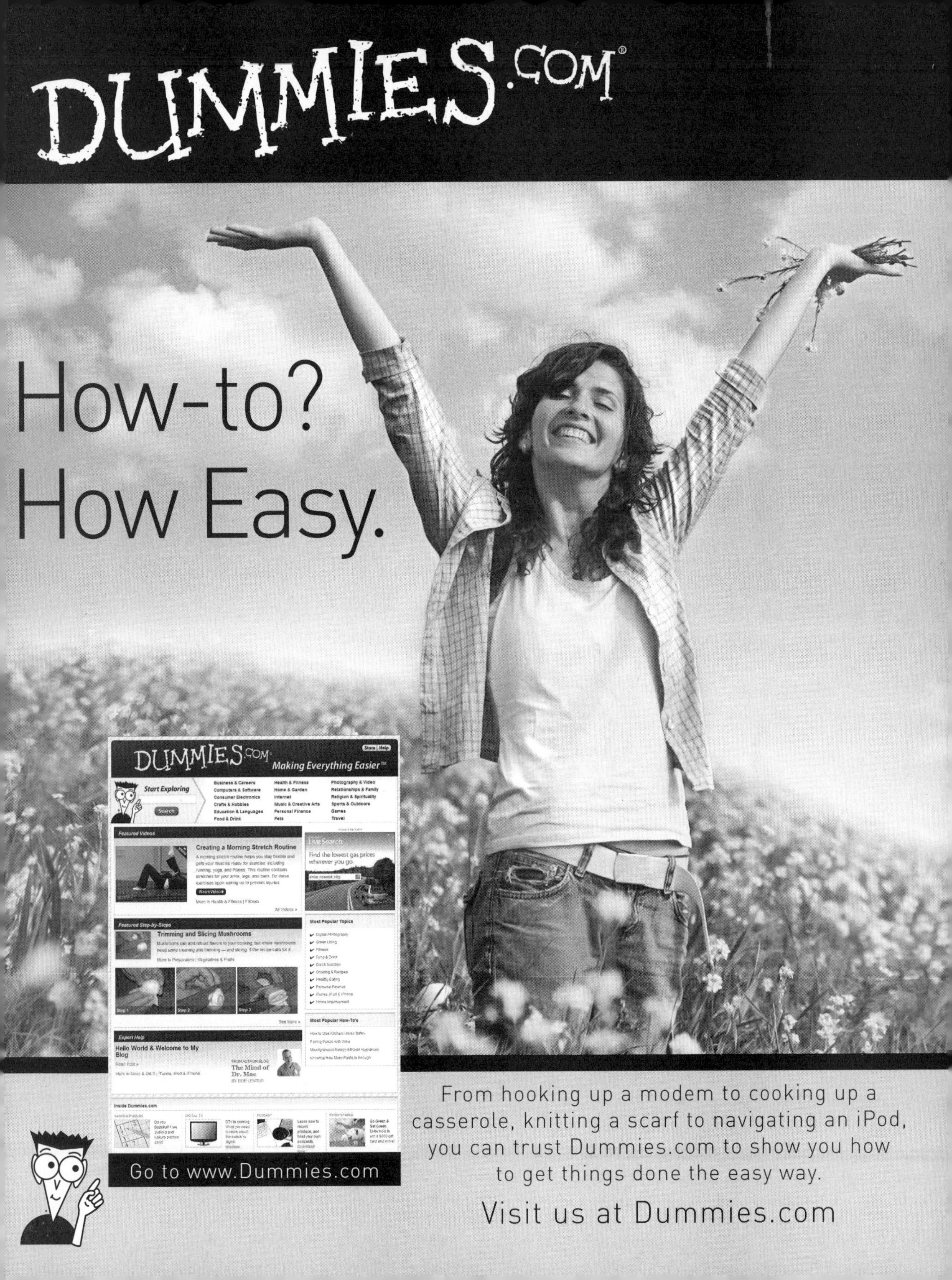
DUMMIES.COM
How-to?
How Easy.
DUMMIES.COM
Making Everything Easier™
Start Exploring
Featured Videos
Creating a Morning Stretch Routine
Featured Step-by-Steps
Trimming and Slicing Mushrooms
Most Popular Topics
Most Popular How-To's
Expert Help
Hello World & Welcome to My Blog
The Mind of Dr. Mac
Inside Dummies.com
Go to www.Dummies.com
From hooking up a modem to cooking up a casserole, knitting a scarf to navigating an iPod, you can trust Dummies.com to show you how to get things done the easy way.
Visit us at Dummies.com

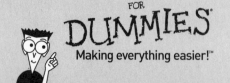

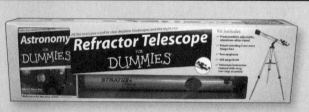

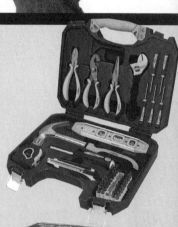